Ohio University

1804–2004

To Compton Reeves,
I hope you enjoy
this version of O.U.
history.
All good wishes,
Betty

BETTY HOLLOW

Ohio University Press   *Athens*

The Spirit of

Ohio University
1804–2004

a Singular Place

Ohio University Press, Athens, Ohio 45701
© 2003 by Ohio University Press

Printed in China
All rights reserved

11 10 09 08 07 06 05 04 03   5 43 2 1

Overleaf (top to bottom): from the scrapbook of Harry Secrest, '17, courtesy Mahn Center; courtesy Jack Moss, '48, and Phoebe Sacheroff Moss, '50; courtesy Mahn Center; courtesy University Photographer's Office; courtesy University Photographer's Office.

Library of Congress Cataloging-in-Publication Data

Hollow, Betty, 1938–
   Ohio University, 1804–2004 : the spirit of a singular place / Betty Hollow.
      p. cm.
Includes bibliographical references and index.
   ISBN 0-8214-1522-0 (cloth : alk. paper) — ISBN 0-8214-1523-9 (pbk. : alk.
paper) — ISBN 0-8214-1544-1 (deluxe ed. : alk. paper) — ISBN 0-8214-1545-X
(presidents' ed. : alk. paper)
   1. Ohio University—History. I. Title.
   LD4191.O82.H59 2003
   378.771'97—dc21
                                                                    2003049886

The publication of this book in commemoration of the two-hundredth anniversary of Ohio University is made possible through a gift from Leona Hughes Hughes, '30, '01. The gift honors all those who have helped make Ohio University what it is today and those who will be the building blocks for the coming centuries.

March 8, 1973

Dr. A. Compton Reeves
305 East State Street
Athens, Ohio   45701

Dear Dr. Reeves:

It is a great pleasure to inform you that you will be granted tenure at Ohio University at the beginning of the new academic year on September 1, 1973.

This letter welcomes you as a permanent member of our faculty and brings you personal as well as official congratulations and best wishes.

Sincerely yours,

Claude R. Sowle
President

CRS/ljs

February 7, 1973

Dr. A. Compton Reeves
305 East State Street
Athens, Ohio   45701

Dear Dr. Reeves:

It is a great pleasure to inform you that you will be promoted to the rank of Associate Professor of History, effective September 1, 1973.

This advancement comes to you in recognition of your effectiveness as a teacher and a scholar and because of your other contributions to the work of the University. I wish to extend to you personal as well as official congratulations and best wishes.

Sincerely yours,

Claude R. Sowle
President

CRS:ljs

THE RECOGNITION THAT OHIO UNIVERSITY
IS A SINGULAR PLACE WITH A HISTORY,
SETTING, AND DISTINCTIVE CHARACTERISTICS
WHICH LARGELY DETERMINE ITS FUTURE
IS A CONSTANT IN THE FACE OF CHANGE.

—Colloquium on the Third Century 1987

Contents

Preface

In 1804 the new state of Ohio, in one of its earliest acts, chartered the first university in the Northwest Territory. Four years later the Ohio University opened with three students and one instructor. Today Ohio University is a large, complex entity with six campuses, thousands of students, and many constituencies. And yet, in spite of its size, this university maintains a sense of community and a democratic spirit that inspire people of diverse backgrounds and interests to create their own spaces, follow their own urges, invent their own programs, speak their own minds. There is about it a spirit of fun and freedom that sometimes erupts in sheer exuberance.

Do the brick streets of small-town Athens and the peaceful College Green encourage this? Is it perhaps because this university with a global reach remains isolated in the hills of its home in southeast Ohio? Or is it simply that the spirit of the founders and early students lingers in the corridors of Cutler, Wilson, and McGuffey Halls?

As you read the story of Ohio University, you may be able to determine how the spirit of this living, changing university—this singular place—was formed and how it has managed to claim and hold so many hearts.

Acknowledgments

In anticipation of Ohio University's bicentennial celebration, President Robert Glidden approved a proposal from David Sanders, director of Ohio University Press, to publish a collaborative history of the university—a "mosaic portrait," depicting the lives that have peopled the institution and the ideas that have kept it vigorous for two hundred years. I am deeply grateful to President Glidden for his strong support of the project and to David for inviting me to organize it.

During the three years the book was in progress, I called on university staff, faculty members, alumni, students, and friends for guidance, information, and contributions of essays, topical sketches, photographs, art, and memories and was consistently met with interest, cooperation, and generosity. An advisory committee—Ralph Amos, Assistant Vice President/Executive Director, Alumni Relations; Crompton B. Burton, Associate Vice President, University Communications and Marketing; Vibert Cambridge, Interim Chair, African American Studies; Nancy Crist, Director, President's Office; Nicholas Dinos, Professor Emeritus, Chemical Engineering; Katherine Jellison, Associate Professor, History; Daniel Riffe, Professor, Journalism; and Julia Zimmerman, Dean, University Libraries—offered counsel, comments on the text, and, in some cases, the expertise of their staff members.

Judith Johnson, Connie Romine, and Tiffany Boles of the Office of Alumni Relations facilitated interviews with alumni. Mary Alice Casey, Tracy Corrigan, and Rick Fatica of Communications and Marketing provided publicity, a website for memories, and access to archival and contemporary photographs. George W. Bain, Head, The Robert E. and Jean R. Mahn Center for Archives and Special Collections, Ohio University Libraries (abbreviated Mahn Center in credit lines), gave me working space and unrestricted access to all areas of the archives. His colleagues—Sheppard Black, Janet Carleton, Karen Jones, William Kimok, Douglas McCabe, and Judith Connick—made me welcome, directed me to obscure documents, and offered their knowledge of the university's past.

Throughout the book, essays on unique aspects of Ohio University's development enhance the chronological account. The following essayists graciously agreed to research and consolidate information on topics and themes of particular interest: Ted J. Foster, Associate Professor Emeritus, Interpersonal Communication: "The Literary Societies and Their Legacy"; Vattel Theodore Rose, Associate Professor, African American Studies: "The African American Experience at Ohio University"; Douglas McCabe, Curator of Manuscripts, The Robert E. and Jean R. Mahn Center for Archives and Special Collections, Ohio University Libraries: "From the Asylum to the Ridges"; Guido H. Stempel III, Distinguished Professor Emeritus, Journalism: "Student Publications at Ohio University"; Crompton B. Burton, Associate Vice President, University Communications and Marketing: "Ohio University Athletics"; Judith Baxter Daso, Librarian Emerita, Ohio University Libraries: "Women at Ohio University"; Robin Pickett, Marching 110 historian: "The Marching 110"; Charles P. Bird, Vice President, Regional Higher Education: "Regional Higher Education"; Marjorie S. Stone, author of *Getting to Know Athens County:* "Ohio on the Hocking"; Felix V. Gagliano, Professor Emeritus, Political Science, and Mary Anne Flournoy, Associate Director Emerita, Center for International Studies: "Ohio University and the World: Two Hundred Years of Global Connections."

Shorter sketches also add texture and flavor to the history, and again I received overwhelmingly positive responses to my requests for profiles of Ohio University people, places, and programs. These contributors are: Phyllis F. Field, Associate Professor, History: "Thomas Ewing"; John Kotowski, Assistant Vice President, Facilities Planning Office: "Samuel Sullivan 'Sunset' Cox"; Ralph Amos, Assistant Vice President/Executive Director, Alumni Relations: "Archibald Green Brown and the Ohio University Alumni Association"; Frank Robinson, Assistant Director, Residence Life, Director's Office: "Margaret Boyd: Ohio University's First Female Graduate"; Connie R. Perdreau, Director, Education Abroad: "Edward and Mattie Berry and the Hotel Berry"; Marjorie S. Stone, author of *Getting to Know Athens County:* "The Civil War Monument"; Jack G. Ellis, Vice President Emeritus and Associate

Director, Manasseh Cutler Scholars Program: "Grosvenor House/Konneker Alumni Center"; Don Swaim, '59: "WOUB: Radio Days"; Tom Gosiorowski, '65: "The Ice Age at Ohio University"; Robert Hynes, Director Emeritus, Auxiliary Services: "Helen Mauck Galbreath Memorial Chapel"; Nancy Crist, Director, Office of the President: "Marie White"; George R. Klare, Distinguished Professor Emeritus, Psychology, and Louis Wright, Professor, Physics: "Faculty Senate"; Richard McFarland, Russ Professor Emeritus, Electrical Engineering: "Avionics"; Roger Finlay, Distinguished Professor Emeritus, Physics: "John E. Edwards Accelerator Lab"; Will Dewees, intentional community resident: "Hamsa"; Alvilda McWilliams, Ph.D., Journalism: "Ohio University's Spring Festivals"; David Wight, Director, Edison Biotechnology Institute: "Edison Biotechnology Institute"; Nicholas Dinos, Professor Emeritus, Chemical Engineering: "Fredrick Hagerman"; Dean McWilliams, Hamilton, Baker, and Hostetler Professor of Humanities, English: "Kermit Blosser"; Michael Grow, Associate Professor and Director, Contemporary History Institute: "Contemporary History Institute."

Sketches of each college and of the University Libraries provide insights into the direction and growth of the university over the years. For them I must thank sketch writers George W. Bain, Head, The Robert E. and Jean R. Mahn Center for Archives and Special Collections: The Ohio University Libraries; Diana Beeson, Communication and External Relations Coordinator: College of Arts and Sciences; Mark L. Carter, Assistant Dean for Development: College of Education; David Descutner, Dean: University College; John P. Barr, Director of External Relations: College of Business; Corinne Colbert, Coordinator of Public Affairs: College of Fine Arts; Drusilla Riley Evarts, Professor of Journalism, Guido Stempel III, Distinguished Professor Emeritus of Journalism, and Lorie McCormick, External and Alumni Relations Coordinator: College of Communication; Jan Cunningham Hodson, Assistant Dean: Honors Tutorial College; Michael A. Weisner, Associate Director of Communication, and Carl Denbow, Director, COM-Operations: College of Osteopathic Medicine; Linda L. Lockhart, Communications and Operations Coordinator: College of Health and Human Services; Mark A. Smith, Director of External Relations: Russ College of Engineering and Technology.

Other writers who have my thanks for their contributions are Margaret Channell, Director of Events and Communications, Office of the President, who produced new profiles of Ohio University's presidents, and Christy E. Johnson, '04, who cheerfully searched for information and produced profiles on just a few of Ohio University's outstanding alumni.

Other student assistants were Denis Flaschner, who transcribed interviews; Katie Fitzgerald, who checked contributor lists; Polly Reincheld, who volunteered as a preliminary proofreader; and members of Doug Partusch's audio production class, who, under his direction, braved an unusually cold Homecoming Day to interview alumni and friends.

Alvilda McWilliams, Dean McWilliams, and Nancy Jones Roe, '50, conducted a number of excellent interviews, using guidelines supplied by Professor David Mould. David Summers and Hollis Summers Jr. graciously gave permission to use a poem by their father, Hollis Summers. Betty Pytlik and Mary Kaye Jordan offered their help by regularly quizzing me about the book's progress.

Artists and owners of drawings, watercolors, paintings, and photographs related to Ohio University enthusiastically lent them to create a visually more interesting history. Though not every work was used, my sincere thanks go to Paul Bradford for his watercolor; Drusilla Evarts for L. C. Mitchell's painting; Patricia Green for a Sue Wall painting; Michael Major for his sketch of the academy building; Alvilda and Dean McWilliams for a June Carver Roberts watercolor; Gary Pettigrew for his rendition of uptown buggies; Don Roberts for a June Carver Roberts watercolor; Charles Scott for photographs of the 1970s riots; Marjorie S. Stone for a Paul Bradford watercolor; Margaret Thomas for an Ursula Lawson painting; Joanne Prisley, Director of the Athens County Historical Society and Museum (abbreviated as ACHS&M in credit lines) for glass slides from the Snow Collection and photographs from the James Anastas Collection; Dan Dry Associates for photographs; and the *Athena Yearbook* for work by many of its talented photographers.

A number of people made the text more accurate and readable. Peg Black and Florence Riffe shared information on President Charles Ping's administration. Readers Samuel and Susan Crowl, Willard Elsbree, Alan Geiger, Elizabeth Hollow, George and Judith Klare, Joanne Prisley, and Bruce Steiner caught errors, asked questions, and offered suggestions. Karen Williams not only read the text and helped organize graphics, but took notes on one hundred years of minutes from trustees' meetings. Beth Pratt, production manager of Ohio University Press, skillfully translated the raw graphics into publishable formats. Nancy Basmajian, managing editor of the press, did a masterful final edit, making the text tighter and the book a manageable size. Chiquita Babb is responsible for its excellent design.

My children, Patton, Elizabeth, and Joseph, get extra credit, as well as my love and appreciation, for listening to stories of Ohio University throughout their lives and, during this project, for listening patiently to hundreds more. The newest members of my family, Sylvia and John, get my love and gratitude for occasionally redirecting the conversation.

Finally, the many people who supplied information, photographs, memorabilia, and especially their memories of Ohio University have my heartfelt thanks, for it is their reminiscences—sometimes amusing, sometimes poignant—that bring to life the men and women who have shared the Green and shaped the institution. Unfortunately, only a portion of these wonderful stories could be included, and those were often edited in the interest of space. I hope their contributors, as well as those whose names were undecipherable or possibly omitted, will be forgiving.

Anonymous • —
Anonymous • '49
Anonymous, Jack • '60s
Anonymous • '68
Anonymous • '80s
Anonymous • '94
Adkins, Charlie • staff
Adkins, Tommy • staff
Alberghine-Gergely, Vicki • '94
Alden, Vernon R. • administrator
Allen, Carolyn Berger • '72 and administrator
Allen, Jessanne Timon • '71
Allen, William • '69, '77 and administrator
Allensworth, John • '67
Amato, Angela Luca • '94
Amato, Gerald M. • '63
Anderson, Dorothy • administrator
Anderson, Ora • friend
Armentrout, Laura M. • '64
Asik, Raymond J. • '63
Asik, Sandra Kovanes • '65
Baker, Thomas R. • '86
Baker, Tom • friend
Ball, Huey L. • '67
Barnett, Jerry B. • '56, '58

Baumann, Arthur • '41
Beasway (?), Paul • friend
Binns, Barbara L. • '43
Birkhimer, Barbara Lee • '69
Blauvelt, Michael • '01
Blinder, Jody • '83
Blosser, Kermit • '32 and faculty
Blount, Frances Holly • '68
Bolden, Adonis • '01
Bonaccorso, Rose Galambos • '83
Bowman, Dolores Neff • '51
Brackett, Jacqueline M. • '79, '93
Brennan, David J. • '90
Brooks, Douglas R. • '90, '91
Brown, Catherine L. • '69, '70 and administrator
Brown, Pamela Lehman • '87, '91 and administrator
Bruning, James • faculty
Burkhardt, William R. • '85 and faculty
Bush, Kenner • trustee
Camplen, Lisa Visnic • '89
Cao, Ellen Birkhimer • '98
Carter, Holly A. • '99
Cernock, Lois Ramser • '66
Cernock, William • friend
Channell, Frances Gensley • '37

Channell, Margaret A. • '73, '80 and administrator

Chaddock, Jeffery D. • '88

Chezem, Jane • '93

Cisneros, Luisa C. • '82

Clark, Mary V. Myers • '44

Claussen, Tammy • '93

Clemmons, Walter F. • '84, '85

Coady, James • faculty

Cohn, Margaret • administrator

Cohn, Norman • faculty

Cole, Kenneth G. • '60

Connick, Judith A. • '79, '91

Connick, Kathleen D. • '82

Corrigan, Tracy Green • '89

Coster, Karen Unfried • '58

Creps, Richard H. • '44

Crowl, Samuel • faculty

Crowl, Susan • faculty

Crupie, Beth Jo • '96

Cunningham, Jean • '76, '81 and administrator

Cunningham, John K. • '49

Czeczok, Heather • administrator

Dailey, Edward • friend

Daughriety, Wanda • friend

DeMonye, William G • '51

deSilva, Donnajean Williamson • '69

Dewald, Howard • faculty

Diles, Mary • friend

Dilley, James • '55, '56

Donaldson, Dianna L. • att '64–'65

Donleon, Elmer • '42

Dong, Daisy • '95

Doxsee, Gifford B. • faculty

Duckworth, Susan Vittel • '86

Dupre, Mary-Blair Truesdale • '70

Dupree, Monica Walker • '79

Dybvig, H. Eugene • '47, '51

Eachus, Madge Acord • '20

Edwards, Thomas B. • '90

Eisel, Mary • '96

Elk, Frank A. • '70

Ellis, Elizabethann Schultz • '48

Ellis, Frank P. • '54

Elsbree, Willard • faculty

Ergood, Bruce • faculty

Essman, Joseph E. • '57, '61 and faculty

Essman, Joseph E., Jr. • '82

Fails, Eva • '78

Farbeann, Mary L Happoldt • '51

Farmer, Jean Waters • '74

Farr, Roger • '63

Fay, William L. • '51, '54

Fialko, Gregory A. • '91 and administrator

Fieberts, Jane E. • '70

Findlay, Loren L. • '36

Finnegan, Anne • '75

Flores, Sara Mari • '04

Follrich de Aguinaga, Gerlinde • '62–63

Francis, William C. • '72

Frank, Christina M. • '01

Fraser, Donald A. • '40

Frattaroli, Antonio • '95

Freeman, Edward • '95

Fulks, Anna Morrison • '43

Gaddis, Barbara • friend

Gamblee, Ellsworth B. • '43

Gault, Janice A. • '50, '70 and faculty

Gebhart, Kara • '01

Goddard, James E., Jr. • '54

Gonzalez, Dr. William • '55

Gosiorowski, Thomas W. • '65

Gray, Helen McLaughlin • '32

Grean, Patricia Anthony • '75

Grosenbaugh, Richard • '59

Guilbault, Francis W. • '61

Gurnick, William C. • '65

Gusteson, Raymond • faculty

Hammell, Donald C. • '41

Hammond, Maria Linhart • '91

Harrington, Molly • '01

Harrison, Richard P. • '82 and administrator

Hart, Miriam (Mimi) • '71, '91 and faculty

Hawkins, Joan Kotapish • '75

Hebert, Carole Vana • '61

Hendricker, Sara Ague • '79, '85

Hendrie, Richard E. • '63

Herpy, James G. • '75

Hess, Mary Caroline • friend

Hesson, Martha E. • '43, '48

Hicks, Charlene Murray • '83

Hodges, Brenda Barnett • '78

Hodson, Jan Cunningham • '73, '96 and administrator

Hope, Harry • '30–31

Horton, George R. • '53

Houk, Clifford C. • '55 and faculty

Hughes, Leona H. • '30

Hughes, Robert E. • '73

Huntley, Joy • faculty

Hurst, W. Jeffrey • '69

Isler, Amy Shough • '00

Jankowski, Sara M. • '93

Jeffers, Ruth Workman • friend

Jeffery, David • '65

Jeffery, Sally • friend

Jeffery, Susan Keck • '65

Jenkins, Jean Hairston • '68

Johnson, Lynne Haley • '69

Johnson, Michael L. • '67

Johnson, Rolland C. • '70

Jolley, James A. • '99

Jones, Beverly E. • '69, '75

Jones, John M. • '49

Kaplan, Ronald • '78

Karikas, James J. • '49

Keck, David M. • '69

Kekich, George V. • '38

Keller, David N. • '50

Kerr, R. Kenneth • '75

Kessler, Amy Lynn • '96, '97

Khollarp, Jirapha J. • '95

Kircher, Patricia Irwin • '51

Klare, George • faculty

Kliesch, M. Lee Brague • '60, '65 and administrator

Kliesch, Ralph E. • '56, '61 and administrator

Kopp, Stephen • administrator

Koshal, Manjulika • faculty

Kowalchik, Richard • '64

Kraft, James M. • '57

Kraft, Sarah Bowling • '61

Krause, Alyn R. • '68

Krino, Gary M. • '65

Kuby, Thomas E. • '54

Lacy, Robin • faculty

Lafollett, Cynthia A. • '85, '87

LaFollette, Anne Downing • '56

Lairson, Timothy S. • '69, '71

Laurie, Donna Collura • '66

Lausche, Darrell R. • '97

Lawson, Ranaldo • '65

Lee, Janet Ann Rutherford • '41

Lee, Terry • '58

Lewis, Lori • administrator

Loh Pola, Angelina • '91

Lohmueller, Mary Ann Samad • '80, '81

Long, Deborah • '68

Lord, Mary Goldsberry • '28

Lynch, Thomas • '85

Mahn, Robert • administrator

Marks, Lester • faculty

Martin, Caretta J. • '79

Martin, Dorothy Trosset • '37

Martin, Gary • '71

Masada, Sandra Penix • '84, '92

Massa, Michael A. • '82

Mayer, Herbert C. • '36

McArthur, Larry F. • '53

McGregor, Jean Runyan • '47

McLaughlin, Joseph • faculty

McMillan, Jean Irwin • '46

Medleau, Laura Wickham • '83

Meeting, Sally A. • '75

Mendat, Randall F. • '70

Mendat, Virginia Burkes • '70

Merrell, William W. • '66

Michelbrink, Bernard H. • '53

Mills, Mark R. • '81

Mills, Virgilene Brown • '83

Mitchell, Darnell • '68

Mitchell, John W. • '55

Moller, Patricia Scheer • '78

Montana, Christine • '90

Moore, Bill • '68

Moore, Veanise (Gina) Ruffin • '79

Morris, James • '77

Morris, John M. • '85

Morris, Mark A. • '78

Moss, Herb • '68

Moss, Jack S. • '48

Moss, Phoebe Sacheroff • '50

Mulcahey, Becky Zielasko • '80

Muntean, Richard S. • '81

Murphey, Terry • '73

Murphree, Carolyn • friend

Mustafa, Hamina Dona • '75

Myers, M. E. Lasher • '42

Netschke, Megan • '05

Norton, Robert P. • '78

Olson, Barbara Kimberly • '60

Pace, Loren L. • '36

Page, Clarence • '69

Paoletta, Robert A. • '68

Parchmann, Mark C. • '83

Parill-Oliver, Linda L. • '98

Peltola, William • '63

Perry, Erek • '95 and administrator

Prasad, Michael • '87

Prisley, Alexander • '54, '58

Prisley, Joanne Dove • '53, '54

Pruitt, Peggy • administrator

Pugh, Michele • '92

Quattrochi, Edward • faculty

Ramirez, Alicia • '03

Raney, Jesse • '04

Ratelle, Eleanor Hazlett • '36

Rawnsley, Bernetta Close • '57

Rebok, Barbara Amos • '61

Reeves, Mary Anne • friend

Reveal, Nikia Fisher • '99

Rex, Malinda • '87

Reynolds, Kristin Nicole • '97

Rienerth, Janice • '66

Riley, Mary A. Wolfe • '58

Rishel, Stephanie Lee • friend

Robbins, Frances Hartman • '40

Robe, Eleanora Komyati • '54

Rocard, Marcienne and Jean Michel • friends

Roe, Nancy Jones • '54, '63 and administrator

Rose, Tom • friend

Rosen, Nat • '78

ROTC Department

Roth, Michael • '70

Rothermel, R. Jerry • '38

Rothgeb, Becky • friend

Rothschild, Beryl Shapiro • '51

Rudolph, Richard H. • '43

Runyan, Kristan Collins • '93

Rutter, Carolyn Saner • '79, '82 and staff

Rutter, Victor L. • '66, '67 and faculty

Sampson, Rodney • '69

Sands, Angela Hoisington • '00

Sands, George W. • '57

Sato, Reiko • '95

Saunders, Margaret Elliott • '58

Schaeffer, Laura • '95

Schuler, Geneva Elliott • '35

Seitz, Donald E. • '73

Sexton, Renee Standera • '93

Sharrock, Anita Wrentmore • '78, 79

Shelley, Robert • faculty

Shmishkiss, Pearl Bernfeld • '37–39

Shorr, Jeremy • '02

Siegel, Lois S. • '68, '70

Sinclair, Reid • faculty

Sinz, Cheryl K. • '66

Sloan, Jeanne Chapin • '59

Small, Irvin G. • '33

Snider, Tom • '78

Snyder, Kenneth W. • '93

Snyder, Kimberly A. • '93

Spencer, L. Dale • '49

Spolrich, Frank • '67

Stafford, Rebecca Terrell • '68

Stark, Matthew • '51

Stelling, Marilyn Glenn • '51

Stelling, Richard • '51

Stempel, Guido III • faculty

Stephan, James J. • administrator

Stone, Marjorie S. • friend

Stoneburner, Ida Mae • staff

Stringer, Eugene C. • '52

Stupack, Edward W. • '44

Susko, Margaret Parsons • '81

Swardson, Mary Anne • faculty

Swardson, Roland • faculty

Swirsky, Charles T. • '76

Thomas, Rose Marie Pescham • '51

Thomas-Maddox, Candice • faculty

Tilton, Timothy C. • '78

Todd, Corey • '01

Tracy, Lane • faculty

Treudley Hall

Trussell, Teresa • staff
Underwood, Frank E. • '54
Wagner, Pat Hallett • friend
Walker, Dale W. • '58
Walker, Mary Jane Shaw • '58
Walters, John T. • '52
Walters, Nancy M. • '84
Warchol, Mary Beth. • '93
Warner, Kathy • M.A. '95
Webb, Anthony • '76
Weckman, George • faculty
Wenclewicz, Stanley J. • '71
Wertman, Edith Wulf • '40

West, Floyd R. • '43
Westrick, David A. • '76
Westrick, Nanci Ferrante • '79
Whan, Edgar • faculty
Whealey, Robert H. • faculty
Whitacre, Vickie • '67
Wickham, Robert C. • '36
Wilcox, Leo A. • '50
Wildeck, Paul L. • '84
Williams, David • faculty
Williams, Robert L. • 47
Williams, Ronald G. • '67

Williams, Susan • '67
Wilson, Gerald E. • '61
Wise, Nancy Canfield • '51
Wolf, Gomer A. • '41
Wolfe, Arnold A. • '50
Wolfe, John H. • '61
Woodrow, Jane Zartman • '66, '73
Woosley, Royce • Ph.D. '66
Yoshino, Kazuya • '95
Young, Robert • '51
Yuhas, Dave • '59
Zhou, Baolin • '95

Ohio University
1804–2004

1

A Grand Conception

A University in the Wilderness, 1787–1824

The bare idea of founding, hundreds of miles away from any center of civilization, in the heart of a dark forest, full as yet of Indians and wild beasts, a "university," for the future amelioration of a State not yet born, was itself a sufficiently grand and disinterested conception.
—A. B. Walker, Reminiscences, 1876

In June 1804, Edwin Tiffin, the first governor of the recently organized state of Ohio, made his way on horseback from the capital in Chillicothe to Athens. Although there were deer, panthers, wolves, and bears along the forest trail he followed, there were virtually no people, for the new state was very much a wilderness, with only 45,000 white settlers. On a hill rising above the Hocking River, Tiffin found the few scattered log cabins that defined the tiny settlement of Athens and made his way to the home of Dr. Eliphaz Perkins.

Dr. Perkins, a New Englander, had brought his family to Athens in 1800 on the strength of rumors that the town would be the home of the first university in the Northwest Territory.

Painting by L. C. Mitchell.
Courtesy Drusilla Riley Evarts.

A copy of the act of February 18, 1804, to establish a university in Athens. *Courtesy Mahn Center.*

The rumors proved correct. On February 18, 1804, the state's general assembly chartered the Ohio University in the clear conviction that "institutions for the liberal education of youth, are essential to the progress of arts and sciences, important to morality, virtue and religion; friendly to the peace, order and prosperity of society, and honorable to the government that encourages and patronizes them."

The governor and six trustees of the future university were meeting in the town created as its home. As local historian Charles M. Walker observes, "They had traveled fifty, seventy-five or a hundred miles, by blind paths or Indian trails through dense forests, inhabited only by wild animals, to this embryo village, for the purpose of establishing an institution of learning"—evidence of their "appreciation of the value of education, and their honest devotion to the welfare of the new country." As some of the earliest settlers on this western frontier of the United States, they were determined to use an endowment of some 47,000 acres of land to create the university that would educate the ministers, teachers, lawyers, and politicians of their new state.

The idea for a university in the Ohio land had originated years earlier through Dr. Manasseh Cutler's association with General Rufus Putnam and the Ohio Company. Cutler was an educated New Englander who so appreciated "the value and pleasures of learning, [that] he regarded the diffusion of knowledge not merely as a source of individual happiness, but as a chief element of political liberty and a necessary part of the policy of a free state." He had pursued a number of professions and served as a chaplain during the Revolutionary War. Putnam had little formal education, but he had served with distinction under George Washington and won the general's respect.

At the end of the war both Cutler and Putnam found they had "an abundance of liberty but no property, and their occupation gone." Hoping to emigrate to the vast Northwest Territory that the defeated British would have to forfeit, Putnam petitioned the Continental Congress to honor its promise to pay soldiers for their military service with grants of land. Three years later, Congress still had not drafted a satisfactory plan for distributing land and governing the Northwest Territory. Putnam decided on a new tactic. He would try to buy land in the Ohio territory, specifically in the

Manasseh Cutler, Teacher,
Clergyman, Lawyer, Physician,
and Botanist
1742–1823

Courtesy Mahn Center.

Cutler, born in Killingly, Connecticut, was a Renaissance man of wide interests and
accomplishments. After earning a degree at Yale in 1765, he taught school, opened a
store, and began to practice law. Developing an interest in the ministry, he studied
divinity and was ordained as the pastor of a Congregational church; during the War
of Independence he served as a chaplain. Afterward, to supplement his meager income, he took up medicine. In 1786 he joined Rufus Putnam's Ohio Company. As its
lobbyist to the Continental Congress, he not only added significant amendments to
the Northwest Ordinance of 1787 but successfully negotiated the company's generous land contract, which, because of his belief in the value of education, included
the gift of two townships for the endowment of a university. Cutler planned to
name this institution the American Western University. However, Ohio's new legislators preferred the name Ohio University.

Rufus Putnam, Soldier and Pioneer
1738–1824

Putnam was born in Sutton, Massachusetts. Orphaned at an early age, he acquired most of his skill in reading, writing, mathematics, and surveying on his own. At age nineteen he enlisted in the French and Indian War, serving three years. In 1773, hoping to redeem the land warrants he had acquired for that service, he joined the Military Company of Adventurers in an unsuccessful attempt to acquire lands for a colony in West Florida. He served as an officer throughout the War of Independence and, in 1783, drafted the Newburgh Petition, requesting the Continental Congress to grant lands for a soldiers' colony in the Ohio Country. In 1786 he formed the Ohio Company and purchased 1.5 million acres of land in the Muskingum valley, where he founded Marietta, Ohio's first settlement. Putnam selected the two townships that endowed the Ohio University, laid out the town of Athens, drew the plat of the university, and served as one of its trustees from 1804 to 1824.

Portrait by Charles Warner Slack from a John Trumbull miniature.
Courtesy Campus Martius Museum, Marietta, Ohio.

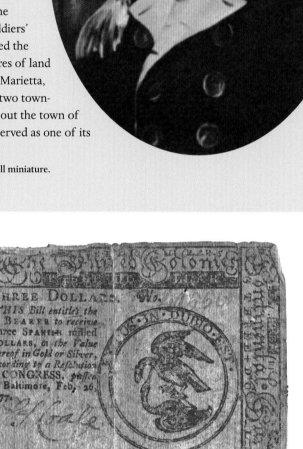

Three dollars in Continental money.
Courtesy Mahn Center.

A GRAND CONCEPTION

Muskingum valley, which he had been told was fertile. Consequently, he placed an "Information" in Massachusetts newspapers, inviting veterans of the Revolution who had been promised land in "the delightful region" of the Ohio Country to send delegates to a meeting at Boston's Bunch of Grapes Tavern, where they would form an association to purchase lands from Congress.

Manasseh Cutler attended the meeting on March 1, 1786. He and other delegates drew up articles of agreement for a land company that would raise $1 million in devalued Continental certificates through the sale of shares priced at $1,000 each. It seemed safe to assume that Congress, desperate for money, would accept the certificates in exchange for land. By the following June, the company had raised $250,000, and Cutler traveled to New York to negotiate the purchase.

His timing was fortunate. The members of Congress were finally ready to decide on a form of government for the new territory. A bill had been prepared, and a copy sent to Cutler "with leave to make remarks and

General Rufus Putnam, *eleventh from right,* with General Horatio Gates, *center,* and Revolutionary War officers. *The Surrender of General Burgoyne.* Painting by John Trumbull. *Courtesy Yale University Art Gallery. Lent by Mahn Center.*

The Bunch of Grapes Tavern, Boston. *Courtesy Mahn Center.*

INFORMATION.

The subscribers take this method to inform all officers and soldiers who have served in the late war, and who are, by a late ordinance of the honorable congress, to receive certain tracts of land in the Ohio country —and also all other good citizens who wish to become adventurers in that delightful region; that from personal inspection, together with other incontestible evidences, they are fully satisfied that the lands in that quarter are of a much better quality than any other known to New England people; that the climate, seasons, products, etc., are in fact equal to the most flattering accounts that have ever been published of them; that being determined to become purchasers and to prosecute a settlement in this country, and desirous of forming a general association with those who entertain the same ideas, they beg leave to propose the following plan, viz: That an association by the name of THE OHIO COMPANY be formed of all such as wish to become purchasers, etc., in that country who reside in the commmonwealth of Massachusetts only, or to extend to the inhabitants of other states as shall be agreed on. In order to bring such a company into existence, the subscribers propose that all persons who wish to promote the scheme, should meet in their respective counties at 10 o'clock A.M. Wednesday, the 15th of February next, and that each county meeting then assembled choose a delegate or delegates, to meet at the Bunch of Grapes Tavern in Boston on Wednesday, the first day of March next at 10 o'clock A.M., then and there to consider and determine on a general plan of association for said company; which plan, covenant, or agreement being published, any person (under condition therein to be provided), may by subscribing his name become a member of the company.

RUFUS PUTNAM
BENJAMIN TUPPER

From William E. Peters, *Legal History of the Ohio University,* 1910.

propose amendments." The bill approved July 13 was the Northwest Ordinance of 1787, which had important consequences for the vast tract of land west of the Alleghenies. The ordinance excluded slavery, set terms for preliminary government, and provided for the eventual creation of three to five states with rights equal to those of the original thirteen states. Most of Cutler's proposed amendments had been adopted, including the idea that "religion, morality and knowledge, being necessary for good government and the happiness of mankind, schools and the means of education shall forever be encouraged."

With the plan for governance in place, Manasseh Cutler redoubled his efforts to negotiate a favorable land purchase. Using the leverage of his allies, politically expedient alliances with other land companies, threats to break off talks, and a final ultimatum, he forced the financially strapped Congress to agree to his terms. He had what he had come for and more: 1.5 million acres of fertile land at a cost of less than seventy cents an acre. More important for the future Ohio University, the contract included Cutler's stipulation that "two complete townships [be] given perpetually for the purpose of an university."

Though seventeen years passed before the founding of the university, Manasseh Cutler and Rufus Putnam did not waver in their determination to see it become a reality. By the spring of 1788, Putnam had gathered fifty laborers, surveyors, and boat builders and proceeded to the mouth of the Muskingum River, near Fort Harmar, where he founded Marietta, the first settlement in Ohio. The following year, the Ohio Company's directors urged Putnam and Cutler to seek "the establishment of Instructors in the university," to "procure a charter for that Seminary," and to "fix the townships which the Directors are obliged to Set apart for the support of a University." However, it was not until 1795, after General Anthony Wayne's devastating campaign against Ohio's Native Americans—the Shawnee, the Miami, and

The Northwest Ordinance, passed July 13, 1787.

Map of Ohio Company
Purchase by William E. Peters,
*Legal History of the Ohio
University*, 1910.

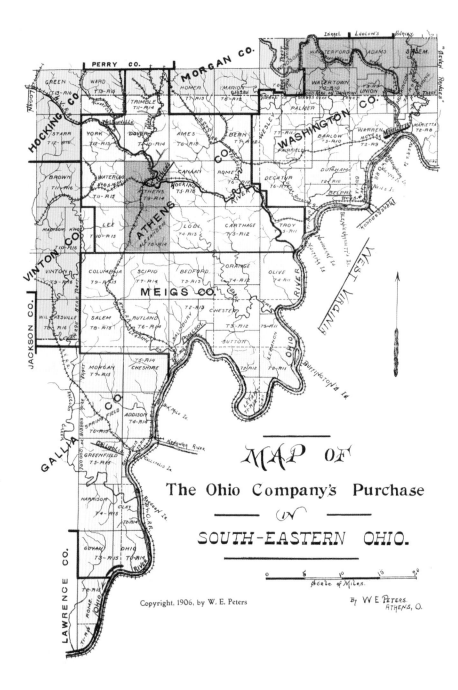

the Delaware—that Putnam could complete a survey and select the two
centrally located townships for the university's land. When he persuaded
about twenty "substantial men" to pole their way up the Hocking River in
1797, the slow settlement of the area began.

Americans were now pouring out of the crowded seaboard states to seek
their fortunes in the New America, but many rejected this hilly terrain in

Ohio Company Land Office, Marietta, Ohio.
Courtesy Campus Martius Museum.

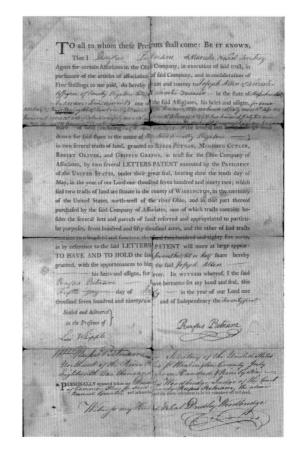

Deed signed by Rufus Putnam, July 5, 1796.
Courtesy Mahn Center.

favor of more fertile regions farther west. Nevertheless, Putnam surveyed and laid out a town to provide a home for the future university. On December 6, 1800, when "there were not more than five or six cabins occupied on the town plat," the territorial legislature passed an act establishing the town of Athens. There was to be a square for the college; lots to accommodate the president, professors, and tutors; and commons, or public grounds. Reverend Thaddeus M. Harris, who visited the area around this time, described the town as "regularly laid out, on elevated ground, of easy ascent, round which the river forms a graceful bend."

When Governor Tiffin and those six trustees, one of whom was Rufus Putnam, gathered for their first meeting four years later, their first task was to raise operating funds by leasing university lands. Consequently, they appointed appraisers and planned the first of several public auctions of town and farm lots for renewable, ninety-nine-year leases. Annual rents, to be paid

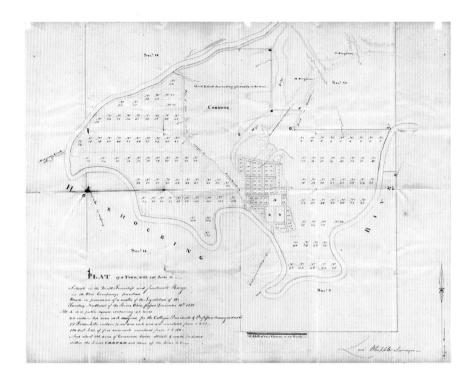

Plat of Athens by surveyor
Levi Whipple, 1800.
Courtesy Mahn Center.

An act establishing the town of
Athens, December 6, 1800.
Courtesy Mahn Center.

in cash, were set at 6 percent of the land's appraised value, with the important provision that reappraisals (and certainly higher rents) would occur at the end of thirty-five and sixty years.

By General Putnam's calculations, rents would bring in $5,529.60 a year, but it quickly became apparent that settlers had little incentive to sign university leases when they could lease land outside the university townships with no threat of reappraisal and increased rents. They could even purchase similar property and pay for it in installments, often at a price lower than the university's $1.75 per acre. When the first auction was unsuccessful, the trustees made a practical but ill-fated decision to rescind the requirement for future reappraisals. After a second auction in 1806, most of the lots inside the town were leased, but profits amounted to only $800. The land was proving to be a poor source of income and a time-consuming management problem. As Robert L. Daniel explains in *Athens, Ohio: The Village Years,* the leaseholders were in constant conflict with the university trustees, "landlord of every resident of Athens village as well as of Athens and Alexander townships."

In spite of these difficulties, in the spring of 1806 the trustees optimistically began preparations to open an academy intended to prepare local pupils for college work. Jacob Lindley, an active trustee, drew a plan for a two-story,

A GRAND CONCEPTION

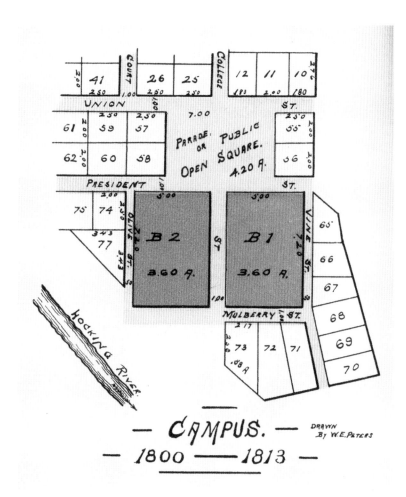

brick academy building, twenty-four by thirty feet, to be constructed on the east side of the green (a site now marked by a sundial behind Galbreath Chapel). Within two years, local builder Jehiel Gregory finished the job at a cost of $500. In the spring of 1808, Lindley, an ordained Presbyterian minister with a degree from the College of New Jersey (now Princeton), accepted the position of preceptor of the academy for a salary of $500. Soon after, though there was little cash in this isolated community, the trustees paid Alexander Stedman to dig and stone a well and Alvan Bingham to clear the college green, "reserving suitable trees for shade." On August 11, 1808, the *Ohio Gazette and Virginia Herald* of Marietta announced that "an appendage" of the Ohio University would open on the first Monday in October.

News story reporting opening of an "appendage of the Ohio University." From the *Ohio Gazette and Virginia Herald*, August 11, 1808. *Courtesy Ross County Historical Society, Chillicothe.*

Three students—John Perkins, Joel Abbott, and Brewster Higley—enrolled. Each of them had developed the self-reliance and practical skills demanded by the hardships of their lives on the frontier. John was seventeen. The son of Dr. Eliphaz Perkins, the university's first treasurer, he had made the trip to Marietta from Connecticut in 1799 with his father, his pregnant mother, and his seven siblings. Their harrowing journey took five and a half months and included long delays, illness, a week's walk through an uncharted forest, a terrifying river ride, the birth of twins, and finally the death of John's mother from a "nervous fever." Arriving in Athens in 1800, John's family moved into the only house they could find—"a log cabin with one room, one window, and one door."

Joel Abbott, who was probably several years older than John, was the owner of one of the earliest brick houses in town. He dug the "necessary" for the academy (for eighty-seven dollars) and later transported its new books and surveying instruments from Marietta to Athens (for another eight dollars). Brewster Higley, from Leading Creek, Ohio, helped survey and appraise university lands in both 1804 and 1807. All three of the first students left the university after a few years, without completing the course.

But what of the days they spent at the academy? Their preceptor and only instructor, the Reverend Jacob Lindley, was described as "not himself a very profound scholar." Charles Walker considered him "an earnest thinker

Receipt for lease of lands, 1816. *Coe Collection, courtesy Mahn Center.*

The academy building, rendered by Michael Major, '71. *Courtesy of the artist.*

and conscientious worker" with "an inflexible and unswerving devotion to moral principle" and control of his students that was "extraordinary, and always marked not less by gentleness of manner than firmness of purpose."

Reverend Lindley's purpose was to give his pupils basic skills in writing, mathematics, public speaking, geography, Latin, Greek, logic, and philosophy. For this they were charged two dollars per quarter for firewood and expenses such as candles, but no tuition. To aid in their studies, they had a set of globes, some classical texts, and Reverend Lindley's strict rules. Six days a week they recited, once a term they were examined by the trustees, and once a year they appeared in a public exhibition. To receive a degree, they needed proficiency in Virgil, Horace, Cicero, Xenophon, Homer, the Greek Testament, geography, logic, arithmetic, algebra, conic sections, natural philosophy, the general principles of history, jurisprudence, English grammar, rhetoric, belles lettres, criticism, and, more pragmatically, surveying and navigation.

Jacob Lindley, Ohio University's first preceptor and instructor.

Early Greek and Latin textbooks. *Courtesy Mahn Center.*
Photographed by Rick Fatica.

As the number of students increased —to fourteen in 1812—the trustees considered plans for a larger building, though money was scarce, as university leaseholders often paid their rents late or with cattle and hogs rather than dollars. Worried that Athenians were overcharging students for room and board, the trustees advertised appropriate rates in local newspapers. They ordered a bell to signal class changes, hired a tutor, and paid for a stage to encourage the debates and orations of the Zelothians, a secret literary society organized by the students, so they could practice their skills in writing and public speaking in an entertaining way.

A. G. Brown, a charter member of the society, reminisced about some less formal pastimes. "Our principal amusement was a peculiar game of ball. One party would knock the ball against the brick wall of the building and the others would attempt to catch it. This was considered a very exciting game at that time." He also recalled that "William W. Petit, who was one of my classmates, was a great joker. . . . He in the company of Harry Perkins [John's brother] . . . made a raid on a sugar camp near town and broke all the legs off the kettles. They were found out and brought to a strict account of their fun."

To control the high spirits, new rules spelled out forbidden activities as well as the punishments that would be applied to rule breakers. Among the proscriptions were possessing lascivious books, lying, drunkenness, unlawful games, and gross immoralities; insults to others; possession of "spiritous"

I enter the [academy] building and there I see the heavy tables and benches where we used to thumb the Lexicon and ply the pencil and slate in solving the knotty problems of Arithmetic and Algebra. There stands the rostrum and the little poplar pulpit. I see as of old the small library in the northwest corner of the building, with its terrestrial and celestial globe standing in the window and a small case of surveyor's instruments, the only apparatus of the then infant college.

—Solomon S. Miles, graduate of 1816,
from a letter to Professor W. H. Young in 1860

liquors or attendance at taverns, alehouses, and beerhouses without permission; destroying property; and wearing disguises such as women's clothes. Apparently these rules were effective, because the trustees' minutes of the next year reported "perfect harmony and a noble spirit of emulation."

On examining several students in 1815, the trustees found that Thomas

Selected Rules of 1814

No student shall possess or exhibit any lascivious, impious or irreligious book or ballad, nor sing or repeat verses of like character; and if any student shall be convicted thereof or of lying, profaneness, drunkenness, theft, uncleanliness, playing at unlawful games or other gross immoralities, he shall be punished according to the nature and heinousness of the offense by admonition, public reprehension, or expulsion from the University.

If any student shall quarrel with, insult or abuse a fellow student or any person whatever he shall be punished according to the nature of his fault.

No student shall keep by him, nor bring nor cause to be brought into the University on any occasion any spiritous or fermented liquors without the expressed permission of the president.

No student shall go to a Tavern, Alehouse, Beerhouse, or any place of like kind for the purpose of entertainment or amusement without special permission from someone of the faculty; nor shall he, on any occasion, keep company with a person whose character is notoriously bad under penalty of admonition, and if the practice is continued, of expulsion.

It is required of the students to treat all persons whatsoever with modesty, civility and due respect; but more especially, to exhibit at all times the most respectful deportment to the officers of the University, and if any student shall willfully disobey an officer of the University, in his lawful commands, or shall either in speech or action manifest disrespect towards the president, he shall be admonished and make due acknowledgement to the offended party, or be suspended, as the faculty may decide.

Any student remaining in University or in town, in time of vacation shall be subject to all the laws respecting decent and orderly conduct; and shall be under the control of such officers of the University as many reside there during the vacation.

No student shall disguise himself by wearing women's apparel, or in any other way whatever under such penalty as the president and any two trustees may see cause to inflict.

Whenever and as often as it may be necessary or expedient for any or the whole of the students to board in private families, care should be had, that none be permitted to board at improper or disorderly houses . . .

Ewing and John Hunter had performed exceptionally well and deserved to be awarded the first B.A. degrees at a formal commencement ceremony. The school had its first official graduates. At least one other student of that period, Giles Samuel Booth Hempstead, had completed his course work and examination in 1813. Hempstead later insisted that he was actually the first graduate. But because Ewing went on to an illustrious public career (Hunter died young), it was Ewing who retained the title of first alumnus.

In another momentous decision that year, the trustees agreed that a new building, eighty-two by fifty-five feet, should be built at the highest point of the Green to provide more classrooms and some accommodation for students. Architect Benjamin Corp of Marietta designed a simply styled, late Federalist building—the College Edifice. After some difficulties, he completed it in April 1818, at a cost of $17,806—money that the trustees did not actually have.

As a university building approached reality, it was time to expand the faculty and curriculum. In 1817 Joseph Dana was hired as professor of languages, and by 1819 a new curriculum promoted the "evolution of intellectual and moral faculty and the formation of habit" as the primary objects of education and set demands for punctuality, exactness, and regular progress.

The College Edifice (later the Center Building and now Cutler Hall) was completed in 1818. A bell was added to the tower in 1820, and students earned a few dollars by ringing it to mark class changes. In 1940 chimes were added to play "Alma Mater, Ohio" at noon daily. *Courtesy Mahn Center.*

Thomas Ewing
1789–1871

Thomas Ewing's earliest memories were those of a pioneer: a flatboat floating down the Ohio, bear and venison stews cooked over an open fire, the bloody head of a scalped neighbor. Ewing's father, an educated man from New Jersey who had served as an officer in the American Revolution, came to the Ohio Country by way of Pennsylvania (where he taught school) and West Virginia (where Thomas was born in 1789). By 1798 his family had located on a hardscrabble farm near Amesville in Athens County.

Thomas Ewing, a bright, athletic, and practical boy, understood that his future depended on his own efforts. He read every book that passed his way and contributed ten skins to help purchase the initial books for the famous "coonskin" library in Amesville. In 1808 he headed to the saltworks in Kanawha to earn the money needed to attend the new college in Athens. For the next seven years he alternated work with schooling. He parlayed his math courses into surveying jobs, did odd jobs for Jacob Lindley, and studied French and Latin on his own during breaks, deciding to prepare for the law. Ewing's examination by the trustees in 1815 persuaded them to regularize degree granting.

Courtesy Mahn Center.

Ewing had a long career of professional and public service. Within a year of graduation he was admitted to the bar, practicing in Lancaster, Ohio, and frequently arguing cases before the Supreme Court in Washington, D.C. He was elected to a term in the U.S. Senate in 1830, served as secretary of the treasury under William Henry Harrison and as secretary of the interior under Zachary Taylor, and completed the U.S. Senate term of Thomas Cerwin, opposing the Compromise of 1850. During the Civil War he counseled President Abraham Lincoln on legal points, and during Reconstruction he advised Andrew Johnson in his conflicts with the Radical Republicans. Ewing and his wife, Maria Boyle, raised twelve children, including five children of relations or friends, among them the Ewings' future son-in-law, Civil War general William T. Sherman. Ewing died in 1871, a worthy son of Ohio University.

For the first time, students were divided into freshman, sophomore, junior, and senior classes. The emphasis was on Latin and Greek studies, with English composition and rhetoric or declamation required each year. However, the faculty soon realized that many of their southeast Ohio students were "irregular" not just in their often sporadic attendance, but in their preference for practical courses over the regular classical course of Latin and Greek. By 1822 classes in anatomy, mineralogy, botany, and "chymistry" were part of the curriculum.

Administrative duties were also restructured and clarified. The president was to superintend the buildings, grounds, and properties; report to the trustees and preside at board meetings; plan commencements and sign diplomas; teach the senior class; and instruct all classes in English composition, with themes due every two weeks. Faculty members were required to teach five and a half days a week and assume the onerous task of maintaining discipline. Students (who now had to pay tuition) were to attend prayers at sunrise and in the evenings and go to church on Sundays.

Though they were not always prompt in answering roll call at these events and irritated their strict professors by breaking windows, damaging furniture, and pouring water on passersby, students were usually more constructive than contentious. In 1819 they founded the Athenian Literary Society, probably as an outgrowth of the earlier, short-lived Zelothian and Polemic societies. Their purpose was to "pursue the attainment of knowledge, the improvement of the mind, in taste, genesis, and criticism, the cultivation of morality and friendship, and the perfecting of the power of eloquence and reasoning." Meetings were held each week, with members writing themes and essays, giving original orations, and rigorously judging each other's performances. The rules were strict and infractions were punishable by fines. This group and the Philomatheans, who organized in 1822, included the president and professors as ex-officio members, creating a learning community that extended beyond the classroom. These societies and their successors generated most of the social and cultural life of the school for the next one hundred years.

In 1820, just as the new college seemed organized, Jacob Lindley tendered his resignation, citing the weight of his duties and failing health. The trustees considered adding another professor to the staff but lacked the funds. After a year's delay, they hired James Irvine as professor of mathematics and cre-

Medal awarded William Parker Cutler, grandson of Manasseh Cutler, by Athenian Literary Society for achievements in oratory while a student, 1829–32. *Courtesy Mahn Center.*

ated the college's second department. When the board realized the funding deficit might be caused, in part, by Lindley's failure to turn over some tuition monies paid to him, they elevated Irvine to the presidency and continued Lindley as professor of rhetoric and moral philosophy.

During the two years of Irvine's presidency (1822–24), the board expressed the conviction that among the state's universities "Ohio University has the precedence in the confidence of the public." And, in fact, the little school was sending out graduates who were succeeding admirably in their careers as ministers, lawyers, and statesmen. However, the trustees lamented that the university needed but could not afford a larger faculty, philosophical apparatus, and additions to the library; they noted the urgent need to collect debts, lease more lots, and raise tuition. In April 1823, their notes fairly shout: "Our finances are in a deranged state—our Treasury is exhausted —we are in debt." But in the next sentences, they propose to add a botanical garden and the first medical school in Ohio.

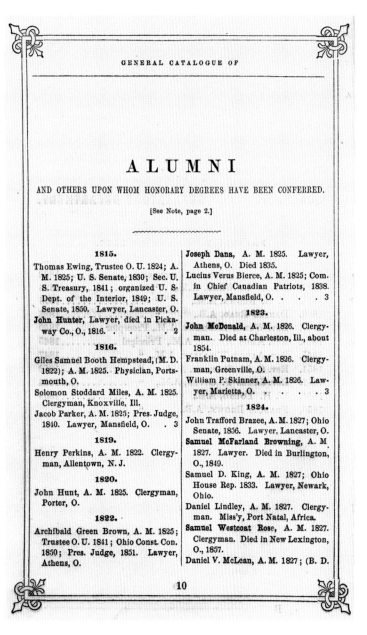

List of alumni, 1815–24, including their accomplishments. From *General Catalogue of the Ohio University from the date of its charter in 1804 to 1857*, 1857. Courtesy Mahn Center.

President Irvine's resignation in 1824 marked the end of the first phase of Ohio University's life. The academy had become a college, and whether by intention or happenstance, much of its character and future were set. By Rufus Putnam's design, the Ohio University took form in southeast Ohio, a place of "pleasing prospect." Encompassed by hills and adorned with a variety of hardwood and evergreen trees, the college lands, once the hunting grounds of Ohio's Native Americans, were quiet and isolated, and they

Athens Ohio University

First day evening, 9 mo. 30, 1821

Dear Father:

. . . I will first give you some account of my journey. Jason will have informed how I got to Chilecothe. I started from that place about two o'cl. I understood that it was 70 miles to Athens. . . . And so I set out alone a long strange road, that far from home yet going still farther with indeed some tender feelings. . . . However, I did not for a moment entertain a wish that I had not started but crossed the bridge with as much composure as I could command. . . .

I observed at a considerable distance behind me a footman coming on the road. . . . I asked him if he went through Athens. Yes. This is good luck for me. . . . We came eleven miles that evening and stopped at an old Dutchman's house where our bills were but twelve and one half cents each. Next morning we went to Adelphia, five miles where we breakfasted. . . . Walked on nine miles further and entered the wilderness. The people told us that there were bears, panthers, and plenty of deer in it. Here, how glad I was that I had Charles with me. It was the most lonesome road that I had ever traveled. . . .

Dear father, I have been looking at the incredible things of my coming here and I shall remark on. I know that thou must have some feelings on handing out to me the necessary for my abode here. It is the profits of thy hard labor. It is then very reasonable and natural that thou should be averse to parting with it and casting it into the hands of others. The man that acquires a fortune by a favorable occurance without his personal labours may scarcely know the worth of these things and may therefore be less thoughtful about spending it, but thou who hast gained all that thou hast by the hammer and the file may feel quite otherwise. . . . Be not afraid father. . . .

I am thy son,
Owen Evans

would remain so. Secured by Manasseh Cutler's efforts and expected to provide a rich endowment, in reality they produced little revenue. They were the source of ongoing tension, and even conflict, as landlord and tenants struggled to establish an equitable relationship.

The university's students—from Athens, Lancaster, Belpre, or Circleville —had known few luxuries, and many were poor. They were pioneers who had grown up hunting in virgin forests; surveying, clearing, and farming the land; or sometimes working in salt or coal mines. Leaving these responsibilities to pursue higher education and professional careers was a sacrifice for them and for their families and marked them as forward looking and independent minded.

The university's founders and Presbyterian professors were committed to the idea of a university in a residential community where education would enhance the "evolution of intellectual and moral faculty" and provide the foundations of happiness for individuals and good government for the state. They insisted on rules, religion, and morality, but they were also resourceful adventurers willing to make pragmatic decisions to ensure that education was available on the new American frontier—not for the elite, but for the sons of farmers, surveyors, and merchants. Their determination laid the foundation of a community that would persist.

"Climbing Bittersweet." Watercolor by June Carver Roberts, from *Season of Promise: Wild Plants in Winter*, 1993. *Courtesy Don Roberts.*

The Literary Societies and Their Legacy

Ohio University's distinguished forensic program, sponsored by the School of Inter-personal Communication, traces its roots to the days when the university enrolled its first students. With little to do except study, those young men formed literary societies —the university's first extracurricular organizations—and spent hours honing their skills in debate, oratory, essay writing and reading, and interpretation of literature. With the help of Jacob Lindley, they secured twenty-five dollars to promote their public speaking activities in 1811 and sixteen dollars for a stage in 1812, when the Zelothian Literary Society was founded. By 1819 the Polemic Society had replaced or joined the Zelothians. The Athenian Society began in June 1819 with a meeting that dissolved the Polemic Society; the Philomathean Society was organized in January 1822. Though other societies developed and disappeared over the years, the formi-dable Athenians and Philomatheans persisted until 1923, making them two of the longest-lived literary societies in the United States.

During their heyday, the literary societies' weekly meetings included the business of planning future programs, fund raising, acquiring books for their libraries, and fur-nishing their meeting rooms. The Philomatheans purchased a carpet in 1842; a rarity at Ohio University, it was loaned out for special occasions—to the university for grad-uation, to Athens women's clubs for meetings, and even to the rival Athenians for an exhibition.

The chief purpose of the meetings, however, was talk about topics of the day stimulated by a member's reading of an essay, or perhaps a reading from a book or a debate between members. Essays might be on corporal punishment, political party spirit, or universal suffrage. Debate topics were a mix of current events, eternal co-nundra, and the frivolous. The early Athenians were concerned with whether fame produced good or evil, whether Washington City should be selected as the national capital, and whether aristocratic rule is preferable to monarchial. The early Philo-matheans argued such topics as property qualifications for holding public office, whether it is ever permissible to lie, and whether slavery can be justified. Although the societies ostensibly kept their regular meetings secret, they held public exhibitions from time to time, and their debates became the highlight of commencement week festivities.

The competition for new members could be intense, as J. Stanbery, an Athenian, reported (ungrammatically) to L. Poston in March 1857.

> We have about one hundred and 10 or 15 Students this term We have got Six into our Society and have the petition for three or four more the philos have got about Six I think that we will get more than them there is two Young men by the name of Gutherie the philoes are Sticking around them all the time but we have there pe-tition for the next fryday night they are a going to come in our society. Baker said that he saw one of them with a philoe a hold of each arm and another walking before a giving him candy.

In 1878, the Athenians and Philomatheans jointly donated their sizable book collec-tions to the university's library. By the 1870s, women were participating in the literary societies and, in 1890, formed the Adelphia Literary Society, restricting membership

In 1890 Ohio University women formed the exclusively female Adelphia Literary Society. *Courtesy Mahn Center.*

to women. They gave as their chief reason the inhibition they felt in expressing their ideas in groups dominated by men and stated that this kept them from fully developing their potential, particularly in parliamentary procedure, oratory, and debate. The Adelphians became coeducational in a few years but dissolved in 1898.

In 1894, the faculty reacted to a decline in student interest in the traditional literary society training by making membership in a literary society a requirement for graduation. Additional literary societies that formed at the beginning of the twentieth century, the Senate, the Crestomatheans, the Oyo's, and the Platonians, were short-lived. The further decline in membership after the World War I suggests that the graduation requirement was dropped or ignored, since this was a period of high enrollment that should have swelled membership. By the end of 1923, the societies were dead.

ATHENIAN.

Some attributed their demise to the arrival of the roaring twenties and "jazz" in Athens. However, there were other reasons. In 1875, Ohio University had joined the Ohio Oratory league to participate in intercollegiate competition. Two debating clubs formed in 1898—the Hyptia Society for women and the Ewing Club for men. As courses in public speaking, debate, and declamation were added to the curriculum and student interest in competition grew, Ohio University professors and students took advantage of easy train transportation to test their skills against students from other schools. By the early twentieth century, as cars replaced train transportation, forensic competitions and tournaments were a feature of life on many of the state's campuses. By the 1920–21 academic year, intercollegiate forensic competition was so well established that all colleges and universities debated a single national debate topic.

Literary society tokens.
Courtesy Athena Yearbook, *1892.*

Largely under the guidance of L. C. Staats, the years between 1924 and 1945 were a growth era in Ohio University intercollegiate forensics. Ohio University students won numerous state championships in men's and women's debate as well as state and national championships in oratory, Staats's great strength. In addition, exhibition debates between Ohio University and nationally and internationally recognized debate teams brought attention to the outstanding program.

At the peak of the forensics program in the 1970s, Ohio University debaters qualified annually for the National Debate Tournament. Between 1968 and 1978, Ted Foster and Raymond Beaty Jr. repeatedly led the forensic program to first or second place in national quality ratings of forensic programs. Ohio hosted three major college tournaments, frequently hosted one of the state's intercollegiate championships, and became the headquarters of the Ohio High School Speech League and host of the league's state championship tournament.

Today, Ohio University's forensic program sends thirty students to twenty-five intercollegiate tournaments, hosts two tournaments under the direction of Jerry Miller, and is consistently ranked among the best in the country. In 2001 senior Erica Mason became one of fourteen students in the country to be inducted into the National Forensic Association's Hall of Fame. Although the nature of forensic activities has changed, students at Ohio University continue to enjoy, extend, and benefit from a tradition that began in 1812 and has lasted for almost two hundred years.

PHILOMATHEAN.

Obstacles and Embarrassments

1824–1845

> The endowment made by Congress was generous, deserving
> the most respectful remembrance of our times; but . . .
> the college has encountered obstacles and *embarrassments,*
> which for a time hindered it in its progress.
> —*A. B. Walker,* Reminiscences, *1876*

As Ohio University entered the second phase of its life in 1824, Andrew Jackson and John Quincy Adams were campaigning for the presidency, and the Erie Canal was nearing completion. The Ohio General Assembly was debating the merits of emancipation and colonization of slaves, while in Athens, citizens were working to improve local roads, control the livestock that roamed the muddy streets, and discourage the immoderate use of alcohol.

At the university, another Presbyterian minister, Robert G. Wilson, was inaugurated as president. In reporting the "auspicious" event in the town's first newspaper, the *Athens Mirror and Literary Register,* editor A. G. Brown, an 1822 graduate, boasted that the university had instructed more than seven hundred students and graduated nineteen. He assured his readers: "We may entertain pleasing anticipation of the reputation and usefullness of the University. Its officers are all filled, and its departments in regular and successful operation. In addition to the Public Library, the two Literary Societies composed of the Students, have each a valuable collection of books. A Museum

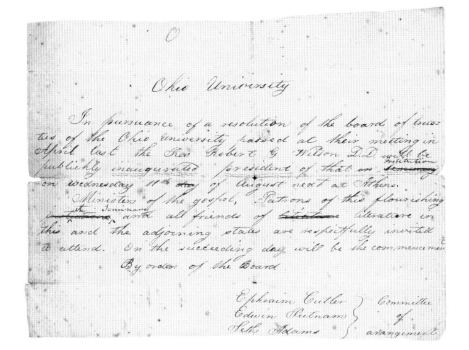

of Native Antiquities and Curiosities has been established. . . . In fine, there is every reason to believe, that the University of Ohio will be . . . eminent for 'the instruction of youth.'"

It was true that Ohio University had come a long way in its first two decades, and during the first years of the new president's administration, editor Brown's predictions of continuing success were borne out. However, after 1832 "obstacles and embarrassments" seemed to accumulate until, in 1845, the university, at odds with the community, "stripped of its birthright of land," "unable to attract a president or students," and with debts it could not pay, was forced to close its doors to all but academy students.

The greatest obstacle to progress was lack of funding. In 1824 a trustees' committee predicted "unpleasant consequences" if expenses did not decrease, and in 1827 Wilson's own report to the trustees indicated a continuing deficit. The founders' assumption that university lands would create an ample endowment had not proved correct. Some lands had never been leased, some had reverted to the university when tenants defaulted, and rents—still based on

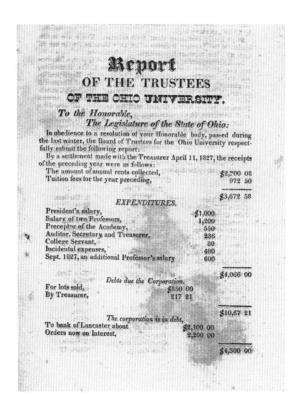

Notice of lands reoffered for lease because of delinquent rents, *Athens Mirror*, April 15, 1825. *Courtesy Mahn Center.*

Report of the trustees, 1827. *Courtesy Mahn Center.*

Story on new Ohio University programs, *Athens Mirror*, April 18, 1829. *Courtesy Mahn Center.*

The Board, as we learn with great pleasure, among other less important measures have determined upon the establishment of a new Department of Study, in which young gentlemen may receive instruction in mathematical science generally, and in all the minor studies requisite to complete a good and substantially useful education, not including the Latin and Greek Languages.

This course will require much less expense of time and money, and, we are confident, will be congenial to the wishes and feelings, and auspicious to the interests of the community.

Suitable arrangements will be made to carry it into effect at the next College Term, which commences on the 12th day of May next.

This department, we understand, is not to interfere in any respect, with the prosecution of the regular course of classical studies hitherto pursued in this Seminary.

1804 land values—were inadequate and hard to collect. Moreover, tuition receipts could not be counted on to fill the gap; fees were low, and the number of young men in southeast Ohio seeking a classical education was small and fluctuated from term to term. Exacerbating the situation were the questionable accounting procedures that left the trustees confused about their finances and open to critics' charges of improprieties.

President Wilson quickly began efforts to reduce the obstacles to solvency. In 1826, 5,000 acres of remaining university lands were put up for sale, and Jacob Lindley was asked to retire. Two years later a number of town lots were reoffered for sale. A rather bold request to the U.S. Congress for a gift of two additional townships went unanswered. Students faced a new one-dollar-per-term assessment for housekeeping services; the number of "charity students" admitted tuition-free was reduced to six; and the trustees agreed to curb expenses.

An indirect route to better funding lay in increasing the public's confidence in the university's mission and character. In 1825 Wilson launched a public relations campaign, writing releases informing the public of graduates' successes and the usefulness of education, and sending ads as far away as Mississippi. He hired an "agent" to travel around Ohio and inform the public that although Ohio University was a state institution it was no "less attentive to religion and good morals than other seminaries established by particular denominations" and, conversely, that although it was run by a Presbyterian minister and Presbyterian professors it did not, in fact, espouse the doctrine of any denomination.

Other practical measures followed. Grades of A, B, and C ("barely tolerable") were instituted, and in 1829 the curriculum was expanded to include two programs of "useful education" for "irregular students." Instruction in mathematical science was designed to require "less expense of time and money and be congenial to the wishes and feelings and auspicious to the interests of the community." An English department (really the beginning of an education school) for "those who have neither the time nor disposition" to pursue the regular course helped train teachers and improve the "efficiency of Common Schools." In 1830 classes in French were offered, and the next year President Wilson, aware of the new science of gymnastics, declared that Ohio University students needed exercise. It took several years to launch the experiment, but during 1834–35 a few students worked in the new cooper's shop, turning out barrel staves for two hours a day in what might be described as either the first physical education program or the first work-study jobs.

The students' living conditions also needed attention. Wilson called for repairs and improvements to both buildings, including the addition of lamps in the hallways and whitewash for the students' rooms. The well was cleaned and an agent was hired to oversee the buildings and grounds. By 1828, all the rooms in the College Edifice were occupied, and the president worried about the expenses, morals, and diligence of students who might have to rent rooms in town. Athenians who provided board for students were urged to resist price gouging and reduce their rates to $1.25 per week.

That same year, the president began a ten-year effort to enclose the Green, including the Commons—a wide strip of lawn adjacent to Union Street where townspeople hitched their horses and grazed their livestock. He told the trustees that an enclosure

Cooper's workshop, woodcut. During 1834–35 some students turned barrel staves in a campus cooperage shop for extra income and exercise.

Advertisement for a new boardinghouse in Athens, *Athens Mirror,* April 1823. *Courtesy Mahn Center.*

Boarding.

WIDOW **ELIZABETH GIL-MAN**, will open a Boarding House the commencement of next College Session, in the house formerly occupied by the Rev. Jacob Lindley.— Boarding, $1 25 per week, in advance, or $1 50 at the end of the Session.

Athens, April 1823.

Ordinance for the regulation of swine, *Athens Mirror*, May 2, 1829. *Courtesy Mahn Center.*

Notice of wild animal show, *Athens Mirror*, May 2, 1825. *Courtesy Mahn Center.*

would "enable us to prevent the accumulation of filth about our doors from sheep, hogs and cattle, and would present a view to the passing traveller, calculated to impress him favorably toward literature, taste and advantages of the Institution." The trustees were willing, but the townspeople were not, and since Rufus Putnam's original plat of Athens had been lost, the dispute over ownership ended in a stalemate that continued until 1896.

Students were also busy during this period. They began their days with prayers and breakfast before six, followed by recitations and study six mornings a week. Dinner was from noon until one-thirty, when recitations and study resumed. After evening prayers and relaxation before and after an early supper, students were confined to their rooms to study "with diligence" until an early bedtime. Sunday worship was required, and attendance at revival meetings was common.

Somehow there was still time for recreation. Students petitioned the faculty to abolish Saturday recitations and to allow them to use relaxation time to practice military tactics. They played a kind of soccer, kicking a ball through the trees on the Green, and a rudimentary football game was popular. John Brough, who attended during 1830 and went on to become a journalist and then Ohio's governor during the Civil War, was famous for his ability to kick a ball over the College Edifice. The nearby river and the growing number of stores on Court Street provided other diversions. Occasionally a traveling show brought exotic animals and other curiosities to town.

Students also formed temperance and Bible societies, and at their weekly meetings, the literary societies often debated serious questions of the day. The issue of slavery was close at hand, for students regularly saw ads in the *Mirror* offering rewards for the return of runaways, and one of their classmates, John Newton Templeton, was a freed slave. Enrolling in 1824, he lived not in the College Edifice with the other students but in President Wilson's house, where he worked to pay expenses. He seems to have been accepted, for he was a member of the Athenian Literary Society, and when he graduated in 1828, becoming the university's first and possibly the nation's fourth African American graduate, one of his classmates commented on his performance at commencement: "I have been attending this afternoon the

John Brough

John Brough, who attended Ohio University in 1830, was said to have been a fine footballer who could kick the ball over Cutler Hall (then known as the College Edifice). After leaving school, he organized the *Western Republican* in his hometown of Marietta, owned and operated the *Ohio Eagle* in Lancaster, and published the *Cincinnati Enquirer*. In 1837 he was elected to the Ohio General Assembly; two years later he began five years of service as Ohio's auditor; and in 1864 he became Ohio's governor. He served only one year and died in office.

From *Athens Home Coming Reunion*, 1904.

Twentieth-century students attempt to replicate Brough's 1830 feat of kicking a football over Cutler Hall.
Courtesy Mahn Center.

Boaters on the Hocking River.
Courtesy Athena Yearbook, *1931.*

Commencement program,
September 17, 1828, listing
John Templeton as a speaker.
Courtesy Mahn Center.

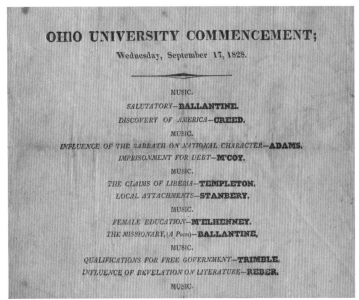

OHIO UNIVERSITY COMMENCEMENT;

Wednesday, September 17, 1828.

MUSIC.
SALUTATORY—**BALLANTINE.**
DISCOVERY OF AMERICA—**CREED.**
MUSIC.
INFLUENCE OF THE SABBATH ON NATIONAL CHARACTER—**ADAMS.**
IMPRISONMENT FOR DEBT—**M'COY.**
MUSIC.
THE CLAIMS OF LIBERIA—**TEMPLETON.**
LOCAL ATTACHMENTS—**STANBERY.**
MUSIC.
FEMALE EDUCATION—**M'ELHENNEY.**
THE MISSIONARY, (A Poem)—**BALLANTINE,**
MUSIC.
QUALIFICATIONS FOR FREE GOVERNMENT—**TRIMBLE.**
INFLUENCE OF REVELATION ON LITERATURE—**REBER.**
MUSIC.

public speeches of the graduates, and my
time has been spent agreeably until now,
late in the evening. . . . There was considerable talent discovered by them in general, and some were deserving of much
applause. . . . Templeton delivered a very
well composed speech with 'The Claims
of Liberia' for his theme."

The African American Experience at Ohio University

Nestled among the foothills of the Appalachians—at considerable distance from most urban centers—Ohio University might at first seem an unlikely site for a long and significant association with Americans of African descent. Yet their association began just twenty years after the university's founding, when John Newton Templeton, a freed slave, enrolled.

Little is known about Mr. Templeton's experiences at the university, except that he lived in President Wilson's household—perhaps because he could not find suitable accommodations elsewhere—and that he was a member of the Athenian Literary Society, suggesting that the local racial climate was not totally hostile to blacks. At the time, however, advertisements for runaway slaves were carried in the Athens newspaper, and soon after, minstrel shows, with vicious portrayals of African Americans, took hold of the American imagination. "Scientific racism," calculated to "prove" the inherent inferiority of black Americans, was about to make its appearance.

Nevertheless, Templeton received his diploma in 1828, becoming Ohio University's first African American graduate and probably the nation's fourth. Whatever his personal experiences, he graduated with knowledge and skills that enabled him to pursue a productive career as an educator and political activist and a story that is, in many ways, paradigmatic of the experiences of other African Americans who have since studied at Ohio University.

Edward J. Roye, who became the fifth president of the Republic of Liberia, followed Templeton in 1833, but attended only that one year. It was to be twenty years before the second African American, James Carter Corbin, graduated. He became the publisher and editor of a newspaper and in 1875 the first president of Branch Normal College—now the University of Arkansas at Pine Bluff—the state-supported college for African Americans.

In the nineteenth and early twentieth centuries African Americans' involvement with Ohio University was not limited to the classroom, for between 1885 and 1911 three African Americans became members of the university's board of trustees. John R. Blackburn served from 1885 to 1892; the Reverend John F. Moreland served from 1892 to 1896; and James E. Benson served from 1892 to 1911. After a long hiatus, Donald Spencer, Lewis R. Smoot, Howard E. Nolan, and Patricia Ackerman were appointed to the board in the latter part of the twentieth century.

The years 1900 to 1920 saw a small, steady flow of African American students. Arthur Carr played on the successful 1903 football team. Martha Jane Hunley (Blackburn) became the university's first female African American graduate in 1916, and was honored, along with John Templeton, in 1999 when the Templeton-Blackburn Alumni Memorial Auditorium was renamed for them.

The increase in the number of African American students in the early 1920s led to two questionable decisions by the board of trustees. A 1923 board resolution states, "Ohio University declines to admit as students in such university any citizen or resident of any state other than Ohio which said citizen or resident is not eligible for admission as a student in the state university of the state of which such student is a citizen or resident." The immediate purpose of the policy was to prevent African

Notice of runaway slaves, *Athens Mirror*, December 10, 1825.

$200 Reward.

RAN-AWAY from the subscriber at Parkersburg, Va. on the night of the 23d ult. two negro men,

TOM AND HENRY.

TOM is a low heavy-set on a country made Coat and Pantaloons with a black cape on his coat, he is 27 years old about 5 feet, 7 or 8 inches high.—HENRY is of a lighter color, slender made and nearly as tall; with a suit of the same kind, and a variety of genteel clothing, and a drab fur hat, he has the nail recently mashed off from his left ring finger, they have both strong shoes with nails all round;——They were seen four miles East of ATHENS, on Sunday last.

Whoever will apprehend said negros and deliver them to HENRY I. PRENTISS, keeper of the HOTEL in Parkersburg, Va. shall receive the above reward, or one hundred dollars for detaining or committing them, & sending word to said Prentiss, (who is authorized to receive them,) and in proportion for either.

PHILIP ALEXANDER, *Late of Prince William Co. Va.* Athens, Dec. 2d, 1825.   34-3w.

Americans from segregationist states from attending Ohio University. As a 1928 letter to the Ohio governor attests, the trustees felt "the danger of having an undue number of colored people apply for admission to Ohio University" would make "the University less attractive and, therefore much less serviceable to the young people of our own state." A group of black ministers from Columbus wrote to the governor to protest, but to no avail.

The second decision affected African American students in the College of Education. On closing the university's own model school, the trustees contracted with the city of Athens to place its student teachers in the city's schools. One provision of the contract was that no African American students would do their practice teaching in the Athens school district. As a result these students had to travel great distances and incur considerable expense to acquire the training they needed to become teachers.

In January 1939, Richard K. Fox, a 1924 African American graduate, condemned the university for negotiating such a contract with the city of Athens when "it could very easily have . . . protected the interests of its Negro students if it had so desired." As a practice teacher in the university's own secondary school in 1923, Fox had been given little responsibility and few opportunities to handle the class. He also charged the university with refusing to serve black students in the cafeteria and reminded President James of the earlier policy that had limited black enrollment. Again, his protests had little effect.

Despite these policies, the number of African American students grew dramatically from the 1940s to the 1960s. With this growth, housing emerged as a critical issue. Like other northern universities, Ohio University was unwilling to integrate its housing except as a last resort. A policy adopted in 1944 stated that the university would seek to place its black students in university-approved homes of local black residents. However, the policy conceded that "If the number of negro [sic] students should become large enough to make it practicable in a financial way, it is possible that a separate housing unit—perhaps a cottage—may be set aside for colored men and women."

After World War II, the university and the nation witnessed changes in the racial climate, and the number of African American students increased, as did their dissatisfaction with the housing situation in Athens. They were joined in their fight by white members of the community; Mrs. Elsa Sylvester, for example, wrote to President John C. Baker, expressing her concern about discrimination in Athens housing and barbershops. He assured her that the university was doing everything it could to advance the cause of racial tolerance on campus and added that "this has been done without controversy and, in my opinion, that is one of the best ways of proceeding."

In 1962 the "Approved Housing Standards Booklet" laid out a policy of nondiscrimination and advised owners of university-approved private rental properties that violation of the policy would result in removal of their names from the list of approved housing. This initiative was probably the result of the passage of the 1961 Ohio Public Accommodation Law; however, in the end, the new policy was not enforced. Although students no longer had to submit photographs with their applications, they were still allowed to state a racial preference for roommates. Unsurprisingly, the result was continued separation of students by race.

In spite of these problems, many African American students of the 1960s and 1970s remember their years at Ohio University as among the happiest of their lives. In interviews conducted at the 2001 Black Alumni Reunion, graduates of these years recall the camaraderie that existed among them. Faced with a world that was not always accommodating and comforting, they turned to one another for support and thus created a world within a world, a world which provided them protection against treatment that might otherwise have proved destructive of their self-esteem and purpose for attending Ohio University.

The 1960s brought widespread recognition of the consequences of racist ideologies and a simultaneous commitment to the ideals of the Constitution and the Declaration of Independence, the overturning of many long-enduring racial practices in the nation, and growing demands by African Americans for equal rights. It was in this climate that E. Curmie Price, the university's first African American faculty member, was hired by the English department in 1963. The next year brought James Barnes to the political science department and Ronald Williams to hearing and speech. In 1967 the first steps were taken toward the creation of a Black Studies Institute. Representatives of black organizations met with President Alden to present a set of proposals for correcting what they saw as areas of neglect. The proposals called for a separate dormitory for black students; courses in black history; the hiring of black faculty, administration, and resident assistants; the inclusion of more works by African Americans in the library; and attention to programming and cultural events for black students.

Vice President James Whalen recommended outright rejection of an exclusively black dormitory, saying it would be in violation not only of federal law but of an executive order banning discrimination in housing backed by federally insured loans and the university's own policy of nondiscrimination and integration. He did suggest, however, the creation of a "black curriculum," and spelled out the means for its implementation.

While the university administrators planned, the students became radicalized, and proposals became demands. Even so, they eschewed the confrontation politics of other universities and organized "based on constructive militancy," forming the Black Students Action Coordinating Committee, with Professor Barnes as faculty advisor. Following a series of local racially motivated incidents and galvanized by the assassination of Martin Luther King Jr. in April of 1968, students pressed their demands for a Black Studies Institute and for courses and faculty who could represent the African American experience in a fully rounded way. In July, Professor Edgar Whan, then the director of the Honors College, offered assurance that in the fall the university would offer at least thirty courses that dealt in some way with the racial situation in America. Commendable as such offerings were, what the students sought was a program of study and ancillary activities that went far beyond course offerings.

After protracted negotiations, heightened tensions, bruised feelings, not-always-polite rhetoric, and the unwavering resolve of those committed to its creation, the Black Studies Institute emerged in the fall of 1969 with William Sutton as its first director. It was one of the first such programs to exist. In looking back at this tense period, Huey Ball, a student who was involved in pressing for these changes, now gives credit to President Alden.

> To this day he is to be respected for his social conscience, his commitment to fairness and diversity before it was . . . politically correct; his commitment of University resources to a disadvantaged population; and the integrity in which he provided opportunity to develop character and leadership for a generation of minority students who were challenged to go into the job market and continue the struggle for equality and the fulfillment of the American Dream.

Since its creation, Black Studies has undergone several name changes, has seen some of its functions assigned to other campus units, and in 1980 moved into the College of Arts and Sciences. Its core mission—providing students of all races with an understanding and appreciation of an important dimension of the American experience—has remained largely unchanged. The African American experience at Ohio University has continued to evolve, and the university has made strides in addressing the concerns of its black student population. These have ranged from special efforts to recruit and retain African American students to recognition of their special needs—hence, targeted cultural programming. Retention is supported through both university and departmental scholarships. The former include the King-Chavez-Parks Scholarships, directed to African American and Latino students, and the Templeton Scholars awards, which emphasize academic excellence, leadership, and campus involvement. Several colleges, including Arts and Sciences, Engineering and Technology, Health and Human Services, and Osteopathic Medicine, administer their own programs designed to enhance minority enrollment and retention. Recruiting and retaining black faculty is an ongoing concern.

Since the 1960s there has been a general increase in the number of black faculty, administrators, and staff, as well as an increase in the level of responsibility some have assumed. Hilda Richards's appointment as dean of the College of Health and Human Services in 1979 marked the first time an African American outside the Black Studies Institute had held such a position at Ohio University. Since then African Americans Dora Wilson and Raymond Tymas-Jones have led the College of Fine Arts. Barbara Ross-Lee's leadership of the College of Osteopathic Medicine marked the first time a black woman had been appointed as the chief administrator of a college of medicine in the United States.

The relationship between African Americans and Ohio University now goes back 180 years, encompassing much of the nation's history. Despite the sometimes less than ideal circumstances in which they studied, African American graduates of Ohio University have had a record of achievement. Many, including syndicated columnist Clarence Page, artist Nelson Stevens, actress Vanessa Bell Calloway, and television anchor Leon Harris, have achieved national reputations in their fields. That Ohio University has played a significant role in this record of achievement is attested to by the alumni themselves. Problems notwithstanding, they say, Ohio University was important in their intellectual and social development.

Although Templeton's attendance caused little stir, the arrival of students from other regions created tensions. Eventually President Wilson would blame outside agitators for some serious problems. In 1829 Charles Arbuckle of Virginia complained in a letter to his brother:

> I have written in all my letters anterior to this that I was satisfied with my situation. At the present I am not very well satisfied. The reason why is that the inhabitants of the town are so selfish: if they get their own thing performed they are satisfied; they are the most miserly set about the town and the yankees of the institution I ever saw. If any of these yankees happen to get a room with a Virginian they spunge entirely and better ones I have never seen if they want quills rather than buy them they will run all over college if they want apples they will go and ask in all the rooms in college almost and if they have any they instantly ask where they are and eat as free as it they had bought them. . . . And if it was not for the Virginians the students would in a manner die off.

The faculty tried to deal with these ordinary problems of student life. In 1824, they discussed the need for some supervision in the Edifice, for it seemed Manasseh Cutler had been right in predicting that "chambers in colleges are too often made the nurseries of every vice and cages of unclean birds." The next year, when President Wilson reported to the trustees that there had been "more calls than usual for the exercise of discipline during the last term," both he and the faculty were commended for "the judicious and inflexible administration of discipline." The trustees, worried about the "extensive mischief" caused by suspended students who lingered in Athens, advised that "the offender should be moved at least some miles from the Institution" but offered no suggestions for how to achieve that solution.

"Inflexible discipline" was no more consistently effective in Athens than elsewhere. Around the country, university students railed against their professors' paternalism, attacked their tutors, and destroyed property. In 1826 Ohio University students staged their first riot. Apparently President Wilson returned a literary society member's unsatisfactory composition for correction, causing insurrection. The trustees, determined to maintain control, expelled the offenders. Their heavy-handed response must have drawn some criticism, because the board soon published an article in the *Ohio State Journal* offering a defense of their actions.

These dramatic eruptions were rare, of course, and in general the college seemed to prosper until 1832, when its difficulties began to mount. The buildings were in poor condition, with rooms that were prone to fill with

WHAT IS REQUIRED OF STUDENTS

IN THE

OHIO UNIVERSITY.

1. Obedience to the laws of the University, and the authority of its Officers.

2. Diligence and faithful application to study.

3. Regular and punctual attendance on all College duties.

4. To be in their respective rooms during the hours of study, and after 9 o'clock at night, unless leave of absence shall have been obtained.

5. To retire to rest at or before 10 o'clock at night, and in no case, except in sickness or special permission, to have lights burning in rooms after 10 o'clock at night.

6. To keep their rooms neatly and in good order; and to avoid sweeping into the Halls, or throwing from the windows ashes, water, or filth of any kind.

7. To occupy rooms in the College Buildings, unless by permission of the President; and not to remove from the particular rooms assigned them, except by the same permission.

8. To attend College Examinations.

9. To take such part in College Examinations as shall be assigned, and to speak only such matter as shall have been previously approved by the Faculty.

10. To abstain from smoking tobacco in the College Buildings.

11. To respect the Sabbath and religious institutions.

12. To attend reverently the worship of the Chapel, and public worship twice on the Sabbath, including the Lecture in the Chapel on Sabbath afternoon.

13. To avoid profanity, obscenity, and vulgarity.

14. To observe polite and decorous deportment toward each other, and toward all other persons.

15. To observe cleanliness, both as it respects person and dress.

16. To give testimony when called upon by the Faculty, concerning irregularities and transgression of College order.

17. To be responsible for damage done to their respective rooms, and for general damage done where the perpetrator cannot be discovered.

Rules of the 1840s.
Courtesy Robert Mahn.

smoke, and there was a "paucity of students." The trustees were sure the lack of students was not "owing to any peculiar expense" at Ohio University, or to "any deficiency in the prescribed course of study" or "in the fidelity of the Instructors," or to the unhealthiness or lack of morals. Rather, the blame must lie in the "moderate circumstances of the surrounding population," rumors of lack of harmony among professors, or reports that the trustees had defrauded the university. Though the administration agreed to publish reports on the university's condition in an effort to counter these suggestions and restore the public's confidence, rumors apparently continued to swirl, and the administration's displeasure with student behavior intensified.

According to the trustees' minutes, in the spring of 1834 "the preservation of order in the Institution has been attended with unusual difficulties.

Booklet containing the rules and regulations of the Independent Court of Ohio University, organized by students to settle grievances and improve speaking, and presided over by "judges," "attorneys," and a "sheriff." *Courtesy Mahn Center.*

A disposition to wantonly destroy the Glass Windows of the Edifice and to deface the Walls, has been manifested again and again." Though the trustees decided that "discipline reasonably consistent and firm is the only corrective for this evil," the situation had not improved by the fall meeting, when they said: "At no former time have our Youth manifested dispositions so ungovernable."

The difficulty may have resulted in part from students' dissatisfaction with some of their professors. The Athenians lodged a protest against Mr. Wall, a mathematics professor, who had been investigated earlier when students accused him of "hurting their feelings" with his harsh comments about their poor recitations. (One student even boasted later of giving the professor a much deserved "whipping.") Now, though students accused Professor Wall of improperly entering the Athenian Hall, the trustees supported him; it was the students, they said, whose behavior had been "boisterous, disorderly & reprehensible." The behavior of Mr. Amasa Read and Mr. McElhenney, especially, was deemed "highly improper, very disorderly & in a peculiar degree censurable." Read's brother Ezra wrote the trustees on Amasa's behalf: "I hope the Honorable Board of Trustees, will give his case a careful examination, and if consistent with the regulations of the Institution, will have the kindness to confer his degree—a favor that will be acknowledged with gratitude. He is the fifth member of our family, who look to the O. University, as their Alma Mater, all of whom with this exception, I think gave entire satisfaction to their Professors, and were careful in their obedience to the laws of the Institution."

President Wilson wrote his nephew about other behavior—especially that of students from other states—that drove the trustees to a decision they quickly came to regret.

> The college is not now in a very prosperous state. Last summer we had a large number of Virginians and some from other parts, not accustomed to Government, who carried on much disorderly mischief: such as rolling stones or brickbats in the college halls in the darkness and silence of the night —fastening up the doors of the recitation rooms, so that the teachers could

not enter in the morning—carrying off, hiding, and sometimes destroying blackboards—by loud & tumultuous noises in and about college—and even while the board was in session, during a recess of that body, their table, benches etc. were thrown from a window of the third story of the college edifice and broken to pieces. . . .

The Board resolved that every student here after admitted would be required to sign the following declaration—we and each of us, do declare it to be our purpose to be quiet, regular, and orderly in our deportment—to obey the laws of the University—respect the authority of the faculty and render our aid in detecting and suppressing disorder. This last, all our Virginians and Kentuckkians & four of the state of Ohio, refused to sign & went away.

After this crisis only thirty students remained—not enough to "justify the ordinary & unavoidable expenses of the Institution." As President Wilson said, unless steps were taken to promote it, "the institution must go down and be no more a public blessing." He proposed repairing the Edifice, constructing an additional building (which would require a loan), establishing some "convenient communication with the Ohio River," and a plan to reduce

Minutes from Athenian Literary Society meeting of January 1834, reporting the concerns of the Philomatheans about Professor Drake, whose services were "discontinued" several months later.
Courtesy Mahn Center.

debts. All faculty members were dismissed except the president and Daniel Read, the head of the academy. The two of them would be responsible for all recitations.

President Wilson also had to admit his responsibility for the Athens Town Council's last-minute refusal to quit its claims to the section of the Green that had been disputed since 1828. Negotiations to transfer ownership had been under way when a "stranger had applied for liberty to erect a tent for a Circus on the College Green." The president refused permission, but the tent went up anyway. Wilson entered a charge of trespass against the stranger and won. However, his unilateral action irritated the town, and the negotiations collapsed. The president ordered a small, neat fence to be erected near the buildings, but it did not enclose the Green, and the town still claimed the Commons. As A. B. Walker would later remark, the people of southeastern Ohio were stubborn.

Perhaps it was this stubbornness that allowed those responsible for the university to keep it open in spite of these obstacles and to begin some measure of renewal over the next few years. By 1838, when Wilson first tendered his resignation, free tuition scholarships were offered to one student from each county. Three faculty replacements were in the classrooms: Daniel Read (previously the head of the academy) in languages, Rev. Alfred Ryors in math-

Drawing of the Center Building and the two wings by Henry Howe, 1846.
Courtesy Mahn Center.

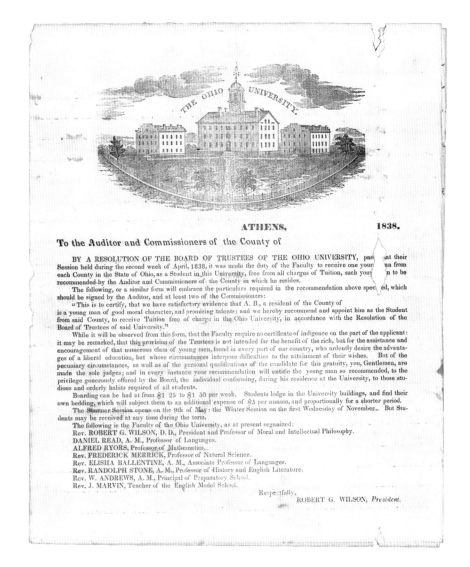

Circular advertising county scholarships, 1838. *Courtesy Mahn Center.*

ematics, and Rev. Edward Smith in natural science. Courses in American history had been approved; a model school to assist in preparing teachers for common schools was open; and a new building, the East Wing, was complete. The next spring, the West Wing was also finished, and President Wilson retired. Though disappointed that the number of students remained small, he was optimistic. Advertise, he said. Open a good boardinghouse with reasonable prices. Continue to admit one student tuition-free from each county to accommodate those whose "pecuniary resources are limited," because it is from them "that our colleges receive the majority of their students and from them, the public is supplied with its most illustrious and useful members."

In September 1839 the trustees inaugurated a new president, William Holmes McGuffey, a teacher of moral and mental science, a preacher, and the author of the *McGuffey Eclectic Readers*. During his first year, he roused Athenian ire when he took it upon himself to beautify the college grounds. He planted seventeen young elm trees parallel to East Union Street, but far enough back not to intrude on the disputed Commons. However, according to a family history, *The Story of the McGuffeys*, when he erected a fence to protect the trees, "to his utter astonishment" the "touchy villagers . . . stamped into the office and ordered him to take away that fence. He flatly refused, and from then on there was open animosity. William received threatening letters and was jeered at and hissed in the streets. When he had to go into remoter country for preaching or weddings, he armed himself with a horsewhip."

Other changes during McGuffey's administration had fewer personal consequences. The trustees appointed a finance committee of three to manage the university's debt. The academy was integrated into the college, and ungraded classes became the norm. The faculty was reorganized, and a new department of rhetoric and English was added. The academic calendar, with two long terms and a late fall commencement, was modernized to include three terms and a more convenient August commencement. The daily schedule became even tighter, and McGuffey's insistence on instructing students in "the Christian religion" alienated many people who might otherwise have supported the university.

McGuffey's strict views extended to student behavior. Since the crisis of 1835 had failed to eliminate students' misbehavior, the administration escalated its reprimands, suspensions, and expulsions. Minutes of the faculty's meetings, first recorded in February 1837, are filled with notations of "whispering in the time of worship," throwing water and ashes from the windows of the college building, absences from recitations, and "withholding testimony necessary for the prevention of disorder." In 1840 Edward Adams, a senior accused of filling the halls with mown grass, was expelled for "negligence and insubordination"; his friends protested his innocence and denounced the president's refusal even to hear his case. One classmate wrote a long letter to the *Scioto Gazette*, accusing the faculty of delighting in tampering with students' rights and showing an unjustifiable disrespect for their feelings.

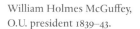

OHIO UNIVERSITY.

INAUGURATIONS.

Wednesday, Sept. 18, 1839—2 o'clock, P. M.

MUSIC.

PRAYER.

Address by JAMES HOGE D. D., to the President Elect, informing him of his election.

Administration of the Oath of office, by the Hon. N. C. READ.

Address to President McGUFFEY, by R. G. WILSON D. D. late President, and delivery of the charter and keys.

MUSIC.

Inaugural Address of President McGUFFEY

MUSIC.

Inaugural Address of Professor MERRICK.

MUSIC.

Inaugural Address of Professor BALLANTINE.

MUSIC.

PRAYER.
BENEDICTION.

ALUMNI-PROCEEDINGS.

WEDNESDAY EVENING, 7 O'CLOCK, P. M.

PRAYER.
MUSIC.

Address of the Hon. THOMAS EWING, to former Students of the Ohio University.

MUSIC.

MEETING OF THE ALUMNI.

Program for the inauguration of William Holmes McGuffey, September 18, 1839. *Courtesy Mahn Center.*

William Holmes McGuffey,
O.U. president 1839–43.

Sketch of McGuffey house at the corner of Court and Union, facing the Green (from William E. Peters, *Athens County, Ohio,* 1947), and same sketch superimposed on the building occupying the site today. *Courtesy Mahn Center.*

Under these conditions, the problems continued. Mr. J. Brice and Mr. Wallbridge left the college without permission and found, when they returned, that they had "cut themselves off from the Institution." So did Mr. Flanner. Mr. Pickens insulted "a citizen, and a company—partly of ladies" and was dismissed. Later the East Wing and Edifice (now called the Center Building) were found to be much disfigured by the vulgar practice of "scribbling on the walls." Three students who had been found to be drinking wine and beer suffered public admonishment, but not expulsion.

Of more consequence, because of the number of students involved, was Mr. Wesson's case in 1841. He had been missing recitations, and his refusal to return to classes when ordered to do so resulted in a petition to the president and faculty from ten of his friends who respectfully requested an honorable, rather than a dishonorable, dismissal for him. When their petition was denied, they left the campus, were deemed to have left without permission, and were added to the list of the dismissed.

Though their departures thinned the ranks of an already depleted student body, it was inadequate funding that most threatened the college during this time. Desperate to increase revenues, Trustee William Medill presented a resolution in 1841 proposing a return to the terms of the 1804 charter, which called for periodic reappraisals of leased college lands. He also argued that land already sold should be taxed at a rate equal to the state tax. In spite of opposition from several Athens trustees and serious concern from President McGuffey and former professor Joseph Dana, now a local attorney, the resolution passed. Important landholders were thoroughly upset and contended that the right of reevaluation had been repealed in 1805. To try to reach some

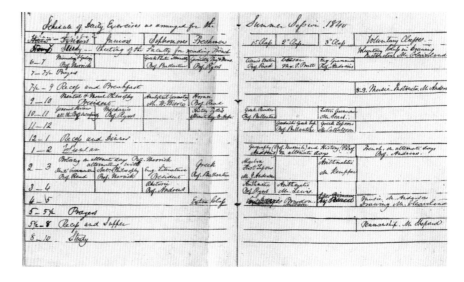

Students' daily schedule for the summer session, 1840. *Courtesy Mahn Center.*

OBSTACLES AND EMBARRASSMENTS

THE ECHO
AND UNIVERSITY RECORD.

The first student publication, the *Echo and University Record* of February 1843. *Courtesy Mahn Center.*

Removal of the College

It is probably well known by our readers that a proposition had been made in the Ohio Legislature to remove the Ohio University to Mansfield, Richland county, by Senator Bartley. The inquiry naturally arises why has this movement been made. . . . It is true that difficulties have arisen, now and then, between the College and the people [of Athens], but they have been very few and that which now exists, is evidence of no unkind feeling on either side. . . .

Why then remove the Ohio University to Mansfield? IF IT IS to be removed, let it be to Zanesville, Columbus, Lancaster, or some other equally central place—where the citizens possess wealth and enterprise and would subscribe a sufficient amount to erect suitable college buildings. Then, and NOT UNTIL THEN will the Ohio University take a rank among the Literary Institutions of the land, consistent with its lofty name and the character of the distinguished men who conduct its affairs.

solution, the two sides agreed to a "test case" in the Ohio Supreme Court, with Festus McVey bringing suit against the university.

As President McGuffey waited for the outcome in January 1842, he wrote to Ezra Walker, describing the situation:

> The revaluation question has created such a state of feeling around us, towards the college, as renders it next to impossible for those connected with the O.U. now, or for years to come, to have the cooperation of the citizens. . . . I, from the first, held it exceedingly problematic whether any man—or set of men—could build up the college. . . . The irritations which exist and must continue, if not increase, cannot fail to make it unpleasant for those who hold office under the Board. . . . Our neighbors censure *us* for what they deem the unjust proceedings of the Board—and the students transfer it to our modes of governing them and conducting their studies.
>
> P.S. Two more colleges are 'being founded in Ohio' . . . So it seems we hadn't enough of colleges in the State.

The court decided for the university, but the disgruntled lessees implored the board of trustees to rescind the order to revalue and, failing in that effort,

Samuel Sullivan "Sunset" Cox

When Samuel S. Cox was a student (1843–45) living in the West Wing (McGuffey Hall), he might well have inspired faculty complaints about "scribbling on the walls" by painting a wall-sized mural in his room. His model was the famous Hellenistic sculpture of Laocoön, a priest of Apollo at Troy, and his sons in a death struggle with sea serpents. Cox was considered "a brassy student" whose pranks included spiking one of the cannons on the Green so that it could not be fired by Athens citizens celebrating their legal victory over the university in 1843. He left Athens in 1845 when this victory contributed to the university's closing. A year later Cox graduated from Brown University in Providence, Rhode Island, and returned to Ohio to read and then practice law. But he was drawn to journalism and became the editor and owner of the *Ohio Statesman* in 1853. His fanciful description of a sunset in that newspaper won him the nickname of "Sunset" Cox. In 1856 he was elected to represent central Ohio in Congress. When he lost that seat in 1864, he moved to New York City and was returned to Washington in 1868, serving effectively as a member of the House of Representatives for many years, including one year as Speaker pro tempore in 1876.

On February 1, 1931, the *Ohio Alumnus* reported that "for many years hidden deep under layer upon layer of various wall coverings and at the present time obscured from view by a single thickness of paper, is an interesting work of art painted on the south wall of the northwest corner room, second floor, of the West Wing. Few, if any, of today's undergraduates know of its existence while only a comparatively small number of alumni are aware of it."

In 1983, McGuffey Hall was renovated for use by the university's Office of Development. The fate of the Cox mural was discussed at length. Because of the condition of the masonry in McGuffey (the building was near collapse at the time), the wall and the painting proved difficult to save. Removing the painting and applying it to another wall in better condition was deemed cost prohibitive, so restorers attempted to correct problems with the wall and save the mural. Before work started, both were photographed. Unfortunately, the effort to save the mural paralleled the struggle of Laocoön and his sons against the sea serpents. Neither was successful.

Samuel Sullivan "Sunset" Cox and the mural he painted on the wall of his room in the West Wing (McGuffey Hall). *Courtesy Mahn Center and John Kotowski.*

took their arguments to the state legislature. The Athenian lobby was strong, and the legislature, on March 10, 1843, ruled that by the binding Act of 1805 the trustees could never revalue their lands. With inadequate income from its property and little support or sympathy from the state, the university had no recourse but to economize and refinance the debt of $13,518.64. Salaries were drastically reduced, including McGuffey's, although he had warned that "competent men cannot be retained but upon adequate salaries." On September 19, after months of facing the animus of a community that blamed him for their troubles—even to the point of attacking him in the street with mud-balls—he resigned, leaving a legacy defined by controversy and the McGuffey Elms.

In spite of the problems of the early 1840s, Ohio University's first fraternity—Beta Theta Pi—was organized in 1841. *Courtesy* Athena Yearbook, 1892.

In the face of this "crippling blow," professors Read and Ryors also resigned, and some twenty students followed them. In early October a group of those remaining held a public meeting, demanding assurances of stability. The trustees' call for a special meeting of their own suggested crisis rather than continuity, and another twenty students left. In the meantime, Athenians met to deny reports that the university's "embarrassments" stemmed from their own "cherished and bitter hostility" toward the school. And in November they presented a resolution to the trustees (published in various newspapers) proffering their sincere "regret that even a momentary cloud should come upon its prospects." Their actions, they argued, were not intended to unsettle the community, and they were sure that only a very few persons—who were more likely to be from the townships than the town itself—had evidenced any animosity.

By January 1844, the financial situation could not "but excite deep concern and anxiety." But the trustees noted the university's long history of struggles and that it had "triumphed over these." Apparently they expected triumph again, for they had already selected the Reverend Alexander T. McGill as the next president. Unfortunately, McGill delayed his acceptance, causing increasing uncertainty throughout the winter, spring, and into the summer of 1844. Finally, in late July, he declined the position.

The faculty and trustees struggled on. But the situation was too dire,

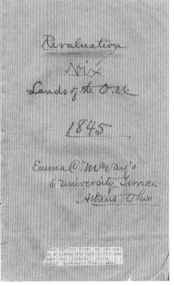

Booklet of the revaluation of Ohio University lands, 1845. *Courtesy* Mahn Center.

The McGuffey Elms.
Watercolor by Carl F. Riter,
circa 1943. *Courtesy Barbara Lee
Binns, '43.*

and on April 2, 1845, the trustees made a decision: "In view of the present depressed condition of the University, in consequence of its financial embarrassments, the falling off in the attendance of students, and other unfavorable circumstances," it was "indispensable for a time to suspend the ordinary collegiate operation of the Institution." The length of the suspension was to be three years. The academy was to remain open to continue preparing students for collegiate work and in the hope that its revenues, along with those from rents, would help pay off the institution's debts. The plan was to begin with a clean slate in 1848.

3

Innovation and the Struggle to Survive

1848–1872

The question thus comes up with great interest to the trustees, faculty, and Friends of the University. "What can be done? What can we do that the wants of this part of the State can be met?"
—*President Solomon Howard, 1867*

When Ohio University celebrated its reopening with the inauguration of Alfred Ryors as president in 1848, the country was alive with issues and innovation. With the end of General Zachary Taylor's successful three-year campaign against Mexico, the United States had acquired territory in the southwest and California that increased its size by one-third and greatly intensified the debate over slavery. In New York, Sojourner Truth, a former slave, spoke at camp meetings, raising questions about both race and gender. Elizabeth Cady Stanton organized a forum on women's rights, and author Margaret Fuller argued for women's independence. The sewing machine had been invented, and Samuel F. B. Morse had sent his first telegraph message. The New York Nine, playing by the new rules of baseball, had soundly defeated the Knickerbockers. A potato blight in Ireland propelled thousands to America's eastern shore, while religion, land, and gold drew others west to Utah, Oregon, and California.

The citizens of Athens were aware of and interested in these issues and had their own as well. The growth in population and prosperity that early

Letterhead from stationery used by President Alfred Ryors in 1851. *Courtesy Mahn Center.*

Alfred Ryors, O.U. president 1848–52.

A Court Street business owned by W. H. Brown was housed in one of two brick buildings that halted the great fire of 1877. *James Anastas Collection, courtesy ACHS&M.*

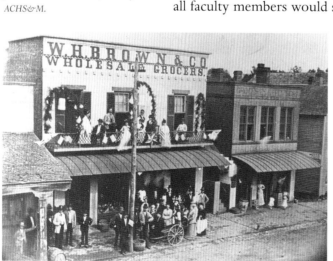

settlers had anticipated seemed to have moved to the north, leaving them behind. Nevertheless, the town was slowly growing, new businesses were opening, businessmen were speculating about railroads, and virtually everyone except the drinkers worried about taverns and drinking.

The two most pressing issues before the university were, as usual, funding and public confidence—how to pay down the debt and convince Ohioans of the great importance and worth of higher education. The new president, thirty-six-year-old Alfred Ryors, yet another Presbyterian minister and an Ohio University mathematics professor from 1838 to 1843, was familiar with these abiding problems and began to make changes immediately. He issued a catalog to publicize the university's programs and virtues. He instituted an early version of a practice now known as "writing across the curriculum": all faculty members would share the burden of teaching English composition. They, rather than trustees, would examine students at regular Friday afternoon rhetorical exercises. The president, with some assistance, would lead a Bible study.

The faculty still held responsibility for discipline and at weekly meetings recorded student misbehaviors such as buying whiskey, engaging in "conversation of a grossly profane and infidel nature," and even "setting fire to the Center Building." However, attitudes seemed relatively lenient. Faculty members agreed, for example, "that College duties be dispensed with the day of the approaching Thanksgiving, except for morning worship." In an innovative turn they began to offer "premiums for excellence" to "stimulate their young charges to highest efforts."

At the end of his first year, Ryors reported that forty-nine students had been in attendance—"discouraging," but not a cause of particular concern. To boost enrollment and help reduce the continuing debt of $15,000, the trustees agreed to a scholarship program similar to ones offered by other colleges. Purchased for thirty dollars each, the scholarships entitled the holder to nine terms, or three years, of instruction. But because thirty dollars was the regular price of one year's tuition, the scholarships simply reduced potential profits by two-thirds. Surprisingly, initial sales were small. Not surprisingly, the inherent flaw in the plan soon became evident; even so, the program continued intermittently over several years.

By 1852, with money from the scholarships, room rents, more lot sales, more vigorous rent collections, and careful economy, the debt was reduced to $8,482.32. At this point, the young president resigned. He had been reasonably successful in reviving the university, but serious problems remained. Although university alumni had built significant reputations in law, politics, journalism, and the ministry, their numbers were small. In its nearly fifty years of existence, Ohio University had graduated only 145 men while rival Miami University had graduated 469. An *Athens Messenger* article under the byline "Viator" asked why Ohio University, so rich in so many resources, had so few students. The answer was apparently that it lacked ease of access, adequate publicity, sympathy from the citizens of Athens, and a clean,

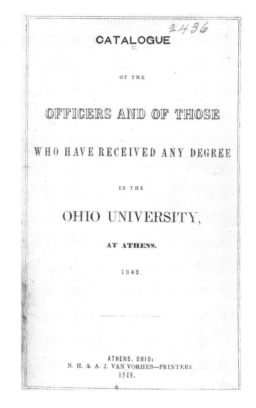

Catalog of 1848, printed for the reopening of the university. *Courtesy Mahn Center.*

Excerpt from minutes of faculty meeting, 1849, noting students' request for a Thanksgiving holiday. *Courtesy Mahn Center.*

Solomon Howard, O.U.
president 1852–72.

Diploma for Bachelor of
Science degree, 1856. The
new, practical degree was
designed to meet the needs of
students from southeast Ohio.
Courtesy Mahn Center.

attractive locale. Both the filthy town and the dilapidated school needed a thorough cleanup, especially of the "squealing menace" presented by the pigs that dug up the Commons and toppled pedestrians.

Later that year the board of trustees, which now included some Methodist members, chose Solomon Howard, a Methodist minister and natural science professor, as president and new problem solver. It was a bold move for a school that from its inception had been dominated by Presbyterians.

Among the early issues confronting President Howard was a lawsuit brought by John Matheny and 770 other leaseholders who objected to the university's attempts to collect tax on their leased properties. The measure had been approved by the legislature in 1852, but the lessees met, raised money, lobbied, contested, and finally won a court decision that denied the university the small endowment that would have accrued from these taxes.

Though the president could not change the problems with the lands, he was determined to make changes in other areas of university life. At his inauguration, he stated his view of university governance. "We believe most firmly," he said, "that as the government of a college conforms to that of the family the better adapted it will be to the end proposed. The parental system should obtain."

He indicated just as clearly that Ohio University would try to "satisfy the popular demand of a learned preparation for different practical pursuits" while maintaining "complete and thorough mental standards" throughout the curriculum. Two "practical pursuits" were arranged almost immediately. A two-year scientific course, similar to the one Wilson had begun earlier, allowed students to prepare themselves for business and teaching without taking the usual courses in Greek and Latin. In 1853, a summer institute was organized with Marietta College to prepare teachers for common schools. This effort later became the South Eastern Normal Institute, where for four dollars (men) or three dollars (women) schoolteachers and local residents could study with regional instructors during a four-week summer session.

Discussions of a medical school in Zanesville and a law department were short-lived, but in general the university seemed to be improving. At least President Howard was satisfied. In 1853 he reported, "I have never known a company of students who were more devoted to their studies." Furthermore, "the faculty had infused life and health into all the Departments." He was just as pleased the next year when the renewed sale of scholarships reduced the debt to $6,119.54. The total enrollment had reached 142, the "spirit of insubordination [was] unknown," and there was "not one case of disorder." By 1855, though a Marietta paper pronounced both Athens and the university "dead," there was enough evidence of prosperity to allow talk of a new chapel or library and perhaps raises for the faculty. The students were even said to be more mature, a notion at least temporarily belied (or perhaps proved) by two incidents of "highly improper conduct": first "a woman of disreputable character" was found in college rooms, and soon after, another student was accused of "admitting to his room by previous arrangement at the hour of midnight, a notorious prostitute."

Were the young men of Ohio University then a group of rude ruffians from the "Huckleberry Knobs," or were they serious, even pious, seekers of knowledge? Obviously, their behavior was not always perfect, at least in the

The Ohio University.

The Board of Trustees also agreed upon disposing of 500 Scholarships, (embracing a term of three years,) at the rate of fifteen dollars each, which is so extremely liberal as to bring the opportunity for an education at this institution within the reach of all. Agents will soon be engaged in disposing of these Scholarships, and we hope before long to see a great increase in the various departments of study pursued in this University.

Other measures were suggested, and which will probably be consumated, having in view the increased interest and usefulness of the University.

A program offering nine terms of instruction for only thirty dollars provided needed funds for the short term and deficits over time. *Athens Messenger,* August 13, 1852.

Group portrait of class of 1856. *Courtesy Mahn Center.*

The Ohio University Libraries

Edwin Watts Chubb Library.
Courtesy Mahn Center.

The Ohio University Libraries system dates back at least to 1814 but came into its own during the university's second century. Since the opening of the first library building—the Carnegie Library—and the appointment of a full-time library director—Charles Matthews—in 1905, the library has grown and transformed itself in many ways from the time of typewritten catalog cards to today's online databases.

The Carnegie Library, now Scripps Hall, served as the library from 1905 to 1931, but more alumni can remember the Edwin Watts Chubb Library, 1931–69. Its designed capacity was 250,000 volumes, but it relinquished some 550,000 volumes when the current Vernon R. Alden Library opened in early 1969.

The Alden Library has operated as a centralized library since its construction. There are no more dormitory libraries, and the Music-Dance Library in the Music Building has been the main exception as a branch library. With continuing collection growth, however, the physical plant has expanded. Today library operations also include the Hwa-Wei Lee Library Annex on Columbus Road, which opened for service in 1998. The libraries on the five regional campuses are also integrated into a university-wide library system with well over 2 million volumes.

But the library is more than a physical structure: it is a central campus hub for learning. Years ago this required a good card catalog (with authors, titles, and subject classification scheme), reference desk, and reserve room. Today, with the rapid growth of computers and electronic technology, this concept has greatly expanded. The Ohio University Libraries now provide information to a global community on a twenty-four-hour, seven-day-a-week basis. Alden Library opened its online catalog, "ALICE," in 1983 and employed its first instructional librarian in 1985. Now, with OhioLINK, students and faculty have quick access to more than 20 million volumes and thousands of electronic journals from more than seventy-five campus libraries across the state. Far more people today connect with Alden virtually than by actually coming into the building. Librarians are concentrating on new methods for working closely with faculty members and on strategies for interactive classroom use, as well as providing more personal attention to in-house visitors. Libraries and librarianship will continue to change, but the link with service will remain a constant.

Vernon Roger Alden Library.
Courtesy University Photographer's Office.

The college regime was simple and rigid. Each class spent two-thirds of its time each day on the "advanced lesson" and one-third on the review of the lesson of the previous day. At the end of two-thirds of the term, they went back to the beginning of the term's work and reviewed it, taking just twice as much each day as they did on the "advance." The class work was all oral, except that while the student first called on was reciting, others, as many as could find room at the blackboards, wrote an analysis of the portions which the professor had assigned to them. They were then called upon to recite, one after another, first the advance lesson for the day, and then a review of the last previous lesson. . . .

A revolution was introduced at the end of the next term. Prof. Eli T. Tappan became the professor of mathematics, and he proposed written examinations.

—President William Henry Scott, recalling his days
as a student (1850s) at Ohio University

eyes of their minister-professors, who tried to serve as examples of moral excellence. But in many ways, they fit the description that Colin B. Burke gives of students of this period in *American Collegiate Populations:* "aggressive, mobile, and involved in the development of the American society." Even from the days of the academy, they had eagerly contributed their labor and spoken their minds. In those earliest days, they had been land appraisers, deliverymen, barrel-stave makers, and faithful chapel attendees. In more recent times they had actively promoted temperance, rejected the Fugitive Slave Act, distributed Bibles, and been converted at revivals. Some of the upperclassmen (future university president William Scott, for example) taught in the preparatory school for up to three hours a day. Most recently one or two of them had "fitted up" the "dilapidated and ruinous condition" of their college rooms, starting a trend that quickly resulted in some seventy rooms being newly "fitted up." The advantage to the university was obvious, and the president decided that the remodeling efforts merited reduced room rents.

These young men lived in a close community where it was possible to be introduced to the president in the morning and have his advice on classes and career in the afternoon. Under these circumstances they felt free to petition professors and the trustees for changes in the calendar, for leniency on

Students were active in temperance societies such as this one during the 1850s. *Courtesy Mahn Center.*

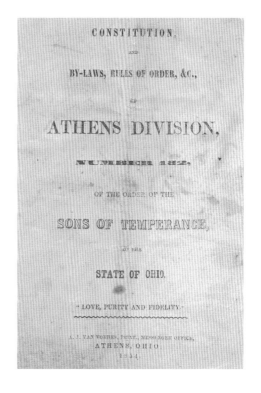

CONSTITUTION,

BY-LAWS, RULES OF ORDER, &c.,

ATHENS DIVISION,

NUMBER 182,

OF THE ORDER OF THE

SONS OF TEMPERANCE,

STATE OF OHIO.

"LOVE, PURITY AND FIDELITY."

A. I. VAN VORHES, PRINT., MESSENGER OFFICE,
ATHENS, OHIO.
1854.

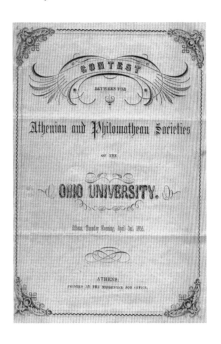

behalf of classmates accused of misbehavior, for hiring or retaining particular professors, and for time off to attend the new county fair. They had created a short-lived publication and two very long-lived literary societies that supplemented classroom instruction and entertained the town with public exhibitions and pre-commencement debates.

In several ways 1856 was a banner year. President Howard was able to say, "We take pleasure in announcing to the Board, that the debt which we owed to the State, and which as an incubus has for years weighed us down, has been . . . relinquished. We are now, I believe nearly, if not quite free from debt." And, at last, the problem of access seemed relieved, at least from the east and west. The long-awaited Marietta & Cincinnati Railroad, with an engine named *Athens,* reduced the trip to Cincinnati, in theory, from a day and a half to six hours. In William Scott's experience, however, the reality of train travel did not match the theory. When he and his father left their home in McConnelsville to enroll him in the university,

Excerpt from minutes of faculty meeting, October 4, 1859, noting students' request for time off to go to the county fair. *Courtesy Mahn Center.*

Program of literary society contest, April 3, 1855. *Courtesy Mahn Center.*

the steamboat on which we traveled reached Harmar [near Marietta], where we were to be transferred to a railroad train, considerably behind time, and the captain proposed to my father that he with his family and household goods should remain on the boat till the next morning, the boat in the meantime making a trip to Parkersburg and return to Harmar. He assured my father that the boat would return to Harmar in time for him to have his family and household goods transferred to a railroad car before the train left the next morning. But when on our return we caught our first view of the train it was speeding on its way to Athens and Cincinnati. As there was but one passenger train to Athens each day, we could do nothing but wait for the train that would leave the next morning. We spent the time at a hotel and in looking at the town and river from the Harmar hill-side.

By 1858, the university was debt free. The town had its first telegraph line but suffered a major flood. The following year Athens had a brass band; 12,000 people attended the first trotting races at the county fair; and the university officially founded an alumni associa-

The Marietta & Cincinnati Railroad passed through Athens in 1857, reducing the town's isolation and simplifying east/west travel. The Hocking Valley Railroad connected Athens to Columbus in 1870. *Courtesy Mahn Center.*

tion. But 1859 was also a year of rising tension between the North and the South. The next fall, Abraham Lincoln was elected president without winning the popular vote, and within the month, South Carolina seceded from the union. Though Lincoln stressed unity in his March inaugural address, by April he issued an appeal for 75,000 volunteers to quell the "insurrection."

The Athens response was immediate, as students and townspeople met on the College Green to make speeches, call for volunteers, raise money to fund recruits, and unfurl the Union flag. Students adopted a resolution stating, "we relentlessly cling to the pillars of our national union . . . [for] in this hour of treason and impending anarchy there is no neutral ground." Edward

Trotting races became popular in the mid-1800s. Grandstand and race, 1900s, Athens County Fair. Gift of Anna P. Williams. *Courtesy Mahn Center.*

Archibald Green Brown, father of the Ohio University Alumni Association, first enrolled in the Academy in 1812, when he was fourteen years old and Dr. Jacob Lindley was the sole instructor. Brown left after only a few terms, but several years later, when his family moved to town, he became a "regular" student and one of the charter members of both the Zelothian and the Athenian Literary Societies.

Only three years after his 1822 graduation, Brown became, in many ways, the town's most important voice. As editor of the first newspaper, *The Athens Mirror and Literary Register,* he provided local, national, and international news for Athenians willing to pay two dollars a year for a subscription. After that venture, he became Athens County's recorder and, eventually, a lawyer and judge of the 8th judicial circuit. However, in all his adult years, Archibald Green Brown's heart and interest remained with his alma mater and her graduates. Even before he became a trustee in 1841, he used a quill pen to compose communiqués and sent copies to alumni, encouraging them to return for reunions during commencement week.

In 1859, when the university had 171 graduates, the Alumni Association was formally constituted and approved by the university's board of trustees. Appropriately, A. G. Brown was named the organization's first alumni secretary. Since those early days, the Alumni Association has been an integral part of the university's rich and colorful history, as leaders of the association have continued to work to encourage graduates to "fraternize and cultivate more familiar acquaintance among the alumni of the University." Alumni Days, a longstanding tradition, were introduced in 1896; the first alumni chapter was established in 1906; and the alumni records initiative dates from 1908. Long before the award-winning *Ohio Today* magazine kept alumni in touch with the university, the more modest *Ohio University Alumni Circular* did the job.

In the early 1920s the organization mounted an impressive fund-raising effort to contribute a worthy monument to the school. The result was Memorial Auditorium, clear and lasting evidence of the appreciation and affection of alumni. Thirty years later, the association headed a drive to raise $150,000 for the Sesquicentennial Scholarship Fund—$1,000 for each year of the university's life—and surprised everyone by finishing with almost $400,000. The Alumni Association assisted the Athletic Board in the "What's in a Name?" contest to select the green-and-white team's sobriquet of "Bobcats" in 1925.

Now, more than 145 years after Dr. Brown wrote his messages by hand, the Alumni Association maintains its initial purpose of solidifying relationships and serving the university's more than 160,000 alumni worldwide.

Archibald Green Brown, father of the O.U. Alumni Association. *From* Athens Home Coming Reunion, *1904.*

H. Gutherie, head of the preparatory department, and Professor William J. Johnson went to Nelsonville to recruit more volunteers. Ohio University alumni, old and young, enlisted. Professor William Young took leave early and joined the Union Army.

As the war dragged on, feelings about it often ran high. Professor Young's letters to the *Messenger* and other news reports kept students and townspeople informed. The only threat to the Athens area came in July 1863, when Morgan's Raiders swept through Nelsonville. Later a group of students got into a fight at a Democratic meeting. They booed the antiwar speaker, Judge Allen G. Thurman, and then, to prevent the flag that adorned the premises from being defiled by Judge Thurman's lack of patriotism, they tore it down. Since the flag was the work of civic-minded Athens women, other members of the audience took offense, and a fight was on. The *Cincinnati Inquirer* scolded: "The young men of the Ohio University do not possess the least shade of good breeding. Neither is it taught at that Institution."

Enrollment declined as young men who might have become students became soldiers instead. For a time the loss of revenue was offset by the

Portrait of Lincoln inscribed "Sold by a wounded soldier." *Courtesy Mahn Center.*

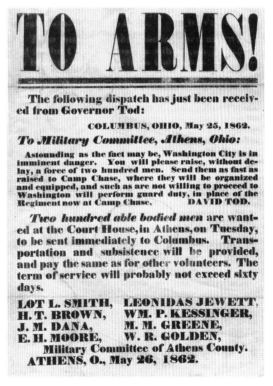

With President Lincoln's call for recruits, faculty members, students, and townsmen enlisted in the Union army. *Courtesy Mahn Center.*

Thomas Ogden Osborn: Civil War General

Thomas Ogden Osborn was born in Licking County, Ohio, in 1832 and graduated from Ohio University in 1854. Seven years later, he helped organize the 39th Illinois Volunteers and soon became their leader. For the next four years, he served bravely under both General Truman Seymour and General Robert S. Foster. In 1864 he was breveted a major general for his gallantry in action and was promoted to brigadier general of volunteers. After the war, Osborn served as treasurer of Cook County, Illinois, for two years before accepting President Ulysses S. Grant's appointment as U.S. minister to Argentina.

Thomas Ogden Osborn.
Courtesy of the Chicago Historical Society. From a 1994 Ohio University Today *bulletin.*

hope that Ohio University and Miami University would benefit from the Morrill Land Grant College Act, signed by President Lincoln in July 1862. By this act, each state was to receive 30,000 acres of public land for each of its senators and congressional representatives. Monies from the sales would then create an endowment to support at least one college of agricultural and mechanical arts.

Ohio University and Miami University began immediate efforts to persuade the state to divide its designated 630,000 acres between the two underfunded state institutions. The trustees, prominent townspeople, other friends of the university, and the Athens press worked hard to win public and legislative support. But year after year of delay made it increasingly clear that once again Ohio University would not benefit from state largess or even receive serious consideration. In 1865, when the state's commissioners sold 575,560 acres of the land for an average price of 53¢ per acre (well below the going price of $1.25), it seemed that much of the endowment had simply been sacrificed. The eventual resolution of the issue came in 1870 when the legislature passed an act establishing an agricultural and mechanical college in Columbus. Also galling was the fact that when the new school opened in 1873, its president was Valentine B. Horton, a long-term trustee of the Ohio University in Athens.

This term opened PROMISINGLY—but has been SERIOUSLY interrupted by the various calls for troups and by the draft. Oh tempora! Oh mores! When CAN the schools of this unhappy land return to their WONTED devotion to learning and literature?

—J. G. Blair, Professor of Natural Science, June 1864

Less weighty events occurring on campus during the war years included founding of a second social fraternity, Delta Tau Delta, in 1862. A charter member recalled its beginnings: "The country was in the throes of the Civil War. Every few months more troops were called. Every young fellow who didn't enlist felt the eyes of the community looking askance at him. Fraternities suffered the obliteration of whole chapters, and such chapters as did not perish were struggling for dear life. The establishing of a new chapter was a rare event." This chapter was organized to compete with Beta Theta Pi, an "airy, uppish set, disposed to be exclusive and flock to themselves," whom the townspeople thought "were the very flower of the school" and to whom the trustees and faculty conceded "an evening of commencement week all to themselves." This evening is described in detail, and disdainfully, in the Delts' history, *The First Ninety Years:*

> On this occasion, its members, active and graduate, gorgeous with long ribbon scarfs of crimson and headed by a brass band, marched in stately procession to Atheneum Hall where some more or less distinguished Beta, alumnus or stranger, delivered a more or less eloquent address to the small but conspicuous body of Betas and a crowded audience of townspeople and visitors. . . . After the address, the chapter held a banquet, to which of course only the fit and few were invited. So this annual function served the chapter well; there was both a glorious publicity and a pretty hint of reserve, exclusiveness, mystery.

Certainly the tone of these remarks presages future competition between the groups—for members, attention, and female admirers. Social life at the university was changing. These two fraternities, along with Phi Delta Theta, which joined them in 1868, contributed to the changes.

As the war ended, veterans returned. In 1863 the trustees had voted to admit wounded veterans without tuition. Now the state approved free admission for veterans who had enlisted as minors. Seventy veterans took advantage of the offer, filling all the college rooms and creating such crowded conditions that some students chose to leave. However, veteran John Lennox McMaster, in a letter to his sister in 1866, sounds content to be away from the war and in a safe place.

MEMORIAL.

———

TO THE SENATE AND HOUSE OF REPRESENTATIVES OF THE STATE OF OHIO.

The undersigned Committee, appointed by the Trustees of Miami University at Oxford, and Ohio University at Athens, to take such action as may be deemed best for the interests of said Institutions, in regard to the grant of land made to the State of Ohio by the Federal Government, by act of Congress approved July 2, 1862, which grant, by act of the General Assembly, has been accepted by the State, beg leave to present to your honorable body the following memorial:

The Miami and Ohio Universities, established by grants of land from Congress and confirmed by action of the State Legislature, are the only two seminaries of learning in the State under the peculiar patronage of the State Government. In both these Institutions the Trustees are appointed by the Governor of the State, by and with the advice and consent of the Senate; and their management and control, as well as the selection of all the members of the Faculty, being under the direction of the Board of Trustees, they are, to all intents and purposes, regulated by the action of the State, and responsible to the Government thereof. The honor and dignity of the State being thus involved in their well-being, it should endeavor by all means to render them worthy of the great educational interests of the people committed to their care. In giving them the name of Universities, it was doubtless intended that they should become seminaries of universal knowledge, subserving the educational wants of all classes of the people. The grant of lands was made in conformity with the act of Congress of 1792, the words of which declare that it was for establishing "an academy and other public schools and seminaries of learning," thus evincing the wide range of instruction intended to be afforded under their management. The progress of science and the demands of an ever advancing civilization, are continually opening new fields of learning, and hence the necessity of enlarging the means and facilities of affording that instruction which the people have the right to claim at the hands of the State.

These universities, founded in the infancy of the State, have long since found their endowments wholly insufficient for the extended field of usefulness which they are expected to fill, and this not from any fault of their own, but by the action of the very laws and regulations under which they have been placed by the State; hence, unless this usefulness is entirely to cease, or at least become very much circumscribed, some means must be adopted to increase their power of doing good, and enable them to occupy the exalted station as seats of learning to which the name of State universities should entitle them. Ohio University owns two townships, containing about 46,000 acres of land, and has an annual income of about $4,000; Miami University has one township of land of about 23,000 acres, and an income of about $6,000; both have large and commodious buildings, pleasantly situated, surrounded with ample and beautiful grounds, and capable, with proper improvements, of accommodating a large number of students in every department of learning. And, inasmuch as the late act of Congress

Memorial from Ohio and Miami Universities to the state legislators, requesting consideration in the distribution of land from the Morrill Act of 1862, establishing agricultural and mechanical schools. *Courtesy Mahn Center.*

Emblem of Delta Tau Delta, O.U.'s second fraternity, founded 1862. *Courtesy* Athena Yearbook, *1892.*

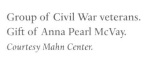

Group of Civil War veterans.
Gift of Anna Pearl McVay.
Courtesy Mahn Center.

John Lennox McMaster, 1869
alumnus, was elected mayor
of Indianapolis in 1883 and
appointed in 1894 to the
Indiana Superior Court Bench,
where he served until 1910.
Courtesy Mary Virginia Clark, '44.

The students as far as I have become acquainted are a very agreable set of fellows and I flatter myself that I am making very fair proggress in my studies although I have to apply myself pretty closely for we are doing one years work in latin in this one term in order to overtake a class which doubled and put six months work in last term. This is a beautiful day everything about our old institution in the shape of vegetation is clothed in a beautiful dress of green. Our college green is a beautiful one It is filled with forest trees of all kinds. It is said to have contained at one time a tree of every species found in the state but some of them have died since but it is still very nice.

Excerpts from another veteran's diary give more details about students' daily life. Not surprisingly, they begin with the difficulty of getting to Athens.

Monday, March 26, 1866

Started to Athens per express. roads almost impassable. arrived at Nelsonville at noon, took dinners, found that the coach did not come up from below, left my trunk, set out on foot in company with R. Trice, made the trip to A. in about 5 hours. . . .

Tuesday, March 27, 1866

Feet sore from the walk. After Chapel in consultation with the Faculty took three studies. Thribble on Latin, Green's Analysis, Mental Arithmetic. Met C. Downing, formaly of 7th O. Batry.

Wednesday, March 28, 1866

Recited in G. Analysis and Latin

Thursday, March 29, 1866

Usual College duties

Friday, March 30, 1866

Initiated into the A. L. [Athenian Literary] Society.

Saturday, March 31, 1866

Fixed up our room. Attended soldiers meeting for the purpose of organizing an association of soldiers.

Sunday, April 1, 1866

Attended M. E. [Methodist Episcopal] Church and Sunday school. Sermon Brooks Pastor. Chapel lecture by Dr. Howard. Took a walk to the semetery.

Tuesday, April 3,

Trunk arrived from Nelsonville. all correct. Finished essay for Saturday.

Sunday, April 8,

Attended Capel class, Sunday school, preaching, lecture, Sunday school quarterly meeting, preaching at night by Revd. M

Handed in my certificate to Proff Gibbons, students leader.

Monday, April 9,

Tolerably successful in recitation engaged heartily in football.

Notice of free scholarships for wounded veterans.
Courtesy Mahn Center.

Two and a half weeks later, the circus was in town, and on May 24, "all business in the O. U. suspended to give the faculty and students a chance to go to the Union S. S. [Sunday school] picnic," where he had a "pleasant time but nothing of special interest."

Another student recalled pleasant days when he and a friend "would occasionally climb away up in the Big Beech, the pride of the campus, establish ourselves comfortably in the buzzy shade, and work our Latin and Greek prose."

On a June morning in 1873, President Scott began his baccalaureate address by saying, "It is a critical hour in a young man's history when he stands on the threshold of home with his childhood behind him and his face to the world." At the time nothing seemed unusual about these words —especially to the six men graduating in the university's fifty-ninth commencement, who knew their place in Victorian America.

But the only woman in the class could not be so certain. Margaret Boyd's presence was not acknowledged until the end of the address, when the president praised the university's first female graduate as the "oldest of a great sisterhood of graduates." Boyd wrote in her diary: "We have a very nice lecture. He tells the boys that they may well be proud that they belong to the class that contains the first lady graduate. I can hardly keep the tears from my eyes. Such a day."

Margaret Boyd's diary was a personal record of university classes, religious services, social visits, and observations about friends and professors. The frequency of references to religious services—prayer meetings, Sunday school, church, chapel at the university, quarterly meetings, and Sunday school teachers' meetings—underlines the role of religion as a centralizing force in Athens and the life of Margaret Boyd. The fabric of religious events and social activity, piety and friendships was nearly seamless.

Despite the importance of family, friends, and religion, Margaret's academic life dominated her diary. Recitations, readings, and examinations provoked her sense of duty: "I can not go to church but must stay at home and study." She occasionally recorded her frustration at not being able to study: "Did not do much today. Did not write any and studied very little. If I could just study all the time, but I find that I can not." Sometimes her sense of responsibility was palpable: "I must write. Vainly I call on the muses."

Boyd's diary also documented her inner life as the first female student in the university. Fears, self-doubts, and fatigue were common. On March 19 she returned home at 9:00 A.M. and studied all day, exclaiming, "O, Butler, how you frighten me." Her study in the Greek New Testament produced more concerns: "Oh! I wish I were a more thorough scholar." On commencement day Boyd said, "I was so very frightened before I went up on the stage that I thought I would fail completely. I did much better than I feared."

Recurrent illness and melancholy were also noted. On some dates, the problems were physical: "I am sick today and so stay at home all day" or "have a headache at night." On other days, the expressions were about emotions: "I feel lonely today" or "I feel sad today." At times Boyd was uncertain in her self-diagnosis: "I can not tell what is the matter with me this term. I believe I have the 'blues' half the time and cannot tell why either." Margaret worried about the academic consequences: "I feel so sick and bad. No wonder I am not marked as well as the boys." However, she added, "I could do as well as they if I were as strong." A month before graduation at the age of twenty-eight, pressured by the need to find a teaching position and aware of her dissipating strength, she wrote, "I am a little afraid will give out before the close of the term."

From enrollment in the spring of 1868 to commencement in 1873, the first woman at Ohio University was aware of herself as an alien. Margaret Boyd's enrollment was recorded in the university catalogue as "M. Boyd" and was the subject of local discussion. While the faculty had no objection, there was "some fear that the public might be unfavorably influenced" by the presence of a female student. Later, when the faculty realized there was "general approval of her presence," Margaret Boyd's full name was printed. Nearing commencement, Margaret was shown her diploma by President Scott and objected to the masculine endings in its Latin text. Her diary for that day summarized much of the history of women in higher education to that date: "What a sad thing it is to be a girl." On June 17 she informed the president, "I do not want a diploma with masculine endings." The endings were changed.

Beneath Boyd's demeanor of determination and conviction were nagging questions and doubts prompted by Victorian ideology, by gender roles, and by the uncertainty of her future. By seeking a college education in 1873 when few universities admitted women, Boyd's courage and perseverance put her on the frontier of changing expectations for women.

The increase in student enrollment did not continue. By 1866–67, there were still 50 veterans but only 176 students altogether. The annual income was about $7,000, while Marietta College boasted $9,400 and Miami $10,300. However, President Howard tried to be optimistic in his annual report:

> The time we believe is near when she [the state] will no longer act as Stepmother towards the University but will recognize her obligations and liberally endow the Institution. Our location is favorable to the building up of a great and prosperous university. All the region of the Country South to the Ohio river, North to the National road, East to the State line and West to the Little Miami river has no institutions of a high grade, with the exception of Marietta College. . . . The question then comes up . . . "What can we do that the wants of this part of the State may be met?"

With no answer by 1868, Howard had to admit that the prospect of help from the state was "remote" and that "the income of the institution is not sufficient to carry on." Perhaps this was one reason the trustees were willing to turn to a new clientele to fill their classrooms. In 1868 Margaret Boyd of Athens took the advice of her two brothers, O.U. alumni, and entered the preparatory school. The diary she kept as a senior records some of the difficulties she faced as one of the first women to study at an American university. By 1870 she was a recognized member of the student body, of her class

Pencil drawing of Athens by H. M. Walker, 1865. *Courtesy Mahn Center.*

Margaret Boyd, '73, with her classmates: John Merrill Davis, Charles Herbert Dixon, Evan Jerome Jones, Ripley Hoffman Kinnison, Moses James Morgan, and Frank Otis Ballard. *Courtesy Mahn Center.*

From the Asylum to the Ridges

Between 1874 and 1988 Athens had the distinction of hosting not one but two institutions devoted to the human mind—Ohio University and the Athens Lunatic Asylum. The first aimed to take minds to the highest of human intellectual levels, and the second tried to raise minds from the depths of despair.

The genus of institutions designed to treat people with mental disturbances began at the turn of the nineteenth century when Dr. Thomas Kirkbride of Philadelphia developed a complete system of treatment, care, and housing for the mentally disturbed. The Kirkbride Plan assumed that a cure for the mentally disturbed required an asylum—a calming sanctuary removed from the noises, tension, and distractions of urban life.

Athens was such a place, and its powerful local representative to the state legislature, William Parker Johnson, was determined to bring the asylum here. After Athens citizens voted funds to buy parts of the Coates and Moore farms on a hill south of town, the state allocated funds so that construction could begin in 1868. Though Dr. Kirkbride had recommended a patient load of no more than 250, politicians and psychiatric professionals prevailed, and the Athens Lunatic Asylum was built to accommodate twice that number. It was finally ready to open in 1874.

One of the first patients was Eli Stevens, who had been a member of Morgan's Raiders during the ill-fated raid through Ohio in 1863. Stevens had been captured in Vinton County and was kept for years as a ward of the sheriff. It appears his mental disability was epilepsy (not an uncommon ticket for incarceration), and he was never repatriated south because none of his family could be located. In 1874 he was sent to the asylum in Athens. He is still there. Stevens is one of the hundreds buried in the asylum cemetery located behind today's Edison Biotechnology Institute.

A persistent legend about the cemetery is that no one knows who is buried where, as the graves are marked only with numbers. Actually, the University Archives has a microfilm copy of the registration book containing the names and causes of death of those buried in the cemetery. Left unexplained is the reason for numbers on the gravestones. Possibly it was cheaper to chisel numbers rather than names on the stones, or perhaps the interred had no family to claim their bodies or represented too

much of a stigma for their families to bury them in their home cemeteries.

It took more than twenty years for the front grounds to be properly landscaped. Many patients worked on the earth moving and plantings under the belief that labor provided mental therapy. The manicured grounds, intended as a setting for "airing" the patients, served the same purpose for people of the community, allowing for a relaxed interaction between the two groups. Other kinds of interactions were conducted at the lakes and nearby "Lover's Lane," as alumni from the 1920s through the 1960s can attest. The four lakes provided more than aesthetic pleasure: as water flowed from the highest to the lowest lake, it was filtered for use in the bathrooms and laundry.

To dispel another legend: the lakes were never in the shape of playing card suits. All plot plans and photographs show the lakes in nondescript shapes. However, three of the four card suits (diamond, spade, and club) show up in the designs of the window gratings on the original asylum building.

Today, the remaining grounds and structures of the Athens Lunatic Asylum represent the evolution of mental institutions. The original idea was to maintain all housing and administrative functions inside one structure. Only the power plant, the horse barn, the dairy, and auxiliary out-buildings were placed away from the massive main building. The center of the main building contained the reception rooms, offices, employee apartments, cafeterias (one for men and the other for women), chapel, a ballroom, and room in the rear for the kitchen, laundry, maintenance shops, and storage. At first, as the patient population grew, new structures were simply attached to the original building. By the 1890s, however, a new concept of care—the Cottage Plan—appeared at the asylum.

Patients with the same mental disturbances were grouped together in smaller, separate buildings. Each cottage had its own day rooms and activity areas, but the

INNOVATION AND THE STRUGGLE TO SURVIVE

individual sleeping rooms were sacrificed for an open dormitory setting. At Athens the first new cottages were naturally grouped near the original building; eventually additional buildings were built up the hill to the west. Topping the hill was the Tubercular Ward, built there to get above the "vapors" of the river valley.

Patient care and therapy also evolved. From the originally popular hydrotherapy to drug therapy, the Athens Asylum encompassed 120 years of efforts by practitioners to get patients healthy and back into society. All of the popular treatments were tried at the institution—from hot- and cold-water soakings, manual labor, arts and crafts, talk sessions, and supervised social events to medical manipulations such as frontal lobotomies, shock therapy, and psychotropic drugs.

Not long after the opening of the asylum, the university became involved with the institution in both official and unofficial ways. The departments of agriculture, nursing, social work, psychology, natural sciences, and performing arts all used the asylum as a training center and laboratory.

Since 1988, when the asylum was deeded to the university and the name was changed—not for the first time—to the Ridges, use of the property has grown steadily. The old Amusement Hall, the first building to be completely refurbished, accommodates dance, theater, and special programs and serves as a venue for the Athens International Film Festival. The former Administrative Building (the center of the original complex) is now named Lin Hall and houses the Kennedy Museum of Art. A major feature of the museum is the Edwin L. and Ruth E. Kennedy Southwest Native American Collection.

Along with exhibits, the museum features curriculum-based programs, tours, special children's programs, and even Museums by Mail.

The most extensive renovation to date is of the former Cottage L (aka The Suicide Ward), which now houses the Edison Biotechnology Institute. EBI combines internationally recognized expertise in molecular, cellular, and developmental biology into an integrated system of basic and applied research for human medical, drug discovery, and agricultural applications. The Innovation Center, a business incubator established in 1983, offers space and support services for new and emerging technology and service or light manufacturing businesses. The Institute for Local Government Administration and Rural Development (ILGARD) provides research, technical assistance, and other services to local governments, community leaders, and nonprofit organizations. The Voinovich Center for Leadership and Public Affairs works with other agencies to improve the economic vitality of the area and provide training for its leaders.

Other services located at the Ridges include the university's facilities planning and construction office, the university mail room and surplus property storage, the Child Development Center (in the old Horse Barn), and even a miniature golf course and a softball diamond.

Facilities Management keeps the 720 acres of grounds at the Ridges mowed and trimmed. A local group has adopted the maintenance of the cemetery. Trails have been opened, and some of the acreage is being used as a land lab. The Ridges is the best place near the city and campus to get out into nature and see the wildlife.

Once reserved as a sanctuary for those disturbed in body and mind, the Ridges now provides a place of refuge and mental stimulation for the benefit of a different community.

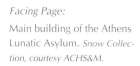

Facing Page:
Main building of the Athens Lunatic Asylum. *Snow Collection, courtesy ACHS&M.*

Picknickers on the grounds of the Asylum, circa 1900.
Courtesy Mahn Center.

of seven, and of the Philomathean Literary Society. When she became Ohio University's first female graduate in 1873, her classmates applauded her.

One of those classmates, Evan J. Jones, describes his own rather typical experiences at the university. He arrived in 1869, attended three consecutive years, and in the fourth year, 1872–73,

> dropped out the first two terms and was principal of the public schools of Burlington, Lawrence county, Ohio, for six months at a salary of $60.00 per month. I attended the Ohio University the spring term of 1873 and graduated in June of that year in a class of seven, the other members of which were Margaret Boyd, the first lady graduate of the University, Moses J. Morgan, John M. Davis, Charles H. Dixon, Frank O. Ballard and Ripley H. Kinnison. . . .
>
> During my college course I boarded myself, except for the last term. My entire college course cost less than $500.00. That included board, lodging, clothes, books, tuition, railroad fare and all other expenses.

A year before Margaret Boyd's eventful graduation, Solomon Howard, the president who had shepherded the university for twenty years, retired. Along with his predecessor Alfred Ryors, he had kept the school alive through difficult times. With a more open attitude toward students and a willingness to innovate to serve the population of his area while still maintaining standards in the classical course, he had regained some public confidence. The faculty, though frequently changing, was strong. Funds remained woefully inadequate, but the draining debt was satisfied. With the creation of two more fraternities and the admission of one woman, Ohio University was on its way to a more varied social life.

Emblem of Phi Delta Theta.
Courtesy Athena Yearbook, *1892.*

A Nod from the State

1872–1901

> The largest achievement of my life, from a material point of view, was the passage of the bill making the first State appropriation to the Ohio University.
> —*President William Henry Scott, 1881*

In the years between Margaret Boyd's graduation and the turn of the century, Ohio University slowly became both a more stable and a more lively institution as it gained support from the state, expanded the curriculum, erected new buildings, and integrated both women and sports into its life. However, in January 1873, Margaret Boyd confided to her diary: "Not too many students out today. I fear for the future of the old O.U." Her fears were well founded. The country's economic depression was having serious effects in southeast Ohio, and a Hocking River flood added to the area's woes. The university's annual revenue from rents hovered around $4,000, and with only forty-four students in the college, income from tuition was low. The campus buildings were dilapidated, with "mouldy" walls and the look of "an abandoned cotton factory," while the Commons remained a filthy hitching ground.

Townspeople view the devastating flood of 1873.
James Anastas Collection, courtesy ACHS&M.

67

The "dilapidated" buildings and Green, with students fighting on the fence. *From "Map of Athens County, Ohio, 1866 from Actual Surveys by E. H. Moore." Courtesy Robin Lacy.*

Memorial to the General Assembly, February 5, 1874, protesting a proposal to reduce Ohio and Miami Universities to preparatory or normal schools. *Courtesy Mahn Center.*

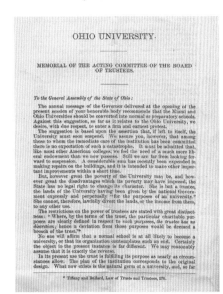

Rumors circulated that the school would have to close, as its sister institution, Miami University, had been forced to do. University officials appealed to the state for help, but the general assembly, its attention and largess directed toward the new Agricultural and Mechanical College in Columbus, offered only the suggestion that Ohio and Miami Universities be converted to normal or preparatory schools.

Ohio University's board of trustees responded indignantly: the state had no right to reverse the direction of this "natural germ of a university." They had, they said firmly, no intention of closing. Rather, they had recently made repairs and, in spite of their poverty, intended to continue making improvements. Funds for these repairs—about $3,000—had come not from the state that had chartered the institution, but from loyal friends—trustees, faculty, alumni, and Athens townspeople. They had responded as best they could when the university's new president, William Henry Scott, an alumnus and native of the area, proposed that the people of Athens, aided by other friends, should raise $50,000 for an endowment. Professor Eli Tappan further suggested that Athenians initiate a plan to have the real estate of the two university townships taxed at the rate of the state tax. In other words, the university's leaseholders should voluntarily begin paying the state tax from which they had been happily exempt for some seventy years.

In March 1875 the legislature responded to the university's lobbying efforts. Reversing the victory the lessees had won in their 1850s lawsuit against taxation, the legislators now passed a law requiring the university to collect the equivalent of the state tax on its lands. The university's rejoicing was cut short as more than two hundred furious lessees, led by J. R. Cable, immediately moved to have the new law repealed. Newspapers ran attacks and counterattacks. Some writers accused the university of treating its tenants as vassals; others denounced the leaseholders as selfish freeloaders who refused to pay their fair share for state services; still others blamed the trustees for a history of leniency toward their renters. A few leading citizens declared that the university's buildings should be burned. After two years of this wrangling, Ohio's Supreme Court ruled in favor of the university. However, the dispute generated more animosity than income. Collections were small, and the university continued to run a deficit. Faculty morale declined as meager salaries were reduced by 10 percent.

Conditions for students, on the other hand, were improving. Although they had little extra money for frivolities, and though the campus was still strongly religious, with regular chapel and church attendance required, they enjoyed a growing variety of activities in town and on the campus. The Hocking Valley Railroad had connected Athens with Columbus in 1870, making the town accessible from the north. The Sells Brothers circus came with seven elephants and twelve camels. Touring theatrical troupes, political speakers, and national figures such as Dorothea Dix attracted large audiences to the Opera House in the new Village Hall. The popular New Orleans Minstrels visited frequently. And when the Athens Lunatic Asylum opened in 1874, it not only stimulated the town's economy but provided an easily accessible, exquisitely landscaped park with secluded paths, bridges, and ponds that encouraged long walks, picnics, and ice skating.

At the college, students sledded behind the Center Building on moonlit winter evenings and enjoyed occasional weekend sleighing parties "finished

President William Henry Scott with the class of 1878. *Courtesy Mahn Center.*

Lawsuit brought by lessees of university lands to overturn a law requiring them to pay the equivalent of the state tax on the lands. *Courtesy Mahn Center.*

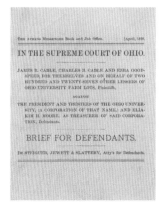

Ice skating at the asylum.
Courtesy Mahn Center.

Advertisement for a circus and balloon ascension, *Athens Messenger,* July 18, 1871.

off with an oyster supper." Fraternity men entertained their female friends at informal parties during the year and escorted them to banquets during commencement week—simple diversions, but as Margaret Kirkendall Campbell recalled, "We believed we were having a lovely evening when we entertained our friends with a banquet, toasts, music, and reading by our most talented members."

At President Scott's urging, students took up the task of publishing a newspaper. In 1874, the *College Mirror,* the first college paper since the *Echo* of 1843, offered local and personal columns and edifying essays such as "The Successful Teacher." One editorial urged town and gown to cooperate in building a walkway to keep the lady students from becoming mired in the mud of a street near the campus. The *Student Magazine* replaced the *Mirror* in 1879, and in 1887 the *Current* was the source of campus news.

Students of the late 1870s were happy to contribute in other ways. When the administration decided that the Green needed new trees, students trekked into the woods and dug up young elms, which they planted on either side of the front walk. (Members of Delta Tau Delta fraternity boasted that they had planted the most.) In 1878 the literary societies tripled the number of volumes in the library when they voted to merge their separate libraries with the university's.

The library merger was not the only change for the literary societies. In 1874 two women joined the Athenians, and the next year Margaret Boyd's

The central walkway of the Green, with elm trees planted by students. *Courtesy Mahn Center.*

Bookplates identifying volumes collected by the Athenian and Philomathean Literary Societies. *Courtesy Mahn Center.*

niece, Ella Boyd, caused a minor sensation when she became the first woman to compete in a literary contest. At her graduation the following year, Governor Hayes was so taken with her commencement oration that he repeated parts of it in his own address to the graduates.

Ohio University coeds of 1873. *Courtesy Mahn Center.*

Only a few years later, President Super could report, "Our experience indicates that the co education of the sexes, far from raising new and difficult problems is a means [of] silently and effectively solving some of the worst of the old ones." But according to Margaret Kirkendall Campbell, at least some of the women moved cautiously on the campus. "[I] tried to walk discreetly so as to avoid criticism. Was not all America watching co-eds? At least we felt the eyes of the townspeople were upon us." Nevertheless, one group of women took the initiative to establish the university's first sorority, Kappa Alpha Theta, in 1876. Pi Beta Phi followed in 1889.

Meanwhile, Ohio University men were caught up in the country's growing interest in sports. Perhaps because of the proximity of Cincinnati's Red Stockings, baseball

Student Publications at Ohio University

The *Athena* and the *Post* are the best-known survivors from a long list of early student publications at Ohio University. Thomas Hoover, in *The History of Ohio University*, lists nine publications that had disappeared by 1892 when the yearbook *Athena* started. Most have left little record and are forgotten, but their very existence is testimony to students' determination to share their stories.

The first publication was the *Echo and University Record*, which started in 1843 and did not survive beyond that year. More than thirty years passed before the appearance of the next publication, the *College Mirror*. Founded in 1874, it lasted only two years, but the name Mirror would reappear twice: the *Ohio University Mirror* published from 1896 to 1900, and the *Mirror*, which began in 1902, lasted at least until 1905. Others that disappeared with hardly a trace include the *Student Magazine*, 1879; the *Philomathean*, 1885; the *Philomathenian*, 1896; the *Current*, 1886–92; the *Daily Yell*, 1890; the *Daily News*, 1891; the *Ohio University Panorama*, 1892–93; and the *Columbiad*, 1895.

The *Athena* was the work of the seventeen members of the senior class of 1892. In the preface, they wrote:

> For this book, the first volume of Athena, we make no apology. Every page may betray its hasty preparation and expose many mistakes. For these we ask the reader's indulgence, but for the book itself, we offer no excuse.
>
> We have endeavored to set forth college life as it occurred during the year '91–'2. If our attempt at wit and humor offend any, let it be said that we erred in our judgment of what is innocent amusement.

The book was 152 pages, and unlike yearbooks today, it was more words than pictures. There were pictures of faculty and staff and the seventeen seniors, but most of the book consisted of essays and poems and miscellaneous tidbits, such as the size and shape of the average senior, who was reported to be 5 feet 9 inches tall and weigh 146 pounds. Names of members of the classes of '93, '94, and '95 were also included.

Staff of the *O.U. Mirror. Top row:* John Lewis Clark, John F. Batterson, John F. Henderson, Rey E. Lash. *Bottom Row:* Florence Craig, Dr. McGraw, Professor Boughton, Charles G. O'Bleness. *Gift of E. M. O'Bleness, O'Bleness Collection, courtesy Mahn Center.*

Through the years pictures began to displace words. Pictorial coverage expanded in scope, and yearbooks soon reached 200 pages, which is about what they are currently. The first full-color photo in the yearbook, in 1941, was of three young women holding skis, but there was no identification of the three women or any explanation of why skiers should be associated with Ohio University.

In 1975 the yearbook changed its name to *Spectrum Green*. The preface explained: "A new concept, a new publication, the new Ohio University yearbook." It indeed was different—more like *Life* or *Look*, with lengthy stories. In addition to the usual campus concerns, it presented off-campus issues of interest to students, such as the Nixon resignation and the end of the Vietnam era. *Spectrum Green* moved away from that concept over the next few years, and in 1983 it became the *Athena* again.

The *Post* started in 1939 as the successor to the *Green and White*, which began as a weekly in 1911 and went to twice-a-week publication in 1926. The *Post* started out publishing four days a week—weekdays except Wednesday. It was tabloid size, with a five-column format, moving to full-size pages and five-day-a-week publication in the 1960s. In its inaugural issue, it called itself "a new paper streamlined and creamlined to keep in step with the rapid progress of the University itself and with the latest developments in news production."

Like the *Green and White,* the *Post* focused on the campus and on sports. As students grew more aware of off-campus events, so did the *Post.* In the later 1940s, the *Post*'s criticism of the administration caused some readers on campus to question whether a paper subsidized by the university should be allowed to criticize the institution. President John Baker met with the editor and the Campus Affairs Committee (CAC), which had oversight responsibility. The result was closer contact between the *Post* and both its adviser and the CAC.

In the 1960s relations between the *Post* and the administration became more adversarial. When the university experienced its first strike by nonacademic employees, the *Post* sided with the employees, finding an Ohio case that disproved the university's position that unionization was not permitted by law. Student activism over the Vietnam War, desegregation, and drug law enforcement raised the inevitable question of whether the *Post* was leading or following student unrest.

On the Friday of Homecoming weekend in 1971, the *Post* ran an unflattering story about Laurel Lea Schaefer, '71, just chosen Miss America. That story led to a reexamination of the governance of the paper. It was taken out of the hands of the CAC, and the Post Publishing Board was created. Consisting of the *Post* editor, two journalism faculty members, and other faculty, administrators, and students, the board retains the function of selecting each year's editor and hearing complaints (fortunately few) about the *Post.*

The *Green Goat,* a humor magazine, published intermittently from 1922 into the 1950s. It was self-sustaining and sold for twenty-five cents a copy. Typical of humor magazines on many campuses in that era—the best known being the *Harvard Lampoon*—it followed the tradition of appropriating ideas and jokes (not particularly funny) from the others.

Sphere, a literary magazine, took a more serious tone. It began publication in 1956, long after campus newspapers and yearbooks had moved away from the tradition of including poetry, essays, and stories. It included both writing and artwork and stated its purpose as encouraging and providing an outlet for the creative talents of O.U. students, as it still does today.

There have, over the years, been other student publications—*Green Jinx, Lamplighter, Caliban, Aquarius, Impetus, Free Voice,* and many more. Most reflect the interests of a particular constituency that feels the *Post* is not sufficient. Usually they are not officially recognized by the university, and most disappear when the students who provide the leadership for the publications graduate.

Looking ahead into the third century, one can conclude that the Internet will surely play a significant role; the *Post* has already established a website. Whatever the form, publications that give voice to student interests, concerns, and talents will continue to be a significant part of campus life at Ohio University.

was especially popular. In 1868 an unofficial Ohio University team had played against the Energetic Club of Marietta and lost 44–38. Most often, the literary societies competed against each other on the steep terrace behind the Center Building, with a thorn bush as backstop and a challenging run uphill to third base. Other teams kicked a ball through the McGuffey elms, and some students had their deportment grades lowered when they skipped study hours to play football.

The faculty, still charged with supervising student behavior, did not encourage these activities. But perhaps there would have been less horseplay in the unsupervised dorms if they had. The new activities there were "stacking" and "smoking." Stacking involved entering a dorm mate's room while he was away and piling as much furniture in his room as possible—an annoying practice, but hardly worth the hours faculty spent trying to catch the perpetrators. "Smoking," which Mrs. David J. Evans says was reserved for "the most conceited and important," posed more serious threats to safety. The most egregious case was in 1877. Mr. Hall was "tied in his room and smoked" as burning paper was thrown into his room through the transom "and fire was put to the door." Of course, the building could have caught fire, but the situation became even more dangerous when Mr. Hall's friends charged down the hall firing pistols to frighten the smokers away. Fortunately, the town marshal heard the disturbance and arrived quickly enough to arrest two students with their guns still in hand.

President Scott wrote himself reminders to be patient: "Let me not suffer the little misdemeanors of students to annoy me. If a few of them steal the tongue of the bell, let me nevertheless do my duties calmly and sleep soundly. If one of them throws a paperball at another during prayer, let me speak to him seriously but kindly; but of what advantage will it be to become disturbed in my feelings?"

Perhaps President Scott could control his feelings about students, but the university's continuing financial difficulties discouraged him. When the idea of merging Ohio State (formerly called Ohio A&M), Miami, and O.U. was voiced openly in 1880, Scott supported it wholeheartedly. He had concluded that it was not possible to fund more than one strong state institution and that the institution would be in

Faculty minutes of January 26, 1875, reporting the burglary and "smoking" of a student's room. *Courtesy Mahn Center.*

Ohio University Athletics

Frank Super, the son of university president Dr. Charles W. Super, took time from his electrical engineering studies to quarterback Ohio's first gridiron squad in 1894. History records the sole loss and, in fact, the only game of that inaugural season as an 8–0 defeat by Marietta. In preparation for the Thanksgiving weekend game at the fairgrounds between the "Athletics of Athens" and the "famous team of Marietta," local businesses and "sympathizers" or fans sported light-blue decorations and ribbons to show their support. Not until two years later, in 1896, did Ohio teams adopt green and white as school colors, chosen by the student body's vote.

O.U.'s first football team, 1894. Frank Super is holding the ball. *Courtesy Mahn Center.*

The inspired leadership of legendary football coach Don Peden produced several Buckeye Athletic Association championships between 1924 and 1946. It was during those glory days that the Green and White found its lasting nickname through a contest with a prize of $10. Hal Rowland, a former student from Athens, put forward the idea that best exemplified the team's tenacity and fighting spirit. The Bobcat was born.

In 1946, Ohio University became a charter member of the Mid-American Conference, along with Butler, Cincinnati, Wayne State, and Western Reserve. Bill Hess's Bobcats took the green and white to the National Small College Championship in 1960 and to the Tangerine Bowl in 1968, each time with perfect 10–0 records. Recent resurgence under Jim Grobe and the excitement of Brian Knorr's arrival continue the gridiron legacy initiated by Super and his teammates.

Admirable graduation rates, responsible compliance with NCAA by-laws and statutes, exceptional facilities, aggressive pursuit of Title IX objectives, and retention of outstanding coaches and staff are all hallmarks of the athletic program's continued evolution. *Sporting News* ranked Ohio thirty-second in the nation for overall achievement in 2001, ahead of such powerhouses as Florida State, Iowa, Kentucky, Georgia Tech, and Kansas.

The 1892 baseball team, the university's first official athletic team. *Courtesy* Athena Yearbook, *1892.*

In 1936 women's athletic activities included fencing, basketball, volleyball, tennis, archery, hockey, and interpretive dancing. *Courtesy Mahn Center.*

NCAA cross-country champion himself, Banton is another outstanding example of the continuity and dedication that distinguish the program.

Also competing on the Athletics Mall, the women's soccer team has climbed to the top of the Mid-American Conference in the few short years since its introduction in 1997, with a MAC regular season title in 2001. And no tour of the Athletics Mall or overview of women's athletics would be complete without mention of the Ohio Softball Stadium, dedicated in 1999. Reaching the 1995 NCAA tournament behind the stellar pitching of Annie Hare and Kandi Rehard, Ohio softball claims a tradition of intensity and competition.

The crown jewel of the Ohio athletics complex, the Convocation Center, was built in 1968 and with a capacity of 13,000 remains the Mecca of MAC arenas and one of the outstanding facilities in the nation. Ohio University women began suiting up for informal games of basketball as early as 1902; in 1995 the 23–7 Bobcats advanced to the NCAA tournament. Sharing the "Convo" with the women hoopsters is the Ohio volleyball program, with three twenty-win seasons in the last ten years.

In Super's day, opportunities for females to pursue recreation and fitness, let alone competition, were confined to membership in the tennis club and participation in the university's annual field day, at which women were eligible to compete in only the baseball throw. Three decades later, women were enrolling in the Department of Physical Education, which had a growing number of offerings. In April 1922, the Women's Athletics Association was formed to promote "physical efficiency, athletic accomplishment, and good sportsmanship among women of the University."

Key among the university administrators building equal opportunities for women through increased funding and scholarship support was Dr. Peggy Pruitt, who retired in 2001 as Senior Associate Athletics Director after twenty-five years of dedicated service. The university's new arti-ficial turf and track facility is named in her honor.

Home to field hockey and lacrosse teams, Peggy Pruitt Field provides state-of-the-art venues that have already produced impressive results. Building upon a tradition that has produced such standouts as Anita Corl Miller-Huntsman, Shelly Morris's field hockey team earned a MAC championship and NCAA appearance in 2001. Dormant for nearly two decades, the women's lacrosse program was reinstituted in 1999 and gains momentum every spring.

Ringing the turf field is a fast new track. Under the guidance of Elmore "Mo" Banton for more than twenty years, Ohio track and field and cross country teams continue to enjoy outstanding success. An Ohio All-American and 1964

Wendy Weeden Devine, the first woman inducted into the Ohio University Athletic Hall of Fame. *Courtesy* Athena Yearbook, *1974.*

When the baskets and net come down, the *mats* come out. Ohio's wrestling tradition is the envy of the conference; its reputation is among the best in the NCAA. With more than a dozen MAC titles and dozens more league champions and All-Americans, the Bobcat mat story continues to write new chapters in sustained excellence.

Grapplers about to be pinned by their Bobcat opponents get a view of the Convo ceiling, where dozens of championship banners hang . . . and a single jersey. It bears the number "54" and is the only number ever retired at Ohio University. It belonged to Frank Baumholtz, a two-sport star and one of the few athletes ever to play two professional sports. Baumholtz and coach W. J. "Dutch" Trautwein led the Cats to the 1941 National Invitational Tournament championship, building upon standards established by Butch Grover during his sixteen-year run as head coach from 1922 to

1938. Larry Hunter belongs to a distinguished list of coaches that also includes the legendary Jim Snyder, whose twenty-five seasons produced 355 wins, conference crowns, and NCAA and NIT appearances.

More recently, players such as Paul "Snoopy" Graham and Dave Jamerson moved from the Convo to tackle the National Basketball Association, and after Gary Trent led Ohio to a Pre-Season NIT title in 1994, he was selected eleventh overall by Toronto in the NBA draft.

Baumholtz's legacy inspires others as well. He was an outstanding baseball player, signing with the Cincinnati Reds in 1941. Tracing their baseball legacy to 1892, the Bobcats have enjoyed consistent success on the diamond. If Frank Super and his teammates approached the Bobcats' ballpark, they would be struck by the signature bronze statue welcoming them to Bob Wren Stadium. Wren, a Bobcat infielder himself, was named Ohio's coach in 1949, and in his twenty-three seasons at the helm, his teams won almost 500 games, never suffering a losing season. Future major leaguers like Phillies' Hall of Famer Mike Schmidt fueled his powerhouse ballclubs. In fact, the 1970 team with Schmidt and future coach Joe Carbone advanced all the way to the College World Series, upsetting Southern California in the first round. Retiring in 1972, Wren gave way to Jerry France, who coached future World Series skipper Bob Brenly of the Arizona Diamondbacks. France won almost 400 games, and his successor, Joe Carbone, has added another 400 victories to the tradition.

The highest honor Ohio University can bestow on a student-athlete is a place in the Ohio University Athletic Hall of Fame, housed in the Convo. The pictures in the main lobby feature the stars familiar to basketball, baseball, and football fans as well as dozens of outstanding individuals who have contributed to the Bobcat winning tradition in other sports such as golf and swimming. Among those enshrined is former men's golf coach Kermit Blosser. An outstanding football player and NCAA wrestling champion, Blosser guided his teams to eighteen MAC championships, developing such talented golfers as future pro Dow Finsterwald. The women's team, introduced in 1996, has quickly built a winning tradition of its own.

Rivaling any winning tradition in the Ohio program is the unparalleled success of Bobcat swimmers. Along the way to eight men's and eight women's MAC team titles, such gifted athletes as Maureen Blandford, Courtney Allen Asher, and Henry Clark joined other gifted Ohio athletes in the Hall of Fame.

Outstanding student-athletes conjure images of memorable performances, and it's a tribute to the Ohio program that fans can ignite a spirited debate about *greatest* games in Bobcat history. Frank Super could describe being within striking distance of the goal line as time expired against Marietta in that 1894 contest. Others might tell of the Tangerine Bowl shootout with the Richmond Spiders in '68. Many fans recall last-second shots in the Convo—none bigger than the one that fell to drop nationally ranked DePaul in two overtimes in 1983. Field hockey fans will argue that the 2001 title game with Kent State, sending Ohio on to the NCAA tournament, is worthy of discussion.

Whatever the outcome, it's clear that Ohio fans are strong supporters of the program—and not just by clicking through the turnstiles. They carry their spirit and dedication beyond season tickets to continue the development of the conference's top overall program. Dr. Steve and Kathy Carin, for example, took the leadership for the Carin Strength and Conditioning Center opened in 1999. Jody Phillips encourages the entire student-athlete experience with support for the Joan and Wallace Phillips Academic Services Center. Ohio athletics remains a product of a proud tradition—a tradition that continues to launch the Bobcats and their fans toward a bright and exciting future.

Football team at the White House with President Herbert Hoover, 1932. *Courtesy Mahn Center.*

The Center Building remodeled in Victorian style. *Courtesy Mahn Center.*

Columbus. Ironically, just a year later, after intense lobbying by alumni and friends, the legislature voted $20,000 to Ohio University, the first state appropriation since 1804. Passage of the bill was a momentous occasion, one that President Scott would still recall years later as "the largest achievement of my life."

The long-awaited state funds were earmarked for a complete overhaul of the Center Building. However, the trustees decided that with $20,000 they could also afford to build a new assembly hall or chapel just west of the West Wing. The rejuvenated Center Building, with new offices, labs, museum, library, and recitation rooms, was ready by August 1882, and by the following October, the chapel was complete and even furnished, thanks to an addi-

Interior of the chapel. *Snow Collection, courtesy ACHS&M.*

tional appropriation from the state. The Green—or at least part of it—was in better shape, with improved grading and a new, paved front walk running between the avenue of elms the students had planted a few years earlier. The unsightly Commons at the front of the campus resisted reclamation and renovation. When President Scott tried, like others before him, to enclose it, town marshals immediately tore down the few panels of fence he had had erected. The galling eyesore remained.

William Scott, interested in more than funds and buildings for his alma mater, wanted to strengthen the student body, the curriculum, and the faculty. He began by raising admission standards and quietly discontinuing the "troublesome students." In 1879, in a practical move to meet the region's need for qualified teachers, he established a better-organized program of teacher training that quickly attracted a number of prospective teachers and became the precursor to the university's normal department.

As for the regular curriculum, the "demoralizing" fact was that the number of students in the more challenging classical course was declining as many students entered the shorter, less difficult scientific course. To establish a balance between the two courses, the scientific course was renamed and reorganized as the Philosophical Course. It now required both modern languages and additional classes in science and consequently lost its reputation as the easier option. Soon, numbers in the more traditional curriculum increased.

The president also reorganized the faculty and, in a particularly bold move, appointed Miss Cynthia Weld, the university's first female professor, as the head of a new department of history and rhetoric. But these successes were not enough to keep President Scott at Ohio University. By 1883 he had come to see his position in Athens as "uncongenial," and when he was asked to be the president of O.S.U., he accepted and left for Columbus. Soon after, he offered Miss Weld a position, and she too joined the newer institution.

After several unsuccessful attempts to attract a new president, the trustees turned to their professor of Greek, Charles Super, in June 1884. They had made a good choice, for he was able to build on his predecessor's successes to make the 1880s and especially the 1890s exciting times at Ohio University.

Following Scott's example, Super began sending relatively small specific annual funding requests to the state, and the state began to respond. In 1886, after intense lobbying by the university's friends, the general assembly approved $5,000 to launch a full-fledged normal department to succeed the simple teacher training program Scott had established. The principal of the new normal department, John P. Gordy, had a background in psychology and pedagogy and believed that future teachers should study the fields they intended to teach. Consequently, he created

Announcement of a course for teachers in the *Buckeye Amateur,* March 1879. *Courtesy Mahn Center.*

Miss Cynthia Weld, first female faculty member. *Courtesy Mahn Center.*

President Charles William Super *(far right in top hat)* with Ohio University students, circa 1880. *Courtesy Mahn Center.*

a course with solid content in U.S. and English history, math, modern languages, English, vocal music, the histories of philosophy and education, and an array of sciences.

Though the university had found creative ways to keep the classical curriculum at its core and practical courses on the periphery, the normal department changed this balance. In Thomas Hoover's estimation, with this bold curricular change, "Ohio University . . . was aligning itself with a world that was beginning to be dominated by science and business." Even the simple addition of the vocal music class had consequences, for it created diversity. Local teachers Miss Eva Norris and Miss Myrtle Stimson taught the music class part-time and began to lead singing groups at college functions. Other women followed: Miss Emily Wheeler in modern languages, Miss Lillian Michael in the normal department, Miss Mary Donnelly in reading and elocution, Miss Anna Lane in drawing and singing, and Miss Catherine Findley in rhetoric. Miss Madalene Ebert from Germany joined Miss Kate Cranz, President Super, and Professor Gordy (who had all studied at German universities) in lending a touch of international sophistication.

As President Super noted, through the 1880s "the undergraduates were a good deal given to 'kicking' . . . and felt impelled to work off superfluous

> A number of cottonwood trees faced our dormitory rooms in East Wing and we had cotton in our clothes, in our food, and in our beds, until we decided to girdle the trees, so the trustees would be forced to cut them down. . . . No punishment was meted out, save that each student was to pay $1 for the cost of cutting away the dead trees.
>
> —Dr. Elmer A. Dent, '88

energies in ways that were dark and tricks that were sometimes nasty." They were, he said, "wont to regard the faculty as a body of oppressors . . . whose chief joy was to take all the joy out of life or at least out of the life of young people." Despite dealing firmly with serious transgressors, Super had a great deal of sympathy for students. Concerned about the high cost of boarding-houses, he created a kitchen and dining room in the basement of East Wing, where a new boarding club saved students $1.10 a week. He contemplated building a house for the women, gave his approval for a rowing team, and encouraged students to raise $450 to build a wooden gymnasium behind the Center Building. (Though crude, this was a great improvement over the few outdoor ropes and railings that constituted the existing "gymnasium.") He even tolerated the unsanctioned, commencement-week news sheets, like the *Galliniper* and the *Daily Yell,* which poked fun at professors.

Then, at the beginning of the 1890s, Athens seemed to catch the new spirit of the times. Women in many parts of the country called for universal suffrage; men played basketball and hockey in addition to baseball and football; Athenians began to pave a few streets with brick and create safer water and sanitation systems. It was possible to sip Coca-Cola at Carpenter and Henderson's marble-topped soda fountain and sample oysters at A. B. Laurie's restaurant or Edward Berry's Bake Shop. A. O. Sloan provided a five-, ten-, and twenty-five-cent store; Cornwell's was known for jewelry and watch repairs; and there was a steam laundry as well as a billiard hall and a bowling alley with Ladies' Night on Fridays.

The university built its own power plant and turned on incandescent lights. Each night two students from the new electrical engineering class supervised the plant's operation, saving the university money and adding practical, hands-on experience to the young engineers' theoretical knowledge.

Both professors and students got organization fever. Professor Dunkle organized a lecture series for the Village Hall, and the men established a chapter of the Intercollegiate Young Men's Christian Association, which was becoming one of the country's foremost collegiate organizations. It offered a Sunday Bible class and quickly became "practically an elective study." One group of

A circular announcing the courses of study at the university, 1886. *Courtesy Mahn Center.*

Clockwise from right: Catherine Findley, Eva Norris, Caroline Sowers, and Kate Cranz joined other women to teach languages, music, and reading, rhetoric, and elementary composition. *Courtesy* Athena Yearbook, *1892*

A few feet from the opposite side of the railroad track was a watering trough, kept full
by a spout from a spring in the hill. This spout was one of the great blessings of life
at the college. The students, remember, lived in the college buildings and they secured
water from this spout, carrying it in large slender stone pitchers, and almost any time
in the day one might see students,—some time singly, but generally in twos, coming
together toward the South Bridge to fill their pitchers.

—Mrs. D. J. Evans, OHIO UNIVERSITY BULLETIN, 1920

Boarding Club membership
card. *Courtesy Mahn Center.*

women established their own literary society, the Adelphia, in 1890, and others petitioned to have the walk and terraces kept free of tobacco spit and smokers.

In 1892 Anna Pearl McVay became the first woman president of the Philomathean Literary Society. She was a senior in a class of seventeen, the largest in the university's history. Describing themselves as "strong, alert, energetic, and enterprising," they wanted to be known as "the class that attends to business before pleasure." Their yell was "Rac-a dac! Rac-a dac! Rac-a dac! O! U! Vive la! Vive la! '92," and their most visible and lasting contribution was the *Athena,* the university's first yearbook, which they dedicated to the memory of Manasseh Cutler. True to its editors' intentions, it "set forth college life as it occurred

The class of 1892, publishers of
the first *Athena. Courtesy Athena
Yearbook, 1892.*

during the year '91–'2." The faculty and president are pictured and praised for "leading us through a garden filled with innumerable varieties of blooming flowers, tempting us with their rich perfumes." There are portraits and bios of the seniors. Members of the other classes are listed, along with their cheers, colors, and brief histories. Fraternity, sorority, and baseball team members are pictured, and lists give the name of those who participated in football, the Annual Field Day, the Poker Club, the Apollo Quartette, the Euterpian Sextette, the O.U. Chorus, and the String Club.

The early '90s also saw the production of the first plays at the university, as Miss Donnelly directed *Fashion* and *Clouds*. Fraternities entertained with elaborate gatherings, such as Phi Delta Theta's progressive euchre party, at which couples danced into the night. And though students still pushed each other on the Old Beech's rope swing and played occasional games of croquet, bigger things were coming. Ohio University joined Miami, Otterbein, Wittenberg, and Marietta in creating the Ohio Athletic Association and fielded a uniformed baseball team that competed in weekly spring games and was a favorite feature of commencement week.

In 1893 the faculty considered an honors course and approved a formal music department and classes in bookkeeping, typing, and shorthand. Students in Professor Atkinson's engineering class installed a pump at the Hocking River to create the school's first running water system. And the sixty-five-year dispute over the Commons was finally resolved when a group of Civil War veterans—with the approval of both town and gown leaders—erected a monument to honor Athenians who had died in the war. As

First Annual Field Day

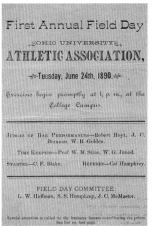

Electrical equipment, supervised each night by students from the electrical engineering department. *Courtesy Athena Yearbook, 1893.*

Program of a Field Day contest. *Courtesy Mahn Center.*

Fraternity party at Hotel Berry. *Courtesy Mahn Center.*

Edward Cornelius Berry.
Courtesy Mahn Center.

Edward and Mattie Berry and the Hotel Berry

In 1907, the Hotel Berry was among the most fashionable establishments in Athens, and its owner, Edward Cornelius Berry, was described by famed educator and author Booker T. Washington as "the leading hotel-keeper of color in this country." Born to a free black family, Berry attended the Albany Enterprise Academy, one of the few schools in the country owned and operated by people of color. However, when he was fourteen, his father died, and Ed left school to help support his mother and eight siblings. First he made bricks for five cents an hour at the Athens State Hospital. Later he was a delivery boy, a waiter, a dishwasher, and then a cook and caterer in Athens. In 1877, at age twenty-three, he married Mattie Madrey, a young woman who shared his desire to succeed as a business entrepreneur.

The Berrys soon started a small ice-cream shop on West State Street. It was very popular, especially with university students. In 1892, Ed bought a major piece of property on North Court Street where he built a twenty-room hotel (later enlarged to fifty-five rooms) complete with an elevator, built-in closets, and an adjoining barbershop run by local black residents. He proudly named it the Hotel Berry. It became a source of employment for many of the area's three hundred people of color, a favorite resting spot for traveling salesmen, and the preferred site for festive dinners and dances given by townspeople and the university's students and staff.

Building a major hotel was an audacious move for a black man at the time. Initially (and periodically throughout his career) Berry was refused credit by local bankers. However, he enlisted the support of at least one local white resident who advanced him the necessary funds to run his hotel. In the beginning, some citizens, primarily competitors, pressured potential guests into boycotting Hotel Berry. Other tradesmen refused to sell Berry the goods he needed to run the establishment and stock his restaurant. Fortunately, these setbacks did not deter the Berrys from their dream of operating the finest hotel in Ohio. They were the first to place Bibles in every hotel room, and the needles, thread, buttons, and pincushions they provided for guests were the forerunner of today's hotel sewing kit. Mattie Berry repaired guests' clothes at night, and Ed cleaned and returned them by dawn the next morning. Their restaurant's food was praised far and wide.

Mr. and Mrs. Berry were generous to both the university and Athens communities. In 1905 Ed Berry led the fund-raising drive to construct Mt. Zion Baptist Church at the corner of Carpenter and North Congress Streets. The couple paid tribute to the university's first black graduate, John Newton Templeton, by contributing handsomely to construction of the Campus Gate.

In 1921 the Berrys sold the Hotel Berry for $100,000. For a while, the hotel continued to be a popular place for university social life, but gradually it declined. In the 1960s it was purchased by Ohio University and converted into Berry Hall, a men's dormitory. In 1974, with amazingly little protest, the once grand hotel was demolished, and a diner and a parking lot took its place. But the Berrys' contributions to Athens and the hotel business remain.

Hotel Berry.
Courtesy Mahn Center.

The Civil War Monument

The artillery soldier standing tall atop the Civil War monument on the College Green since 1893 has witnessed many things—some heartbreaking, sad, controversial, contentious, destructive; others patriotic, sentimental, joyous; and some just everyday goings-on.

The land on which the monument stands was not always a part of the campus, however. When the Ohio University campus was first laid out in 1800 there was a ninety-four-foot-wide strip of land between its northern boundary and East Union Street. As stipulated by the plat drawn for the town in 1800, any land not designated as university campus or town lots was identified as Public Commons. Even though the university technically owned all the land, those open spaces came to be considered part of the town and were used freely by the townspeople.

Teams of horses and oxen were hitched there; livestock roamed loose; traveling circuses erected tents; and as late as 1810 Indian hunting parties rested there. The accumulated filth and litter was a source of constant anguish for the university, but the townspeople insisted it should not be fenced in. Slowly, however, pieces were incorporated until only the section bordered by Court and East Union remained open.

After the Civil War, there was county-wide interest in erecting a monument to the 2,610 men who had fought for the Union, and that corner of the hitching grounds was chosen as the location by the Athens County Monument Association. On July 4, 1893, a grand dedication was attended by seven thousand people who came to see the impressive monument with its sentry topping the forty-five-foot shaft and its life-size bronze statues of an infantryman, a cavalryman, and a sailor standing guard at a base decorated with informational and scenic plaques.

In 1896 the Athens City Council transferred the entire hitching grounds to Ohio University with the provision that the university keep the monument and area in good and proper condition. And so, finally, the square of the College Green was complete.

Placement of the Civil War Monument on the Commons ended a longstanding dispute between the city and the university over control of the public area fronting the College Green. *Snow Collection, courtesy ACHS&M.*

Civil War Monument seen through trees. *Snow Collection, courtesy ACHS&M.*

Athens citizens watched, a towering monument with four military figures was set in place, as if to guard the freedoms of all who entered the Ohio University. Three years later, the land was released to the university with the stipulation that it maintain the area.

At the beginning of 1896, all of Athens was waiting, hoping for passage of the Sleeper Bill. David L. Sleeper, an attorney, former Athens newspaper publisher, and Speaker of the Ohio House of Representatives, had sponsored a bill by which a small annual millage would support Ohio and Miami Universities. To encourage passage of the bill, a group of Athenians invited the state senate's finance committee to an elaborate banquet at the Hotel Berry. Less than two weeks later, the bill passed—and after ninety-two years, Ohio University was guaranteed continuing annual funds. The town and university erupted in celebration. A huge bonfire burned on the campus as people cheered and shouted. Festivities continued as Sleeper and the bill's co-sponsor, George Falloon, arrived the next day for a rally and testimonials amid the pealing of bells and universal rejoicing.

Though for Ohio University this was surely the climax of the century, there was more to come. Women now made up one-third of the student population—and they needed housing. The solution lay with local businessmen, who agreed to construct a women's hall at the corner of College and Union and lease it to the university. The building could house thirty, and that fall, female students and instructors began moving in. The trustees also issued bonds for an elaborate, all-purpose building that would house an auditorium, nine recitation rooms, a president's office, fraternity and sorority rooms, a chemistry lab, an art room, and other amenities. It would stand west of West Wing. Unfortunately, the chapel already occupied that space, so the chapel was simply moved. The process took forty days, affording entertainment for anyone who had time to watch. The new building, named Ewing Hall for the university's first graduate, opened in 1898.

The football team was also organizing during this time. With President Super's son Frank as captain, team members successfully petitioned for a change in class schedules that allowed time for practice every afternoon at four o'clock. They

Ladies Hall (later, Women's Hall), the university's first dormitory, was built in 1896 by the College Place Improvement Company, a group of local businessmen, and leased to the university. It was purchased in 1908 and named Howard Hall in 1916. The site, at the corner of College and Union Streets, is now a park. *Thomas Oldfield Collection, courtesy Mahn Center.*

Moving the chapel to create space for Ewing Hall, 1896. *Thomas Oldfield Collection, courtesy Mahn Center.*

played on the south campus, with Frank S. Remsburg as a player-coach and Charles O'Bleness as manager. When their first away game was scheduled with great rival Marietta, both men and women made the trip to cheer them on. Though this game ended peaceably, fights seemed to be the rule rather than the exception.

By the next year, the team was successful. Saki Taro Murayama from Japan, the university's first international student, bought sweaters to go with the players' quilted vests and high-top shoes. An Athletic Fair with games, darts, and food raised $230 for team expenses. The following year, faculty members were asked to contribute to the team, and the trustees allotted $300 to lease nineteen acres for a playing field. Men's athletics was on its way.

Ewing Hall, completed in March 1898, contained a 1,200-seat auditorium, nine recitation rooms with attached offices, the president's office, a faculty room, a large gymnasium, five society and fraternity rooms, the chemistry lab, and the art room. *James Anastas Collection, courtesy ACHS&M.*

Ewing Hall, O. U.
Athens, Ohio.

Members of an early football team with Charles O'Bleness as manager. *Thomas Oldfield Collection, courtesy Mahn Center.*

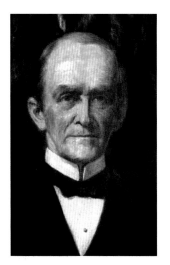

Isaac Crook, O.U. president 1896–98.

Meanwhile, Miss Findley negotiated a change in the daily schedule to provide the young women with their own fifteen minutes of "physical culture."

In June of the momentous year of 1896, President Super retired. His successor was the Reverend Isaac Crook. During his two-year tenure, professors organized a senate to help define faculty status. Under its terms, all faculty members could discuss academic matters, although only heads of the fourteen departments could vote on them. President Crook encouraged the English department to supervise the *Ohio University Mirror* so students could have the experience of managing a paper, and he arranged to house the Coonskin Library at the university. Although he based his administration on faculty participation and recognized the faculty members' hard work, he never gained their trust or the board's and was soon encouraged to leave. Super, perhaps a bit rested, resumed the presidency while a number of his students marched off for remarkably uneventful service in President McKinley's "splendid little war" against Spain. Super's renewed service as president continued only until 1901, when he took the positions of professor of Greek and the first dean of the College of Liberal Arts.

The century was over. Ohio University had survived. The academy that had begun with three students and one instructor had grown into a college. With some support from the state and a decline in sectarian control, this "natural germ of a university" showed promising signs of new strength and growth. A strong pedagogical program that prepared teachers for Ohio's schools complemented the classical course that had long trained legislators, judges, ministers, and professors. The 22 faculty members and 102 spirited collegiate students of 1899 considered themselves "one happy family." They felt they knew the answer when they asked, "Who then can estimate the influence . . . that the thousands who have matriculated at the Ohio University have exerted in behalf of education and humanity, learning and culture?" They and their southeast Ohio school were ready for the twentieth century.

O.U. cheers from 1898.
Courtesy Mahn Center.

Coeds with O.U. banners. (Emaline Goddard Rudolph, *first from the left.*)
Courtesy Richard H. Rudolph, '43.

OHIO UNIVERSITY,
◖1898◗

1. Wa-hoo, wa-hoo, rip rah, O. U. OhiO U-Tiger.

2. O-U, O-U, Rah, rah, rah, rah, O-U, O-U; rah, rah, rah, rah; Hoo-ra, hoo-ra; Bully for the old O-U.

3. Razzle dazzle, hobble gobble, siz boom rah; Ohio University, rah, rah, rah.

4. Ama vivo, ama vivo,, ama vivo vivo vum; Boom get a rat trap bigger than a cat trap, boom get a rat trap, bigger than a cat trap, Boom, boom, siz boom ah, Ohio University, rah, rah, rah.

5. Rah, rah rah, zip rah boom, Ohio University, give her room.

6. Shool, shool, shool I rool, shool i shack a rack, shool I barbe cool. Last time I saw, silly bally eel, dis cum bib-a-la la boom slow reel.

7. Hulla-be-luck (biz), Ko-whack (biz), Whoa-up (biz) diaballoo—Ohio.

8. Hullabaloo, zip, bah; Hollabaloo rip, rah, Hollyboom, Sollyboom, lee rah roe; Rhe rah roe; Ohio; Ohio.

College of Arts and Sciences

The College of Arts and Sciences is often referred to as Ohio University's oldest college, but that label is not entirely accurate. The first degrees awarded by the university, two in all, were Bachelor of Arts and Science degrees. The university's first course offerings included Latin, Greek, rhetoric, English grammar, geography, logic, philosophy, literature, classics, astronomy, and various branches of mathematics, all of which still are offered in the College of Arts and Sciences. But since a liberal arts curriculum was *all* the university offered, the College of Arts and Sciences did not exist as a discrete entity until the university grew to include other colleges; it became a truly separate college—the College of Liberal Arts—in 1902.

During the fall term of 1902, the State Normal College of Ohio University was established and enrolled its first students, but the liberal arts curriculum provided its academic foundation. Normal college students attended the same classes and functions as liberal arts college students. In 1906, a state legislator, Edwin Lybarger, introduced a bill that threatened to fund only the normal schools at Ohio and Miami Universities. The pitched battle that ensued included accusations that Ohio State professors had posed as Ohio University alumni in support of the measure. In the end, President Alston Ellis won the day, and state support was restored for the liberal arts missions at both Ohio and Miami Universities. In 1911 a science hall was dedicated, supporting an increasingly important focus on scientific endeavor.

Charles W. Super, the first dean of the College of Liberal Arts, was succeeded in 1907 by Edwin Chubb, who served in that capacity until his retirement in 1936. During Professor Chubb's thirty-six-year career with the university, he was head of the English department and served as acting president on two occasions, once in 1920 on the death of Alston Ellis and again in 1934 on the death of E. B. Bryan. Professor Chubb, described as "urbane and witty," was cited in the 1928 *Athena* as an advocate of high standards of scholarship. The yearbook article says, "His loyalty to the University is coupled with a secret silent devotion to his students, who remember him long afterward for the length of his service and the breadth of his sympathy."

President Herman Gerlach James created the College of Arts and Sciences in 1936 when he organized the university into five degree-granting entities to eliminate duplication of efforts. The College of Arts and Sciences has been under the leadership of Dean Leslie A. Flemming since 1996. At the bicentennial, the college has nineteen departments offering students a choice of twenty-six majors, twenty-eight minors, seven certificate programs, and fifty-seven career-related programs. The college has twenty programs that lead to master's degrees and eight that lead to doctorates. To help meet the needs of students in an increasingly interconnected world, the college also offers thirty-eight education abroad programs in twenty-eight countries.

All Ohio University students depend on the College of Arts and Sciences for a range of courses in the humanities, the social sciences, and the sciences as the foundation for any degree they pursue within the university. Whether or not the College of Arts and Sciences can claim to be the university's oldest, it remains at its core.

The Normal School Years

1901–1921

Whereas the General Assembly of the State of Ohio has enacted into a law
House Bill No. 369, known as the "Seese Bill," providing for the establishment
of Normal Schools at the Ohio University, and at the Miami University at Oxford,
and has provided for the support thereof: Therefore be it resolved . . . that this Board
will establish and maintain such an institution, and will provide the necessary
teaching force, buildings and equipment therefor at the earliest practicable date.
—*Resolution of the Ohio University Board of Trustees, March 25, 1902*

Throughout the nineteenth century, Ohio University had struggled just
to survive. But those difficult days were recalled with fondness and "overflowing enthusiasm" in June 1904, as hundreds of alumni gathered to celebrate the university's Centennial Anniversary. The event, a notable occasion
on its own, became part of an extravaganza as Athens celebrated its own
centennial with a homecoming reunion replete with decorations, music,
parades, a barbecue, and hosts of eminent speakers. Both alumni and former
Athenians returned to walk the old walks and see familiar faces, and they
joined in George A. Beaton's extraordinary banquet for 3,200 guests. Beaton,
a former Athenian who had suggested the homecoming, shipped eighteen
waiters along with elegant boxed dinners, complete with silverware and
souvenir plates, from New York to Athens, where the seated dinner was
served "with the precision of machinery" in a mammoth tent on the College
Green. *The Athens Home Coming Reunion,* a charming souvenir album, exuded
optimism: "You will rejoice, with all the friends of the University, at the great
prosperity and firm foundation upon which it now rests."

As part of the centennial anniversaries of the university and the town of Athens in 1904, former Athenian George Beaton provided a dinner on the Green for 3,200 people. *Photo by Ada Wickham O'Bleness, class of 1898, courtesy Laura Wickham Medleau, '83, and Robert C. Wickham, '36.*

President Alston Ellis (standing) in his Ewing Hall office with secretary Eugene F. Thompson and Professor Clement L. Martzolff. *Courtesy Mahn Center.*

What had happened in this new century to create such rejoicing and prosperity? The simple answer was the Seese Bill, passed by the Ohio legislature in March 1902. The hotly debated bill, ardently supported by the forceful new president Alston Ellis and many Athenians, addressed the state's increasing need for public school teachers by funding teacher training, or normal schools, at Miami and Ohio Universities. For O.U. it meant an annual increase of $38,000 and new enrollments that quickly triggered a transformation of the university's physical plant, demographics, and culture.

Athens Messenger editor Fred Bush instantly recognized the potential impact of the State Normal College on the Athens economy. By his calculations, an additional 500 students could add "the munificent sum of $100,000 a year" to what students already spent in town. He also predicted, quite accurately, that a fully equipped normal school would give the university "the best chance in its long and useful life to be and do."

The "doing" began immediately. The Normal College opened in the fall of 1902 with Henry G. Williams as dean (the university's second), five new instructors, and 102 students. Less than two years later, when the mostly female enrollments had grown to 180, the new college and its model school, which allowed prospective teachers to

The central section of Ellis Hall, home of the Normal College, completed in 1904. *Courtesy Mahn Center.*

practice their skills on Athens students, moved into its new home on University Terrace. The massive building would acquire its north wing in 1907. When the south wing, with additional classrooms and a 500-seat auditorium, was completed a year later, the building was named Ellis Hall amid complaints that the president was taking too much credit and lacked proper humility. (In 1912 the model school moved into the building that is now named for the university's first professor of pedagogy, John Gordy.)

The normal school's success was evidence that it was meeting the needs of southeast Ohio as well as of the state. It also highlighted the need for a larger, more accessible library for the university's 16,000 volumes. Fortunately, philanthropist Andrew Carnegie was funding public libraries in the early part of the century, and General Charles Grosvenor, a leading Athens citizen and friend of both Carnegie and the university, persuaded him to donate $30,000 for a building. Carnegie Library (now E. W. Scripps Hall) was dedicated in June 1905. The university and the town of Athens pledged to make annual contributions for its upkeep, and the citizens of Athens, including the pupils of its public schools, were guaranteed access to its facilities.

Programs were also expanded. The summer school, which professors Eli Dunkle and Dafydd J. Evans had started quietly in 1892, became a permanent part of the school year. The summer *Bulletin* touted the pleasures of Athens, the beauty of the campus, and the courses at the "best summer school in the state of Ohio." Hundreds of area schoolteachers poured into Athens and paid three dollars for six weeks of instruction. County clubs,

College of Education

When the first settlements were established in Ohio in the late eighteenth century, education was a catch-as-catch-can proposition. Children were taught at home or learned their letters and numbers in one-room schoolhouses. Teachers who received any training learned their craft in local "common schools." Few went to college.

As Ohio changed from frontier to industrialized state, it needed well-trained, professional teachers. Ohio University had created the state's first college-based teacher education program in 1831. In 1886 the General Assembly appropriated $5,000 to establish a normal department at Ohio University, making it Ohio's first state-supported teacher education program. In 1902 Ohio University became one of two official teacher training schools, or normal colleges, supported by the state (the other was at Miami University).

Many campus landmarks owe their existence to the Normal College. Ellis Hall, completed in 1908, was the first state building erected specifically for teacher education. A training school for aspiring teachers, now Gordy Hall, opened in 1912; it was followed by Rufus Putnam Hall in 1926. These buildings not only provided classroom space for teacher candidates but served as schools for local children. From its earliest years, teacher training at Ohio University was based in practice. America's first model school was founded here in 1837, and Ohio's first kindergarten opened on the Ohio University campus in 1907. In 1917 the top floor of Ellis Hall became the home of John Hancock High School, giving teacher candidates practical experience in secondary education. From 1926 to 1972, the Rufus Putnam School served the same purpose for those in elementary education.

Continuing education for teachers also has been a longstanding pillar of the university's mission. In 1892, the university offered its first summer term, giving working teachers the opportunity to hone their skills.

In 1935, when President Herman G. James reorganized the university into five degree-granting colleges, the Normal College became the College of Education. In 1948 Dr. George Hill organized the Department of Guidance, Counseling, and Student Personnel. Today, the college comprises three departments: Teacher Education, Counseling and Higher Education, and Educational Studies. It offers nineteen undergraduate courses of study leading to a bachelor of science in education, primarily in teacher education. There are thirteen courses of study that lead to a master of education degree and six doctoral programs.

Practice remains a cornerstone of the college's approach. Through partnerships with local elementary and secondary schools, education majors begin gaining classroom experience as early as their sophomore year. Many students amass more than 300 classroom hours by their senior year. The college collaborates with the colleges of Arts and Sciences, Fine Arts, and Health and Human Services to offer specialized training in specific subjects.

The college also has a significant commitment to education outreach at home and abroad. It is home to ten centers and research institutes dedicated to adult literacy, improving Appalachian education, development of literacy and language, democracy in education, and professional development. For nearly a half-century, the college has assisted African and Asian nations in developing faculty for their own teacher education programs.

Grosvenor House/Konneker Alumni Center

General Charles H. Grosvenor was one of many early friends of Ohio University whose contributions extended well beyond their own lifetimes. General Grosvenor, who served during the Civil War, became a well-known Athens lawyer and politician. He was elected to the Ohio General Assembly and later spent more than twenty years in the U.S. House of Representatives.

During his years in the statehouse in Columbus, Grosvenor frequently supported the interests of the university, and in the 1880s he joined other Civil War veterans to solve the longstanding problem of the Commons. He also played a part in the additions of Haning and E. W. Scripps Halls to the university campus. Haning, once the Athens Post Office, was built with funds provided by the U.S. Congress to honor Grosvenor on his retirement. Scripps Hall, originally Carnegie Library, was completed in 1904. General Grosvenor, a personal friend of Andrew Carnegie, helped persuade the millionaire industrialist to donate $30,000 for the library project.

General Charles H. Grosvenor and his house on University Terrace, now Konneker Alumni Center. *Courtesy Mahn Center.*

Another legacy from Grosvenor and his family is the house he built at 52 University Terrace in 1901. Charles H. and Louise Currier Grosvenor lived there for seventeen years, entertaining such famous guests as Presidents William Howard Taft and Theodore Roosevelt, Alice Roosevelt Longworth, Joe Cannon, and Mark Hanna. The Grosvenors' granddaughter, Constance Leete, later inherited the house, which she eventually left to the Church of the Good Shepherd.

In 1980 when the Alumni Association was looking for an official home, active alumni Dr. and Mrs. Wilfred Konneker donated funds to purchase the Grosvenor house and issued a challenge grant to renovate and furnish it. In appreciation the Alumni Association and Foundation boards named the building The Konneker Alumni Center. The cottage, purchased by the Foundation, was named Claire Cottage in honor of Claire Oates Ping, wife of President Charles Ping.

Dr. Konneker, a pioneer in the radiopharmaceutical industry, and his wife, Ann Lee, took great interest in restoring the house to its former grand style. Among the many other projects that they supported over the years are the Alumni Board, the Ohio University Foundation, major fundraising campaigns, Manasseh Cutler scholarships, genetic research, and the Innovation Center. Like General Grosvenor, and so many others, they were friends for the long term.

Carnegie Library (now E. W. Scripps Hall), dedicated in 1905 and named for its benefactor, philanthropist Andrew Carnegie. From undated scrapbook, "Ohio University Scenes." *Courtesy Mahn Center.*

There is a charm about Athens that impresses itself strongly upon every Summer School student. The old University itself set in the midst of a grove of trees which would have rejoiced the heart of an ancient Druid; the well-paved streets; the placid Hocking with its willow-fringed banks; the rolling green hills in the distance . . . (Souvenir Edition of the Ohio University Bulletin, Summer Term, 1907)

picnics, the attentive faculty, and evenings spent singing on the Green kept them occupied through the hot days and nights. The extension program, for which professors endured slow travel and missed train connections to provide classes in off-campus settings, also took on new life.

Programs in music, commercial studies, and engineering also benefited from the normal school's growth. Music courses originated in Professor Gordy's pedagogical curriculum, but their popularity led to overcrowded classes. At the turn of the century the School of Music opened, with James P. McVey as director and productions that were both ambitious and accomplished. In 1906 its seventy-five-member chorus enlivened *The Bohemian Girl,* and in 1908 the school offered one of its first comic operas, *Princess Bonnie.*

YMCA picnic on the asylum grounds, circa 1900. *Front left:* Anna Pearl Williams. *Courtesy Robert L. Williams, '47.*

Cast and chorus performing in the comic opera *Princess Bonnie. Courtesy* Athena Yearbook, *1908.*

The practical commercial classes in stenography, bookkeeping, and type-writing were equally popular. Charles M. Copeland, an alumnus, and Mabel K. Brown had first offered them in 1893 as adjuncts to the regular curriculum. Gradually, as more students demanded practical business education, these classes evolved into a two-year certificate program. As for the engineering department, by 1906 it offered courses in electrical, civil, and mining engineering. Though some faculty members were concerned about the strong move toward engineering and other sciences, President Ellis had no objections to either. By 1911 physics and chemistry had moved into Science Hall, their new building on President Street. A year later, the university added programs in agriculture and domestic science. By 1915 they too had their own

Students in the commercial course, initiated by Charles M. Copeland and Mabel K. Brown in 1893. *Courtesy* Athena Yearbook, *1908.*

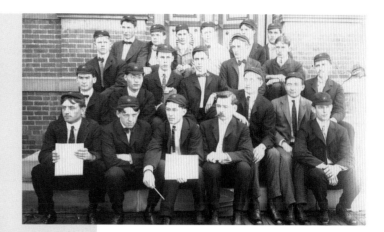

Here are the men who counted in my life . . . Dunkle, Chubb, Elson, Mercer, Super, and Wilson. I was closest to Super and kept in touch with him until he got too old to write. Mercer and he were like elder brothers. Wilson and Dunkle were delightful drill masters who taught us how to learn lessons; Chubb and Elson were clever fellows who could make a young fellow stay up all night reading collateral stuff for the sheer fun of it. Their tricks have lived on in younger bones, and often kept the world from getting out of joint.

—Dr. Grover C. Morehart, '09
(Ohio University Alumnus, November 1944)

Professor Albert Atkinson and freshmen in his electrical engineering class, 1902. *Courtesy Mahn Center.*

Horses and buggies crowd Court Street (looking south from Washington Street). *From* Athens Home Coming Reunion, *1904.*

new building, across the street from the Green on University Terrace.

Improvements at the university paralleled attempts to improve life in the town. Some citizens tried to solve the uptown parking problem by creating hitching areas for horses and wagons. Others, concerned about recreation, opened a swimming hole near South Bridge. A group of men formed the Anti-Saloon League and tried to shut down Athens saloons and run the prostitutes out of town. A number of women formed the Village Improvement Society with the goal of cleaning up the filthy streets, reducing spitting, and controlling the number of signs on trees and fences. Others campaigned for women's rights and suffrage.

University women too were making their presence felt. As their numbers increased in the normal school, the problem of housing them became acute. Ladies Hall (later called Women's Hall and finally Howard Hall), leased from the College Place Improvement Company, had room for only thirty students. A few men still lived in the East and West Wings, but most lived in town, often in dank, dark rooms. Assigning young women to such unsupervised quarters was worrisome. The situation prompted the president to declare that "either additional accommodations must be provided, or the whole dormitory system abolished." In early 1906 he persuaded the legislature to appropriate funds for a new building to house eighty-eight women. It was completed a year later and named Boyd Hall for the university's first female graduate. Zoa

McGuire Pixler, a 1913 graduate, recalled moving in when it still smelled of fresh varnish, sleeping on what she called a "sanitary cot," and eating at dining room tables served by freshmen boys who were working for their own board. She also remembered that "every girl had to be in her room at seven. She could study until ten o'clock but then it was 'lights out.'" Two years later, the trustees decided to buy Women's Hall and increase its capacity to one hundred—a help, but the problem of housing and supervising coeds continued.

Boyd Hall, erected on Mulberry Street (now Park Place) in 1906 and named for Margaret Boyd, the university's first female graduate. *Courtesy Mahn Center.*

A more serious challenge arose in 1906. State Representative Edwin L. Lybarger of Coshocton introduced a legislative bill proposing that Ohio State University, already the state's favored ward, continue to receive full funding while Ohio and Miami Universities receive support only for their normal schools. Though O.S.U. had been established as an agricultural, mechanical, and technical institution, its supporters now wanted it to have exclusive rights not just to those programs, but to the liberal arts as well. As Thomas Hoover explains in his *History of Ohio University,* "By this act the liberal arts colleges at the older institutions would have become meagre adjuncts to the teacher-training departments, or would have been closed entirely."

President Ellis pledged to "fight to the bitter end any attempt to upset the established order of things at Ohio University." Alumni were urged to press for their alma mater's interests. Some 150 Athenians rallied to protect their university. After heated debate in committee, the issue was defeated, but after only a month, a somewhat different proposal, the Eagleson Act, passed. Supporters of this bill—largely O.S.U. alumni and friends—said it would prevent duplication of services and save money. But once again the intention was to restrict operations at Ohio and Miami Universities by limiting their programs to the liberal arts, to the normal schools, and to master's-level graduate study. The old Sleeper Bill of 1896 and the Seese Bill of 1902 were repealed and new funding formulas devised. Ohio University was to receive $86,000 annually, a clear gain, but the school in Columbus was awarded the lion's share.

The whole incident was trying, but President Ellis was more concerned

The Case of Ohio University

Whereas Mr. Lybarger has introduced a bill having for its purpose the taking away of State aid to the Ohio University save for purposes of Normal school work, we, a Committee of the Alumni of Ohio University, wish to present the following facts. We do so with the conviction that fuller information with regard to the history and present usefulness of the Ohio University will not only prevent the unjust impairment of her present efficiency, but furnish her with means for greater effectiveness in the future.

In brief, the alumni and friends of Ohio University protest most vigorously against the passage of the Lybarger Bill because,

1. The Ohio University is a ward of the State.

2. Owing to the fact that the Legislature in the past took away the University's means of support. The State is under moral obligation to support the Ohio University.

3. The State needs Ohio University, which today has greater efficiency than ever.

4. The head and front of all opposition to Ohio University is inspired by the Ohio State University.

5. A just and wise educational policy should lead the O. S. U. to confine her energies along the lines of her original foundation instead of trying to rob her sister institutions of their rights and opportunities.

Furthermore, we send out this fragment of information with the deep conviction that neither the present Assembly nor the people of Ohio whom they represent, when once acquainted with the facts, will permit the passage of a bill which, to quote the language of James A. Garfield in reference to the passage of the act of 1843, is "unjust to the character and honor of the State."

To defeat the Lybarger Bill, which threatened to limit programs at both Ohio and Miami Universities, O.U. alumni presented "The Case of Ohio University." *Scott Papers, courtesy Mahn Center.*

Mildred Rice *(left,* with members of Alpha Gamma Delta sorority) was one of many students who taught school while completing college work. She first enrolled at Ohio University in 1916 and earned her degree in 1928.
Courtesy Robert L. Williams, '47.

about preserving O.U.'s threatened engineering programs than about education beyond the master's degree. In fact, a Mr. Babcock, who reported on the state of the university a few years later, remembered Ellis as "unsympathetic with the development of advanced courses . . . and with research by his faculty. . . . He desires a faculty devoted enthusiastically to teaching, and to nothing else. He disbelieves in vacations and sabbatical privileges."

Even though Ellis allegedly disapproved of vacations for the faculty, by 1907 he felt he needed one himself. Along with threats from O.S.U., there were increasing criticisms at home. Long-term ally Aaron Price turned on Ellis and accused him of trying to sabotage the normal school and promote only the liberal arts college. The trustees investigated the university treasurer's books and found that "there seems to have been no well-defined system of making purchases. Anyone connected with the University bought what was needed," but there were no records to show how it was done. At the same time, local contractors charged the trustees with questionable handling of construction contracts. And former president Charles Super, Ellis's most vocal and scathing critic, turned in his final resignation. President Ellis took a month off to visit other universities. At Harvard he noticed the squirrels on the lawn and came home with a plan to get some for O.U.

Students were also encountering their share of criticism. In this progressive era of new buildings, new courses, ragtime, Gibson girls, the Wright brothers' first flight, $850 Model T's, legalized forward passes in football, and the Nickelodeon, they were full of college spirit. The trend had begun in the late 1890s, causing the faculty to pass an apparently ineffective resolution: "[We] discountenance and disapprove of the boisterous cheering and other anonymous practices which have been in vogue in our assembly halls," and "'college yells' are not to be considered in place on such formal occasions as lectures, musical recitals, etc."

A student of 1907 reported that even the literary societies took little heed of these admonitions. At one memorable contest between the Athenians and Philomatheans, Ewing Hall auditorium was packed with students, faculty,

Members of the Athenian and Philomathean Literary Societies. *Courtesy Mahn Center.*

40   STUDENTS' HANDBOOK.

Chorus.

Forever dear, enshrined here,
In hearts true to her name,
Her praise we'll sing, her glory ring,
Her worthy deeds proclaim.

Chorus.

Then take the hymn of friendship true,
In pledge of love sincere;
Let come what must, in faith we'll trust
Our Alma Mater dear.

Chorus for Last Stanza.

Then loved and dear, both far and near,
Repeat the glad refrain;
Wah-hoo-wah-hoo-rip-rah-O. U.
O-Hi-O,-U. again.

COLLEGE YELLS

1 O. U.! O. U.! Rah! Rah!
   O. U.! O. U.! Rah! Rah!
   Hoo-rah! Hoo-rah!
   Bully for old O. U.!

2 Razzle, dazzle, hobble gobble,
   Sis, boom, bah!
   Ohio University, Rah! Rah! Rah!

3 Owski, wow, wow,
   Skinny, wow! wow!
              Wow! ! !

NORMAL COLLEGE.

1 N-O-R-M-A-L
   That's the way we spell it!
   This is the way we yell it!
   Normal! Normal! Normal!

2 One-two-three-four!
   Two-four-three-four!
   What are we for?
   Normal! Normal!

STUDENTS' HANDBOOK.   41

COLLEGE OF MUSIC.

1 Mendelssohn, Liszt,
   Zis: Boom! Bah!
   College of Music.
   Rah! Rah! Rah!

2 Chopin, Chaminade, Bach, Listz,
   Schubert, Schumann, listen to this,
   Handel, Haydn, Rubenstein,
   We're the class of nineteen nine.

PHILOMATHEAN LITERARY SOCIETY.

Onery, twoery, tinkery, three,
You are zero; who are we?
Zip, Zaw, .uscataw;
Philo, Philo, Raw! Raw! Raw!

ATHENIAN LITERARY SOCIETY.

Razzle, dazzle! Hobble, gobble!
Sis, boom, bah!
Athenian! Athenian!
Rah, Rah, Rah!

4 Ama veva! Ama veva!
   Ama veva, viva, vum.
   Ama veva! Ama veva!
   Ama veva, viva, vum.
   Ohio's the best school,
   The rest are on the bum.

5 Hickidilly! Pickidilly! 23 skiddo!
   Razzle, dazzle! Cizzle, spazzle!
       Old O. U.

6 Esse, esse, quam videri,
   Veni, veni et moneri,
   Ecce, ecce, ecce tu
   Quod est factum, ad O. U.

Students' handbook of 1909–10, with songs, yells, and pointers for freshmen. From the scrapbook of William Fenzel, '18. *Courtesy George Weckman.*

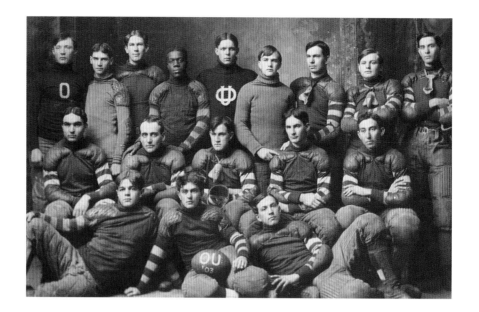

The 1903 football team.
Courtesy Mahn Center.

and townspeople. The Athenians sat in a body on the left of the house; the Philos sat on the right, and both groups hurled "derisive songs and yells on appropriate occasions. The Athenians had fife and drum . . . to supplement its songs and war cries." When they were announced as the winners, they "stood in their places and sang all the songs they knew and yelled all the yells they knew."

Athletics of course inspired more yelling, some fights, and questions of supervision and funding. In 1896 the board of trustees had spent twenty-five dollars to provide showers for athletes in the basement of East Wing. In 1897 they spent $300 to cover the football team's deficit, only to discover the next year that "no member of the faculty knows how the money was expended." The following year the student athletic association asked the faculty for contributions. The faculty established eligibility requirements and reviewed the roster of players before each game to keep "ringers" (non-students and paid players) off the field, though townspeople petitioned against suspension of the ringers.

President Super, who had seen the beginnings of the university's first official teams in the 1890s, felt that only athletics programs at schools near cities with large populations had a chance of coming out ahead financially. Nevertheless, he had gone along with the times. "We have athletics

Baseball games at University Field often pitted faculty members against the senior men.
Courtesy Athena Yearbook, *1919.*

Gymnasium on Mulberry Street, now
Park Place. *Courtesy Mahn Center.*

First men's basketball team, circa 1900.
Courtesy Mahn Center.

1902 women's basketball group.
Courtesy Mahn Center.

ATTENTION

YE WORMS
Of Ye Freshman Class!

LIST ye to your horrible doom, ye vile slimy lizards who have dared to ooze forth from your habitations of filth and rot and wriggle your loathsome carcasses upon our fair Temple of Learning. Hearken ye to your Lords and Masters,

The Sophomore Class.

THE frightful horrors of bloody torture and ignominious death are hovering over you. The foul stench of your decaying bodies shall be cleansed from your balmy atmosphere and your blood-curdling shrieks shall be silenced forever.

HENCEFORTH, you stinking idiots, ye shall no more nauseate us with your putrid presence.

FLEE the mighty wrath to come and bow to the iron decree.

TAKE HEED!   BEWARE!

Flyers littered the campus in 1915 to warn the "worms" of the freshman class of their impending "doom" at the hands of sophomore men. From the scrapbook of William Fenzel, '18. *Courtesy George Weckman.*

At stated times, class fights were the order of the day with the flag pole and also the Tug of War at the hospital grounds. One class would raise its flag on the pole and the other class try to get it down. I doubt if I ever had a greater thrill than the day I climbed the pole and dragged down the flag victoriously. It seems to me now that enthusiasm ran high and love for our college knew no bounds.

—Bob Rucker, '14

One team inevitably ended up in the slimy lake when first-year men tried to best the sophomores in the annual Tug of War at the asylum. *Courtesy* Athena Yearbook, 1932.

with us," he said in 1901, "and it would not be wise to suppress it." Though President Ellis began his tenure by saying that he looked "with great favor on anything that suggests the physical well-being of our students," he came to consider athletics a "necessary evil" that involved only a few students at great cost. By 1909 the students' constant petitions had pushed the president and board of trustees to approve money for a football coach, an athletic director, an athletic field, a grandstand, and a gymnasium on Park Place. Both men and women had basketball teams, and both sexes were able to compete in field day exercises that included a ball toss and egg, potato, and three-legged races. Baseball was a featured event during commencement week, and students often challenged their professors to games.

Class competition added to this new spirit. Freshmen challenged sophomores to flag fights and tugs of war, which took place at the asylum, with a rope stretched across a murky lake and a team—limited to 2,500 pounds—on either side. Losers ended up "struggling thru the slimy water." In the 1913 *Athena,* the junior class bragged: "No one will ever be able to give a 'Junior Prom' such as ours."

Sororities and fraternities also competed, especially for members. As in the old days, fraternity rushing often began at the train station when students arrived in town. Later, when a few students acquired cars, a fraternity group would sometimes drive to Nelsonville and put an active or two on the train to scout likely prospects while the others rushed back to Athens in time to pick them all up at the station. Pledges were subjected to such stunts as standing in the window of Lash's Drug Store "attired in baby clothes, and fondling a nursing bottle" or posing as blind men and begging on Court Street with tin cups and dark glasses. No doubt when some men tied a goat to the roof of the College Edifice, recently renamed Cutler Hall, they meant to show off to competitors.

Program for 1912 Junior Promenade given by the class of 1913. From the scrapbook of Percy R. Stout, '12. *Courtesy Mahn Center.*

There were no such social antics for the few African American students on the campus. It was only in 1915 that Leonard Barnett organized the Du Bois Club, and not until 1919 that nine men established Alpha Phi Alpha, the first black Greek-letter fraternity on the campus. Until then, they had no home in either greek or non-greek social organizations.

The non-greek Barbarians, who constituted the majority of the student body, had little use for the more exclusive greeks. These loosely organized "Barbs" (later the Phrenocons) published a sometimes anti-greek paper called *Sidelights,* and they entertained at inclusive annual banquets and with a new-student reception each term. In May 1908, they took

Members of the Du Bois Club in 1917. *Inset:* 1956 photo of Leonard Barnett, '16, who founded the club in 1915. *Courtesy Mahn Center.*

Members of the Chinese Club, the university's first organization formed by international students. *Courtesy Mahn Center.*

Cartoon mocking the efforts of President Ellis and Dean Edwin Chubb to see that Ohio women behaved in sufficiently ladylike fashion. By Clyde L. White, '10. *Courtesy* Athena Yearbook, *1910.*

Perhaps some of you by being here will have met your future husband or wife. No one can tell how differently your life may be because you have been here. You will take away with you, we hope, some of the spirit of O.U. We wish this spirit so to possess you that you may come back again.
(SUMMER SCHOOL BULLETIN, 1913)

180 students to an all-day picnic. The women made baskets of "good things," and the men arranged for eight hay wagons to take them the four miles to Hibbard's Grove. The day, which began at 7:30 A.M., included swinging, horse-shoes, baseball, the picnic feast, races, songs, readings, and speeches and ended "with a happy heart singing the songs of old O.U."

This idyllic day was, of course, well chaperoned by members of the faculty, for the young women had to be protected. Even so, occasional "unseemly" behavior persuaded President Ellis and Dean Chubb to speak to the young ladies: they should be aware that their reputations were their most precious treasures; they should make every effort to be discreet. Howls of protest rose from the O.U. men. They dubbed Boyd Hall "The Hennery" and lampooned this overprotective attitude in a 1910 *Athena* cartoon with Cupid weeping near the Boyd Hall door. (Mary Goldsberry Lord, '28, says there was "a big panty raid on Howard Hall" about this time, but it may not have been a part of this protest.) Even ten years later, restrictions on women had changed little. Madge Acord Eachus, who was one of only two female

The Barbarians, a non-greek group, on a day-long picnic in May 1907. *Courtesy Wanda Daughriety.*

Carr Van Anda

Carr Van Anda entered Ohio University in 1880, at age sixteen, but abandoned formal education after two years to pursue a career in journalism. In 1904 he joined Adolph Ochs's *New York Times* as managing editor. Over the next twenty-one years, he became known for his prodigious intellect, keen interest in science and mathematics, steady fairness, and ability to select news and gather information quickly.

Van Anda is most often remembered today for his handling of the *Titanic* disaster in 1912. When the ship's distress messages ceased shortly after midnight on April 15, he concluded that the "unsinkable" vessel was indeed going down and ran a banner headline in the morning edition of the *Times*, making it the first paper to break the horrible news.

Courtesy Mahn Center.

biology majors of that period, recalled that even though dancing and movies were becoming popular, smoking was still forbidden, boys could call at the dorm only during certain hours, and "you had to get consent from the dean if you turned around hardly."

In 1912 there was news, published in an exclusive by former student Carr Van Anda, that the *Titanic* had gone down on its maiden voyage. That year, too, Theodore Roosevelt came to town campaigning. The seniors made their devotion visible through their gift of a class gateway. Drama students presented *The Merchant of Venice* and *Hamlet;* the O.U. Choral Union staged *Campus Pinafore,* a highly successful parody of the Gilbert and Sullivan original; and the humor magazine *Green Goat* appeared. Martha Jane Hunley, who would become the school's first female African American graduate, enrolled for classes. In a burst of high spirits, Roger Jones, football star and hometown boy whose father was a trustee, gathered his friends and fired

Alumni of 1862—John L. Hatfield, William H. Scott, Jefferson B. Clayton, and Jefferson Booth—at the campus gateway, a gift of the class of 1912. *Courtesy Mahn Center.*

I seized offered immunity . . . from Billy Hoover's terrifying math classes, only to fall into equal terror in Prof. Atkinson's physics course. . . . Here laboratory proof was demanded for every carefully memorized law, and the electricity induced by experiment was matched by the professor's lightning scorn of scientific retardation. I had delightful and valuable, though occasionally painful, lessons in writing from Mac McKinnon, who taught me English composition with benefit of a certain sparkle as well as correct syntax.

—Greta Lash, '17 (from OHIO UNIVERSITY ALUMNI JOURNAL, 1975)

Martha Jane Hunley (Blackburn), the university's first female African American graduate, 1916.
Courtesy Mahn Center.

Card for the *Green Goat,* a popular humor magazine. From the scrapbook of Carr Liggett, '16. *Courtesy Mahn Center.*

THE · GREEN · GOAT
A Bi-Monthly Magazine of Humor
Published by the Students of
Ohio University, Athens, Ohio

Campus Pinafore, a parody of *H.M.S. Pinafore* by Gilbert and Sullivan, performed by the O.U. Choral Union. From the scrapbook of Carr Liggett, '16. *Courtesy Mahn Center.*

one of the cannons near the Soldiers Monument—not an uncommon trick, but this time the explosion rattled windows all over town, and all those in the houses on University Terrace broke, including his parents'.

The following year President Ellis hired Ohio University's first dean of women. Dr. Irma Voigt, a young woman with a Ph.D. from the University of Illinois, arrived in Ellis's office in the summer of 1913 and made her prophetic announcement: "I'm here for work." That fall Dean Voigt began her thirty-six-year career with enthusiasm, energy, and a penchant for organizing. To her mind, Ellis had created too many rules of the "thou shalt not" variety. She reduced the rules to thirteen and started her campaign to create Ohio University's first student government. All coeds were invited to join a Women's League that would establish standards for the dorms and

plan social events. To help women who needed financial aid, the dean proposed a Women's League Loan and Service Fund and organized the coeds to raise money for it with Skit Shows, complete with elaborate costumes, for an entrance fee of twenty-five cents. The shows became a tradition that thrived for thirty years and left a fund of $10,000. In their earliest days they had to compete with the YMCA's Stunt Carnival, which, though popu-

lar, had become bitterly competitive and somewhat "questionable." At one performance, rivals threw rotten eggs and tomatoes, and as Dean Voigt recalled, "a spray of the contents of the eggs and tomatoes fell like rain as they whizzed over the heads of the audience." The curtain of the auditorium and Dean Voigt's dress were ruined, and Stunt Carnival's days of unsupervised productions were over.

YWCA was as popular on campus as YMCA, and Irma Voigt gradually encouraged its members—including several African American women who were segregated into their own service unit—to take on new projects. Since Athens was part of a large mining community with numerous poor villages, she organized small groups of women for off-campus service projects in the villages. By 1915 students were traveling on a bus to conduct Sunday schools, Saturday story hours, and sewing circles in tiny communities throughout the area; eventually these efforts included visits to the Athens County Children's

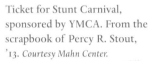

Dean Irma Voigt and members of Women's League traveling to nearby towns for community service. From the scrapbook of Katherine E. Dague (Cocanower), '23. *Courtesy Mahn Center.*

Dance programs. From the scrapbook of William Fenzel, '18. *Courtesy George Weckman.*

Pathfinders were among the cast of eight hundred depicting the history of Ohio and the university in the 1915 pageant. *Courtesy Mahn Center.*

Home. But Dean Voigt was not all seriousness. She loved to dance and was a frequent chaperone at the increasingly popular dances, where the waltz and two-step were giving way to the dangerous tango and bizarre grapevine.

Dean Voigt's organizing skills were further proved in 1915 when the university decided to celebrate the hundredth anniversary of the first graduates in the Northwest Territory, O.U.'s Thomas Ewing and John Hunter. Professor Martzolff asked the young dean to write a pageant for the event. Although there was little money for the production and as a recent arrival Dean Voigt knew little about O.U. history, she agreed and cast eight hundred participants from town and gown in a two-day event. On day one, the glee clubs sang *Elijah* at the Methodist Church. The next day, though the performers had never practiced the pageant together from beginning to end, they rose to the occasion. In the morning they enacted Ohio History from forest primeval to the class of 1915. During the midday intermission, the new alumni gate, with its poignant inscriptions, was unveiled. In the afternoon, the players presented Ethnic Ohio, with a pageant queen, dances by wood sprites and select ethnic groups, a Maypole, and a finale of two hundred schoolchildren performing an American flag drill. As if that were not enough, the Girls' Glee Club entertained in the evening with an operetta called *The Japanese Girls.*

Meanwhile, both local and international hostilities were surfacing. The local battle again involved Ohio State University. Though the 1906 legislative efforts to reduce Ohio and Miami Universities to normal schools had been defeated, the urge to create an educational "monopoly" in Columbus had not died. In the fall of 1913, rumors circulated that friends of O.S.U. would push for consolidation of the three universities, leaving few programs in the older institutions. Within a few months, a further insult was added with the suggestion that Ohio State would change its name to the University of Ohio. Once again the Athens and university communities were outraged. In a special issue of the *University Bulletin,* alumni protested: "We are not going to be swallowed up. There are three things we will not stand for. First our name to be infringed upon; second, our College of Arts to be taken away from us; third, to go under a central board of trustees. For these principles we stand and for these principles we will fight to the ditch. So there!" The move to consolidate and the fight over the name dragged on through 1920 and finally subsided, though both challenges would be renewed many years later.

The greater worry was that war had begun in Europe. As long as the United States was not directly involved, university administrators tried to go about their usual tasks. More land was purchased around the Green; John Hancock High School was created as part of the model school and housed on the third floor of Ellis Hall; plans for Lindley Hall, a new dormitory for 120 women,

Members of the Women's Glee Club closed out the 1915 centenary celebration with a performance of an operetta, *The Japanese Girls.* Louise Cable, seated on the left in the rickshaw, later played the lead in *Music Box Revue* on Broadway. *Courtesy Mahn Center.*

The Memorial Gateway, unveiled in 1915. *Courtesy* Athena Yearbook, *1916.*

Newspapers around the state opposed Senator Lloyd's persistent efforts to change the name of Ohio State University to the University of Ohio. *Scioto Gazette,* February 22, 1917. *Ellis Papers, courtesy Mahn Center.*

Mass induction of students into Student Army and Navy Training Corps (SATC and SNTC). *Courtesy* Athena Yearbook, *1919.*

were under way. As cars became more common, the administration worried that they provided a convenient place for students to misbehave. Athletic competitions continued, and Thor Olson became the wrestling star.

But in the background, there was the war. In 1917 the United States broke off relations with Germany. In April, on the eve of the country's declaration of war, a group of 10,000 gathered at the Athens Armory for a patriotic display. Students immediately voted for compulsory military training and within a month were ready for their first drills. Faculty and students began to enlist, with members of the football and baseball teams leading the way. The university decided to give academic credit to students who left school before the end of the quarter to boost food production by working on farms. All 600 female students enrolled in Red Cross classes in first aid and nursing, and the YMCA pledged to raise $4,000.

By the fall of 1918 enrollment had fallen dramatically from its high of 1,065 in 1916. Ellis wrote the governor that "out of 828 different students we have left but 257 men, and that number is diminishing daily." Army-supervised training units—Student Army Training Corps (SATC) and Student Navy Training Corps (SNTC)—were established, with the student trainees eating in Howard Hall dining room and living in temporary barracks on the Green. An army captain with little understanding of academic culture took charge. When the Spanish influenza epidemic hit the depleted campus, the women were sent home for six weeks, and men who were ill went to nearby Camp Sherman to recuperate.

With so many men absent from the campus, the young women tried to keep things going. To help the Red Cross effort, they knitted scarves and distributed sandwiches and candy bars to troops that came through Athens on the train. They put on a bazaar and raised $800. Not content with these efforts, they readied themselves for the war. To build their stamina, they took up hiking, marching to Chauncey on a day when the temperature was ten degrees below zero. Once, when they undertook a hike after dark, two students got lost and the rest had to search for them for hours. On the next hike, the adventurers took the precaution of carrying a cowbell.

From the scrapbook of William Fenzel, '18. *Courtesy George Weckman.*

Barracks on the Green for SATC and SNTC participants. *Courtesy Athena Yearbook, 1919.*

President Ellis, perhaps frustrated by his many responsibilities and by suggestions from the trustees for a few improvements in his administration, offered his resignation. The trustees hastened to assure him that his performance needed no improvement. He stayed on, and when the war ended in November 1918, he was there for the wild celebration. However, only a year later, as faculty and students returned from camps, battlefields, and other military service, Alston Ellis suffered a heart attack and died.

His administration had happily coincided with the state's need to train schoolteachers and the creation of the normal college. In spite of his predecessor's accusations of vanity and intellectual shallowness, Ellis had been suited for this work, in both experience and temperament. Under his leadership, seven buildings were added; annual subsidies from the state grew

1st Lieut. Grosvenor S. McKee wrote President Ellis from France in 1918 to suggest a design for a medal to honor O.U. veterans of World War I. *Ellis Papers, courtesy Mahn Center.*

Ribbon from Red Cross Fair. From the scrapbook of Lois Hays (Parker), '18, donated by her son, Gene H. Parker. *Courtesy Mahn Center.*

Dean Voigt *(second from left)* with *(left to right)* Cleo Jenkins, Harriette Lemmon, and Peg Dague, breakfasting after a morning hike. From the scrapbook of Katherine E. Dague (Cocanower). *Courtesy Mahn Center.*

from $55,232 to $170,919; and enrollments increased from a few hundred to more than a thousand. Though the campus was larger and its numbers greater, it remained a friendly place where students and professors mingled easily. Increased enrollments encouraged more academic programs, more complex administration, and more student organizations. However, the presence of so many women in the normal school and the decline in the number of men during the war created an imbalance between the sexes that the next president would undertake to correct.

Class of 1921 in academic procession on South Court Street, spring 1921. Leading the seniors are Professor Victor Whitehouse and Mr. Clark Williams. *Courtesy Mahn Center.*

A rite of spring in the early 1900s was the Maypole dance, by a queen and attendants, on the College Green. *Courtesy Mahn Center.*

"Alma Mater, Ohio," by Kenneth S. Clark, won first prize in the school song competition sponsored by the English Club in 1914. Ohio University Song Book, *Courtesy Anne Downing LaFollette.*

Women at Ohio University

Margaret Boyd entered the university's preparatory program in 1868 and began a tradition of courage and perseverance that brought changes in Ohio University women's experiences, roles, and opportunities. Only a few years after Boyd became the university's first female graduate in 1873, there were fourteen women on campus, including Minerva Woodson, who was probably the first black woman to enroll at O.U.

Coeds of the early 1900s at Lindley Hall. *Courtesy Mahn Center.*

A decade later, the East Wing (now Wilson Hall) housed thirty women (at $.50 per week), the janitor's family, and the first female faculty member, Cynthia Weld, who was hired in 1883 to teach history and rhetoric. Beginning in 1902, the new State Normal College (later the College of Education) drew many women who were planning to become teachers. To house them, the university acquired Howard Hall and in 1906 built Boyd Hall. However, the university did not provide a place for Martha Jane Hunley (Blackburn), who graduated summa cum laude with a major in literature and English studies in 1916. Hunley, the first African American woman to graduate, had to find her own housing in town. In 1999 the university recognized her accomplishment by placing her name, along with John Newton Templeton's, on the Templeton-Blackburn Alumni Memorial Auditorium.

By the turn of the century, almost half of the university's students were women. They organized chapters of four national sororities—Pi Beta Phi (1889), Alpha Gamma Delta (1908), Alpha Xi Delta (1911), and Chi Omega (1913); several departmental clubs, including the Home Economics Club and Kindergarten Club; literary associations; and the YWCA, which sponsored activities ranging from volunteering in the community to team sports.

In 1913, with an enrollment of 330 women and nearly 500 men, the university hired its first dean of women. Arriving on her thirty-first birthday, Dean Irma Voigt later wrote that aside from getting a desk in the hallway of Cutler Hall, she received little direction, much less encouragement, from President Alston Ellis. Within three weeks, she had called a meeting of all women students and faculty to discuss organizing a Women's League, which would develop "spirit, loyalty, and standards." During her thirty-six years of influence on the campus, Dean Voigt was also active in the university branch of the YWCA, the Women's Recreation Association, Student Council, and the Panhellenic Council and was the first president of the Athens branch of the American Association of University Women (AAUW). In 1920, when the nineteenth amendment gave women the right to vote, she arranged political forums for women, believing that some men were "sitting back and waiting for us to make a mess out of our enfranchisement." She liberalized women's rules, refereed women's basketball games, and took hiking trips with "her girls." Dean Irma Voigt retired in 1949. Three years after her death in 1953, Voigt Hall was named in her honor.

Leona Wise Felsted and Janice Battin Bixler each served as dean of women for brief periods in the early 1950s. In 1953 Margaret Deppen, an early feminist, was appointed. When the positions of dean of women and dean of men were dissolved in 1962, Dean Deppen took the new title Director of Organizations and Activities, retiring in 1975.

Margaret Deppen, the last dean of women, an early feminist. *Courtesy Mahn Center.*

Once or twice a year, Mrs. Chubb
(Dean Chubb's wife) gave us a talk
on morals, manners, and hygiene.
We thought her most charming and
promised her that we would lean out
our open windows each morning on
arising and take long breaths, sniffing
as if we were smelling a rose.

—Flo Hutchins,
in a 1950 letter to Dean Voigt

The '60s brought a number of changes for Ohio University women. In the spring of 1967, the band director eliminated women from the marching band in order to build "greater esprit de corps," and for the next seven years, the band remained all male. On the other hand, when the American Federation of State, County, and Municipal Employees (AFSCME) went out on strike in 1967, "equal classification of jobs" and more reasonable requirements for cafeteria workers (all women) were among the issues the union wanted to negotiate.

As student enrollment grew rapidly in the 1960s, many women accepted part-time teaching jobs to meet the need for additional instructors. By 1974 they too realized the need to negotiate better working conditions. A group of female part-time faculty members organized a survey of part-timers that documented a history of dead-end jobs with quarterly contracts offering few benefits and low wages, regardless of education or years of experience. Following the group's proposals, the faculty senate made some changes to improve conditions.

Almost everyone on campus was touched in some way during the 1960s and early '70s by debates on the war in Vietnam, civil rights, and women's rights. Students chafed under the university's "in loco parentis" policies, including dress regulations and curfews for women. In 1969, for several consecutive nights, hundreds of women stayed out after curfew. One of the protest leaders, Alicia Woodson, was a relative of Minerva Woodson, who had been an O.U. student almost one hundred years before. Shortly after the demonstrations, Alicia was elected student body president, becoming the first black woman elected to the position. The university ended women's hours in 1972 with little fanfare.

There were other demonstrations and protests. Angered that the university sauna was accessible only through the men's locker room, some women marched straight through and took seats in the sauna; a sauna for women was built within a year. Athens mothers and friends staged a "Baby-In," putting pressure on the university to respond to the growing need for child care. After continued lobbying, committee discussions, and proposals, a university day-care center opened in the fall of 1972 with Julia Nehls as director.

In 1971, the three coaches of women's teams protested women's $2,246 allocation out of the $1,069,992 intercollegiate athletic budget. As a result, Women's Intercollegiate Athletics was formed with Catherine Brown as director, and some changes were made in funding. But it was only after passage of Title IX of the Education Amendments of 1972 that more significant changes began. In 1974 the university awarded its first athletic scholarships to women—some of the first in the country. In 1979 the university began remodeling the ten-year-old Convocation Center to accommodate women athletes. In that same year, Wendy Weeden Devine became the first woman inducted into the Ohio University Athletic Hall of Fame.

In the early 1970s, President Claude Sowle appointed Beverly Price, '69, as special assistant for women's affairs. Her 1972 *Report on the Status of the Women at Ohio University* (the "Price Report") included information on salary equity, hiring and promotion practices, job placement patterns for Civil Service employees, funding for women's programs and athletics, the all-male marching band, child-care needs, pregnancy benefits, and a women's studies program. The historic report and resulting discussions were a watershed of consciousness-raising for the university community. Reactions ranged predictably from enthusiasm to ridicule, but the call for equal treatment would never go back in the box.

A safe, comfortable place for wide-ranging debates during the '70s was United Campus Ministry. Located just off the campus and directed by the Reverend Jan Griesinger, the first female minister in Athens, UCM was the birthplace and frequent meeting place for groups interested in specific issues. For instance, Athens Women Against Rape was founded at UCM in 1974, and the Athens area chapter of the National Organization for Women (NOW) was organized there in 1975.

In 1978, six women in the music school tested the university's commitment to equality for its female faculty by filing a complaint with the Equal Employment Opportunities Commission. An investigation confirmed inequities between the salaries of men and women faculty members, and the women received a total of $30,000 in equity adjustments. Shortly afterward, the provost's office began conducting regular "salary equity studies" to guard against incidents of discriminatory pay.

That same year, the Athens Women's Collective grew out of discussions at UCM. The collective's success in raising the issue of violence against women eventually resulted in the campus Student Escort Service. In 1979, the collective organized the first annual Take Back the Night March, now the responsibility of Student Senate. Each year hundreds of women march to declare that staying home is *not* an acceptable solution to the problem of unsafe streets.

A women's studies program was officially proposed to the university by Patricia Richard, Joy Huntley, and Barbara Daniel in 1978. (There were more than a hundred women's studies programs nationwide by 1974.) Courses such as Women in History and Women and Politics that already existed at Ohio University were popular with students. In addition, women were reading and talking about new research on women's experiences, the importance of role models, and the need for an institutional commitment to equal treatment for women. In 1979 the Women's Studies Program was established as a certificate program, with a $10,000 budget. Nancy Bain of the geography faculty was named the acting coordinator and served until 1980, when Marilyn Atlas was hired as half-time director. By 1980, eighteen women's studies courses were being offered by twelve departments.

In the early 1980s the university received another charge of discrimination, which alleged that Ohio University "discriminates on the basis of sex in its intercollegiate athletic program." A review completed in 1982 documented inequities, and the university made plans for improvement. In 1987 yet another review found that disparities continued—in budgets, scholarships, and coach-

Price: set 'numerical goals'

Urges female hiring

Beverly Price, assistant to President Sowle, issued her report on the status of women at O.U. in the spring of 1972. *Post,* April 13, 1972.

ing opportunities. Whether or not the university was doing all it could to equalize opportunities, improvements in women's athletics were coming slowly.

By 1980 female students outnumbered men 7,735 to 6,474, but the ratio of female to male full-time faculty in 1981–82 was the reverse: professor, 8 women to 248 men; associate professor, 32 to 178; assistant professor, 58 to 81. When the Equal Rights Amendment was defeated in 1982, university and community women staged a peaceful demonstration.

The Graduate Women's Studies Certificate Program was approved in 1985. By then, twenty-four women's studies courses were offered in eleven departments. In 1999 the university hired Susan Burgess as the program's first full-time tenured director.

In 1995, the seventy-fifth anniversary year of woman suffrage, the university responded to a request from campus and community women's organizations and placed a plaque on Memorial Auditorium in commemoration of Susan B. Anthony's 1878 visit to Athens. By the turn of the century, enrollment on the Athens campus stood at nearly 20,000 students. The number of full-time tenure-track female faculty had jumped from 150 in 1992 to 240, and women occupied positions at the university's highest administrative levels. Two hundred and sixty-five women played on eleven intercollegiate athletic teams, and twenty-seven of them had made it into the Athletic Hall of Fame. The university provided a training program to give nonacademic workers the skills and experience to work in the skilled trade shops; an expanded child-care center served the needs of both university and community families.

Ohio University today is very different from the school attended by Margaret Boyd. She herself changed it, questioning traditions with her determination. Women who followed her also had the courage to question roles and traditions, and such women continue today to transform Ohio University.

6

Toward a Modern University

1921–1945

It is certainly a general impression that, with the beginning of this year, Ohio University reached a turning point, and has started a new career of wider use, greater efficiency and higher standing.
—*George W. Reed, '88 (Ohio University Bulletin, 1922)*

*I*n 1922 the impression that Ohio University had reached a turning point was both widespread and accurate. Over the next eight years, both the country and the university would experience unprecedented prosperity and growth. And in spite of the effects of the Great Depression and World War II, by 1943 the institution would emerge with the structure of a modern university.

Between 1920 and 1922 a number of events had signaled the end of the old era. Alston Ellis died unexpectedly after twenty years as president; "Old Beech," the spectacular tree that every student from John Perkins and Joel Abbott to the class of 1920 had known, succumbed to old age; and even the venerable literary societies were breathing their last, as fraternities, sororities, and new debate teams took their members.

Then in 1921, the state legislature's approval of new building funds for its three universities—including $400,000 for O.U. over the next two years—heralded a new era of more generous allocations. In addition, the decision to appoint the university's trustees for limited rather than life terms suggested an openness to new ideas. When the acting president, Edwin Watts

Chubb, turned the presidency over to Elmer Burritt Bryan in 1921, enrollment stood at 1,219, and the future looked bright.

President Bryan was an experienced administrator who had already served eleven years as the president of Colgate University. Though he made an early autocratic announcement that he planned to govern without interference from the faculty, he set a tone of openness and cordiality by calling at the home of every faculty member, holding a monthly open house, and learning the name of virtually every student. He also made his plans clear. "Our motto," he said, "should be 'Creditable work in all departments, and very exceptional work in some of them.' This will give to the University a unique character and standing in the educational world." In the College of Liberal Arts, the schools of music and commerce "should be the long arms extending into society." In the College of Education, he proposed to "make a special feature of the school of physical education," which housed all athletic programs.

Dr. Bryan's decision to foster athletics and programs with masculine appeal aimed to attract men to a campus overpopulated with women. Building a proper athletic program meant replacing the "entirely inadequate" gymnasium on Park Place. For once, funds were already available. On Founder's Day, 1924, the university dedicated the new $260,000 men's gymnasium on

President Elmer Burritt Bryan had a reputation for knowing his students. I realized it was true after I met him in 1933. Dr. Bryan had come to give a talk in Caldwell, Ohio, and since I was trying to decide where to go to college, I went to hear him. After the talk, he invited students who had any interest in O.U. to come up and speak to him. He showed a warm interest in me, and asked where I lived. When I told him, he said he would have his driver return to Athens that way, so he could get a drink of water from our well.

I promptly went home and sat on the front porch swing, watching and waiting. I could not have been more flattered. Nor, as the hours went by, could I have been more disappointed. He never did come, and I supposed I would never know why.

In the fall, I matriculated at Ohio University. On a sunny October afternoon, I was strolling to the library when Dr. Bryan came walking toward me. My mind raced. I didn't know what I should say, or if I should just ignore him. But then he called out to me: "Oh, Miss Elliott, I want to tell you why I failed to come to your house last April. My driver insisted that the route through Marietta was much better than through McConnelsville and Amesville."

I marveled at his memory, his ability to recognize me instantly, and identify me with the right situation. I was convinced that he cared about each and every one of the students at Ohio University. And I know that he was loved.

—Geneva Elliott Schuler, 1933–35

The new men's gymnasium, now Bentley Hall, completed in 1924 as part of the effort to make Ohio University more attractive to men. *Courtesy Mahn Center.*

President Street (now Bentley Hall), with O.U.'s fifty-piece band playing "Stand Up and Cheer" to the wildly excited crowd of 2,500. The old gymnasium was left for the exclusive use of the women, and the university was now "equipped to place proper emphasis on the physical education of both sexes."

Bryan understood that a successful athletic program would require more than well-equipped facilities. In 1922 he hired Ossian C. Bird, a former athlete with both coaching and administrative experience, to head the school of physical education and its athletic programs. At the end of the following year, John C. Heldt and Don Peden joined Bird, Brandon Grover, Thor Olson, and R. W. Finsterwald. These men soon had the Green and White—aka the "Nameless Wonders"—on the minds of sports fans throughout the state.

In another effort to attract men to the campus, the board of trustees agreed in 1922 to buy the old

Masonic Hall at the corner of College and East Union (eventual site of Baker Center) as a headquarters for men, with dorm rooms on the third floor, a "lodge room" on the second floor, a dining hall in the basement, and rooms for student organizations such as Torch (a men's honorary society), the *Athena,* and the *Green and White.* At about the same time, President Bryan encouraged a group of upperclassmen to organize a Men's Union for all O.U. men to cut down on divisive competition between the greeks and the barbs and allow a desirable degree of self-government. The Men's Union controlled the number of activities each organization could sponsor, chose student athletic managers and song- and cheerleaders, and made and enforced the rules for freshmen.

These changes impressed alumni, who, even before President Bryan's arrival, had been thinking of a way to show their appreciation for their alma mater. Many of them had feelings similar to F. C. Kirkendall's: "Ohio University gave to me as a poverty stricken lad

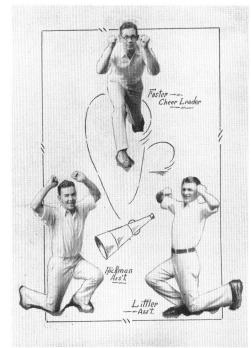

Cheerleaders led enthusiastic crowds in support of O.U. teams by 1925. *Courtesy* Athena Yearbook, *1925.*

Ohio University's first athletic director, Ossian C. Bird *(top left),* with *(clockwise)* coaches R. W. Finsterwald, B. T. Grover, Thor Olson, John Heldt, and Don C. Peden. *Courtesy* Athena Yearbook, *1923.*

The Marching 110

In 1923 student Homer Baird called an organizational meeting for a marching band, and more than forty musicians showed up. Local instrumental teacher Raymond Connett agreed to direct the band for free. Baird said, "Fortunately, we had at least 25 top-notch musicians and the others were coming along fine." The band raised enough money for thirty blue coats and white caps, and members bought their own white trousers.

Around 1927, Curt Jansen took over. One of his lasting contributions was an arrangement for the band of "Alma Mater, Ohio," Kenneth S. Clark's winning entry in the English Club's 1914 song contest. He also established a girls' band, dropped some time later and reestablished by Professor Charles Gilbert, who also added dancing majorettes. In the early 1950s, when men were being drafted into the Korean War, the OUMB briefly became female-only.

The "big switch" came in 1966 when Gene Thrailkill succeeded Charles Minelli as director. The band adopted a trademark pregame "Diamond Ohio" formation and more traditional uniforms. In the fall of 1967, women were excluded from the group. The rationale given was that they could not keep up with the band's new moves or contribute to its esprit de corps. Their removal raised protests in Athens, but according to Tom Edwards, OUMB announcer from 1966 to 1969, at the band's first home-game appearance in 1967 "the student body was absolutely blown away" by the first note of the fight song, "Stand Up and Cheer"—and the controversy quickly died.

Called the "100 Marching Men of Ohio" during its first year, the new band was renamed the "110 Marching Men of Ohio" the next year. But the most significant changes Thrailkill introduced were the athletic marching style and the addition of currently popular music to the repertoire. Alumnus David Keck describes a notable performance of one such song from the musical *Hair*.

It was a Saturday football game against Kent State on a dreary, chilly, overcast day. The game was close until the second half, and the overcast sky reflected the uncertainty of the outcome. . . . Suddenly, with a late touchdown [by Ohio], the game was clearly in hand. . . . The band played the chorus from "Aquarius"— "Let the sun shine in . . ." And, at that very moment, the clouds parted, and a beam of light pierced the sky and shone on the field. For the rest of that year, whenever the game was in hand, the band played that song.

It was not until 1968 that the 110 became "Dancing Fools." Drum major David Fowler began the tradition of dancing to the rock tunes, but because not everyone

Top: An informal concert on the Green. *Courtesy University Photographer's Office.*
Bottom: The 1923 Ohio University band, with its founder Homer Baird behind the drums. *Courtesy Mahn Center.*

could groove as well as Fowler, the rule of thumb was that if the director could do it, the band could too. The first dance piece used by the entire band was "Ain't Been Good," which the 110 still performs. After practicing their new moves all that fall, the 110 Marching Men of Ohio boarded a chartered Boeing 727 on Christmas Day and accompanied the football team to the Tangerine Bowl in Orlando, Florida. According to reports, "For its performance the band received an unprecedented minute-and-a-half standing ovation from the enthusiastic crowd."

Ronald P. Socciarelli, an exceptional director who took the position in 1973, led the Marching 110 for seventeen seasons, traveling with them outside Athens to share the hard-driving marching style and energetic dance routines that captivated hundreds of thousands of fans. His dreams for the 110 took them all the way to Carnegie Hall—the first marching band to perform there.

By 1975 the band had existed as an all-male ensemble for eight years. That fall, Mr. Socciarelli welcomed six freshmen women to band camp. In a *Post* article, Jay Kraker, staff writer and saxophone player, observed that "all of the hassle of the last few years disappeared under the dust and sweat generated by the musicians. The freshman had a lot to learn about the marching style and musicianship demanded of each member; there was simply no time left over for worrying whether one's neighbor was male or female." In the same article Mr. Socciarelli and an alumnus noted that once everyone was on the field, there was no difference to be seen.

Dr. Sylvester Young took over in 1990, continuing the tradition of the Marching 110 that by then was twenty-three years old. During his seven-year tenure the 110 performed at National Football League games and other events around the country, and in 1993 the band danced down Pennsylvania Avenue in President Bill Clinton's inaugural parade.

Richard Suk became director of the Marching 110 in 1996. He has aided in the formation of the Ohio University Marching Band Society of Alumni and Friends and in 2000 led the group to New York City to perform in Macy's Thanksgiving Day Parade. Most important to its fans, he has continued the group's long tradition of success as the "Most Exciting Band in the Land."

Top: The band in 1938. *Courtesy Mahn Center.*
Bottom: "The Most Exciting Band in the Land."
Courtesy University Photographer's Office.

Two O.U.er's never get together without mentioning how beautiful spring is in Athens, or what an incomparable sight the sun setting into the Hocking always was. Living in Athens seemed to be like living outdoors, with a constant awareness of weather and nature. No other city seems to have just that quality, and its effect on student activity is readily realized by the number of picnics, outdoor dances, hikes, and similar affairs.

—Shirley Max, letter to Dean Voigt, 1950

The old Masonic Hall at College and Union Streets, purchased in 1922 to serve as a gathering place for all male students. *Courtesy Mahn Center.*

All Ohio University graduates, students, faculty, staff, and friends were urged to contribute to the fund for the Alumni Memorial Auditorium. Ohio University Bulletin, *1922.*

a chance at a college education, cheaper, considering the quality, than any other place in Ohio at that time offered. I ought not to forget that. At Ohio University I formed a few of the closest friendships of my life. I don't wish to forget that. It was at Ohio University that I met Alice Pilcher. I shall never forget that."

Alumni proposed the gift of a stadium, but Dr. Bryan encouraged them to consider a greater need. Because Ewing auditorium was now far too small for most college events, especially for commencements, the alumni agreed to raise $300,000 for an auditorium that would honor "all the war dead of the University and her famous men and women of the past." Every one of the university's 15,000 living graduates and former students was asked to contribute; currently enrolled students were asked to give twenty dollars each. Virtually every faculty member pledged one-tenth of a year's salary. The campaign committee decided not to name any part of the building for any individual in order to keep it "as democratic in spirit as the University itself."

The successful programs in civil and electrical engineering, led by Professors Lewis J. Addicott and Albert A. Atkinson, also needed new space. In 1926 Super Hall, on President Street, was ready. Rufus Putnam Training School was completed the same year. The normal college training program moved there, leaving its former Park Place home to the music school.

With enrollment continually increasing—to 954 women and 700 men in 1925—the administration added new programs and hired new faculty—23 in 1923 alone. Among them was Professor George Starr Lasher, who taught journalism classes in the English department before becoming the head of a separate journalism department. In 1925 his precedent-setting arrangement with *Messenger* editor F. W. Bush made Ohio University students the first in the country to learn reporting and proofreading by working at a commercial newspaper rather than at a school publication.

In 1924 the president gathered the faculty especially to announce Ohio University's accreditation by the Association of American Universities. This honor made it possible to petition for both AAUW and Phi Beta Kappa chapters and was viewed as "the longest step forward that Ohio University has taken in the past quarter of a century." Scholastic standards were also rising as new state-mandated entrance exams eliminated applicants unlikely to succeed.

Other groups of students were being eliminated by a new policy set in 1923: "The University admits . . . graduates of the four-year high schools in Ohio . . . and all others (either in Ohio or in other states, provided their own

Super Hall, completed in 1926, provided more labs and classrooms for rapidly expanding engineering programs. *Courtesy Mahn Center.*

Professors George Starr Lasher and Isabelle Work, frequenters of college dances. *Courtesy Mary Elizabeth Lasher Myers, '42.*

When George Starr Lasher was the director of journalism, his infamous introduction to news writing was required. It was a demanding, rigorous, cordially hated course. Each semester there were two sections, each with thirty students. At the end of semester, there were fifteen in each section.

We had homework three times a week that took three or four of us a whole evening to work out. We went to class and diagrammed sentences on the board. When Lasher called you there was no saying, "I'm not ready." You went to the board and, with the sweat running down your back, you struggled at the board. And the next time, you came prepared. He was tough in class, but students really, really liked him.

He had a respect for language and a love of the arts. He went to all kinds of activities and dances with Isabelle Work. No matter what kind of music, they were out there stepping. He was a wonderful, wonderful guy.

—Ralph Kliesch, Professor Emeritus of Journalisn

The Float Parade led the Homecoming crowd to the football field for the game. *Courtesy* Athena Yearbook, *1929.*

Football ticket with the team's 1926 schedule, issued to Leona Hughes, '30. *Courtesy Mahn Center.*
Football team in formation. *Courtesy* Athena Yearbook, *1929.*

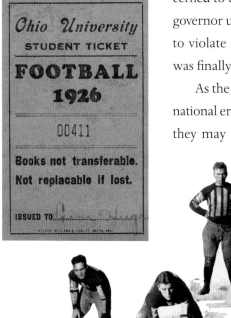

state universities admit them)." The policy eliminated students from states such as New York, New Jersey, and Massachusetts, which did not have public universities, and black students from nearby states such as Kentucky and West Virginia whose public universities did not admit African Americans. In writing about this policy later, Professor Gamertsfelder called it an economic decision. Because out-of-state students paid no extra fees, the administration considered it appropriate to question why Ohio should subsidize other states' students, especially if they crowded out Ohioans.

The unavoidable conclusion, however, was that the motivation was not only economic but racist. Neither the university nor the town of Athens, which had its own small African American community, was particularly receptive to the few minority students who attended O.U. In Dr. Walter Gamertsfelder's words, "the restaurants and barber shops of Athens [including the one owned by African American Edward Berry] were not generally giving service to Negroes nor had dormitories on campus yet been open to accommodate Negro students." Though President Bryan was "concerned to avoid criticism," the board took no action despite protests to the governor urging that the resolution be rescinded. Ohio University continued to violate its usual democratic spirit until the mid-1950s, when this policy was finally removed from the *University Bulletin.*

As the administration upheld the status quo, students embraced the new national era of dance marathons, flappers, and jazz. Though in Athens, Ohio, they may not have felt like members of Hemingway's "lost generation," they recognized that the twenties were roaring and added their energy and enthusiasm to the roar. Dancing, strictly forbidden in 1845 and discouraged for years after, became so much the rage that the Campus Activities Committee had to ration it. Sororities and fraternities were allowed two dances per year, provided that one was a matinee; groups like Women's Athletic Association were allowed one; but Varsity "O," Women's League, and Men's Union could each offer three—and all after dark.

The Homecoming Hop was the culmination of a whole weekend of frenetic activity, which since 1922 had included the celebration of Dad's Day. Friday evening began with a bit of humiliation for first-year men, who marched in the Pajama Parade that preceded the "thuse" (a pep rally) and bonfire. The next morning's gory Sack Rush left the athletic field strewn with bits of clothing from the brawniest freshman and sophomore men, who endured a thirty-minute battle for three sawdust-filled sacks. In the early afternoon, the band led a pep parade of elaborate floats to the field for the game. By the late 1920s, Don Peden's team, known as the Bobcats since the naming contest held in 1925, was clawing its way to the top of the conference and giving fans something to shout about. Finally, after a concert by the band, students danced the night away with Chase's Collegians, or Ted Wildermuth, or, by the end of the decade, the soon-to-be-famous Sammy Kaye and his Ohioans.

J-Prom, or Junior Prom, was the "night of nights"—an occasion for transforming the men's gym into a wonderland of colored crepe-paper streamers and balloons, dressing up, and getting dance cards filled. As one student of the time said, "We had a good time—went at 8 and I mean we went. Exchanged dances. Unheard of now." And, in spite of the fact that carrying hip flasks had become the smart thing to do, "no one who mattered got drunk or at least not very. It was definitely frowned upon."

Dance tokens from the scrapbook of Eleanor Crites, '28. *Courtesy Mahn Center.*

Sammy Kaye, '33, studied engineering and ran track as an Ohio University student. He also formed a band and played regularly at dances and at the Varsity Inn. After leaving Athens, he made music his life. His band and compositions enjoyed great success during the swing era of the 1930s and 1940s. The Sammy Kaye Orchestra often performed on radio and television and sold millions of records, including such songs as "There Will Never Be Another You" and "Remember Pearl Harbor."

Sammy Kaye and his Ohioans.
Courtesy Mahn Center.

Streamers decorated the gymnasium for J-Prom. *Courtesy* Athena Yearbook, *1929.*

The first J-Prom queen, Mariana E. Bing, crowned in 1928. *Courtesy* Athena Yearbook, *1928.*

Serenaders at Lindley Hall compete for the Goldsberry Cup. *Courtesy* Athena Yearbook, *1926.*

The old Skit Show presented ever more inventive performances for Mother's Day Weekend visitors. Tug o' War, the Doll Show, an occasional Halloween party, and the fall Mixer, where newcomers joined "one large joyous family with true college spirit and friendliness," continued, as new social activities evolved. Though smoking had been virtually forbidden only a few years before—Madge Acord Eachus recalled that a young man caught smoking by President Ellis was told never to set foot on the "sacred soil" of the campus again with a cigarette in his mouth—Men's Union now entertained first-year men with an autumn "smoker." O.U. women, who had already bobbed their hair, raised their hemlines, and gone out to vote, now enjoyed cigarettes as well as their twenty-five-cent meatloaf sandwiches at the Bettie Shop. Upset by this unladylike behavior, Dean of Women Irma Voigt wrote a hundred letters to parents, seeking their help in the battle against this new addiction.

The university music and dramatic arts programs flourished. Students tried out for glee clubs, the orchestra, the band, and choral groups. Torch Sing, with the Goldsberry Loving Cup as prize, became a serious competition, and on at least one occasion, Men's Glee Club performed for nine hundred patients at the asylum. Men sang after hours, too, serenading the president at his home as well as the women in

Ruby Mercer, '27, was born in Athens and attended the university when singing was among the most popular extracurricular activities. An operatic soprano, she studied at both Cincinnati's Conservatory of Music and Juilliard. She appeared on Broadway and sang leading roles at the Metropolitan Opera. Moving to Canada in 1958, she sang with the Montreal Opera Company and established herself as an opera critic and commentator, hosting radio programs and in 1960 founding the quarterly magazine *Opera Canada*.

Courtesy Mahn Center.

their dorms. Delta Tau Delta, the singing fraternity, often loaded an old piano onto a truck and made impromptu serenading stops around the campus. In fact, by 1929 serenades had become so frequent that they were "frowned upon by the townspeople and administration" as unwelcome noise forced "upon unwilling listeners during all hours of the morning."

The highlight of student theater in the 1920s came with productions by the Playshop (formerly the Revelers) and a new all-male group of fifty called the Comedians, who began their careers in 1928 with *Hello Happiness*. Their second production, *Dawn O' Day,* with music entirely by the students, included "exquisite singing, extraordinary chorus work, sparkling humor," and dancers with "masculine legs, concealed in opera length chiffon hose terminating in high heeled patent leather slippers." Playshop's production of *Seventh Heaven* that same year drew an audience of 1,600, the largest ever assembled for an O.U. dramatic production, and "surpassed any former one in the history of the University."

President Bryan created some suspense in 1925 when he unexpectedly offered his resignation. Fortunately he was persuaded to stay on to see the fruition, in 1929, of many of his efforts. Enrollment had doubled since 1921; income—now over $2 million—had tripled. The men, who finally outnumbered the women, had a dean of their own. The alumni had completed their campaign for the new auditorium, and the names of all contributors were safely sealed in the building's cornerstone. With the curtain hung, it was time to offer their

The Comedians, an all-male group of fifty, followed their successful production of *Hello Happiness* with the hit musical comedy *Dawn O' Day*. *Courtesy* Athena Yearbook, *1929.*

SEVENTH · HEAVEN
BY AUSTIN STRONG
THE PLAYSHOP
OF OHIO UNIVERSITY
PRODUCED AT THE MEMORIAL AUDITORIUM
FEBRUARY 15, 1929   CURTAIN AT 8:20 O'CLOCK

Program of *Seventh Heaven,*
produced by the Playshop
(formerly the Revelers).
Courtesy Mahn Center.

Alumni Memorial Auditorium,
lighted for an evening production. *Courtesy University Photographer's Office.*

impressive gift. In an "inspiring" ceremony, which included a brass band playing on the balcony of the Men's Union and a hymn with words by Professor Chubb, Alumni Memorial Auditorium was dedicated to "the memories of the lofty and noble men and women who have come and gone in the shadowy past and to the thousands to come and go in the more shadowy future."

In the spring of that same year, thirteen undergraduates were inducted into Phi Beta Kappa and the contract for a new library was advertised. That fall the new stadium was dedicated at a homecoming game in what was to be the first of several undefeated, championship seasons. On November 29, 1929, the stock market's crash put a sudden end to this era of success. The state quickly announced budget cuts of 7 percent. Plans for the library proceeded, but those for a biology building and a men's dorm had to be abandoned. The next budget cut of 13 percent caused the threat of layoffs, which Bryan was determined to avoid. Though some senior faculty proposed letting junior faculty go, he refused. The highest salaries—those above $5,000—fell 25 percent. The lowest—$1,000 —suffered decreases of 5 percent.

Families found it difficult to pay for higher education. Still, with joblessness as the most probable alternative to the classroom, students continued to enroll. Accommodating the added numbers became more challenging for the university as its own resources dwindled. In the painful search for economies, Bryan appointed a committee to review all the university's courses to see if they could be more efficiently organized. Another group worked to secure federal funds for a badly needed men's dormitory. One occasion for rejoicing was the dedication of the new library to Dean Edwin Watts Chubb in the spring of 1931.

In 1934 Bryan's chronic health problems flared, and in October he died, leaving a grieving student body and faculty who had respected, admired, and loved him. According to Thomas Hoover, "He had brought Ohio University out of the century old

The football stadium under construction, 1928–29. *Courtesy Mahn Center.*

In 1929 Irv Small won first place at the Freshman Varsity Track Meet. As a sophomore he ran the half-mile in 2:01.1, and he later set a new Ohio indoor half-mile record with a time of 2:09. *Courtesy Irv Small, '33.*

provincial mists and made it a recognized peer of any school of its size and class in the land." As the trustees began a search for his replacement, Edwin Chubb again stepped in as acting president.

The following spring Herman Gerlach James, president of the University of South Dakota, accepted the position. Though he proved to be more democratic than Bryan had been, his air of "detachment," "impatience," and "inscrutability" contrasted sharply with Bryan's cordiality. When he announced, twenty-three days after arriving in Athens, that O.U. would be reorganized to include a University College in which all freshmen would spend a year correcting any weaknesses in their preparation for university work, the change was "violently opposed" as too abrupt, too indiscriminate, and made without proper advice and consent.

A year later, when President James unveiled the second phase of his reorganization plan, there was further consternation. A graduate college would make requirements for graduate study more uniform across departments. Furthermore, the courses and departments of the two existing colleges, Liberal Arts and Education, would be regrouped into five new colleges: Arts and Sciences, Education,

The new library, named for Edwin Watts Chubb, who served the university as professor, dean of the College of Liberal Arts, and acting president, opened in 1931. *Courtesy Mahn Center.*

In the fall of 1932, I pledged Phi Mu, along with about six others. Our house, where this picture was taken, was on East State Street; the fashion of the day was the fur-collared coat, the Lettie Linton, inspired by a Joan Crawford movie of the same name.

My father mortgaged the house to get money for me to go to college—the Depression was still on, full tilt. He was determined that I would go. I was the first in my family to get a degree.

—Eleanor Hazlett Ratelle, '36

Phi Mu pledges in their Lettie Linton coats. *Courtesy Eleanor Ratelle, '36.*

Herman Gerlach James, O.U. president 1935–43. *Courtesy Mahn Center.*

Applied Science, Commerce, and Fine Arts. Departments in the Education College that duplicated ones in other colleges—math, English, painting, and music among them—would be eliminated. Arts and Sciences, long overshadowed by Education, would regain its position as the core of the institution. To soften the blow to the education college, its dean, Thomas McCracken, was made the first university provost.

President James began making direct budget allocations to each college and meeting regularly with the deans. He also proposed a faculty advisory council to solicit faculty opinion. Both the faculty and the board of trustees debated whether the faculty, composed of independent thinkers who often found it hard to agree, would have the interest, the expertise, and the cooperative spirit for this role. Eventually the decision was made and the faculty added their voices to the mix.

In spite of the positive aspects of these changes, the insecurity they engendered helped set the stage for even wider protests that came with James's 1936 announcement of an ROTC unit on the campus, a decision made by the trustees before his arrival. Antiwar feelings were high, as Americans responded to the spread of Nazism and fascism in Europe with renewed isolationism. Faculty, townspeople, and especially ministers bombarded the president with letters protesting military training for students. In the spring of 1937, students voiced their concerns by staging Irwin Shaw's strongly antiwar play, *Bury the Dead,* and by turning out in great numbers for a lecture by

General Smedley Butler, one of the most forceful antiwar speakers in the country.

Other problems were even more pressing. By 1937 the university was experiencing serious financial difficulties, and reductions in state appropriation bills made planning difficult. Professors' salaries lagged behind those at other Ohio schools. The 3,024 students created shortages of classroom space, labs, offices, and housing. The university needed an addition to Howard Hall, a student union to center the social life of the university, and a natatorium for the men's swim team. None of this was possible; there was not even money to maintain the existing buildings, including Cutler Hall, which had a wide crack from top to bottom and was on the verge of collapse.

The grim state of university finances was evident in the situation of the admissions director and registrar, Frank Dilley. Lacking the money for postage stamps, he would accumulate a number of applications for

Ministers protested the creation of ROTC units on campus. *Athens Messenger, January 7, 1936.*

University College

Since its inception in 1935, University College has played a pivotal part in undergraduate education. The college's original charge was to provide "the most effective instruction, direction, and guidance of Freshmen," orienting them to university life and equipping them with a strong foundation in general education. Initially, the dean of women and the dean of men shared administrative oversight of University College, but in 1941, Einar Hansen became the first dean of the college.

The University College advises all first-year students who have not chosen or been accepted into a major—typically, about a quarter of each entering class. The college collaborates with the Advising Council in advising efforts across campus, and also offers special advising to students with particular needs, such as nontraditional students. In 1986 the National Academic Advising Association awarded University College its prestigious Certificate of Merit.

University College, in conjunction with Residence Life and Student Affairs, plans and executes the Precollege orientation program, inaugurated in 1955, in which all first-year and transfer students participate. University Experience courses, initiated in 1977, introduce more than five hundred first-year students annually to the many dimensions of university life. University College also houses the Academic Advancement Center, founded in 1972, which offers tutoring and courses in reading, studying, and computer skills and coordinates the Supplemental Instruction program and a federally funded College Adjustment Program for high-risk students. LINKS, which began in 1984, aims to improve the retention rate of minority students.

As part of its mission to serve undergraduates, University College supports and recognizes faculty members through workshops, the Center for Teaching Excellence, the Center for Writing Excellence, and its teaching awards. The college is distinctive in bringing together faculty from across campus in new combinations to discuss interdisciplinary issues and curricular reform.

College of Business

When Charles Moffat Copeland entered Ohio University on a tuition-free "county" scholarship in 1893, the institution had been offering courses to prepare students for clerkships and other business jobs for fifty-seven years. During his first year as a student, Copeland established commerce as a formal topic when he taught a non-credit "commercial course including the science of accounts, credits, commercial law and the history of money," in what was called the Commercial Branch of the university.

In 1897 the university founded a commercial department, which in 1901 became the School of Commerce with Copeland as principal. Housed in the Normal College, it had four faculty members and three departments: accounting and commercial law, stenography and typewriting, and penmanship. In 1904, when the university issued its first certificate for completion of a four-year commercial course to Roy T. McClure, it claimed that "no school in the country can show a larger percentage of its graduates at profitable employment." In 1916 the school began offering the A.B. in Commerce. In 1936 Copeland retired due to ill health and A. H. Armbruster was recruited as principal to direct seventeen full-time and three part-time faculty. When President James established the College of Commerce in 1936, it included departments of accounting and economics and the School of Journalism. Enrollment was 323, amounting to about 21 percent of the total university enrollment. By 1949 this number had increased to 1,128 students. In 1950 Armbruster's efforts resulted in accreditation of the college by the American Assembly of Collegiate Schools of Business (AACSB).

In 1952 the work of Professors Albert Gubitz and Edwin Hellebrandt resulted in the creation of a management department. In 1956 Copeland Hall was completed and an MBA was added to the curriculum. An executive MBA followed in 1977. The master's programs received AACSB accreditation in 1969. In 1977 the

A diagram of the university administration after the reorganization of the colleges by President James. *From James Papers, courtesy Mahn Center.*

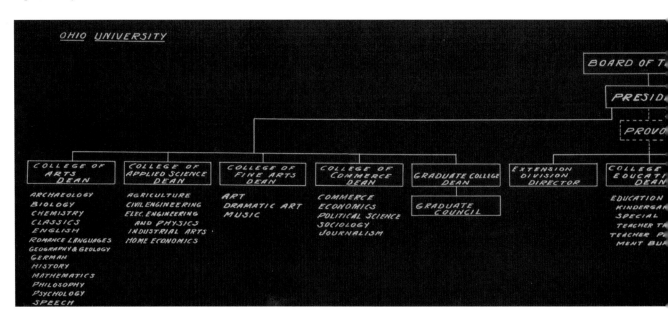

college recruited business leaders to its Executive Advisory Board (EAB). The EAB and the Society of Alumni and Friends (SAF), established in 1982 with Arthur Aspengren, '56, as its first president, advised the college to add majors and to make other changes in the curriculum. The SAF established the Copeland Scholars program in 1983 to attract academically gifted students. The Corporate Leadership Program was created in 1987 to build the leadership abilities of undergraduates.

The College of Business is now organized into the departments of Finance, Management Information Systems, Management Systems, and Marketing, and the School of Accountancy. Admission standards are high and enrollment continues to be limited, with just over 1,800 undergraduates and 90 resident graduate students in 2001.

Special programs provide exceptional opportunities for students.

- The Global Learning Community (GLC), open to all majors, brings together the resources of the colleges of Business, Communication, Arts and Sciences, and Engineering and Technology to offer an interdisciplinary undergraduate certificate program on global issues.
- The Center for International Business Education and Development (CIBED) allows students to earn class credit while working on business projects in foreign countries.
- The Sales Center provides a focal point for leadership in entrepreneurial thinking and sales education.

At the graduate level, The MBA Without Boundaries (MBA/WB), designed to allow working professionals to earn master's degrees through a combination of resident and Internet-based learning, is recognized as one of the best technology-mediated programs in the country. A full-time MBA program is offered in India, and other MBA programs combining in-country and resident coursework are offered in Brazil and China. The College of Business also provides executive education programs for corporate and public sector managers worldwide.

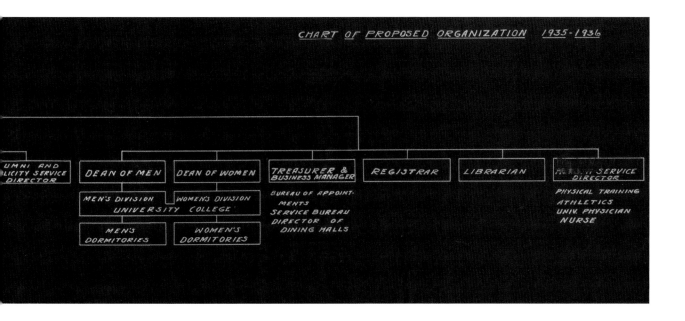

College of Fine Arts

Aspiring artists had a limited role on the campus of Ohio University for most of its first century. The first fine arts classes—in art and music—appeared only in the early 1880s as training for aspiring teachers in the State Normal College or as extracurricular activities. The Department of Oratory offered Shakespeare classes, but only to bolster students' speaking skills.

The first established fine arts unit was the Department of Vocal Music, created in 1889; instrumental music was added a year later. But again, the emphasis was on appreciation: "Those who desire to become performers will be accommodated as far as possible, but the chief attention of teachers will be directed toward the attainment of genuine music culture," warned a department circular in 1893.

Still, interest in the arts swelled. The 1890s saw the creation of the Department of Drawing and Painting and, in 1890, the first campus play. By the turn of the century, some three hundred students were enrolled in the College of Music. (Its teachers, however, were not granted academic rank until 1926.) With the addition of instruction in pottery and sculpture in 1928, the Department of Drawing and Painting became the Department of Fine Arts. In 1930, theater gained more equal footing with oratory in the new Department of Dramatic Art.

Five years later, the arts at Ohio University gained their most important booster: incoming President Herman G. James, an accomplished violinist who played in the university orchestra. James's reorganization of the university into five degree-granting colleges included a College of Fine Arts, comprising the schools of Music, Dramatic Art, and Painting and Allied Arts. He envisioned a community of artists who would not only hone their individual talents but also inform each other's work through interdisciplinary cooperation. Indeed, cooperation was required during the prolonged search for a dean; for six years, an Executive Council ran the college, with the directors of the three member schools taking turns as chairman.

The college found its first leader in Earl C. Seigfred, who became dean in 1942. During his twenty-four-year tenure, the college expanded to include a Department of Fine Arts (later Comparative Arts), offering interdisciplinary studies in the arts, and a School of Architecture. Theater students benefited from the founding of the Ohio Valley Summer Theater in 1950 and Elizabeth Baker's 1958 purchase of the Monomoy Theater on Cape Cod.

The School of Dramatic Art became the School of Theater in 1968, when speech courses were split off to form the basis of the new College of Communication. The School of Dance was established in 1969, followed by the Department of Film in 1973. The School of Architecture was eliminated in 1976.

The college achieved its current makeup of six schools in 1988, when the departments of Comparative Arts and Film were elevated to school status to join Art, Dance, Music, and Theater. The college offers twenty-one programs of study leading to bachelor of fine arts and bachelor of music degrees, as well as twenty master of arts, master of fine arts, and master of music degree programs. The School of Interdisciplinary Arts (formerly Comparative Arts) offers a doctoral degree. College alumni have forged distinguished careers as performers, artists, administrators, therapists, and teachers, and the college serves as a primary source of cultural offerings in southeastern Ohio, with nearly three hundred public performances and exhibitions presented annually.

admissions, take them to the treasurer, and ask if he should respond to them. The treasurer would agree that they should be answered and then count out exactly the number of stamps needed for the replies.

Students tried to take life in stride during these "threadbare thirties." Expenses averaged $400–500 per year, and many men tried to save by creating housing co-ops where they did their own cooking and cleaning. Donald Hammell, '35, says it wasn't so bad:

> Elated by Dean [John Reed] Johnston's waiving the $45.00 semester registration fee, the offer of a National Youth Association job allowing me to make $20.00 a month, and a chance to live in a cooperative, I left Salem, Ohio, with a packed laundry case, put my thumb in the air and headed for Athens. A few hours later, I arrived and made my way to Palmer Hall. The room I was to share was about ten by twelve with a sink, a couple of desks, and chairs, some drawers for clothes, and a double bed. The other facilities were down the hall. Not exactly the Ritz, but to a seventeen-year-old, this was going to college, a privilege offered to only a small percentage at that time.
>
> "Cooperative" meant just that. Your room . . . was expected to be reasonably neat and clean. The "dining hall" was the responsibility of the students—cleaning the floor, setting and waiting on tables, and washing the dishes, pans, and silverware. Two brave women ordered the food, did the cooking, made up the work schedules and figured the costs.
>
> This doesn't sound like college life as described in the brochures, but the room was $1.50 a week and the board averaged about $2.50. Room and board for $17.00 a month! Not the Intercontinental, and some work was involved, but all had the opportunity to get an excellent education. Throw in the job for $20.00 a month and it is easy to see what a wonderful opportunity had been dumped into my lap. Figure out the total financial picture and you are looking at one of the best bargains of all times.

The Tradition that Ohio University is a "poor man's school" was established early in the life of the institution and persists at the present day.

—Ohio Alumnus, 1938

In their off-campus co-ops, many men saved money by sharing food costs and cooking and cleaning chores. *Courtesy* Athena Yearbook, *1940.*

The Baseball Nine of 1937 won 21 of 24 games. *Courtesy* Athena Yearbook, *1938.*

Students took the opportunity to enjoy sports. When Coach "Dutch" Trautwein's Big Six basketball team of 1940–41 was invited to the post-season National Invitational Tournament, some students cut classes to follow them to New York. Fans left behind in Athens followed the games by telegraph at the Hotel Berry. When word came that the Bobcats had advanced to the final, "pandemonium erupted," according to Floyd R. West. "A 'snake dance' of a couple hundred men (the girls were all in their dorms and houses by this time) worked its way up Court Street, . . . entered the Athena Theatre, trooped down one aisle, crossed in front of the screen, and up and out the other aisle. . . . It was an exhilarating event."

Although only $400 was spent on intramurals, "hobby sports" such as wrestling, volleyball, archery, Ping Pong, horseback riding, and golf attracted large numbers of men. Women also became fierce competitors in field hockey, swimming, forensics, tennis, and modern dance in the new Studio Club. Others, like Pearl Bernfeld Shmishkiss, joined the OK Girls, the Butterfingers, the Panty Waists, or the TNTs for intramural basketball.

A patch from the Women's Athletic Association (WAA). From the scrapbook of Eleanor Crites, '28. *Courtesy Mahn Center.*

Frank Baumholtz and the Big Six

Frank Baumholtz, '41, was the first athlete in the country to play two major league sports—baseball and basketball— in one year simultaneously—baseball in spring and summer and basketball in winter. But even before his days as a professional, Baumholtz won lasting fame as the star forward of the Big Six basketball team of 1940–41, which went on to the prestigious post-season NIT. Though Ohio was defeated in the final game against Long Island, Baumholtz scored a record 53 points over the three games and was named Most Valuable Player of the NIT. He completed his major league baseball career with 1,010 hits and a lifetime batting average of .291. His Ohio University number, 54, is the only one ever to be retired, and his jersey hangs from the rafters of the Convocation Center.

Courtesy Athena Yearbook, *1941.*

Both men and women enjoyed soirées at the home of their French professor, Miss Noss. They especially enjoyed dances, which they now attended as "dating" couples rather than in groups of friends. Some parents deplored the new trend of dancing all night with the same person as "selfish," "disgusting," and sure to create a "total lack of joyful, healthful social intercourse in all the U's activities." Nevertheless, bands like Rex Koons's drew students to the Hotel Berry on Wednesday "date nights" as well as to the Varsity Inn beneath Logan's Book Store on Friday afternoons. For the big occasions, such as the ever-popular J-Prom, the big bands of Kay Kyser, Paul Whiteman, Duke Ellington, and Cab Calloway provided the draw.

As students danced, the administration tried to solve the problem of serious overcrowding. Funds from the federal government's Works Progress Administration, established to put the Depression's unemployed to work, allowed the completion of two sections of a men's dormitory in 1936 and another two in 1939—a quadrangle named for former president William Scott. Howard Hall was enlarged to accommodate another seventy-five women, and Lindley got a new wing. Carnegie Hall was renovated, and the basements of other buildings were cleaned out to create classroom space. Students also got an infirmary near the Agriculture Building (now Tupper Hall) and a much-needed student center in the Men's Union, while the

Formal dances at the Hotel Berry were popular events. *Courtesy* Athena Yearbook, *1941.*

Professor of French Mary T. Noss *(left)* performed frequently in outdoor productions sponsored by the Alliance Française, which she initiated at Ohio University. Dr. Noss also founded Le Cercle Français and arranged for the first O.U. students to study in France. The host of popular evening and afternoon concerts, Dr. Noss encouraged music students by financing their travel abroad and often their education, finding them work or providing funds herself. From the scrapbook of the Alliance Française, 1914–57. *Courtesy Mahn Center.*

My earliest exposure to dance band music was at age nineteen, playing at the Varsity Inn beneath Logan's Book Store directly across the street from the main gate of the campus (likewise my first really serious exposure to girls). My second dance band experience was with the Rex Koons Band. I was a piano major, but the mere mention of jazz in the music school during the thirties was an automatic ticket to the front door. Needless to report, once hooked on the joys of performing this type of music . . . I gladly returned to my faithful tenor sax and have been happily married to the same for lo these many years.

—Loren L. Pace, '36

The *Green and White*, January 2, 1937. *Courtesy Mahn Center.*

The jitterbug, swing, and many other new dance styles were popular in the '30s and '40s. Courtesy *Athena Yearbook,* 1941.

Extension Division expanded its services and offered credit-bearing courses at "branches" in Portsmouth and Zanesville.

Unfortunately, one long-festering problem re-emerged. Accusations of prejudice and discrimination against African American students, which had plagued President Bryan ten years earlier, resurfaced and extended to Jewish and Japanese students as well. Complaints came that the university was complicit in the Athens City School System's refusal to allow African American students to do their student teaching locally. There were protests that two professors were making overtly anti-Semitic remarks in their classes. And the presence of two Japanese students on campus drew criticism. The African American students continued their practice teaching outside Athens; the complaints against the professors were not investigated; but the Japanese students were allowed to remain.

Though Ohio University students were well aware that Japan had entered the expanding war, they hardly imagined that it would ever involve them. Then on December 7, 1941, all the usual activities of college life were forgotten. As Mary Elizabeth Lasher, first female editor of the *Post,* recalls, she received a call at the *Post* office telling her that Japanese planes had bombed Pearl Harbor. Within minutes, O.U. men were signing up for mili-

Couples "Coking" at Quick's Drug Store. *Courtesy* Athena Yearbook, *1941.*

tary service. At the entrance to one fraternity house there was "a card table 'staffed' by one fellow in an ROTC uniform and another in sailor garb. Each arrival was being 'signed up' for military service, the only men excused being those who could prove family-man status. That condition was clarified by the table's only decoration, a painted wooden stork with a baby doll slung in a diaper from its beak and a sign round its neck asking: 'Who in the Hell's exemption is this?'"

Some faculty and students left for active duty or government service almost immediately. Others continued in the classrooms, at least for a while, with an accelerated three-semester calendar that speeded graduation rates. They listened to Bob Hope and the Hit Parade and sang "I'll Walk Alone." As one student noted, "We danced more, drank more, made our lowest grades, and few of us gave a damn. We could only hope with all the fervor of youth that we would find ourselves in time." By 1943, when reservists

"The Curse of Drink"

Each day O.U. students sip approximately 2000 cokes, or $100 dollar a day worth of soda water and coke syrup. In one week students spend about $700, enough to send a student through college for one year, with plenty of spending money.

—POST, January 17, 1940

Tickets to a dance at the Varsity Inn where student dance bands played several afternoons and evenings each week. From the scrapbook of Eleanor Crites, '28. *Courtesy Mahn Center.*

I was a vocalist in the college dance band, and we played at many of the school dances and at social functions at several other colleges in southern Ohio. We had a 12-piece band led by the drummer Bill Smith, and it sounded like many of the big-time bands of the era. I was doing well until a guy by the name of Sinatra took my job! I still enjoy singing romantic ballads of the time, like "Serenade in Blue," "I'll Be Seeing You," and "I'll Never Smile Again."

—Ed Stupack, '44

> Dear Ellis Hall! You were my "home" for four years and five additional summers. How I loved your creaking wooden floors, your friendly benches on the second-floor hall (where I often sat to review an assignment), your big classrooms with wooden desk-chairs and blue slate chalkboards, your generous windows overlooking the campus, and your cool, wide staircases!
>
> —Martha E. Hesson, 1939–48

began to be called up, hundreds more departed. The athletic teams were decimated; the cannons from the Green were commandeered for the metal conversion effort. Even President James took leave to participate in a diplomatic mission for the State Department, convinced that "nothing can be mentioned in the same breath that is comparable to the successful culmination of the war." In May, he decided not to return to the university and tendered his resignation.

But spring in Athens still had "the quality of foreverness that makes us one with the past and with the future," and Ohio University carried on, with Walter S. Gamertsfelder as president. The board of trustees insisted that research and administrative costs be kept in balance to ensure teaching of the highest quality. They made plans for an airport, discussed the need

Mary Elizabeth Lasher, first female editor of the *Post*, at the copy desk with staffers in 1941. *Courtesy Mary Elizabeth Lasher Myers, '42.*

for a new student center, and applied for a license to establish a radio station. The faculty reported the need to "turn the heat" on the administration to strengthen weak departments and the graduate college; to offer an honors program, a program of adult education, and terminal degrees; and to prepare a study of space needs for the postwar era. Ohio University's remaining students, who were now mostly female, also did their part. They knitted for the Red Cross, gave up their rooms to the SATC, and counted their ration cards. Though formal dances were eliminated, dance parties with patriotic themes persisted. At Prep Follies, the lyrics of "The Campus Is Lonely" gave perfect expression to a general longing. The *Post* ran a new column, called the *Stars and Stripes,* with news about absent students and professors. As Arthur Baumann remembers, the news was often painful.

Students quickly became soldiers after the bombing of Pearl Harbor on December 7, 1941. *Courtesy* Athena Yearbook, *1944.*

> The war was not kind to my little group of friends. J. E. was the first to leave school. He joined the Navy and was shot down over the Bougainvillea Islands in the southwest Pacific. Charlie joined the airforce and was killed in a California plane crash. Ed Kunzlman saw action in Europe and returned a Captain. I was the last to leave school. Sometime prior, I had made application for Aviation Cadet Training and was accepted, but had to wait for the next class to start. After being commissioned a 2nd Lieutenant, I spent thirty months in North Africa and Italy, returning in 1945 as an Air Force Captain.

About fifteen of us who were R.O.T.C. Advanced Corp officers graduated in January 1943 by simply stopping by the Registrar's office to pick up our diplomas. My processional was from 1 Pearl Street to Ewing Hall in my bathrobe, pajamas and wooly slippers. A handshake from the Registrar sent me back down the hill to the apartment on Pearl Street where I waited several weeks for someone to figure out what to do with us.

Eventually I was assigned to the 31st Infantry Division to chase the Japanese in the southwest Pacific theatre. In the fall of 1946, I re-entered O.U. as a special student and met my wife-to-be, Joanne Duke. In 1947, I watched her graduate under the elms.

—Ellsworth Briggs Gamblee, '43

In the late spring of 1943, most of the student ROTC officers had already left for military service and a few of us were still finishing the semester. . . . I was president of the Men's Union at the time. The officers lived, rent free, in a big room on the second floor of the Student Center Building. The first floor was called the "Grill" and featured a big dance floor, jukebox, and booths around the perimeter. The food was delicious and cheap.

That summer, the army sent men to the campus, and they were housed in the Men's Dorm (later Scott) and Howard Hall. Working with Dean Voigt, a wonderful lady, we arranged dances and other events in the Men's Gym. I also arranged to have Friday evening movies in Mem Aud because of the junky films on the weekends at the two theaters in town. I think we charged ten cents. Fox films was the easiest to deal with (the local houses had tried to block our showings) and I was always kidded about the frequency of showing Betty Grable films, she being the big star at Fox.

—Richard H. Creps, '44

Dance card, "Caught in the Draft." *Courtesy Mary Elizabeth Lasher Myers, '42.*

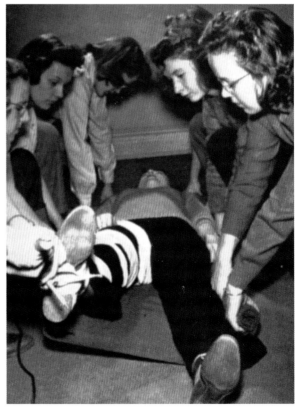

University coeds practice first-aid techniques.
Courtesy Athena Yearbook, *1943.*

TOWARD A MODERN UNIVERSITY

The Campus Is Lonely

The wind through the elm trees is sending a tune
    Of college days carefree and bright;
The tower of Cutler looks white in the moon,
    But the campus is lonely tonight.

I walked up on Court Street, the gang wasn't there;
    The jive was all gone from the grill;
I thought of you then, and it didn't seem fair
    That the campus is lonely and still.

The bugles have sounded and you've gone away,
    And hushed is the beat of my heart;
What is there to do, love, what is there to say
    When we are so far apart?

The couples that linger by old Ellis Hall
    Bring mem'ries and tears to my eyes;
I've tried to forget, but it just isn't right
    That the campus is lonely—
I long for you only,
For the campus is lonely tonight.

—Music by Ernie Mariani and lyrics by Helen Townsend,
written for Prep Follies, 1943. *Courtesy Ernie Mariani and Mimi Hart.*

After a few months as acting president, Walter S. Gamertsfelder was inaugurated with the full authority of the presidency on July 1, 1943. Gov. John Bricker *(right)* attended his inauguration. *Courtesy Mahn Center.*

Though Ohio University lost more than two hundred members of its faculty and students, many, like Captain Baumann, did return to a more modern institution. During the 1920s Elmer Bryan had dramatically expanded the school's physical plant and its extracurricular opportunities for students. In the 1930s Herman James had taken a college of liberal arts and a teacher training program and reorganized them as a university. The College of Arts and Sciences, with its liberal studies curriculum, was reestablished as Ohio University's core, and new, efficiently organized professional colleges complemented it. A

I worked for three years in what was then East Wing (now Wilson Hall) and attended Philosophy and Logic classes in the rooms upstairs. The campus was much smaller then, but I believe more beautiful. The first and lasting impression was of the large, towering McGuffey elms. Never was there a more beautiful sight as the morning sun filtered through the leafy canopy onto the campus green as we rushed to 8:00 A.M. class.

—Donald A. Fraser, '40

graduate college allowed some advanced study, and administrators, faculty, and students had stronger voices in the university's governance.

Within this more modern Ohio University, President Gamertsfelder, the trustees, and the faculty began the search for a new president and made plans for the biggest influx of students the country and Ohio University had ever experienced. They were getting ready for the veterans and a postwar era that would shape campus life over the next fifteen years.

Morning sunlight on the College Green. *Courtesy* Athena Yearbook, *1947.*

TOWARD A MODERN UNIVERSITY

7

Postwar Expansion and the Quest for Quality

1945–1961

There can be no retreat from quality.

—*John Calhoun Baker*

*W*ith the end of the war in sight in 1945, Ohio University faced the challenge of expanding its facilities, its faculty, and its programs to help meet the needs of a country that now stood, as Winston Churchill observed, "at the summit of the world." However, between 1929 and 1945 the school had experienced so many contractions and reductions that the popular admonition to "use it up, wear it out, make it do, or do without" had become a way of life.

Cutler Hall, the centerpiece of the campus, stood boarded up and abandoned. The surrounding buildings and grounds were in deplorable condition. Only 1,300 students, mostly women, were enrolled. The faculty, though well qualified to conduct research, carried heavy teaching loads for salaries that were among the lowest in the state. The programs in engineering, commerce, and journalism lacked national accreditation and, by the terms of the 1906 agreement that President Alston Ellis had struck with Ohio State, the university offered no doctoral programs. Added to these chronic problems was the urgent need to prepare for the thousands of Ohio veterans who were

Enrollment of Veterans to Double
At Ohio University By Second Semester of Current Year

In the fall of 1945, Coordinator of Veterans Affairs Victor Whitehouse predicted a rapid increase in the number of veterans who would use the generous G.I. Bill to attend Ohio University. *Ohio Alumnus, October 1945.*

expected to leave military service over the next few months and years and enter the state's colleges and universities.

When John Calhoun Baker arrived in February 1945 from his position as associate dean of the Harvard Business School to assume the presidency of Ohio University, he focused first on the financial future of the university rather than on the condition of the physical plant or the imminent arrival of the veterans. He asked the trustees to establish a fund, independent of state allocations, that could be used to "raise the sights" of the university community by providing money for travel, equipment, research, scholarships, and intellectual and cultural programs. Board members enthusiastically endorsed the Ohio University Fund, agreeing that it would allow the school to set a goal of "attaining the rank of one of the finest small or medium-sized universities in the United States." Baker also made plans for a faculty lecture series to allow professors to share their scholarship, arranged for key faculty members to study at other universities, and removed the $4,000 cap on faculty salaries. Then he turned his attention to the veterans, his "No. 1 problem" for the next five years.

Classroom buildings and housing were the first concerns. Funds for a chemistry building had already been approved, and its construction could begin as soon as materials were found. A dormitory for women, an engineering building, and renovations to Cutler and Ewing Halls would follow. The American Legion Building at South Court and President Streets and the Schloss Building on East Union were prepared to house the first groups

John Calhoun Baker, O.U. president 1945–61.
Courtesy Mahn Center.

of veterans. Nonetheless, it was clear that the Athens campus could not accommodate all its applicants. Ohio veterans were given admission priority, and out-of-state students, particularly out-of-state women, were limited. A more creative solution, reached after the promise of state support and consultation with other state schools (some of which were less than enthusiastic), was to have Professor Albert Gubitz reopen the "branch" campuses that had operated briefly in Chillicothe, Portsmouth, and Zanesville during President James's administration. Another partial solution came from the Extension Division. Courses that had been offered originally in nearby small towns by enterprising traveling faculty, and then by correspondence to service people

To accommodate more veterans, Ohio University reopened its old "branches" at Portsmouth *(left)* and Zanesville *(below)* as well as a new "branch" at Chillicothe. *Ohio Alumnus, March 1946. Courtesy Mahn Center.*

overseas, were expanded through a contract with the Veterans Administration to provide both high school and college level work to returning servicemen. Negotiations with the federal government made the new aviation department the first training center in the country to provide an accredited course in flight training under the G.I. Bill.

Though only 215 veterans were among the 2,000 students who enrolled in the fall of 1945, another 600 to 800 were expected for the spring semester. Professor Victor Whitehouse coordinated the Office of Veterans Affairs, and Dean A. H. Armbruster worked through government agencies to secure any available surplus materials that seemed useful and as much temporary housing as possible. He ordered twenty-three housing units—enough for 740 men— and a large cafeteria building for a site on the lower ground east of campus. The colony of barracks quickly became known as "Hog Island" because the tons of dirt that had been used to raise the area above flood level became a sea of mud after every rain and spring flood. Numerous office and housing units eventually filled areas on the College Green, near the airport, and along the river and on the town's North Hill.

Meanwhile, enrollment climbed rapidly. By 1946 there were almost 5,000 students, 75 percent of whom were veterans with no place to live. A house-to-house canvas turned up 2,000 rooms in town, but that was still not enough. Men lived everywhere—in the men's gym, the Armory, the stadium,

Regional Higher Education

For approximately 15,000 students each year, five regional campuses and the Division of Lifelong Learning provide the face of Ohio University. These students enroll in courses and pursue degrees or certificates through traditional coursework offered on the campuses, as well as through Independent Study and other flexible formats designed to help them reach their educational goals. Thousands more attend workshops, conferences, and noncredit courses in Athens and on the regional campuses. The communities served by the regional campuses benefit from a wide variety of cultural events, lectures, and economic development activities. Today, more than 150 faculty members and a large number of support staff work as part of Regional Higher Education.

All of this activity has its origins in the establishment of an extension department by President Alston Ellis in 1909. In 1910 fifty students were enrolled in extension courses taught by regular Ohio University faculty members in the communities of Jackson, Logan, Nelsonville, and Pomeroy. In 1914 three faculty members were hired full-time to spend their weeks riding circuit around southern and southeastern Ohio delivering courses. C. L. Martzolff was appointed the first director of extension in 1916, and by the early 1920s more than 1,000 students were enrolled in at least seventy different centers.

Teaching full-time in the extension department must have been quite a challenge. A typical schedule might require catching a train from Athens to Chillicothe on Monday morning. After teaching a class in Chillicothe, the faculty member might catch a trolley to Circleville for an evening class and then ride overnight in a sleeper car to Wheeling. Proceeding from town to town, the faculty member would teach a total of ten two-hour classes during the week, returning to Athens by early Saturday afternoon. The total cost of transportation, food, and lodging for the week averaged about $30.00 per faculty member.

In 1924 the role of the extension department expanded significantly when the university began to offer correspondence courses. That first year, fifteen instructors made forty correspondence courses available. Under the direction of Simeon H. Bing, the program grew rapidly to 159 courses just six years later. Students could count up to 36 credit hours (later raised to 64) earned through extension courses or correspondence toward completion of a baccalaureate degree.

At the encouragement of J. Floyd Dixon, who became director of the Ohio University Extension Division in 1937, two "evening divisions" were established in Portsmouth and Zanesville to offer a wider range of courses. Local high schools provided the necessary physical facilities at no charge, and students used the high school science labs and libraries. The plan was to offer two years of instruction, with all courses taught by regular Ohio University faculty members. The divisions were designed to be self-supporting; the Portsmouth division, at least, was expected to develop into a "day junior college." However, in 1941 the university closed both divisions and returned them to the status of extension centers. Other state universities' concerns about spreading limited funding too widely combined with the effects of the depression to end this early experiment in "branch" campuses.

Nevertheless, the Extension Division thrived, offering evening and Saturday courses on the Athens campus. What came to be called Independent Study through

Correspondence grew to serve more than 2,500 students each year. Extension centers decreased in number but continued to exist at least into the 1960s.

The return of World War II veterans prompted Ohio University to reconsider the possibility of establishing branch campuses outside Athens. In 1946 Governor Frank Lausche asked the presidents of all universities in Ohio to do everything they could to accommodate every Ohioan who wanted to go to college. President Baker and other administrators developed plans to open "residence credit centers" to offer freshman and sophomore coursework in less congested parts of southeastern Ohio and added a third site at Chillicothe to the earlier Portsmouth and Zanesville evening divisions. To head this new endeavor, President Baker appointed Albert C. Gubitz, a faculty member and head of the economics department. President Baker made it clear to Governor Lausche and to presidents of other universities that these "campuses" were a temporary measure to deal with the emergency situation. When classes opened in the fall of 1946, 859 students, at least half of them returning veterans, enrolled at the new residence credit centers. Instruction was provided by a combination of Athens faculty members and local teachers qualified to offer particular courses. As expected, enrollment began to decline after 1948, reaching a low of 458 students in 1952.

Although the university had intended to close the branches, Gubitz and the communities served by the centers argued forcefully for their continuation, and President Baker persuaded Governor Lausche to allow operations to continue. With a title change to Dean, Gubitz worked aggressively to promote regional campus enrollment. Finances were precarious, but the branches not only paid their way but began to develop a modest reserve. Full-time directors were appointed at the campuses, and resident faculty members were hired. New branches opened in Ironton and Lancaster in 1956 and in Martins Ferry in 1957. Enrollment reached 5,366 in 1965, the last year of Gubitz's tenure.

As demand for courses and programs continued to grow, the university considered creating permanent physical facilities in the communities served by the centers. In 1965 Edward M. Penson was named Dean of Off-Campus Programs (OCAP) by President Vernon Alden and directed to pursue vigorously the development of the branch campuses. Local communities provided land for the construction of permanent academic buildings. (It was during this period that the Martins Ferry operation switched to its current location in Belmont County, near St. Clairsville.) Although the OCAP operation eventually proved to be expensive and cumbersome, Penson's objective was to create modern campuses with a faculty, new libraries, and significant future potential. During his three years as dean, five academic buildings were opened, creating the Chillicothe, Belmont (later, Eastern), Lancaster, Portsmouth, and Zanesville campuses. Course offerings continued in Ironton, as well, although an official campus did not come along until much later.

In 1971 OCAP changed its name once again, to the Office of Regional Higher Education, and Beaumont Davison was named as its vice president. He began to

The Extension Division

CLASS WORK

The Extension Division has extended the O.U. Campus to include all of southeastern Ohio. Each semester evening classes taught by resident faculty are conducted in the larger southeastern Ohio towns.

Annually from 200 to 300 students earn standard transferable credit in this way.

CORRESPONDENCE INSTRUCTION

The Correspondence Department annually teaches from 1000 to 1200 students by mail. Many of these students are members of the Armed Forces or veterans under the G.I. Bill of Rights.

CREDIT

In extension classes and in correspondence study a student may earn as many as 40 of the required 124 semester hours for a bachelor's degree.

RECOGNITION

The Extension Division is a member of the National University Extension Association. This association is composed of the extension divisions of 60 colleges and universities of national standing.

The N.U.E.A. promotes and upholds standards by strict procedures for admission.

For further information write to: Director, Extension Division

OHIO UNIVERSITY
ATHENS, OHIO
"OLDEST UNIVERSITY IN THE NORTHWEST TERRITORY"

The Extension Division expanded its services as World War II veterans returned. Ohio Alumnus, *December 1946.*

dismantle the relatively large central office structure, asking campus directors (later, deans) to assume broad responsibility for local operations.

As the campuses continued to develop, programming opportunities expanded. Baccalaureate programs in education and business became part of the curriculum. Technical associate degree programs began with the now-defunct engineering program at Zanesville in the late 1950s, followed by programs in nursing and radio-television. Although the technical mission did not expand beyond this point at Zanesville, and never developed at Belmont (Eastern), on the other campuses these two-year degree programs have continued to be an essential part of the curriculum.

In 1976, James C. Bryant was named Vice Provost for Regional Higher Education, after serving two years as interim vice president. (Some years later, Dr. Bryant again became vice president, the current title for the position.) Programming continued to expand, with the introduction of new degree options at the associate and baccalaureate levels. Ohio University also created an efficient cohort model for delivering master's degree programs at regional campuses, in which a group of students moved through a program together, generally over two years, before the program shifted to a different campus.

Bryant also recognized the critical role that communities played in the creation and continuation of regional campuses. Regional coordinating councils made up of leading citizens of the community were strongly supported at each campus. The physical plants continued to grow, although not to the extent that was imagined in the 1960s. In 1975 the Portsmouth campus left the university, developing into what is now Shawnee State University. However, the Ironton campus finally opened its first building in 1985 and quickly grew into the largest of the regional campuses.

Dr. Bryant retired in 1998, having served the extension/regional campus effort longer than any other leader. Vice President Charles Bird, appointed in 1999, now leads the regional campuses and the Division of Lifelong Learning. Today nearly two dozen associate degree programs, at least ten baccalaureate programs, and a broad range of cohort-based master's degree programs are available on various campuses. Interactive video classrooms, first introduced in the mid-1980s, allow some courses to be delivered to smaller groups of students at each campus. Computer labs, strong libraries, and support services, as well as a dedicated faculty and staff, have allowed the regional campuses to think of their mission in new, more complex ways.

The Division of Lifelong Learning also offers classes in a variety of formats to meet the needs of adult learners. Thousands of students continue to take traditional correspondence courses, even as electronic-based alternatives are developed. Ohio University Without Boundaries brings graduate programs and certificates to individuals who would be unable to relocate to Athens, and Adult Learning Services uses a variety of methods to help undergraduate students achieve their educational objectives. Distance education programs and international programs, such as the Hong Kong Center, promise to help carry Lifelong Learning into an exciting future.

Methods of delivery and the range of programs have changed since the first faculty members boarded trains to visit the communities of southeastern Ohio, and the "region" served by Regional Higher Education is now global in scope. Yet, the original commitment to a mission of outreach and access has served for nearly one hundred years, providing a sense of continuity and purpose.

Army surplus buildings provided a home for veterans in the low-lying area east of campus. *Courtesy Mahn Center.*

in every nearby town, and in government housing units as far away as Point Pleasant, West Virginia. John K. Cunningham was typical of married men who took advantage of the G.I. Bill to enroll at O.U. that fall. He was offered housing in Point Pleasant, but he and his wife were from Glouster, which was closer, so they stayed there.

Temporary housing for veterans was erected on a foot of fill dirt that turned into mud after every rain—hence the name Hog Island. *Courtesy Athena Yearbook, 1947.*

> I didn't have a car, so I and a few other guys from Glouster . . . would go to the Wonder Bar early in the morning, have a cup of coffee, and try to find someone who was driving to Athens. . . . I was often late to class and sometimes a

As the number of veterans increased, men were everywhere, some with no place to live. *Courtesy Athena Yearbook, 1948.*

400 ROOMS ARE NEEDED NOW!

Meeting this emergency is a challenge that should be shared by the people of Athens and neighboring communities. Ohio University does not want to turn away these young men who wish to enroll here. But they cannot be accepted, if rooms are not available.

If you have one or more rooms that can be rented to students, or to a veteran and his wife, please notify Ohio University Special Housing Committee, telephone 990 or 712, immediately.

The University has completed plans to provide regular bus service for students rooming a considerable distance from the campus in Athens and arrangements can be made to assign students owning cars to homes in neighboring communities.

Please don't delay. Every room made available means that another young veteran can attend Ohio University.

Opening your homes to these young men will not only be an unselfish move and a real help to our veterans, but it is, furthermore, our responsibility in this crisis. They earned the right on the battlefield and at sea to continue their education. And lastly, it is necessary for the continued growth of Ohio University and the income of the county. You will, of course, receive immediate return in room rentals.

Flyers urged Athens citizens to open any available rooms to veterans. *Courtesy Mahn Center.*

prof would try to make me feel bad, but I didn't pay any attention. I was twenty-one years old, and I had been to the war, and I didn't care what they said to me.

The independence and urgency of these men, who were often a bit older and who had seen something of the world, affected the campus atmosphere in a number of ways. They crowded into practical and technical fields—commerce, engineering, and the sciences—escalating the demand for equipment, labs, library resources, and at least twenty-five new, well-qualified faculty members. Their willingness to work hard created serious competition in classrooms.

The huge number of single men also revitalized campus social life. Mary Lou Happoldt Farbeann, a freshman in 1947, says: "I thought I was in heaven! There were five men for every girl on campus. They all got a monthly allowance from the government, and on the first of the month, groups of fellows pooled their money, hired a band, and had a dance. . . . Most of the guys who came back didn't talk about the war. They wanted to party and have a good time. The war was behind them." When the Varsity Theater opened a year or so later, its "dating seats" were wide enough for two and "quite cozy" when a "guy put his arm across the back."

Veterans with wives and children lived in temporary housing on East State Street. *Courtesy* Athena Yearbook, *1948.*

I was enrolled in an English Lit class taught by Professor Paul Kendall. He was always an energetic lecturer and his enthusiasm made it a class I never wanted to miss. In the course of the semester, we finally got around to Shakespeare. Until that time, I had very limited exposure to the Bard and recall our first reading assignment was HENRY V. I did plod through the assigned reading with very little appreciation for the play.

The day following my reading of HENRY V Professor Kendall gave a lecture that turned things around for me. When he discussed Henry's speech to his troops before the battle of Agincourt he read the text with such fervor and so much passion I could hardly believe that he was reading the same play that I had read the night before. I was ready to go into battle with Henry. Then when he got to the battle he waved his imaginary sword and raced across the room doing battle in front of the class until the fighting was done.

That one lecture opened the whole world of Shakespeare for me. It showed me that Shakespeare could be dramatic and full of action. Since that time I have played roles in Shakespeare productions and directed a few. Without this one lecture, I think I would have shied away from the Bard in place of appreciating him.

—H. Eugene Dybvig, '47, '51

Professor of English Paul Murray Kendall. *Courtesy* Athena Yearbook, *1947.*

The asylum's wooded grounds hid partiers with "gin-jugs"—gin and juice mixed in large milk cans. Practice rooms in the music building and a clearing in Dean Voigt's overgrown garden offered privacy for a campus Casanova who was reputed to resemble Gregory Peck. Of course, the few men with cars had the advantage. Nancy Canfield Wise remembers living in Lindley Hall, "when there was a certain way you could drive through the alley between the men's gym and Lindley, and after hours some women would jump from their dorm rooms into convertibles, and go off and do—I don't know what! Then they would come back and someone would have to pull them back up into the room. As a freshman, I thought it was quite scandalous."

President Baker and wife Elizabeth were also scandalized. The Kissing Circle—that peculiar zone on the Green where any man could kiss any woman who was passing through at the same time—was bad enough. But the view from the Bakers' temporary College Street apartment was worse. From there, they could see Howard Hall, where courting couples necked in the few minutes before the women's ten o'clock curfew. Both Bakers found these public displays unseemly, inappropriate, and cause for intervention. The president chose not to lecture the coeds on virtue, as President Ellis and

Couples enjoyed the freedom afforded by the few cars on campus. *Courtesy* Athena Yearbook, *1941.*

Dean Chubb had done. Instead, he invited campus leaders to his office, expressed his concerns, and asked them to write an acceptable code of student conduct. They agreed—even to having the campus police speak to couples seen lying on the Green. Impressed with their cooperation and convinced that "any president who depends on official channels for information is not getting full information," he included students on most of the university's key committees—an unusual move for the times.

Students took responsibility in other areas without being asked. Some individuals concerned themselves with civil rights, battling Dean Voigt for the coeds' right to wear slacks and, more significantly, insisting that pictures and religious preference be omitted from admissions applications. Other students continued to operate the radio station they had helped construct

Public displays of affection led to a new Student Code of Conduct. *Courtesy* Athena Yearbook, *1948.*

in 1942 despite Trustee Arthur Johnson's worries that the $2,500 investment in broadcast equipment could create "one million dollars of headaches." The Men's Independent Association (MIA) expanded on the Men's Union practice of offering Friday evening movies, raising ticket prices to fourteen cents and adding Wednesday and Saturday showings. Most profits (an eventual total of $5,000) were earmarked for the fund for a new student union. O.U. students were so eager to see the ugly, inadequate Student Union replaced that

WOUB: Radio Days

WOUB came about in a time when radio stations signed off at midnight with "The Star-Spangled Banner," a patriotic custom reflecting the axiom admonishing stations to broadcast in the "public interest, convenience, and necessity." We were no competition for the 50,000-watt clear channel stations that thundered into the farmlands of Ohio brandishing big-city names. No matter, WOUB was *our* station, and Athens, well, if it wasn't our town, it was where we lived.

WOUB—for "We're Ohio University Broadcasting"—began in 1942 as a student-run contraption wired into the dormitories, little more than a public address system. An FM companion, WOUI, took to the air in 1949, but virtually no one in those days owned an FM receiver, and it was not until 1957 that WOUB positioned itself on the AM dial with a 100-watt signal that at last could be heard by the local community. The station was headquartered in an army surplus Quonset hut before it moved to the relative luxury of the basement of the Speech Building, later Kantner Hall.

Plans for a television operation were still on the drawing board. By the mid-fifties TV had reduced radio to a superficial cacophony of simplistic music, rip-and-read headlines, and fast-buck commercialism, but that didn't deter us. In Studio A sat a nearly obsolete device, an enormous sound-effects console on rollers, with all the paraphernalia for making one noise sound like another.

Our programming was eclectic. We offered radio dramas, a colorful ensemble program for kids, jazz, big band, pop, classical, play-by-play. A legion of us produced an all-weekend broadcast (*Weekend*) influenced heavily by *Monitor,* an NBC public affairs broadcast.

We were hot shots, often abrasive, naturally competitive, sometimes infuriating, throwing our names back and forth as if we were programming only to ourselves. It got so bad that the faculty head of the department barred us from using our names on the air—under threat of suspension. For some of us, grades suffered as the result of our extracurricular labors as announcers, newscasters, disc jockeys, sports reporters, and backup personnel. Some of us were paid station department heads. I was Special Events Director, earning $16.75 a month.

It was a rare learning experience at a university that teetered somewhere between a liberal arts school and a trade school. That so many of us who worked at WOUB in the fifties actually went into broadcasting professionally and succeeded is proof that a radio station, even a college station, is more than dials, switches, wires, and tubes.

—*Don Swaim, '59*

A Quonset hut on the College Green housed WOUB in the '40s. Established by students in 1942, the station expanded to include FM station WOUI in 1949. *Courtesy Mahn Center.*

Courtesy Mahn Center.

4,000 of them signed a petition to the trustees proposing a $5-a-semester "center fee."

The new student center would not be a reality for several years, but during 1947–48, the university's great building program began. Cutler Hall, restored to its original design, was rededicated, and President Baker decreed that all future O.U. buildings would conform to its style. By midyear the chemistry building was complete and the women's dorm (Bryan Hall) on University Terrace was under construction. Properties near the campus, which the trustees had sold years before, were purchased as quickly as they became available. With two million dollars for new buildings from Ohio's general assembly, the trustees stepped up plans for the engineering building, a speech building, the health center, and a natatorium.

Dancing in the Grill at the student union. *Courtesy* Athena Yearbook, *1949.*

Cutler Hall in the process of being restored to its original design in 1947. It was placed on the National Register of Historic Places in 1966. *Courtesy Mahn Center.*

Next, the administration focused on strengthening the faculty and student body. Competition among universities for well-qualified instructors was extremely heavy, and Ohio University salaries remained low. President Baker pushed for more equitable salaries, interviewed prospective hires himself, and encouraged tighter standards for promotion and tenure. The efforts paid off. More than forty new faculty and staff joined the university community in 1947 and another forty-eight arrived the following year.

The university had less flexibility in selecting its student body. Admissions priority could be given to veterans and the number of out-of-state students restricted, but as a state institution, the university was obligated to accept Ohioans who applied. To broaden these students' cultural horizons, President Baker invited statesmen, writers, musicians, artists, and actors to the campus. Students from other countries were welcomed, and their International Forums and International Nights fostered friendships.

Ohio University in 1949. Temporary buildings front the College Green. The barracks of Hog Island are on the left, and to the right the river flows dangerously near the campus. *Courtesy Patricia Irwin Kircher, '51.*

To counter many students' inadequate high school preparations, especially in writing, faculty and administrators devised an English Proficiency Program, which required several writing classes and proof of writing competence for graduation. Academic advising, offered during the week-long registration periods, directed the less-prepared freshmen into the new two-year Associate of Arts programs and the most able into honors work while also allowing students to establish relationships with some of their professors. President Baker considered the program so valuable that he eventually took on some advisees himself.

Evelyn Coulter Luchs, '27, a teacher, writer, and lecturer, became the university's first female trustee in 1949. *Ohio Alumnus,* June 1956.

Of course, the times influenced the kinds of advice students received. Women, for example, were sometimes urged to play it safe and avoid careers that might require evening hours, direct competition with men, or an investment in graduate school. Some later regretted that they had not been encouraged to follow their dreams. As Nancy Canfield Wise put it many years later, "Now I wonder what would have happened if I had been told that I could go ahead and do something with psychology. At that time it was rather implied that our education was mainly to fit in with the man's roles as a working person."

By June 1950 it was easy to agree that "the campus has never been as beautiful as this spring, nor have there been as many evidences of growth and expansion—physically and otherwise—as now." Trustee John Galbreath's

Registration in an army surplus building on the College Green, counseling by professors, and the Registration Hop defined Freshman Week. *Courtesy* Athena Yearbook, *1952.*

initial gift of $50,000 for construction of a nondenominational chapel swelled the Ohio University Fund. The speech building was under way; contracts had been let for the south wing of Lindley and the first of eleven dormitories that would gradually transform Hog Island into the East Green. New oak trees replaced the College Green's dying McGuffey elms. Students even got a much-appreciated footbridge across the Hocking. However, across the country the exuberance of the postwar years was subsiding. Americans were increasingly preoccupied with communism and suspicious of intellectuals, including professors. Enrollments at college campuses declined as World War II veterans finished their studies and new draftees left to fight in Korea. At Ohio University, as elsewhere, the drop in the number of students and a rise in inflation strained budgets and temporarily slowed the frenetic pace of expansion, if not student activity.

Among the many popular activities on the Athens campus was the annual Powder Bowl game between two sororities—Pi Beta Phi and Alpha Xi Delta. Until they were discontinued for fear the women would be hurt, these hard-fought scrambles attracted as many as 2,500 fans and raised between five and six hundred dollars for the Damon Runyon Cancer Fund. The varsity teams, revived in full force after the end of the war, were intensely popular. On Migration Day in 1950, 1,000 students followed Coach Carroll Widdoes's football team to Miami University. In 1952 so many students wanted to see the "Snydermen" play basketball in the Men's Gym (now Bentley Hall) that admission had to be limited to every other game. However, avid fans like John T. Walters and William Demoyne would not be denied. When Walters and his friends could not find seats, they would just "get up in the ceiling and lie across the rafters to watch the games." Demoyne and eleven other veterans went underground. They sneaked into the university heating tunnels, and after several abortive attempts to find their way, popped up in the gym. Though they swore to keep their route secret, word got out, and "a group of other students used our system to visit Bryan Hall, a women's dorm, in the middle of the night, and after that the heating tunnels were secured against all future excursions."

President Baker often said he considered sports at Ohio University "de minimis," but he supported both intramural and intercollegiate teams as a part of the educational program and for their character-

The College Green's famous elm trees, planted by President McGuffey in the 1840s, fell victim to old age and disease in the 1950s. *Courtesy Mahn Center.*

In late November 1950, just as students were about to return to campus after Thanksgiving break, a huge snowstorm shut the university down. Many students did not get the word that classes were cancelled for a week and somehow made it back to campus. They arranged dances, open houses, and swimming hours; built snow people (including Mae West on President Baker's lawn); organized a snowball fight on the Green; and, of course, borrowed cafeteria trays for sledding on E. Union hill (now Jeff Hill). *Courtesy* Athena Yearbook, *1950.*

Members of Pi Beta Phi and Alpha Xi Delta compete in an annual Powder Bowl game to raise funds for the Damon Runyon Cancer Fund. *Courtesy Mahn Center.*

Below: Fans filled the Men's Gym (now Bentley Hall) to see the hoopsters coached by three alumni: Jim Snyder, Kermit Blosser, and Bob Wren. *Courtesy Athena Yearbook, 1952.*

Right: Courtesy Terry Lee.

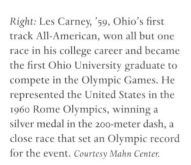

building potential. However, persistent rumors of ringers, open payments, and dishonesty in the recruitment and retention of athletes at other Ohio schools caused him to insist "that we play in a conference and compete with teams that have the same objectives and standards that we have" and that it was easier and more responsible to turn students into athletes than athletes into students.

Among the student-athletes who were recruited in 1950 were Frank Underwood and Charlie Wilson, the first African Ameri-

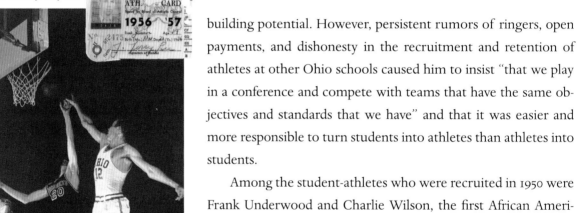

Right: Les Carney, '59, Ohio's first track All-American, won all but one race in his college career and became the first Ohio University graduate to compete in the Olympic Games. He represented the United States in the 1960 Rome Olympics, winning a silver medal in the 200-meter dash, a close race that set an Olympic record for the event. *Courtesy Mahn Center.*

The 1953 football team, champs for the first time in their six years in the MAC. *Courtesy* Athena Yearbook, *1953.*

cans to attend Ohio University on football scholarships. Although they were popular on campus, their social lives were limited to hanging out in their rooms or in the rec center on the Green, watching MIA movies, or occasionally visiting a club or bowling alley in a nearby town. Underwood says he was not bothered by his minority status, even though he did not always feel welcome in local shops and he and Wilson were not always allowed in restaurants to eat with the team when they traveled out of town. He chooses to remember President Baker's attention to how he was doing, Dean Maurel Hunkin's help in getting him onto the men's disciplinary committee, Kermit Blosser's "life lessons," the Mid-American Championship of 1953, and especially that the small campus was a place where "you meld."

Carroll C. Widdoes, Ohio College Coach of the Year, 1953–54. *Courtesy* Athena Yearbook, *1954.*

According to the student handbook of the day, the school had a reputation as the friendliest campus in the country. It was "a wonderful place to be—just beautiful." Perhaps its friendliness and beauty made up for the difficulty of getting to Athens over winding, dusty roads, for the frequent spring floods, and for overcrowded dorms. In Lindley Hall, a women's dorm, each room for two was shared by three. There were two desks, two dressers, a set of bunk beds, and a single bed. One coed recalls that only two of the three mattresses were adequate, and residents were advised to switch beds every six weeks in order to distribute backaches equitably. Because of "hours," women spent a great deal of time in their dorms. They studied there, organized dorm government and ran for offices, played endless games

of bridge, suntanned on the roof, decorated their rooms for holidays, entertained professors at dinner, and enjoyed fraternity serenades that were "just like a fairy tale." Twice a year each dorm arranged a dance, complete with band, decorations, formals, and corsages. And every spring they made floats and campaigned for J-Prom royalty with clever skits—at least until

1952 when the event was threatened. That year, a member of Delta Tau Delta decided to set a record for sitting at the top of a flagpole. Students determined to dislodge him stormed his perch with "tear gas, eggs, tomatoes, [and] fireworks," causing Student Council President Wayne Adams to call for more becoming behavior.

Student Council members also directed the cheering card section at ball games, a Campus Chest Drive, Mother's Weekend, and a campus bridge tournament. The Men's Programming Board arranged each fall's Freshman Mixer and the Registration Hop, Migration Day, and Homecoming festivities. Not to be outdone, Women's League held a Leadership Conference, the Coed Ball (women invited the men), and informal parties. More than a hundred smaller groups —from honor societies and Charlie Minelli's university bands to student-led bands, theater groups, a swim club, and debate clubs—contributed their activities to the mix. Among the most popular were groups with a religious

Because of the forthcoming Junior Prom, classes were dismissed at noon. Indeed, because of the excitement connected with serenading and the preparation of floats for the parade tomorrow, very little work has been done for the last two or three days.

—Professor Raymer McQuiston, diary, April 12, 1957

Pete Tompico, campaigning for the title of J-Prom king in 1957. *Courtesy Mahn Center.*

affiliation, such as the Westminster Foundation, the Wesley Foundation, Canterbury and Newman Clubs, and Hillel. The Campus Religious Council sponsored large campus events such as Religion in Life Week and Faith in Action Week, as well as midweek chapel in the Music Hall and a radio program on the university station. Every Sunday evening found a great many students eating, singing, or performing in local meeting rooms or church basements.

The seventeen fraternities and ten sororities provided such an active social life for some students that the *Post* ran a column called "The Nightlife of the Greeks." Joanne Dove Prisley, '53, '54, remembers circus parties, gay nineties parties, roaring twenties parties, a Bowery party, and a Casino party; she says she was constantly making costumes—everything from Greek slave to weight lifter. The highlight of all this activity was the annual Greek Week, kicked off by a marathon from Logan to Athens with

Homecoming float, 1954. *Courtesy Leona Hughes, '30.*

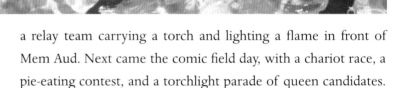

A performance by the Dolphin Club. *Courtesy Mahn Center.* *Inset:* Patricia Irwin Kircher, '51. *Courtesy Patricia Irwin Kircher.*

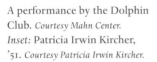

a relay team carrying a torch and lighting a flame in front of Mem Aud. Next came the comic field day, with a chariot race, a pie-eating contest, and a torchlight parade of queen candidates.

A variety show in the auditorium, dances on Friday and Saturday nights, and the crowning of the queen capped the week. As the number of African Americans on campus increased (to about fifty in 1954), the reactivated chapter of Alpha Phi Alpha and a new local sorority, Kappa Alpha Alpha, joined in at least some of the greek activities.

Organizations with religious affiliations were among the most popular on campus. *Above:* Students at a Hillel Foundation service. *Courtesy Athena Yearbook, 1950. Right:* A student choir. *Courtesy Mahn Center*

In 1953, O.U.'s first Greek Week featured a marathon from Logan to Athens, a chariot race *(left)*, a pie-eating contest *(below)*, and a parade of queen candidates. *Courtesy* Athena Yearbook, *1953.*

It seemed there was something and some place for almost everyone at Ohio University. Robert Young, '51, explains it well.

I arrived at Ohio University on the B & O Railroad at midnight in early February 1948 in the middle of a terrible snowstorm, all my worldly goods packed in a steamer trunk. . . .

Being a southern boy from [Virginia's] coal fields and farms, I was somewhat intimidated by the prospect of Ohio University. I wondered if I could cope with the North, with a big university, with a more sophisticated crowd than I was used to, and whether I could pass the courses. I slept a fitful sleep.

The next morning dawned bright and clear, and I walked up the hill to the College Green and experienced a most extraordinary feeling of exhilaration. It was so beautiful and so different that all my fears and apprehensions dissolved, and I decided that I would make it no matter what the effort. This was My Place. I walked back down to the station and told them to deliver my trunk.

The new University Center (now Baker Center), opened in 1953, provided ample space for dancing. *Courtesy* Athena Yearbook, *1955.*

Faculty members also felt at home in Athens. According to Carolyn Murphree, both President and Mrs. Baker

saw their domain as a family-like community. Walking across campus, they greeted faculty, staff, and more than a few students by name. . . . Mrs. Baker could easily drop in on faculty newcomers, pop in to

The College Green in morning light. *Courtesy University Photographer's Office.*

see a new baby, phone to say "can you come up for dinner—we need another couple." President Baker might get acquainted with a new faculty member by requesting company on a trip to the Columbus airport that included a stop for bean soup at his favorite Canal Winchester restaurant.

The feeling of family carried over into all-campus parties and Saturday night buffets at Baker Center. Both were arranged by Margaret Davis, who was in charge of feeding and housing all students, maintaining and furnishing all buildings, and landscaping the grounds, as well as running Baker Center's faculty dining room. Her Saturday night, family-oriented buffets, with toddlers, teenagers, and parents, were picture-book feasts, with abundant flowers, linen, a groaning board, and a price to fit an instructor's salary.

This was the tranquil state of affairs in the summer of 1953 when President Baker and Professor Willard Elsbree traveled to Geneva, Switzerland, where Baker had been invited by President Dwight Eisenhower to serve as U.S. delegate to the United Nations Economic and Social Council. Both he and the trustees agreed that such service to the nation should not be refused, but it is unlikely that any of them realized the impact President Baker's three summers in Geneva would have on his intense interest in international affairs and on Ohio University's future connections with other countries.

That September, the long-awaited Ohio University Center opened. Students could now bowl, play billiards and Ping-Pong, steal a kiss in the 1954 Lounge, and rip out a tune on the piano in the 1804 Lounge. They loved the sophistication of the ballroom, saw the cozy Cavern as a "wonderful place to chat with a date," and trooped to the Frontier Room between classes to play the jukebox and sip cups of coffee.

A few months later, in February 1954, the year-long Sesquicentennial Celebration, designed to draw attention of Ohioans to the university and to the value of education, began. The first event was on Founders Day, February 18. *The Green Adventure,* a play by Charles Allen Smart, O.U.'s first writer-in-residence, chronicled the origin of higher education in Ohio. With music and a cast of 150, Rufus Putnam, Manasseh Cutler, and Eliphaz Perkins came to life on stage. A few days later, the university's symphony orchestra premiered *American Rhapsody,* composed by the acclaimed Ernst von Dohnányi, who had been visiting the campus each spring since 1949. Homecoming that fall and Ohio Education Days offered two more occasions to show off the oldest university in the Northwest Territory. Professor Thomas N. Hoover's *History of Ohio University,* the second publication of the Ohio University Press (after *The Green Adventure*), made the institution's whole story available for the first time.

It was a good year. Not only were the official events successful, Coach Widdoes's football team won the MAC championship and Ohio University became the only school in the country to offer both B.F.A. and M.F.A. degrees in photography. When Trustee Fred Johnson led a drive to raise money

Elizabeth Baker, wife of President John Baker. A theater supporter, she purchased the Monomoy Theatre in Chatham, Massachusetts, for the university in 1956. *Courtesy Mahn Center.*

The new student center—later named for President Baker—opened in the fall of 1953. *Courtesy Dan Dry Associates.*

1954 Lounge. *Courtesy Anne Downing LaFollette, '56.*

Ernst von Dohnányi conducted
the Ohio University orchestra
as part of the sesquicentennial
celebration. From the scrapbook of Maurel Hunkins.
Courtesy Mahn Center.

SESQUICENTENNIAL
HOMECOMING
BALL

Dance program from the
Sesquicentennial Homecoming
Ball. *Courtesy Terry Lee, '58.*

for a Sesquicentennial Scholarship Fund, 3,788 alumni,
faculty, staff, students, and friends responded generously.
Asked to contribute $150,000—$1,000 for each year of
the university's life—they surprised themselves by contributing almost $400,000.

A further reason to celebrate in 1954 was the administration's decision to offer doctoral degrees. By the
mid-fifties, young faculty members, like Roland Swardson of the English department, welcomed this new
scholarly climate. As he said, "We didn't want gentility
[teas, dinners, and conversation]; we wanted brains. . . .
We wanted brains that worked very much in the latest
way. And we wanted a place at the table."

Along with increased interest in research came more resources to support it. The Ohio University Fund subsidized some projects, and more faculty received grants from outside agencies and published highly regarded
work. In 1956, the chemistry department's ten young faculty members, all
with Ph.D.'s, organized the university's first doctoral program and accepted
Joseph Denham as its first student. For President Baker the new program
was "but the start of advanced graduate study on the campus." He was correct, for in 1957, the speech department, with a respected faculty and his-
torically strong forensic program, organized the second Ph.D. program. The
following year, the College of Education's departments of Administration
and Supervision, Guidance and Counseling, and Elementary Education were
also approved to offer advanced degrees. Baker was able to tell the trustees
that "the academic climate has never been more vigorous."

Gratifying as these successes were, they also created challenges. By 1956
Ohio University had become one of the fastest-growing universities in the
country. Combined enrollment had reached 6,100 and was expected to ex-
ceed 10,000 within the next few years. The Faculty Advisory Council studied
the feasibility of limiting the size of the university, but advised against it,
causing President Baker, who was committed to quality over quantity, to
worry about the consequences of unlimited growth. "It is our hope," he
told the trustees, "that Ohio University will not become so large that its historic role in Southeast Ohio will be disturbed or destroyed. Above all we
wish to preserve that friendly and personal relationship between the student

As unlikely as it sounds, my soccer experiences on Coach John McComb's varsity soccer team were coupled with the excellence of the education that I received in civil/structural engineering.

Coach John McComb required players to inform their professors of pending class absences on dates of out-of-town games. These absences were unacceptable to Professor Carl Shermer. Immediately following the first out-of-town game, he began to question me in class regarding homework assignments, technical principles, and related topics. This pattern of questioning continued for the next four years! Thus, I prepared well, in self-defense, for Dr. Shermer.

In the spring of my fifth year, Dr. Shermer spied me sweeping the sidewalks in front of Cutler Hall. He remarked that he didn't know I was a working student. The daily questioning suddenly ended. More than thirty years later, I still hold fond memories of Dr. Shermer. He expressed a concern for his students that I will never forget. Perhaps he would be pleased that I still practice structural engineering.

—William W. Merrell, '66

and university which has become so much a part of a tradition dating back more than a century and a half."

President Baker was not alone in his concerns. A generation of "baby boomers" in the nation's elementary schools and a Supreme Court decision that declared "separate but equal" education unconstitutional prompted both President Eisenhower and Gov. C. William O'Neill of Ohio to appoint commissions to study the future of higher education. Their charge was to recommend policies to ensure equal educational opportunity while preserving educational excellence.

Herman Leonard, '47, spent much of his time at Ohio University working as a photographer and photo editor for the *Athena*. Later, he melded his passions for photography and jazz to create a place for himself in art history. He has worked for *Playboy* magazine and with the likes of Marlon Brando and famed portrait photographer Yousuf Karsh, but he is best known for his portraits of American jazz greats. His images of Miles Davis, Charlie Parker, Billie Holiday, Duke Ellington, and others are preserved in *The Eye of Jazz* and *Jazz Memories*. *Courtesy* Athena Yearbook, *1947*.

The Ice Age at Ohio University

In 1956 President Baker approved a request from the Athletic Department for a field house for indoor football, baseball, and track. After the building was completed, it was found to be unsuitable for its intended purposes. Elizabeth Baker, the president's wife, enjoyed ice skating and thought Ohio University's women students would, too. In 1958 the floor of the field house was flooded and frozen for the first time, and the Ice Age began at Ohio University. Bird Arena, named for former athletic director Ossian C. Bird, became the site of skating classes, open skating sessions, intramural and local youth hockey, and the home of Ohio University's ice hockey team.

John McComb, an O.U. physical education teacher who had played hockey at Boston University, recruited the first team members. One Sunday morning, on a frozen pond at the old Asylum grounds, John gathered the boys playing there and told them about his vision for hockey at Ohio University. As Elmer Gates, one of the original team members, put it, "That's when all of the student pond players began to realize how little we knew about playing college hockey."

At that time only one other university in the state had an indoor rink, so the Bobcat team had a chance to distinguish itself, winning its first game in December 1958 by a score of 22 to 1. The second year the Bobcats won the Ohio Intercollegiate Hockey Association Championship, and for the next two years they repeated as champions.

John McComb coached and managed the team for eighteen years and won 176 games, pushing for increased funding and nurturing the team to varsity level; he helped establish the Central Collegiate Hockey Association (CCHA), the Division 1 College Hockey League in the Midwest.

In the '70s, when hockey lost its varsity status due to budget constraints, the team languished. A series of stand-out coaches—Mike L'Heureux, Tiff Cook, and Craig McCarthy—reestablished the team's reputation. In 1995 the team won its first National Club Hockey Championship.

For most of its forty-plus years, the hockey team has been a club sport with a budget that makes it hard to buy equipment and pay travel expenses. The Sands A.C. Social Club offered support in the early days by helping players secure low-rent housing and selling ten-cent programs and twenty-five-cent beer at games. Today the Blueline Boosters Club conducts innovative fund-raising programs and communicates with fans via a website.

Since 1958 Ohio's hockey team has represented the university in more than a thousand intercollegiate games, winning 65 percent of those games and bringing countless league championships and three national championships to Ohio University. More than a thousand players have suited up in the Bobcat uniform. Standing-room-only attendance at home games has been the norm, with almost one million students, parents, visitors, faculty, and staff attending. Few other colleges or universities can boast such a long and successful hockey history or a campus-wide tradition that is so cherished.

Ice hockey, a club sport, proved popular with Ohio University students. Spectrum Green, 1966. *Courtesy* Athena Yearbook.

At Ohio University, new facilities were still being added as rapidly as possible. The eleven-dorm complex on the East Green was nearing completion, and a new commerce building—the tallest on campus—was open. The health center, the larger engineering building, an education building, and an ice rink (thanks to Mrs. Baker, who thought skating would be fun for the women) were being planned. As for equal opportunity, Ohio University had, except for the period from 1923 to the mid-1950s, been open to students of every color and creed. In spite of this, the student body remained white, middle class, and Christian, except for approximately 50 African American students, 250 Jewish students, and a few dozen students from other countries.

The university's efforts to broaden its constituency were more visible in programs that extended beyond the regular school year and beyond the Athens campus. The summer workshops, for example, were extremely popular and attracted thousands of high school students, teachers, bankers, and businessmen each year. WOUB, now with both FM and AM capabilities, provided news and entertainment throughout the area. The Extension Division allowed students to take courses without leaving home. The branch campuses, reopened as temporary sites to serve veterans, were now self-supporting. The university reached an even broader audience in 1957 when it signed its first contract for work in another country. At the request of the International Cooperation Administration of the U.S. Department of State, the Ohio University administration agreed to provide teacher training for the rapidly growing education system in western Nigeria.

That same year, demands for excellence in higher education increased dramatically when the Soviets surprised the world by sending the satellite Sputnik into orbit around the earth. At Ohio University, the trustees moved ahead with plans to create the larger engineering building they had been discussing for years. They also saw a new life science building as equally important, welcomed Mrs. Baker's gift of the

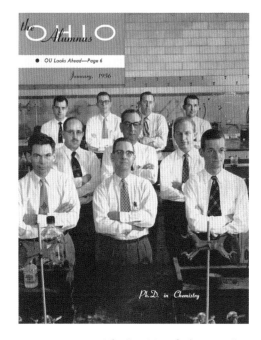

The "Big Ten of Chemistry," who organized Ohio University's first doctoral program in 1956. *Left to right, 1st row:* Robert F. Sympson, Lawrence P. Eblin, Wendell V. F. Brooks; *2nd row:* Jesse H. Day, Donald R. Clippinger, William D. Huntsman; *3rd row:* Robert K. Ingham, Bill Smith, Robert J. Kline, Thomas H. Curry. Ohio Alumnus, *January 1956.*

The East Green replaced Hog Island and gradually expanded to include privately owned Lakeview Apartments in the late 1960s. *Courtesy Dave Westrick, '77.*

Helen Mauck Galbreath Memorial Chapel

When President John Baker arrived in Athens in 1945, he was struck by the fact that though the university had a strong foundation in religion, it had no chapel. By the early fifties, he found support for the idea of a nondenominational chapel that could be a sanctuary for all students and staff. The obstacle was a lack of funds.

John Galbreath, a 1920 graduate and an outstanding trustee, agreed to build a chapel in memory of his late wife, Helen Mauck, a 1919 graduate and a dedicated alumna. Deciding on a location for the building presented a problem, as President Baker's notes from a 1955 trustees' meeting indicate: "Only point of agreement: Where John Galbreath wants it." Folklore has it that Galbreath chose the site between Memorial Auditorium and Ellis Hall because he and his wife had courted there. True or not, by 1956, the site was settled.

The Greek Revival building, with its octagonal nave and 120-foot spire, was dedicated on June 7, 1958. The Reverend Roy A. Burkhart spoke of the "woman of excellence" who had inspired it and of the many who would benefit from its use. "There was a chapel in the heart of Helen Mauck Galbreath. This chapel in her name is now dedicated that all who seek knowledge may find wisdom; that those who rush toward their destiny as if it will not wait, may find a sense of direction; that worshipping here, they will come to know a sanctuary within the soul of each one in time that it may be dedicated in the soul of humanity."

Helen Mauck Galbreath Memorial Chapel, the gift of trustee John Galbreath. *Courtesy Dan Dry Associates.*

For almost fifty years, the chapel has been available to anyone associated with Ohio University. It has quietly graced the College Green with its beauty. It has served as a venue for poetry readings, recitals, community events, memorial services, joyful weddings, and solitary reflections. In 1983, a rededication service affirmed its importance in the university's life. In 1997 Jody Phillips, the Galbreaths' daughter and a university trustee, enhanced her father's earlier gift by donating a new 1,200-pipe organ, the J. Wallace and Joan Galbreath Phillips Organ, dedicated "in loving memory of Helen Mauck Galbreath with great admiration for John W. Galbreath."

Monomoy Theatre in Chatham, Massachusetts, and did not abandon plans for an arts building (Seigfred Hall), a new heating plant, and—because of President Baker's commitment to a "live-in" university—a new residential green off Richland Avenue.

Students reacted to these changes in their own ways. The members of Alpha Phi Alpha and Los Amigos worked to reduce discrimination in Athens. Participants in the biennial Religion in Life Week considered the role of religion in everyday life.

Marie White

Marie and Jim White were the first couple to marry in Galbreath Chapel. It was 1958 and only eight days after the chapel's dedication. President Baker walked Marie down the aisle, and Maggie Davis, director of residence services, provided flowers and helped with the reception. Marie was a member of the president's office staff and had been since the day after she earned her Associate of Arts degree in secretarial studies in 1952. Beginning as the receptionist, she stayed to work as secretary and administrative assistant to Presidents Baker, Alden, Sowle, Crewson, and Ping, in a career that spanned forty years.

The first wedding in Galbreath Chapel united Marie and Jim White in June 1958. Ohio University Today, *Summer 1995.*

Marie White credits the university's secretarial department for training her well. She also says her first employer, President Baker, taught her "to be flexible, to respond to whatever came along, and to learn to work with many different types of people."

President Baker returned the compliment: "Marie White quickly became a most important member of my administration, until the last day I was there, and has proved to be the same indispensable person to all four of my successors." The successors agree that her handling of the president's office was exemplary. She offered firm direction for the office staff and, as the first point of contact for faculty, visiting dignitaries, heads of state, and major donors, was invariably calm, poised, and impeccably discreet.

In 1992, Marie White retired and was awarded a Medal of Merit for her long and excellent service to her alma mater. But even after her retirement, she continued serving Ohio University, for in 1994 she was a member of the presidential search committee that recommended Robert Glidden.

There was no mass movement to either the sciences or engineering. Instead, education became the most popular major, enrollment grew most rapidly in the graduate college, and the *Page* (an off-campus initiative) received enough poetry submissions from students (and faculty) to support weekly publication. Lectures by world-renowned figures such as authors Pearl Buck and Robert Frost, physicist and Nobel laureate Dr. C. N. Yang, Assistant Secretary of State Francis Wilcox, Ambassador to Germany James B. Conant, U.N. Secretary General Dag Hammarskjöld, and civil rights leader Martin Luther King Jr. provided a variety of perspectives on the world. Politically, most Ohio University students remained staunchly Republican. They voted for Eisenhower in their mock elections of 1956 and, although

President Baker on Nigerian television, following the presentation in March 1960 of the first Ohio University degrees to Nigerian students. *Left to right:* President Baker; alumnus J.A.F. Sokoya; Peter Proudman, head of WNTV; alumnus A.T.O. Odunsi; and F. N. Hamelin, dean of Ohio University's College of Education. *Courtesy Mahn Center.*

U.N. Secretary General Dag Hammarskjöld talked with students on a visit to O.U. in 1961. *Courtesy Mahn Center.*

some 5,000 cheered Senator John Kennedy as he campaigned in Athens in 1959, the majority of eligible voters supported Nixon in 1960.

Formal dances, with big bands like Woody Herman's, still brought young women in evening gowns of tulle and lace out on the arms of clean-cut young men bearing corsages. Groups like Dave Brubeck, Fred Waring, The Four Freshmen, Count Basie, Duke Ellington, and Louis Armstrong played in Mem Aud to full houses. Even Concerts under the Elms by their own symphonic band were well attended by Ohio University students. They did not appear to be adversely influenced by Bill Haley, Elvis Presley, or Little Richard.

The president and his staff worried, however, about the amount of time and energy Ohio University students lavished on extracurricular events. Though many of the events (such as Circle K's 1959 Jazz Concert) raised money for worthwhile causes, there was a strong move after 1956 to curtail the number of events. The Orange Riot of 1958 provided evidence that the efforts were doomed to fail.

The Orange Riot, which drew national media attention, began innocently

Left: Martin Luther King Jr. at the Ecumenical Conference, Baker Center, December 1959. *Below:* Buses arriving for the conference. *Courtesy Mahn Center.*

enough. According to Jerry Barnett and Barbara Amos Rebok, it started on the East Green when a couple of boys began to toss the oranges served at Sunday night supper. Gradually, more and more people joined the fun until a two-man ballgame became a minor war. When campus police put an end to the battle, the East Green gang was miffed. They, and many of their friends, gathered on the corner of College and Union. Soon there were from three to five thousand students milling about. At that point, Barnett, ARD of Read Hall, and student council president George Voinovich got a bullhorn from the Athens police, stood on the steps of Baker Center, and "made a pronouncement to the roaming hordes to cease" their ridiculous behavior. The crowd, however, paid no attention and headed off to various women's dorms to urge the only coeds still indoors to toss out their underwear. Hours later, the good-natured crowd finally dispersed, and the weary police went home.

Left: Senator John F. Kennedy campaigned in Athens in 1959. *Courtesy Mahn Center.*

Below: Pearl Buck, author of more than seventy books and winner of the 1938 Nobel Prize in literature, spoke on campus in 1961. *Courtesy* Athena Yearbook, *1961.*

By 1959 the administration's concerns about student activities extended to drinking. St. Patrick's Day Weekend was getting out of hand as students invited friends from other colleges to join them

SEE AND HEAR!

U. S. SENATOR
JOHN F. KENNEDY
AT
Ohio University Student Center
FRIDAY, SEPT. 18, 1959
9:00 P. M.
On Steps At Main Entrance of Student Center
Open to Public

The Military Ball. *Courtesy* Athena Yearbook, *1955.*

in Athens and spend a day and night drinking green beer in local bars.

On a happier note, a generous gift from Trustee Edwin L. Kennedy and his wife, Ruth, both alumni, funded the Distinguished Professor awards to recognize faculty members whose outstanding research brought distinction to the university.

A year later, a team of Ohio University faculty members traveled to Cambodia to consider establishing a technical institute there. The Portsmouth campus opened its first official building and added daytime classes to its schedule of evening courses. The university and the city of Athens applied for urban renewal funds to purchase Richland Avenue properties and construct a West Green. Faculty members from several departments planned to publish a humanities journal, the *Ohio University Review,* and Edwin and Ruth Kennedy endowed the Kennedy Lecture Series. President Baker saw the Ohio University football team defeat rival Miami for the first time since 1942.

At the end of 1961, John Baker retired. During his sixteen years in Athens, enrollment had quadrupled. His greatest challenge had been to expand the university's facilities and continually revamp its programs to meet the changing needs of a growing student body while maintaining, or even enhancing, quality. He had overseen construction of fourteen dormitories, a classroom building for each college, a student center, a health center, a physical education center, an ice arena, a natatorium, and housing for married students. He had seen a shift from humanities, to the sciences, to

George Voinovich *(second from right),* '58, was active in campus affairs during his student days and as a senior was president of the student council. Since then, he has enjoyed a distinguished career in public service and an immense popularity in Ohio. Before becoming governor in 1990, he held a series of elective posts, including Ohio assistant attorney general, state representative, lieutenant governor, and mayor of Cleveland. In 1994 he was reelected governor, capturing 72 percent of the vote. He was elected to the U.S. Senate in 1998. *Courtesy* Athena Yearbook, *1958.*

The Bobcat

In 1925 the athletic board, tired of having Ohio athletic teams known as the "nameless wonders" or "the green and white," sponsored a contest and offered a prize—ten dollars—for the name that "best exemplified the fighting spirit of Ohio University." Hal H. Rowland entered the name "Bobcat" and won.

It took thirty-five years for a Bobcat mascot to appear. In 1960 the men of Lincoln Hall were hesitant to enter the Homecoming float competition because, as Tom Schantz said, "We just didn't have the time or know-how. Yet we wanted to donate something permanent to the University—something that would last." They decided to bring the Bobcat to life. Schantz, a fine arts major, created patterns for a papier-mâché head and for pants and gloves. Companies in Philadelphia agreed to make the pants, the gloves, and a hand-knit oversized sweater. (The colors were green and white, of course, because student preference prevailed over the trustees' choice of gray and blue.)

After discovering how hard it would be to have a head made in the U.S., the enterprising men of Lincoln had one constructed in France. Total cost, including long-distance phone calls: $250. The costume was hot—and small. No one taller than 5' 11" could wear it. Dan Nichols, another Lincoln Hall resident, was the first Bobcat, joining the cheerleading squad as a spirit builder and setting a longstanding tradition of choosing the Bobcat from among the men of Lincoln Hall.

In 1968 a Howard Hall project sent Bobkitten Francesca Femia to cheer beside the Bobcat, but now the members of Chi Omega bring her out only occasionally, and not as an official member of the cheerleading squad.

Since 1996, women as well as men have been auditioning for the role of Bobcat and often winning the chance to chase off intruders in Bobcat territory, gyrate with the band, and send kisses to the crowds. No matter how the mascot's suit is restyled or who wears it, the wily Bobcat is one of Ohio University's most popular ambassadors.

Mr. Bobcat came to life in 1960, thanks to the men of Lincoln Hall. *Courtesy Mahn Center.*

From 1968 through the '70s the Bobcat often made appearances with the Bobkitten. *Courtesy Mahn Center.*

The Ohio University Bobcat, circa 2002. *Courtesy University Photographer's Office.*

Acacia fraternity members try to set a record for cramming a VW bug. *Courtesy Carole V. Hebert, '61.*

Hula hoops created another new fad. *Courtesy Barbara Kimberly Olson, '60.*

business and education. He had pushed for creation of Ph.D. programs, for a more research-oriented faculty, and for private funding. President Baker involved the university in service to the region through branch campuses, an airport, and an expansion of radio services. His interest in international affairs had fostered connections with other countries and encouraged Ohio University students to look beyond their comfortable local world. John Baker's efforts had contributed to making Ohio University "a place of beauty, a home of freedom, a source of wisdom, and an institution of excellence." It would be up to Vernon Roger Alden, the university's next president, to manage the challenges that would come quickly during the '60s.

Trustee Edwin L. Kennedy, '26, and his wife, Ruth, '30, established the John C. Baker Fund in 1962 to provide Distinguished Professor Awards, Baker Fund Awards, and the Kennedy Lecture series. Their gift of southwest Native American art became the impetus for the Edwin L. and Ruth E. Kennedy Museum of Art at the Ridges in the 1990s. *Courtesy Mahn Center.*

Change, Confrontation, and Crisis

1961–1974

> More than any other period in our history, it is essential for
> all of us to understand the components of change. We must
> prepare to manage change; otherwise change will manage us.
> —*Vernon Roger Alden*

In 1962 the nation's youngest elected president, John F. Kennedy, was in the White House. He spoke confidently of a New Frontier and sent men into space; he worried about the spread of communism into Southeast Asia and ordered Green Berets to Vietnam; he challenged a new generation of Americans to ask what they could do for their country and created a Peace Corps. In the South, Martin Luther King Jr. and James Farmer preached nonviolence and pushed for desegregation and civil rights. The children of World War II veterans—the baby boomers—filled out college applications and danced the Twist. The federal Food and Drug Administration approved a birth control pill.

But despite these changes in technology, foreign policy, race relations, demography, and mores, the early '60s in isolated Athens were barely distinguishable from the idyllic '50s. Student life was still ruled by traditional attitudes. On most evenings, coeds were locked into their dorms at an early hour. Each spring and fall, they and their male cohorts dedicated weeks to building floats, practicing skits, and arranging dances for Homecoming and J-Prom. The unexplainable tradition of exuberant seasonal riots—such as

In the early '60s, Homecoming was a popular event. *Courtesy* Athena Yearbook, *1963.*

A coed competing in the popular Greek Games. *Courtesy* Athena Yearbook, *1964.*

the Orange Riot of 1958—continued. Each spring, St. Patrick's Day celebrants, some from as far away as California, poured into town (now called the Fort Lauderdale of Ohio). Ohio University had acquired the reputation of a party school.

However, there were occasional glimpses of a new sensibility. Jane Woodrow, '66, remembers an early '60s Homecoming where "competition to have the best float was high. The elaborate parade, featuring a queen and court, was almost over when two students in scruffy clothes joined it. Their 'float' was a child's rusted red wagon full of straggly corn shucks." Jane felt she had seen a small sign of rebellion against the '50s.

In 1962 Ohio University inaugurated its fifteenth president, thirty-nine-year-old Vernon Roger Alden, who was planning ambitious changes for the 158-year-old institution, its students and faculty, and even its southeast Ohio home. He held an MBA from the Harvard Business School and had served as associate dean of the school, where he co-founded an institute at which college and university administrators analyzed their campus problems. With his experience, he felt prepared to lead Ohio University into a "New Frontier" of excellence and national prominence.

Some time in the early morning hours of a day in 1962 I painted the Kissing Circle that was just east of the old library (Chubb Hall). It was a BIG tradition for fraternities and sororities to paint the circle. I believe that I started a tradition by painting the circle for a special person. Soon after I left my message to Sandy, others chose to follow my lead.

—Ray Asik, '63

The Kissing Circle on the College Green. *Courtesy Sandra Kovanes Asik, '65, and Raymond Asik, '63.*

At the beginning of Alden's tenure, Ohio University's annual budget stood at $12.9 million. There were 399 permanent faculty members and 13,600 students—9,600 in Athens and another 4,000 at the branches. Enrollment was expected to climb to 26,000 within a decade, and this enormous change would necessitate a larger faculty, new programs and buildings, and a broader funding base. President Alden intended not only to provide these essentials but to attract better students—"innovative doers"—and faculty whose work would enhance the school's academic reputation. Further, he hoped to provide roads, hospitals, and desperately needed flood control and to encourage tourism and research-oriented industry for the region.

Over the next few years, the president pursued his agenda with energy and enthusiasm. In his inaugural address, he began the push for academic excellence by stating the most important task of his administration: creating "a climate in which the best minds are stretched and superior students aspire to even greater accomplishment." He announced plans for an honors college, a substantial new library, more doctoral programs, and sabbaticals and travel to revitalize the faculty.

Though the university was obliged to accept all qualified Ohio high school graduates, President Alden initiated a selective admissions policy for the fall of 1962: the best students would be admitted in the fall, the less prepared would be deferred until second semester, and out-of-state admissions would be held below 20 percent. The president urged students to limit their extracurricular activities and help their housing units win one of six scholarship trophies. To cut down on disruptions and bad press, he approved a new policy that banned dorm guests on St. Patrick's Day weekend.

In the fall of 1964, when enrollment increased 28 percent, the Honors College, under the direction of Professor Samuel Jasper, admitted twenty-three students. Soon after, the innovative Ohio Plan offered a few carefully

Coming from a family that had no experience of college, I'd decided to attend Ohio University mostly because a friend's older brother went there. I signed up without ever having laid eyes on the place. Getting in wasn't a problem. In those days, O.U.'s open admissions policy gave entry to anyone with a diploma from an Ohio high school. Many of us were from blue-collar ethnic families nourished by the factories of such places as Cleveland, Youngstown and Steubenville, my hometown.

O.U. was an ordinary state school. During my time there it was in tremendous disarray as it swelled to embrace the ballooning student body. The lovely old core campus was ringed by construction sites. Students had to be tripled in dorm rooms. Almost every spring the Hocking River added to the chaos by flooding large sections of the campus. But to me the place was magic. Compared to the sooty steel town where I'd grown up, the core College Green, with its towering oaks and sycamores and red neo-Georgian brick building with white steeples, was a dream of beauty.

There was plenty of intellect around for the likes of me. Even freshmen had access to full professors such as Carl Gustavson, chairman of the history department. My God, here was a place where the plays of Samuel Beckett were performed. A place with people who could speak knowledgeably of Malthus and Mill, Heidegger and Hegel, Whitman and Waugh. These names were not exactly on everyone's lips in Steubenville. . . . Ohio University cracked open the door of my mind as widely as middling hinges would allow. It harrowed my interest in things vastly beyond my personal experience and instilled in me a yearning to prove, to myself as much as anyone else, that I could function in a much larger world.

—James Ricci, '67,
from an article in OHIO UNIVERSITY TODAY, Summer 1992

selected students a chance to discuss significant issues with distinguished leaders from around the country, and the English department added thirty sections of an advanced freshman English course.

Although students, or at least *Post* writers, said the new president's attempt to replace the nickname "O.U." with "Ohio University" or "Ohio" was "absurd," they described him as friendly, open, and willing to talk to them. A year after his arrival, they reported that standards were toughening up and both the "party school" label and "Mickey Mouse" courses were "fast disappearing." They were impressed when he was interviewed on national television programs and praised in *Life* magazine and *U.S. News & World Report.*

Typical O.U. students were still more likely to protest the administration's removal of Delt pole-sitters than the war in Vietnam. However, they occasionally took up causes. They applauded President Alden's defense of freedom of speech on college campuses. As the country reeled from the assassination of President John Kennedy, 2,800 of them petitioned to have a building named in his honor. The Young Democrats took complete charge of bringing students from more than a hundred nations to a two-day mock United Nations. In general, there was greater awareness of the issue of civil rights. As the administration actively recruited African American students, their numbers rose to several hundred. Dorm rooms were integrated, a few students joined southern civil rights marches, and discussions of campus and community discrimination became more frequent. In a special 1963 issue, the *Post,* now the state's top-rated college newspaper, devoted six pages to civil rights, saying, "We feel the civil rights issue is the most significant story of the times in America today." However, several *Post* stories also noted a high degree of self-segregation and what E. Curmie Price, the one African American member of the faculty, called a "conspicuous lack of communication between Negro and white students."

When President Lyndon Baines Johnson visited Athens in 1964, most of the thousands who crowded the Green were students, and they shouted their support when he asked them to create a "Great Society" with basic rights for all Americans. Movement toward this goal was slow, even on a campus that seemed sympathetic, and by the end of the decade Ohio University's black students would grow tired of waiting and demand attention to their needs.

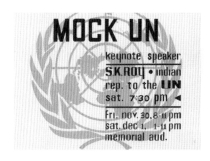

In 1962 the Young Democrats organized a two-day mock United Nations that brought student delegates from more than a hundred countries. *Courtesy Mahn Center.*

The Alden administration actively recruited African American students in the early '60s. *Courtesy* Athena Yearbook, *1966.*

One of the things about O.U., being a minority, we all just kind of bonded together. I was just going some place and walking with someone, and I didn't speak to another black student. And they said, "Debbie, you didn't speak." And I said, "I don't know him." And they said, "Hey, if it's black and it walks, you speak." So we kind of narrowed down the size of the campus just by bonding together. There were no more than 500 black students on the whole campus, and probably by the end of the first year, you knew just about everybody.

—Debbie Carol Long, '68

President Lyndon Baines Johnson announced his plan for a "Great Society" on a visit to Ohio University in May 1964. *Courtesy Mahn Center.*

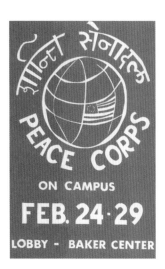

Poster announcing a campus Peace Corps meeting. *Courtesy Mahn Center.*

As students began to question their world, the faculty was modernizing the curriculum. The new school of architecture, in the recently completed art building, admitted its first class. English, clinical and counseling psychology, and fine arts (later comparative arts) welcomed their first doctoral students; the fine arts degree, which combined several areas of the arts into a broad program, was called "unique in American education and one of the most promising." Meanwhile, the colleges of applied science and commerce became the College of Engineering and Technology and the College of Business Administration.

The university's international connections were also expanding. The success of the teacher training center in western Nigeria brought requests for additional programs in eastern and northern Nigeria, as well as in South Vietnam and Cambodia. In early 1962 President Alden signed the first of several contracts with the U.S. government to train Peace Corps volunteers in Athens for service in foreign countries. In June, Sargent Shriver, the director of this idealistic Kennedy administration venture, greeted volunteers from around the country and congratulated them for choosing Ohio University's program, which was unique in administering its own programs in the field and allowing volunteers to earn academic credit during their service.

The faculty's increased research efforts also gained attention, with the department of electrical engineering leading the way. Dr. Roger Quisenberry's team of engineers and physicists joined the space age with highly acclaimed work on leak detection in Saturn and Apollo missiles. A satellite tracking station operated on Radar Hill on the old asylum grounds. One

President Vernon Roger Alden *(left)* with Sargent Shriver, director of the newly organized Peace Corps, who announced a Peace Corps Training Center at Ohio University. *Courtesy Mahn Center.*

CHANGE, CONFRONTATION, AND CRISIS

JUNE '62: I have won a Fulbright Scholarship at Ohio University! The Americans in Vienna for whom I have been babysitting say, "You are lucky! O.U. is a good school!"

SEP. '62: After a one-week boat trip, a couple of days in New York, and a tiring train ride to Athens I have arrived! I explore my new environs: Voigt Hall, my classrooms, the library, the R.C. church, Galbreath Chapel. . . . And there are so many lovely and friendly people. None of my teachers in Austria ever invited me to their homes. Here they do, and this creates a wonderful relationship between them and their students. In April '63 the Hocking floods the lower parts of Athens and Prof. Hultgren's private library. Those of us who have time, run there to help.

There is a large cultural offering at O.U. My friends and I watch old movies, listen to chamber music, take part in the Mock United Nations, admire Helen Hayes. I myself have joined the Chorus.

Sometimes I go window-shopping. Of all those wonderful things I see I can only afford toothpaste and soap. The pocket money my parents gave me "for America," which was an awful lot for them, is worth nothing here. America: Sugar candy mountain for the Americans—but not for me. Yet, there are so many things that cost nothing: the wonderful friendship of so many people, the beautiful countryside of Ohio, studying in the library, the smell of popcorn (unknown in Austria in those times), and especially my deep feeling of gratitude toward all those people who contributed to my scholarship.

JULY '63: Back to Austria . . . and an incurable homesickness for Athens.

—Gerlinde Follrich de Aguinaga, '63

hundred physicists attended a local conference on high-energy particles. During 1963, the faculty's research output exceeded that of any preceding year, despite heavy undergraduate teaching loads and relatively low salaries.

In 1963 the Ohio University Press, which had published two celebratory books during President Baker's administration, was formalized to provide an outlet for faculty work and to enhance the institution's reputation. Cecil Hemley, co-founder of Noonday Press, was chosen as editor, and Professor Taylor Culbert became director. Supportive alumni endowed three professorships: the O'Bleness Professorship in Economics, the Robert Morton Professorship in Mathematics, and the Rush Elliott Professorship in Anatomy (funded by his former pre-med

Ohio University extended its international connections with a program in South Vietnam in the early '60s. *Courtesy Mahn Center.*

A satellite tracking station on Radar Hill, the gift of Standard Oil of Ohio in 1965, expanded university scientists' involvement in the space age. *Courtesy Mahn Center.*

Cecil Hemley became the first editor of Ohio University Press. *Courtesy Mahn Center.*

The first editorial board of Ohio University Press: *(left to right, standing)* William U. Snyder, Claude E. Kantner, Donald C. Darnton, John F. Cady, George E. Hill, *(seated)* Paul M. Kendall, Carl L. Shermer, Taylor Culbert, Edward Stone, and William D. Huntsman. *Courtesy Mahn Center.*

students). In 1964 President Alden asked the board of trustees to replace the faculty advisory council, initiated by President James, with a faculty senate. The board cautiously agreed. The new senate, with a constitution and a handbook that defined faculty members' contracts with the university as well as their role in its governance, was unique in the state. It gave the faculty a stronger voice, which was soon raised to protest a number of the administration's decisions.

During this time, students were pouring in. In 1965 the freshman class alone totaled over 5,000 students, so new facilities were a high priority. President Alden was, as he said, "fearless" in asking the legislature to fund Ohio University's capital needs—among them a dormitory complex on a new South Green. The Ohio University Fund bought almost a million dollars' worth of property along Richland Avenue, and the state transferred 216 acres to the university from the old asylum grounds. As the West Green dorm project neared completion, a new engineering complex began. Private investors added the Ohio University Inn, Lakeview Manor Apartments, Monticello Apartments, and Bromley Hall. The new library, promised as a first priority, was delayed.

Plans for the development of southeast Ohio moved ahead quickly. President Alden wanted to change both the image and condition of this isolated area and intended Ohio University to take the lead in spurring its economic development. In the earliest days of his administration, he persuaded 450 leaders from surrounding communities to work together for improved roads, medical care, tourism, flood control, and a healthier economy. Within a year, Vice President for Development Martin Hecht announced grants from the Area Redevelopment Administration. Soon after, the city of Athens received an urban planning assis-

CHANGE, CONFRONTATION, AND CRISIS

tance grant and the university received more than one million dollars to develop a new South Green. In 1964, the Institute for Regional Development began working with 150 community groups and set a national precedent in its transformation of a twenty-one-county area in southeastern Ohio. Two years later the Office of Economic Development funded a Center of Economic Development at Ohio University. In the middle of these exciting developments, President Alden was called to Washington and invited to participate in developing the Job Corps, a part of Lyndon Johnson's War on Poverty. For several months, he spent two or three days a week meeting with business leaders and academicians around the country, arranging job training centers for urban youth and publicizing Ohio University.

These years were an exciting "up" time. Departments added new faculty almost as quickly as they could find them; a big department like English, for example, might add more than ten new members a year. The town was

Faculty Senate

On November 23, 1964, the *Post*'s lead article read: "President announces new Faculty Senate." In the story that followed, President Vernon Alden announced that the university's board of trustees had recognized the need for faculty participation in university affairs by unanimously approving a constitution for a faculty senate.

Previously the faculty had participated in university governance through a variety of largely advisory organizations. During most of the nineteenth century, the university's few professors met with the president each week to discuss academic matters. By 1896 the faculty had grown, and professors assigned the heads of the fourteen departments to vote on academic matters. In 1920 a chapter of the American Association of University Professors, with Professor William Bentley as chair, became a vehicle for faculty participation. Then, during President James's administration, a budget crisis led him to suggest a more efficient way for faculty to help establish university policy. The result was the Faculty Advisory Council (FAC), organized in January 1937, with Professor Gaige Paulsen as its first chair.

President James and his successor, John Baker, emphasized the advisory nature of the FAC, but the creation of Faculty Senate gave faculty a formal role in university governance. The board's action also recognized the *Faculty Handbook*—with its provisions for protecting academic freedom and tenure—as part of the contract of the faculty with the university and agreed that any changes to it must be initiated by Faculty Senate.

Professor Robert Morton prepared a strong constitution, and bylaws written over the summer of 1965 established election procedures and a committee structure that is still in use. President Alden and Provost Tom Smith also began a practice that is still current by meeting with the senate each month during the academic year to report on the status of the university and take questions from senators.

The members of the senate indicated at the outset that they intended to play more than a "housekeeping role" in university governance. Over the years, they have participated actively in decisions facing the institution, including budget allocations and, especially, curricular matters. The senators have created a useful partnership with the administration and helped to further academic excellence. Faculty Senate's role in Ohio University's governance is recognized by outside observers as one of the strongest faculty voices in any public institution.

From the students one hears that Professor Rush Elliott is a Master Teacher.

From the successful physicians and dentists all over the country one hears that it was the influence and guidance of Rush Elliott that carried them to medical school and supported them through the demanding and difficult curriculum.

From medical school admissions officers one hears that . . . Rush Elliott, with his drive and special interest, has made Ohio University one of the leading pre-professional schools in the nation.

From hundreds of Ohio alumni one hears that it was from Rush Elliott that they acquired their inspiration toward scholarly achievement and their motivation toward a more fruitful life.

—From the announcement of the Rush Elliott Professorship, endowed by his former students, 1966

Professor of Anatomy Rush Elliott.
Courtesy Mahn Center.

Through the Institute for Regional Development, community leaders of twenty-one southeast Ohio counties worked to improve the area. *Courtesy Mahn Center.*

overflowing, and housing was scarce to nonexistent. Faculty spouses such as Marjorie Stone took on the job of searching for places for new faculty members to live, sometimes reading obituaries or following moving vans around the town, hoping to find a house that someone was leaving. Graduate students had to take what they could find. Royce Woosley recalls coming to Athens in 1962 and moving into a small house equipped with a coal-fired furnace but without a source of potable water. He and his wife collected water from the roof for bathing and carried water from the chemistry building for cooking and drinking.

By 1965 the university's annual budget was $28 million. Further improvements to the Athens and branch campuses and more new doctoral programs were in place or being planned. Faculty salaries and fringe benefits had improved markedly, and the university's athletes had won the Mid-American All Sports Trophy three years in a row.

In spite of these successes, the mood of the campus was changing. One group after another seemed to catch the revolutionary spirit of the times and protest the status quo. A student's letter to the *Post* questioned the

Avionics

In the 1960s, it was becoming clear that the reliability and
capability of the nation's aircraft fleet were increasingly
dependent on its electronic equipment—in today's lexicon
called avionics. In 1962 Ohio University addressed this
outside need for increased capability in both landing and
horizontal navigation by blending the talents and experience
of personnel in aviation and electrical engineering to
address critical problems. It also saw this technical area as
one that would justify a Ph.D. program in the Department
of Electrical Engineering.

 Some of the technical issues to be addressed related to
adverse effects of undesirable environments on navigation
performance. Ideally, navigation paths are straight lines, but
in practice these paths are corrupted by signals reflecting
from objects such as nearby hills and buildings. Early problems related to everyday factors such as snowfall and trees.

 Ohio University, surrounded by hills and trees, was the
ideal place to bring students into the quest for solutions.
Graduate students, in particular, needed challenging technical
problems for their theses and dissertations. The university
sorely needed sponsors for the production of major technical papers, such as
dissertations, because experience had shown that in the avionics field it cost about
$100,000 to get a dissertation produced. The federal government was willing to fund
such efforts simply because it got at least that value in technical product and the
additional byproduct of a well-trained prospective employee.

 Initial success was due in large part to cooperation from the
Ohio University administration, which provided funding—some
from the Stocker Endowment—for basic lab equipment, an aircraft,
and seed money. A key ingredient also was the assimilation of a
small group, which grew to become the present Avionics Engineering
Center, with distinct talents for creating, marketing, and implementing solutions. Growth, in terms of outside support and technical
personnel involvement, has been steady.

 A national need, an identified university need, and available
resources from the FAA, U.S. Army, U.S. Navy, NASA, and industry
allowed the Avionics Engineering Center to develop, prosper, and
grow to significantly serve society by improving air transportation
and flight capability.

Electrical engineer
Richard McFarland of the
Department of Avionics.
Courtesy Mahn Center.

An ad for the new aviation department's
flight training course, the first in the
country to be offered under the G.I. Bill.
Ohio Alumnus, April 1945. *Courtesy Mahn
Center.*

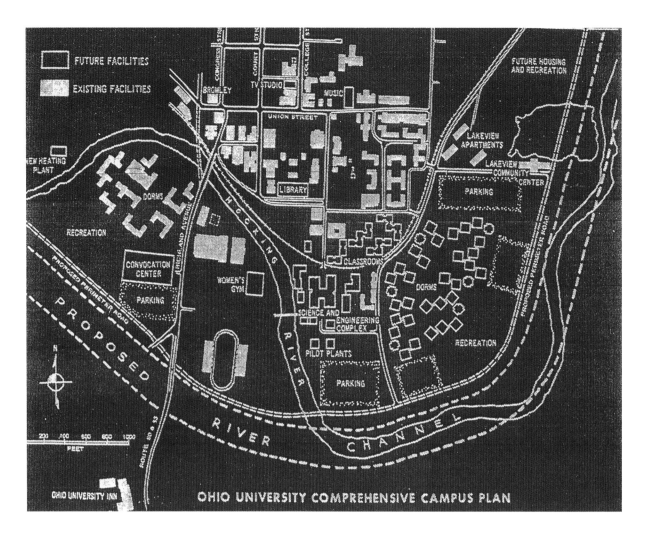

A Comprehensive Plan
of the campus, early '60s.
Courtesy Mahn Center.

Bob Wren, 1965 Coach of the
Year. *Courtesy Mahn Center.*

rapid rise in the number of administrative positions. Previous presidents had functioned with small administrative staffs, but President Alden created new positions and brought in a sort of "think-tank" of young Ivy League graduates—known as the "Upper-Tupper" group (because their offices were in Tupper Hall). By 1964 students complained that "every day a new policy is levied that encroaches on our freedom" and railed against the "paternalistic" policy that required them to live in approved housing until age twenty-three. Although the age was lowered to twenty-two on the advice of a faculty committee, the issues of approved housing and women's restricted hours represented a growing generation gap.

Faculty concerns focused on the lack of adequate housing and medical services in the area, the continual

CHANGE, CONFRONTATION, AND CRISIS

Left, above: Track star Elmore Banton later became the university's first African American coach. *Courtesy Mahn Center.*

Right, above: Soccer competition.
Courtesy Athena Yearbook, 1962.

Left: Basketball coach Jim Snyder.
Courtesy Athena Yearbook, 1967.

Below: A Bobcat cheerleader.
Courtesy Athena Yearbook, 1964.

inefficiencies in registering students for classes, and class closeouts. In 1965 the announcement of plans for a 14,000-seat convocation center—dubbed "Stonehenge" by some faculty members—reminded them of the president's early promise to build a library to support the rapidly growing graduate programs and the frequent announcements that the project was delayed.

In an effort to exercise more control over the university's direction, the faculty senate adopted a resolution requesting the administration and board of trustees to reconsider the decision to allocate funds to a convocation center when other needs were more pressing. However, President Alden declined to submit the resolution to the board, and the project was approved.

My favorite professor was Abraham Clearfield, who taught chemistry. I took his freshman-level course and can remember going in to complain to him that I only got a 98 on the exam instead of 100. He very gently reminded me that no one was perfect. I ended up working for him one summer, doing research on titanium. It was a wonderful experience in spite of almost burning myself up in one of the experiments.

—Vicki Whitacre, '67

Acclaimed pianist George Katz was an artist in residence in the music school in the mid-1960s. *Courtesy Cheryl K. Sinz.*

David L. Hostetler, '49, is a renowned sculptor and carver and former O.U. professor whose bronze and wooden representations of the American woman are displayed in the university's Wolfe Garden and in Alden Library. *Courtesy Mahn Center.*

I had dreamed of becoming a piano student at Ohio University. But Professor George Katz, internationally acclaimed pianist and O.U.'s artist in residence, interrupted my audition after only a few minutes. "You certainly need more than half-hour lessons; you definitely need one hour a week. But I'd be happy to help you if you're willing to put the time into it."

I was in! And I was tremendously motivated by Professor Katz's vote of confidence and by his trademark enthusiasm. He had a tremendous knowledge of piano literature plus the ability to prescribe just the right compositions to challenge me. . . . Today in my own piano studio, I take great pride in the way I teach. But then, I had the consummate example.

—Cheryl Kimes Sinz, '66

Unfortunately, a $1 million gift designated for the building did not materialize, and as the prosperity of the 1960s collapsed into a recession in the 1970s, the debt on the building would become a debilitating burden.

The following fall, the faculty spoke out again when President Alden announced that the Ohio Board of Regents (the state's new higher education planning agency) had asked all state universities to change from the semester system to the quarter system, effective in fall 1967. The president thought the change would not only make better use of facilities but "require every faculty member to redo his course," thus "freshening up the whole academic environment." The *Post,* however, reported that students and faculty alike felt left out of the discussion.

The faculty had already studied alternatives to semesters and rejected them. Most faculty members thought quarters would create even more crowded classrooms, and they resented the unilateral decision by the board of regents. In October 1966, the faculty senate adopted a formal resolution protesting the

Faculty protests switch by Regents to quarters

Many faculty members opposed the change from semesters to quarters. *Post, October 11, 1966.*

I taught the large classes of Intro. Psych in Memorial Auditorium a total of four times. Each class had a total of approximately 3,000 students; over 2,000 typically took it at 1:00 and slightly more than 1,000 took it at 2:00. Memorial Auditorium in those days had dim lighting, a poor sound system, and, of course, no writing tables attached to the seats. In spite of these difficult physical conditions, attendance was excellent, and the course generally was a success, in large part because of the outstanding graduate students who taught the weekly "small group lectures" and because of the good humor of students taking the class. (Remember, this was in the late '60s and early '70s when protesting was a well-practiced activity on all campuses.)

On one occasion, as 3,000 students filed out of their dorms and headed toward the Convo together to take their exams, one student with a perceptive sense of humor pointed speakers out of a window above the front entrance, turned up the volume full blast, and played the whistling theme from The Bridge on the River Kwai. Hearing the "Colonel Bogey March" probably didn't make the exam any easier, but everyone did enter the Convo smiling.

I want to thank all of you who are alumni of the largest classes ever taught at Ohio University. Those classes were hard work under difficult conditions, but your good humor, plus a desire to learn and perform well, made the special effort worth it. Thanks to you, I enjoyed teaching the classes and look back now with fond memories.

—James Bruning, Provost Emeritus and Trustee Professor, Psychology

Frustrated by crowded classrooms and dorms, students staged a protest in 1964. *Courtesy Mahn Center.*

During his years at Ohio University (1962–66), Hungarian-born Joe Eszterhas was one of several dynamic editors of the *Post* who drew attention to student concerns and helped make the campus newspaper the best in the state. The William Randolph Hearst Memorial Foundation named him America's outstanding college journalist. Eszterhas became a star writer at *Rolling Stone* and then one of Hollywood's most successful—and controversial—screenwriters. Included among his best-known films are *Showgirls*, *Flashdance*, *Basic Instinct*, *Jade*, and *Sliver*.

Courtesy Athena Yearbook, *1966.*

decision, arguing that the change from semesters to quarters was based on political, administrative, and financial considerations rather than on academic concerns. A few days later Ohio Board of Regents Chancellor John Millett told the *Post* that he had not yet asked university presidents to change to a different calendar. By the time he did eventually mandate quarters, the dispute had cost President Alden a great deal of goodwill.

On another front, the nonacademic employees decided to try again to improve their working conditions by forming a union. They had made this effort several times between 1943 and 1965, but the trustees had never been willing to meet with them. Their complaints were that the university had no adequate grievance procedures for them, no regularized system for assigning people to job classifications, no system for promotions or rights to bid on jobs, and no regard for seniority. As Ida Stoneburner, a cook, recalls, "No one was paid overtime until the time clocks were installed to make it legal, [and] no one really knew what the pay scale was."

According to Tommy Adkins, who had experience with unions, when

The controversial Convocation Center, completed in 1968.
Courtesy Dan Dry Associates.

CHANGE, CONFRONTATION, AND CRISIS

I started to work in food service October 15, 1957, for $.75 an hour at Edge Hill Cafeteria, an old army barracks building. We fed around 900, with one choice of menu. I wanted to learn all I could, but the older cooks were reluctant to help us since they resented the fact that we got the same $.05 raise that they did, though they had been there longer.

Soon, Edge Hill burned to the ground in the night. But Jefferson Hall was almost complete, so we were reassigned and established in

Cooks in East Green's Jefferson Cafeteria, built in 1957. *Courtesy Ida Mae Stoneburner.*

a new environment. Jefferson was the hub of all workshops and visitors. Companies competing for business put on all kinds of workshops with new cooking techniques to sell their products. We had the Livestock and Meat Board of Chicago, Standard Brands, Procter and Gamble, and others submitting recipes for cooks to try. One of the companies' chefs was John Zinker, who baked President Kennedy's birthday cake. He stayed with us a week and taught us all kinds of cake decorating.

We did all our own food preparation, portioning steak, peeling potatoes, cleaning vegetables. Bakery was fresh from the oven to the food line. Salads were plated individually. Main entrees were cooked in ovens and steamers and put in warmers. We worked until everyone was fed and the kitchen cleaned up—nine hours' work for eight hours' pay, since an hour was taken out for lunch and dinner.

At some of the large summer workshops we often prepared special foods like lobster tails and prime rib. I once cooked 1,000 pounds of prime rib for 1,000 members of a Garden Club Workshop. When students were off between semesters, we shaped up the dining facilities, cleaned ovens, scoured pans, refrigerators, and pan rooms. It was a time to laugh, joke, and vie for the cleanest units.

I'm glad I had the experience.

—Ida Mae Stoneburner

Cooks in Edge Hill Cafeteria, a wooden structure that preceded the modern facilities in Jefferson Hall. *Courtesy Ida Mae Stoneburner.*

When nonacademic workers went out on strike in 1967, they asked for and received strong support from students. *Courtesy* Athena Yearbook, *1967.*

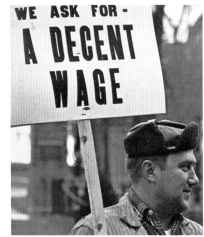

the question of forming a union came up again in 1965, a small group of employees contacted officials of the American Federation of State, County, and Municipal Employees (AFSCME) in Columbus and learned that 75 percent of the 1,300 nonacademic employees needed to sign union cards requesting direct deduction of dues from their wages. Using the campus heat tunnels to keep their activity secret, the organizers gathered signatures. That fall one of their representatives met with President Alden and showed him 500 signed cards and a copy of a 1959 senate bill that gave all Ohio public employees the right to assign part of their earnings to an employee organization. The president did not present the employees' request to the trustees, assuming they would reject the proposal.

When union officials approached the president again about a year later, he cited the advice of legal counsel that a 1947 Ohio Supreme Court decision invalidated payroll deductions for civil service employees. To clarify the ambiguity between the 1959 and 1947 rulings, the Inter-University Council would have to seek the opinion of the state's attorney general, William Saxbe. When the next Inter-University Council meeting adjourned without a decision to seek the attorney general's opinion, Ohio University employees let Alden know they would strike. The next morning —Sunday, March 5—sign-carrying picketers stood in the rain at strategic points around the campus.

The faculty senate called a special meeting and passed a motion urging Alden to seek Attorney General Saxbe's opinion. The student congress, led by Dan DiNicola, quickly voted its support for the striking workers; the *Post* followed suit. President Alden expressed his commitment to keeping the university open and his respect for the workers' right to dissent. However, as the days passed, there was no movement on either side.

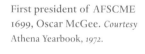

Students left campus for an early spring break because of the 1967 strike. *Courtesy Jessanne Timon Allen, '71.*

Four days into the strike, picketers were at their posts around the clock; they solicited students' support, asking them not to substitute in the kitchens and dining halls. Most construction and deliveries by non-university workers stopped. Striking employees told the media they did not understand Alden's position: "[He] is on all these poverty programs and he has men working for him who live in poverty." Alden responded that, according to his legal counsel, he could not approve the dues check-off. Then, saying the university was "close to a serious state of emergency," he sought a restraining order to prevent further picketing and urged union officials to settle the matter in court.

On March 9, *Post* writer Tom Price confirmed a UPI story that quoted Attorney General Saxbe's personal opinion that the university could approve the dues deductions. Soon after, the trustees set a meeting in Columbus for the following week with the attorney general. On the Friday before the meeting, the president announced that the university would close immediately for an early spring break. Within twenty-four hours, the campus was deserted except for the picketers, who held their ground.

First president of AFSCME 1699, Oscar McGee. *Courtesy Athena Yearbook, 1972.*

When Saxbe reiterated his opinion that the trustees could grant payroll deductions, their executive committee accepted President Alden's recommendation to grant the deductions. Two days later, after negotiations between AFSCME representative Edward Dailey and university officials, nonacademic employees were back at work, and the eleven-day strike was over.

As the university tried to return to normal that summer and fall, it seemed clear that the definition of normal had changed on campuses from coast to coast. Some students were accepting Professor Timothy Leary's message to drop out and get high to the music of The Doors, Jimi Hendrix, and Janis Joplin. Others, galvanized by nightly television reports of death and destruction in Vietnam and race riots in Watts, Atlanta, Chicago, and Detroit, joined organized protests around the country, only to be beaten by police and chastised by the government. Young people around the country turned their growing frustration on their increasingly impersonal universities.

At Ohio University, *Post* reporter Clarence Page had already explained Black Power. Now, Joel Forrester explained Student Power. Many of the student "doers" President Alden had recruited said student power did not exist on their campus. Though they volunteered responsibly for the Children's Home, the Mental Health Center, and President Johnson's War on Poverty and challenged Mayor Shephard to examine discrimination in local housing, they were treated like children and excluded from decisions that affected them. They were kept in the dark about how the university spent their student fees and seen as computer digits rather than individuals. *Post* writer Tom Price said Ohio University students should stop asking what they *could* do and tell the administration what they *would* do.

The administration was hardly unaware of this growing disaffection or the need to address it. By the spring of 1968, committees were planning ways to maintain a sense of community, liberalize and broaden the curriculum, and answer both faculty and student questions about the school's budget and priorities. Residence life staff focused on making each green a personalized "student community" where smaller groups could connect. Provost Thomas Smith proposed eliminating a number of university requirements, including the practice of requiring students to spend a year in University College, and the faculty considered pass/fail grading. The College of Communication and the School of Theater were created. The English department boasted a new program in creative writing that included Hollis Summers, Jack Matthews, James Norman Schmidt, Walter Tevis, author of *The Hustler* (made into a movie starring Paul Newman), and Daniel Keyes, whose novel *Flowers for Algernon* was the basis for the movie *Charly*. President Alden convinced the legislature to equalize its appropriations to state universities, and

My father was a janitor and my mother was a cook. I was a cold war baby who was pretty aware of events of the times: My high school was integrated. Had about 500 black students out of 2,400. JFK's assassination happened in my junior year of high school. The Beatles were on the Ed Sullivan show; there was the Berkeley free speech movement and the Mississippi freedom summer.

I was looking at O.U. (1965) because it offered five phases of journalism and it had an independent paper rather than a lab paper. There were about 400-500 black students out of 15,000 at O.U. We drove over on a Sunday and I fell in love with the place. I was used to a small town. I also didn't limit myself to any one group. I became a Postie-Toastie as soon as they would let me. They had to run me off. I was devoted to it.

I remember the demands thing—the storming of Cutler and the big rally in front of the place. It was probably caused by a number of things. At Cornell students had taken over a building with rifles. There were over 400 race riots around the country—Cleveland, Dayton, Cincinnati—while I was at O.U. Johnson's War on Poverty, Black Pride, Black Power, Black Is Beautiful were in the air. . . . Those were exciting times. We gave Blacks a chance to say: "We are here."

—Clarence Page, '69

Clarence Page, '69, began his journalism career as a high school student with stints at the *Middletown Journal* and the *Cincinnati Enquirer* and became a regular fixture in the *Post* newsroom during his days at Ohio University. After completing his degree, he began work at the *Chicago Tribune* and was part of a *Tribune* task force series on vote fraud that won a Pulitzer in 1972. In 1987, his column was syndicated; in 1989, he was honored with a Pulitzer of his own. Since then he has appeared regularly on several television news shows, offered biweekly commentary on National Public Radio, and continued publishing his prize-winning syndicated news column.

Courtesy Athena Yearbook, *1967.*

Simon and Garfunkel in performance at Ohio University.
Courtesy Mahn Center.

for the first time Ohio University and its sister institutions could expect per-student subsidies equal to Ohio State's. However, a Priorities Committee was questioning the administration's spending plans.

In April all local changes were overshadowed by dramatic national events. First, President Johnson, beset by criticism of the war, announced that he would not run for reelection. Only a few days later, civil rights leader Martin Luther King Jr. was brutally murdered in Memphis. As the campus reacted to news of King's death, President Alden addressed the university community at a mass meeting. Afterward, two hundred grieving students and faculty members staged a sit-in at the corner of Court and Union Streets. When police threatened to move them by force, only the intervention of Vice President James Whalen and a quiet discussion of future action by student leader James Steele averted a riot.

A "sit-in" at Court and Union followed a memorial tribute to Dr. Martin Luther King Jr. Athens Messenger, *April 7, 1968.*

A month later, a riot did erupt in very different circumstances. In this case, the trigger was the decision of the year-old nonacademic employees' union (1699 of AFSCME) *not* to strike. When students realized on the night of May 19 that the strike they had expected to close the school and send them home early would not materialize, some began a good-natured protest. East Green residents gathered friends

College of Communication

In 1968 the College of Communication was created by merging the School of Journalism, formerly housed in the College of Business, and the areas of public address, radio-TV, and hearing and speech sciences from the College of Fine Arts. Such restructuring was occurring at other universities and combining these areas of common interest promised to produce stronger undergraduate programs and an expanded Ph.D. program at Ohio University.

The former director of McGraw-Hill World News, John Wilhelm, who had recently come to Ohio University as director of the School of Journalism, became the college's first dean. Claude Kantner, former director of the School of Dramatic Arts and Speech, and Presley Holmes, former chair of the radio-TV area within that school, were appointed associate deans.

By the late '70s, the college began experiencing some changes: the School of Hearing and Speech Sciences left Communication and joined the College of Health and Human Services; photojournalism became an institute in 1978 and the School of Visual Communication in 1986; communication systems management began in 1981 as a center, achieved school status in 1986, and became the J. Warren McClure School of Communication Systems Management in 1988. Thus, the college now consists of the five schools (Communication Systems Management, Interpersonal Communication, Journalism, Telecommunications, and Visual Communication) and the Telecommunications Center (WOUB-AM-FM-TV).

The faculty of the College of Communication has doubled since its inception—from thirty-six tenure-track faculty members in 1968–69 to seventy-two in 2001–2. The number of students has more than doubled, increasing from 1,052 in the initial four schools to 2,607 in 2001–2, and the programs have adopted selective admission standards as they have grown. The Telecommunications Center (NPR and PBS stations) adds more than 60 staff members and 200 student volunteers.

The college's visibility and reputation have been enhanced, both on campus and beyond, by its annual spring Communication Week. Walter Cronkite was on campus in the fall of 1968 for the inauguration of the college, and such communication notables as Marshall McLuhan, Harry Reasoner, Katharine Graham, John Chancellor, Helen Thomas, Charles Osgood, Ellen Goodman, Ted Turner, and Christiane Amanpour have been speakers and guests.

In 1981 Paul Nelson succeeded John Wilhelm as dean. That decade saw substantial growth of the faculty as well as expanded facilities. In 1982 the School of Journalism received a $1.5 million endowment from the Scripps Howard Foundation. The following year the industry-university cooperation program, introduced by newly inaugurated Governor Richard Celeste, recognized the relationship between Scripps Howard and the School of Journalism with a $3 million state appropriation to renovate Carnegie Hall for that school. The name of the building was changed to E. W. Scripps Hall, and the E. W. Scripps School of Journalism occupied it in January 1986.

Four times in the 1980s, the Ohio Board of Regents invited all thirteen public universities to compete for its Excellence awards. Ohio University's College of Communication won five awards, possibly exceeding any other single college of any university in the state. Some other highlights of the college: twenty-two Pulitzer Prizes among faculty and graduates; the nation's first advertising-supported, totally student-run radio station in a public university, ACRN, and the student-run Athens Video Works; consistent regional and national recognition of Interpersonal Communication's debate and forensics teams; a NASA satellite entrusted to the Communication Systems Management faculty and staff; more Hearst Competition and College Photographer of the Year contest winners among Visual Communication students than any other college in the country; and eighteen student professional organizations, some of which have won awards as the best student chapters in the nation.

These successes have been continued since 1996 under Kathy Krendl, the college's third dean. With additional emphasis on research, grants have increased. In addition, college-wide facilities have been implemented with the Scripps Howard Survey Research Center, a state-of-the-art telephone interviewing facility, and the Scripps Howard Multi-Media Laboratory. The college continues to add leading-edge equipment, new hands-on learning experiences, and new research opportunities to provide students with the skills to carry out tasks in today's job market, as well as to further the scholarly study of communication.

Riot Rocks Ohio University

Union Stand Brings Action

ATHENS, Ohio 2—Residents of Ohio University students romped over the campus and downtown area Sunday night—quiet was not getting an anticipated early reaction.

The students toward President Vernon Alden's home in the main downtown infrastructure, throwing bricks, stones "and anything else they could get their hands on," Police Chief Fred James said.

NINE PERSONS were injured, most of them hit by flying missiles, the university Health Center said.

Wood fights and numerous students were smashed, including those at Alden's home. Alden and his family's own home, but remained locked into all brains were hurled through the windows. He was not injured.

James said no arrests were made. He estimated between 1,000 and 1,500 students swept over the campus protesting a lunchtime demand that student unions not to go on strike. The university has 16,000 students.

THE STRIKE had been...

Ohio University students publicized their grievances against the administration.
Post, May 22, 1968.

Columbus Evening Dispatch

When nonacademic employees decided not to strike in the spring of 1968, students who had expected the university to close staged a demonstration that ended in a riot. Columbus Evening Dispatch, *May 20, 1968.*

on West Green and massed two thousand strong in front of the president's house, shouting, "Let's go home" and "We want a strike." President Alden, his wife, and their young children waited inside as police moved the crowd away. After a brief stay on Court Street, students returned to Park Place, where they gathered on the construction site of the new library across the street from the Aldens' house. This time, some lit fires in the street while others picked up bricks and lead pipes from the site and hurled them through the president's windows.

Vice President James Whalen called the display "disgusting." The *Post* agreed "it wasn't good," but challenged the administration to understand that underlying the ridiculous call to "go home" was "FRUSTRATION! Alienation." The next evening, more than 400 students protested outside Baker Center as 650 National Guardsmen stood by at the county fairgrounds. A day later, 3,000 students signed a list of almost 100 demands to which the president was somehow supposed to respond within only a few days.

President Alden was understandably shaken. In September, as the library and new South Green progressed and plans to reroute the troublesome Hocking River took shape, he announced his resignation, saying the university was at a turning point where future goals and priorities might best be set by a new president.

Students did not take this announcement as a reason to abandon their demands. In the fall, when Trustee Fred Johnson made clear that he had no

With the war in Vietnam dragging on and LBJ out of the 1968 presidential race, students campaigned for Nelson Rockefeller, Robert Kennedy, and Eugene McCarthy. *Courtesy Mahn Center.*

intention of including students on the presidential search committee, *Post* editor Bill Sievert declared that "students must—and will—have a direct

Former O.U. student Paul Newman "came home" to campaign for Senator Eugene McCarthy. *Courtesy Mahn Center.*

voice in determining who the next president will be." In the winter, as he and other leaders fought for and finally won a chance to participate, black students led by Sam Fowler, chairman of the Black Student Action Coordinating Committee, quietly approached the administration with a list of six demands: a black dormitory, a black curriculum, admission of every black applicant with financial aid if needed, a black scholarship and recruitment program, a black resource center, and a black student growth fund drawn from student fees. Prepared to institute a more militant "Phase II" if necessary, they were surprised to find the administration willing to listen. The black dorm was never considered, for

both social and legal reasons, but a planning space was provided, a planning coordinator, Jesse Arnelle, was hired, and by the end of April, $250,000 was pledged to a Black Studies Institute, which had been approved by the University Curriculum Council.

In April, women spoke out. At the end of a "spring fever" disturbance on the West Green, a group of them proceeded to Alden's house with demands

The year 1967 became a pivotal year in the struggle for both integration and identity. Malcolm X's auto-biography had recently been published and gave rise to a new awareness. Militancy entered the accepted activist mindset. We became initially Afro-Americans, then African-Americans, then "Black and Proud," then Black, which was a bold departure from being Negro or Colored. The "struggle" transitioned from an evolutionary confrontation to a revolutionary demand for immediate change. . . .

While other universities were responding to politics of confrontation, Ohio University Black students were organizing based on constructive militancy. The Black Student Action Coordinating Committee was formed. Its leaders were McKinley Broadus, Leon Hogg, James "Prophet" Steele, and Janice Pace. President Alden assigned Dean Margaret Deppen as the university liaison to work with students in planning and conducting a month-long Negro History Celebration during February 1968. Dr. James Barnes also acted as a mentor to BSACC. He provided intellectual confirmation and access to administration resources, and was instrumental in formatting the Negro History events, which included the Alvin Ailey Dance Theatre, comedian Dick Gregory, and the editor of EBONY magazine, Lerone Bennett Jr. Ohio University has to be one of the first universities in the country to sponsor a Black History celebration.

—Huey Ball, '67

At Omega Psi Phi's Sweetheart Ball in May 1967, students asked President Alden for a meeting to discuss the needs of African Americans on campus. *Courtesy Huey Ball, '67.*

for "no hours." A few days later, saying "there are no educational, social or legal reasons for confining women students in dormitory residences between arbitrary time limits," 850 of them defied their curfew. With Alicia Woodson as their leader, they stood outside their dorms beyond the closing hour for several nights. The administration threatened them with letters of reprimand; Trustee Fred Johnson said "rules are rules" and refused to eliminate hours. Within the year, experimental visitation polices were tried, but it was 1972 before women's hours were finally eliminated.

By the time President Alden said goodbye in June 1969, Ohio University's total enrollment had grown to more than 22,000 students. Its annual budget exceeded $50 million, and the value of its physical plant had increased from $40 million to $153 million. Seventy-five percent of the faculty had been recruited in the past seven years. New graduate degrees, innovative undergraduate

In September, 1969 I moved into Ryors Hall, an all freshman women's dorm on the West Green. Life there was relaxed and wonderful—like one big pajama party. When we were in our rooms, we left the doors open, keys in the locks. We never worried about theft or security. Boys were not allowed on the floor, except during an occasional "Open House" on Sunday afternoons. We would clean up our rooms, make the beds, and sweep the floors. Boys could come into our rooms as long as the doors were open and everyone "had at least one foot on the floor." This led to some very interesting contortions, but for the most part, we were all on our best behavior.

"Women, it's a minute after twelve and we're liberated."

—Alicia Woodson, quoted in the Post, April 18, 1969

Women's "hours" meant we had a curfew each night. Our R.A. would go through the halls and check that everyone was accounted for. If we wanted to spend the night elsewhere, we had to write down where we would be, put it in a sealed envelope, and give it to the R.D. Supposedly, the envelope would only be opened if there was an emergency and we had to be found. One night I was out past hours. The front door of Ryors was locked. I pecked on the ground floor window and the girls in that room pulled me through the window.

When I see the dorm rooms of today with their computers, microwave ovens, and mini-fridges, I laugh. We only had electric popcorn poppers and hot plates and kept our food cold in winter by putting it outside on the window ledge. We had no air conditioning—only fans in the windows. We did have stereos and radios; people with typewriters were very popular.

During my freshman year, we all wore dresses or miniskirts to class. Jeans were just beginning to catch on. By my sophomore year, that's all we wore. We ate in the Boyd Hall cafeteria and always dressed up for dinner because all the boys from Sargent Hall ate there. I thought the food was great! Occasionally, we had fried shrimp, and there was a chocolate milkshake machine. Healthy eating was not a focus back then.

★ ★ ★   ★ ★ ★   ★ ★ ★   ★ ★ ★

Spring: Ohio maidens bewail imprisonment

'No Women's Hours'

POST photos by: Gary Rings Al Kamuda

In April 1969, Ohio University women, led by Alicia Woodson, violated their midnight curfew and declared themselves liberated. Post, *April 18, 1969.*

During my sophomore year, I had an 8:00 A.M. class that met Tuesdays, Thursdays, and Saturdays. Saturday classes were normal and no one thought anything about it. Thursday night was not a party night; most of us had a full day of classes on Friday.

I didn't attend my graduation ceremony. None of my friends did either. It seemed that it was considered "uncool" back then. Also, during those years of '69–'73, few students wore O.U. sweatshirts or anything that had the O.U. letters, colors, or mascot on it. Also, not cool. School spirit was considered corny. Nevertheless, I feel fortunate to have attended O.U. from 1969 to 1973. It was an exciting time to be a student.

—Jan Cunningham Hodson, '73

programs, and growing international connections provided exciting academic opportunities. The Appalachian Highway was under construction; a larger university airport was being built in Albany; a new community hospital was almost finished; and the trying Hocking was on the verge of being tamed. The changes Vernon Alden had brought to Ohio University and southeast Ohio were enormous, but as he had discovered, some changes were beyond his command.

Any new president would have to face the problems Alden was leaving and some new ones as well. Inflation was becoming a national concern. In Ohio, where support for higher education was among the lowest of the fifty states, Governor James Rhodes and the board of regents proposed raising tuition and restructuring seven of the state's two-year branches into four-year institutions, effectively creating competition for the existing four-year institutions. At Ohio University, grants were drying up, and a budget deficit of almost a million dollars was predicted for the 1969–70 school year. Some faculty members worried that too much money was spent on administration at the expense of academic departments. Others, like John Cady, Robert Whealey, and Giovanni Previtali, conducted teach-ins against the war, and Professor Gerald Scully invited SDS founder Tom Hayden to participate. Gradually, the campus was developing a reputation as a hotbed of progressive thought, becoming, as Clarence Page recalls, "the Berkeley of the Backwoods."

Attorney Claude R. Sowle, the university's new president, was willing to confront these challenges. As he said on accepting the position, "In these times of troubles one accepts the presidency of a major university with mixed emotions, and yet, my basic feeling today is one of optimism." He had taught at Northwestern University, served as dean of the law school at the University of Cincin-

Claude Sowle, O.U. president 1969–74. *Courtesy Mahn Center.*

nati, and written about the problems of student unrest. His plan for the university was to reexamine and reshape its foundation, creating space for discussion by both faculty and students. The hallmarks of his administration were to be honesty and openness.

Six task forces—on academic goals and priorities, student life, budget and goals procedures, university resources, university services, and university facilities—were established to conduct "an institutional self-study." An advisory council of administrators, faculty, and students was created to keep the president abreast of concerns. Innovative academic programs, such as the Honors Tutorial College (based on the "Oxbridge" system), the Black Studies Institute, a Residential/Experimental College, the Bachelor of General Studies degree, a University Professor award, and liberal pass/fail and ABC grading systems (which meant freshmen could not fail a course), were welcomed. The budgets of each unit of the university would be presented in unprecedented public meetings.

> I remember taking a Communication Law class in the home of Mrs. Sowle, the president's wife. Hers was probably the BEST class I took at Ohio University. She made the subject come alive for me.
>
> —Jean Waters Farmer, '74

To deal with the potential deficit, President Sowle made three unpopular decisions: to increase fees; to put a limit on hiring faculty, administrators, and classified staff; and to reduce expenses at the new airport by selling five of the university's six airplanes and eliminating some aviation training programs. The trustees approved the first two decisions, but two board members opposed him on the third. Sowle objected to their interference, and the board agreed to review the policy—but not before the president threatened to resign.

Katie Sowle, wife of President Claude Sowle. *Courtesy Mahn Center.*

Honors Tutorial College

Although the foundation for an honors program at Ohio University existed as far back as 1945, it was not until 1959 that an Honors Program and Awards Committee was established to set rules for and supervise honors courses conducted by various academic departments. These courses were open only to juniors and seniors with a 3.0 accumulative average. In January 1964, President Vernon Alden first authorized the Honors College with Professor Samuel J. Jasper as its first full-time director. He was followed in the late 1960s by Professor Edgar Whan. Enrollment grew from 23 in its initial year to 430 students in 1969.

English professor Edgar Whan directed the Honors College (later Honors Tutorial College) and pushed for innovations such as Pass/Fail and ABC grading and the Bachelor of General Studies.*Courtesy Mahn Center.*

Initially, enrollment was limited to 5 percent of the student body, and students were required to have a 3.5 accumulative average. Honors College courses for sophomores were similar to regular university courses except that classes were small and more was expected of Honors College students. For juniors and seniors, courses were interdisciplinary and often designed by students and faculty. Under Dr. Whan's direction, the college began to invite freshmen to participate in special seminars to satisfy an English requirement.

In the 1970s, during President Claude Sowle's administration, there was much discussion about the direction of the Honors College. In 1972, Professor Ellery Golos, who had served as assistant director under Dr. Whan, sent President Sowle "A Proposal for a Tutorial System" to "provide the best education for the highly gifted, highly motivated undergraduate student." This proposal, based on a study of the British tutorial system, was approved by the curriculum council on May 9, 1972. At this point, the Honors College became the Honors Tutorial College, adopting the tutorial format, which allows for tutorials in the major sequence, courses as required by academic departments, electives as desired, and the possibility of completing a degree in three years.

The first group of tutorial students began in September 1973 with Professor Golos as director. Dr. Margaret Cohn took over leadership of the college in 1977 and served for fourteen years. Professor Joseph Berman was her successor. In 2003 Dean Ann Fidler oversaw a program offering twenty-six majors to 250 students.

Ohio University is the only institution in the United States with a degree-granting college incorporating all the essential features of the traditional tutorial system.

I graduated in 1969, the height of Vietnam and, unfortunately, one spring celebration got out of hand, necessitating the need to call out the National Guard and patrol. I remember the sign, "Ohio U. welcomes the National Guard" and smile since I feel the sign reflected the mood and character of Ohio U. at that time.

—W. Jeffrey Hurst, '69

Students on the College Green observed the national Vietnam Moritorium Day, October 15, 1969. *Courtesy* Athena Yearbook, *1970.*

Except for some class walkouts in conjunction with the national Vietnam Moratorium Day on October 15, the campus was relatively quiet until the early months of 1970. Coach Snyder's winning basketball team brought cheers, but increasingly voices were raised in discontent. Students protested the proposed fee increase with a takeover of the first floor of Cutler Hall, a brick-throwing melee with Athens police, and a bomb scare. Although state senator Robert Corts did not mention the *Post*'s Sunday edition, which listed local drug prices and called dope the "biggest business in Athens conceived and run by students," he lambasted the *Post* for printing "pure unadulterated smut" in its report on a campus sex symposium. More than a quarter of the university's one thousand black students responded to a report on the new Black Studies Institute's effectiveness with

Students protested a proposed fee increase in early 1970. *Courtesy Mahn Center.*

Students demonstrated against the presence of ROTC on campus in the spring of 1970.
Courtesy Mahn Center.

a list of five serious grievances. The report from the task force on student life, which pegged the true costs of intercollegiate athletics as $2,203,911 a year and suggested reducing all sports except basketball to club status, generated a controversy that eventually involved the president and trustees in another showdown.

When the university curriculum council met on April 29 to "review the academic merits" of the ROTC program, about 400 anti-ROTC students attended the meeting, heard the heated debate, and witnessed the narrow defeat of a motion to force ROTC off campus and make it an extracurricular activity. The council did, however, stipulate that instructors of ROTC have rank in academic departments and that no university funds or rent-free facilities be used to subsidize the ROTC programs.

The next day, President Nixon announced that several thousand American ground combat troops had entered Cambodia. With that—and the killing of four students by National Guardsmen at Kent State four days later—the campus saw an escalation of incidents that resulted in the closing of the university on May 15.

In the subsequent months, the university worked out arrangements with the Department of Defense enabling military instructors to apply for and receive academic rank. There was a distinct improvement in the academic standards of the ROTC curriculum, and it was determined that tuition subsidies for cadets from the Department of Defense exceeded the program cost incurred by the university.

Three decades later, I would guess that most of us who worked so hard to get rid of ROTC would now welcome their presence on campus. But if the U.S. ever again gets involved in a war as unpopular as Vietnam, we might expect a renewed attack on all manifestations of the university's cooperation with the military on campus.

—Bill Burkhardt, Associate Professor Emeritus of Sociology

In the spring, as uneasiness grew about the appropriateness of ROTC on campus, nine students disrupted an ROTC class and were arrested. Though fifty students protested the arrest of "the Athens Nine," President Sowle refused to drop charges against them. When President Richard Nixon sent troops into Cambodia, protests erupted all over the country. Governor Rhodes sent the National Guard to restore order at Kent State University, and on May 4 guardsmen shot and killed four students.

Kent State closed immediately, and Governor Rhodes urged all state schools to close if they were experiencing unrest. At Ohio University, President Sowle was determined to show there was "at least one university in this country that can discharge its responsibilities and, at the same time, peaceably attempt to influence the course of events in this country." On the afternoon of May 4, thousands of students gathered on the College Green and, after hours of talk, decided to strike peacefully by cutting classes the next day. On May 5, from 25 to 30 percent of students stayed out of classes. That afternoon and evening, President Sowle met with large groups, explaining that classes would remain in session to protect the freedom of students who wanted to attend them.

Rumor had it that, while O.U. was staying open, outsiders and non-O.U. students would be coming to Athens to close down the campus and cause riots and destruction. So the president formed a volunteer "student patrol" group to help out Campus Security. I participated in that patrol for five days. We were given flashlights, two-way radios, and an area to patrol. We had no arrest powers, but our mission was to report any unusual happenings. It was sort of reminiscent of military duty—four-hour watches, then eight hours off, with most of the patrolling at night.

—William C. Francis, Ph.D. '72

In the first days after Kent State, there was a demonstration in which several thousand students and faculty carried candles around town and campus in memory of those who died and to protest the secret bombings of Cambodia. That march received NO national or regional television coverage. The following night ONE student threw a brick through the bookstore window and every regional television station and all three networks gave coverage to the event. It was a lesson in what is important to the mass media.

I don't know if anyone not there at the time can understand the confusion. However, seeing the National Guardsmen with bayoneted rifles standing at each parking meter made most of us realize how fragile the freedoms are that most of us take for granted. It is hard to explain to people not around at that time how fragile our democracy can be and the roles which the media can, does, and should play.

—Rolland C. Johnson, Ph.D. '71

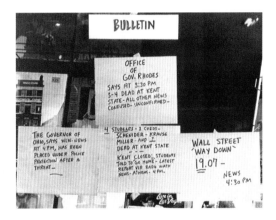

News of the Kent State shootings was posted in the window of Koons Music Store. *Courtesy Athena Yearbook, 1970.*

On May 4, students called for a strike of classes to show solidarity with Kent State students. President Sowle addressed students at Mem Aud. *Courtesy Mary-Blair Dupre, '70.*

One student wrote her parents: "About the strike. It's an open-ended, 'protest anything' idea. The big thing is to wear an armband signifying your concern for any problem in the U.S. (the situation in Cambodia, the killings at Kent State, pollution, etc.)."

The third day after the shootings, students harassed local businesses, demanding that they close, and some 2,500 trekked through town in a "March against Death." On the afternoon of May 7, two firebombs exploded in an ROTC supply room in Peden Stadium, and Governor Rhodes told Sowle that he would send National Guard troops only to help close the university, not keep it open. After a weekend of relative quiet, 2,500 students gathered on Monday for a rally led by John Froines of the Chicago Conspiracy Eight, following which 100 students broke into Chubb Hall (now empty and awaiting renovation) and proclaimed a Free University.

When the colleges in northern and central Ohio closed after Kent State, many of the students chose to move to other campuses in Ohio rather than go home. We had elaborate plans for assimilating the rabble-rousers and keeping things calm, so we tried to figure out how many of them each of us could accommodate—in beds or sleeping bags. But as the angry hordes from other places descended on Athens, they opted for the streets instead of accepting the offers of housing. Finally, we closed and became another campus with the National Guard on every corner.

However, as the other students returned to their schools to finish out the year, we were told not to return until fall. There were rules for how to finish the term—how to accept the grade you had or work to change it. For seniors like me, it was pretty much a done deal. I did not come back when the class of 1980 invited us to "walk" with them—somehow the memories I hold of the way these sobering times affected me seem to be what I need to hold on to.

—Mary-Blair Dupre, '70

CHANGE, CONFRONTATION, AND CRISIS

In the early morning of the next day, a firebomb exploded on the South Green, causing damage to two buildings. Again, the governor refused troops to keep Ohio University open, but the situation was growing more serious. Students from Ohio schools that had closed had poured into Athens. Wary of their motives and knowing they had little involvement in O.U., the provost called on "marshalls" to help protect buildings, and a strict curfew was imposed. When seven students were suspended that night for breaking the curfew, Sowle refused student and faculty senate demands to drop the suspension. Late that night the first real violence erupted as 250 students threw bricks at local businesses and police, and police fired back with tear gas and pepper guns.

On the evening of May 13, campus tension erupted in a confrontation between students and police. *Courtesy Mahn Center.*

The evening of May 14, police attempted to disperse several hundred students who had gathered in front of Baker Center. After a three-hour battle, twenty-three students needed treatment at Hudson Health Center, fifty-four were

In May 1970 came the bombing–Kent State crisis, and all hell broke loose. I spoke every day on the College Green. The talking continued from about 9:30 A.M. to 4:00 P.M., for about a week. Every night there were massive rallies at the Memorial Auditorium. Some of my colleagues supported the informal intellectual discussions on the Green because they helped keep some of the protesters quiet and out of mischief. Others thought I and the other faculty doves were escalating the problem. . . .

With the benefit of hindsight, I would say President Sowle made a tactical mistake in pledging to keep the campus open. Many universities shut down for a day of mourning for the Kent State martyrs, but soon reopened. . . . Sowle's tactics made O.U.'s demonstrations one of the more militant campuses in the country.

—Robert H. Whealey, Professor of History

On May 14, a battle between students and police resulted in injuries, arrests, and a decision to call in the National Guard and close the university.
Courtesy Professor Charles Scott.

under arrest, and the administration called for help from the National Guard to close the university. At 3:00 A.M. students were told to vacate the campus within twenty-four hours.

The closing was unsettling and somber. Students, parents, friends, and enemies sent letters of support, of dismay, of outrage. One senior lamented the canceled graduation: "President Sowle, I implore you! please hold graduation ceremonies this year. I'm sad enough about missing my last 4 weeks of instruction." An alumna wrote: "I would like to suggest that 'I'm Tired of the Tyranny of Spoiled Brats,' by K. Ross Toole . . . be made required reading for all professors." An alumnus wrote, "Your stand on keeping OU open and expelling five chronic agitators is a beacon in a sea of darkness, a return to sanity and an inspiration midst news which indicates most universities have turned their schools over to the inmates and abdicated their

On the morning of May 15, the National Guard patrolled the campus and Athens city streets as students quickly left the campus.
Courtesy Professor Charles Scott.

At about 3:00 A.M. Friday morning, President Sowle came on the radio to announce that the school was closed and we were to be off the campus by noon Saturday.

I went uptown that morning to view the damage. It was a shock to see Ohio National Guardsmen at parade rest with fixed bayonets on their M-1 rifles standing every ten feet along Court and Union Streets. My uncle came down from Columbus to "rescue" me. On our way out of town, we passed Peden Stadium, where a helicopter was parked on the football field. We passed two large military convoys on US 33.

After that, things were never the same again in Athens.

—Donald E. Seitz, '73

responsibilities." A parent sent the president a letter he had written to his son: "Unfortunately I feel you have been robbed of a truly positive education and been forced to accept an ersatz sort of make-do learning which emphasized only the negative issues." Another said: "I just thought that it would be only fair for the university to reimburse me for the room and board which was paid for and not fully received." *Athens Messenger* editor Kenner Bush wrote, "We are today expressing full support of President Sowle and urging our readers to stand behind the president of Ohio University with us. This town and this university simply must stand together."

As the university resumed life after the riot, the administration focused on improving campus communication, giving students more power in decision making, and solving budget problems. Campus security was doubled; the *Campus Communicator* and a communications control center were created. An administrative senate was approved. Students were added to a new university council (a replacement for the president's advisory council), and Professor Lester Marks took on the job of resolving campus problems as university ombudsman. The student judiciary system was streamlined, and the remaining "in loco parentis" regulations were gradually eliminated.

No cap and gown ceremony, no saying goodbye to teachers and friends, and most of us seniors just starting the interviewing processes having to leave campus with no jobs. I can still hear the radio stations and the National Guard advising us to be off campus in 24 hours.

War affects us all. Let us strive for world peace.

—Randy Mendat, '70

I recollect President Sowle's 3 A.M. directive to leave campus within twenty-four hours. Being from Connecticut, all I could do was hitch a ride with some friends to a town I'd never heard of. I phoned my mother, told her what had happened and where I was. She said, "Where's Apple Creek, Ohio?" I said, "I have no idea. I think it's south of Cleveland." Intrepid, but also bitter at the dissolution of the graduation ceremony for her only daughter, she drove to Ohio and retrieved me.

It was only years later that I realized how pivotal that experience was. Exiting Lindley Hall under the watchful eyes of bayoneted National Guard troops, who allowed only the use of crosswalks to transport our possessions, I left with memories of having sponged down kids overcome by tear gas who stumbled into our dorm's lobby during each of three nights of violence preceding the shutdown. For us white, middle-class kids, shielded by college, it was the closest thing to actually being in Vietnam any of us would experience that spring. O.U. would have become another Kent State in just one more day; of that I am sure.

—Jane E. Fieberts, '70

Students quietly went through registration in Grover Center in the fall of 1970. *Courtesy Mahn Center.*

Some much-needed positive publicity came from announcements that the physics department had received a Tandem Van de Graaff accelerator and that students had selected Professors Edgar Whan, James Bruning, and Richard Doolen as the first University Professors. The university council opposed the controversial student life task force recommendation to eliminate most major sports and President Sowle agreed (perhaps reluctantly) to maintain the budget for intercollegiate athletics.

By midwinter, budgets were a growing concern. A report by Earl F. Cheit of U.C. Berkeley said that "higher education has come upon hard times" and placed Ohio University in the category of "headed for trouble." The trouble was evident at the university's second open budget hearings when Vice President and Dean of Faculties Taylor Culbert had to remind the university community that "all other parts of the University exist to serve the academic area" as he asked for a transfer of $465,000 from nonacademic to academic areas in order to hire desperately needed faculty. A short time later, Gov. John J. Gilligan's Ohio Plan proposed asking Ohio students to repay their state subsidy after graduation; his budget called for even higher tuition rates and elimination of all subsidies for out-of-state students—a move that would cost Ohio University $1.3 million.

In the spring, as students planned a Southern Ohio Folk Festival featuring Doc Watson, Pete Seeger, Tim Hardin, the Youngbloods, McKendree Spring, and Kate Taylor, academic deans scrambled to stretch teaching budgets by delaying new hires and increasing teaching loads of current faculty. Other administrators worried that housing contracts for the coming fall were down by 1,300. They contemplated closing Howard, Scott, and Lindley Halls and requiring both freshmen and sophomores to live in university housing.

With the opening of school in September, AFSCME Local 1699's president Oscar McGee led the union in a nine-day strike, and the enrollment report showed a drop of 2 percent. President Sowle reorganized his administration, ordered a salary freeze for faculty, and revoked a previously announced increase for twelve-month contract personnel. In addressing other

The experimental nuclear and particle physics program at Ohio University has been a long-running show of at least three acts. Act I featured a tiny particle accelerator housed in the abandoned Ford tractor garage on Richland Avenue. The show ran well enough to secure a few years of National Science Foundation funding, produce the first few Ph.D.'s, and establish the basis for future growth.

Act II: Construction of the John E. Edwards Accelerator Laboratory with its Tandem Van de Graaff particle accelerator. The Tandem was purchased in 1969 with a million-dollar grant from the Atomic Energy Commission (now the Department of Energy). With more faculty and increased funding, the experimental nuclear physics faculty produced about seventy-five doctorates in nuclear physics. The powerful neutron production and detection techniques at the Edwards Laboratory are still in demand with Department of Energy scientists and other groups interested in, for example, the basic physics of cancer therapy and the role of nuclear reactions in supernova explosions.

Act III commenced with the establishment of the Institute of Nuclear and Particle Physics in 1991. The INPP is the administrative vehicle by which experimental and theoretical programs at Ohio University can communicate and collaborate on projects of much greater scope than were ever possible at the Tandem laboratory. Ohio scientists are active leaders and participants in frontier studies of the quark substructure of the neutrons and protons of Acts I and II. They can be found at world-class facilities from Japan to Europe and across North America. Any accelerator time at the Tandem made available by the outward-bound nuclear scientists is promptly claimed by the W. M. Keck Thin Film Facility, which now shares the expanded Edwards Laboratory with the nuclear scientists.

Nuclear physicists Roger Finlay *(center)* and Jacobo Rapaport with the Tandem Van de Graaff particle accelerator, purchased in 1969 with a grant from the Atomic Energy Commission. *Courtesy Mahn Center.*

concerns, he rejected a proposal from the dean of the Center for Afro-American Studies to fill 50 percent of current and future vacancies with blacks and appointed Beverly E. Price, a recent graduate, to prepare a report on the status of women at Ohio University.

What Price revealed six months later in her hundred-page report was that women were "underemployed and underpaid within the faculty and staff of the University." More specifically, her report showed few women in faculty positions and fewer in the upper ranks, no women in top administrative positions, little chance for advancement for women

Beverly E. Jones [Price], author of a hundred-page report on the status of women at the university. *Courtesy* Athens Messenger.

In the early '70s, the Convo was one of the largest music venues in Ohio and drew popular performers. To many people, the 1973 music festival was "something akin to Woodstock." *Posters courtesy of Michael Prusad, '87, and Kathy Connick, '82.*

in civil service positions, and an educational environment that was less rich for women than for men. The report also noted the lack of funding for women's athletics and the exclusion of women from the 110 Marching Men. Price's recommendations included "numerical goals" for recruiting, hiring, and promoting women, an equalization of domestic workers' wages, a drastic reduction of aid to male athletes within the Mid-American Conference, and admission to the band of all qualified applicants of either sex.

To show commitment to solving the problems cited in the "Price Report," President Sowle put Beverly Price in charge of university equal opportunity programs, allocated money for a day-care center and an administrative internship program for women and minorities, and proposed adding Women's Intercollegiate Athletics to the Intercollegiate Athletic Budget. The athletic director and some of the trustees apparently opposed this decision. When Sowle discovered that a subcommittee of the trustees was considering overturning it, he threatened for the second time to resign. A few days later, campus edginess increased when some 250 students renewed their protests against the Vietnam War and ROTC by occupying Lindley Hall. After eighty of the activists defied orders to leave the building, police arrested them.

Once again, the fall term opened amid turmoil and some bad news. The university was involved in prosecuting the spring's protestors, now known as "The Athens Seventy-five." Professor James Barnes had accepted the deanship of Afro-American Studies, but successful baseball coach Bob Wren had resigned, citing cuts in athletic scholarships and staffing. The Board of Regents proposed tuition reductions at two-year state schools and increases at four-year schools. And for the first time in twenty years, enrollments

dropped precipitously—from the projected 18,774 to 17,549. To make up for lost fees and subsidies, the university needed to cut well over $1 million.

Winter quarter brought more bad news: there would be another cut in the 1972–73 budget. Again, the president reorganized his staff, eliminating some positions and creating the position of executive vice president for Taylor Culbert, who warned at the third annual budget hearings that the College of Arts and Sciences might have to cut at least sixteen faculty positions. Virtually simultaneously the trustees passed a special resolution protecting intercollegiate athletics from proposed cuts. As the president contemplated closing five more dormitories, he noted that Miami University had wisely chosen stabilization over growth, and admissions director Jerry Reese added that the 1960s' $50 million building program was now "a neo-Georgian brick around the University's neck."

Dr. Daniel Ellsberg was among the Kennedy Lecturers for 1972–73. *Courtesy* Athena Yearbook, *1973*

In spite of mounting financial problems, 1972–73 was a lively year. WOUB got a larger radio-TV tower. The ten Edwin and Ruth Kennedy lecturers included Bella Abzug, Daniel Ellsberg, Brit Hume, and physicist Dr. Geoffrey Burbidge. Writers Robert Bly, Leslie Fiedler, and Joyce Carol Oates drew a literary crowd for three days of readings and discussions. An international festival, the Miss Bronze contest, and Black Awareness Week fostered diversity, while a Student Workers Union organized to support the United Farm Workers in a boycott of non-union grapes and lettuce. The forensics team was named the nation's most outstanding. The Cavern was a popular student hangout; Jethro Tull, McKendree Spring, The Eagles, Bruce Springsteen, the Beach Boys, Argent, and Blood, Sweat and Tears provided plenty of music. Baseball star Mike Schmidt was gone, but the rugby team still promised bone-shattering fun. Unfortunately, the year ended with another brick-throwing skirmish against Athens police.

When President Sowle presented his biennial report in the fall of 1973, he asked the university community, alumni, and friends to pay at least as much attention to the institution's strengths as to the "pressing problems of the moment." However, when fall enrollments fell to 15,844 (below even the lowest projections), it was difficult to shift the focus. Executive Vice President Culbert presented an "academic blueprint" that reaffirmed Ohio University's commitment to liberal studies as the "intellectual foundation of responsible citizenship." He suggested cutting weak departments and urged professional colleges to prepare students for careers rather than for entry-level jobs.

By the early '70s, the Graffiti Wall behind Super Hall had replaced the Kissing Circle as a message center. *Courtesy Mahn Center.*

When figures showed only 13,100 students preregistering for winter quarter—a drop of 7 percent from fall to winter—it was

Mike Schmidt, '72, was recognized as a "keeper" by Ohio University's baseball coach Bob Wren. In 1970, Schmidt and his teammates were ranked fourth in the nation and became the only O.U. team to play in the College World Series. In an eighteen-year career with the Philadelphia Phillies, Schmidt distinguished himself as a great third baseman and a particularly gifted hitter. His career home run record of 548 surpassed the records of Mickey Mantle, Ted Williams, and Willie McCovey. Schmidt was a twelve-time All-Star, won three National League Most Valuable Player awards, and was named MVP of the 1980 World Series. When he retired in 1989, his Phillies jersey number—20—retired with him.

Courtesy O.U. Athletic Department.

inevitable that more dorms would close and some first- and second-year faculty members would be let go. The exhausted president laid at least some blame for attrition on the *Post,* which, he said, searches out "the most bizarre student behavior and gives it prominent display." An anonymous commentator agreed, saying, *"The Post* has a death wish for the university."* To counteract public criticism, President Sowle called for freshman dorms and quiet hours. Students saw the move to appease conservative opinion as a step backward. A horde marched on President Sowle's house and later burned his effigy. Unfortunately, the president's angry response drew more negative media attention. On a snowy day in February, eight or nine hundred students again appeared at his house and pelted him with snowballs.

Rugby became a popular club sport for both men and women. *Courtesy* Athena Yearbook, *1973.*

During the winter's tumultuous open budget hearings, the academic vice president predicted a drop in full-time faculty from the existing 762 to 652 in 1975–76. Faced with a projected fall enrollment of 13,650, the administration floated proposals to close the architecture school (which had lost its accreditation) and perhaps to eliminate the linguistics department. As many as twelve tenured faculty members found their names added to the list of untenured faculty who were to receive terminal contracts. Faculty

Students confronted President Sowle at Baker Center on May 14, 1974, to demand more sensitivity to the needs of African Americans on campus. *Courtesy* Athena Yearbook, *1974.*

Senate officers argued unsuccessfully that the university had not proved financial exigency—the only legal condition for dismissing tenured faculty.

Spring brought no relief. After a music festival, students built a fire in the middle of Court Street and engaged in a rock- and brick-throwing riot when police came to put it out. On May 14, black students decided to confront the president about the university's lack of sensitivity in providing appropriate entertainment and cultural programming for its black students. A group marched on Baker Center, where the president was attending a luncheon, and insisted on seeing him. Amid angry exchanges that somehow came to include the frustrations of the Student Workers Union's Bruce Mitchell, '75, the infuriated students shouted epithets at the president and stormed out. Two days later, reenacting the drama that had preceded President Alden's 1969 departure, a coalition of student organizations confronted President Sowle with a list of fifty-one demands and a further demand for a response within twenty-four hours. Among other things, he and much of his senior staff were to resign.

To the surprise of the student coalition, and certainly of both the university and Athens communities, President Sowle did just that. On May 19, he sent notification of his resignation to the board of trustees, saying, "Universities are among the most fragile institutions in our society. It is unfortunate that in such a setting the dedicated selfless efforts of so many can be nullified by the senseless acts of so few."

The climate of change, confrontation, and crisis of the '60s and '70s had, for the moment, overshadowed many of his accomplishments as well those of his predecessor, Vernon Alden. Yet only two months earlier, a ten-year review of the institution by a committee of the North Central Association paid far more attention to the strengths of the university's programs than to its problems with enrollments and funding. The positive report credited "a strong and effective administration, a good student body and an open decision making style . . . which emphasizes participation and wide dissemination of information." Of particular note were the open budget hearings, the Honors Tutorial College, strong arts and science programs, a dramatically changing education college, and a notable fine arts college. Moreover, the report approved Ohio University's accreditation as a doctoral-level institution, with eighteen "mature" graduate programs.

The members of the university and its many friends could only hope that the coming year under the leadership of economics professor Harry B. Crewson would be a healing one in which they too could focus on the strengths of a greatly expanded, better-known, innovative, but troubled, institution. The trustees had to trust that they would find a new president who would be able to solve the university's financial problems and restore both its reputation and its sense of community.

Courtesy Professor Charles Scott.

CHANGE, CONFRONTATION, AND CRISIS

Ohio on the Hocking

Newcomers to Athens are often told that Ohio University was to be located on The Plains but that the surveyors laying out the university lands were drunk and put the flags in the wrong place. There is no truth to the story, even though the flatboat the surveyors poled up the Hocking River that fall of 1795 did carry—along with the pork, flour, and beans—forty gallons of whiskey. The flags were placed correctly—as near the center of the Ohio Company of Associates' purchase as possible.

Boaters motored through the West Green in the flood of 1964. *Courtesy Mahn Center.*

Settlers soon came up the river to the university land, built houses, and established a town that extended from the high hills on the north to the flood plains of the Hocking River, which meandered around the other three sides of the town. An 1803 visitor commented: "This settlement commenced in 1797. The town is regularly laid out, on elevated ground, of easy ascent, round which the river forms a graceful bend. The situation is healthy, and the prospect delightful beyond description."

In those early days, the river, flowing more deeply than now, provided a means of transportation for the pioneers in their scows and flatboats. In 1805 it began to provide a means of industry also. The state legislature authorized the building of the first dam across the Hocking to serve the gristmill that opened at what today would be the eastern extension of Mill Street. In 1816 another dam was authorized and built on the western side of town at "the ripples," or shallow falls, of the Hocking. A large milling operation there continued to serve a wide area for more than 150 years. Today, White's Mill, at that same location, is the scene most frequently painted by Athens artists.

Commerce on the Hocking River continued to grow, and in 1843 the Hocking Canal—bypassing unnavigable sections of the river and extending north from Athens—was opened. An industrial complex developed at the turn-around, and a large warehouse, at the location of the present-day Athens Station Apartments, stored southbound products off-loaded from canal boats as well as northbound goods brought in by flatboats.

That commercial connection between Athens and the Hocking River ended not long after the Civil War. Agricultural produce continued to be taken downriver for years, but the Hocking Canal lost business to the developing railroads, and the end came in 1873, when much of the canal bed and towpath were ruined by a flood.

Many stories were told of happenings in the town during flood times. In 1873 the old 1839 lowland bridge across the Hocking on what is now Richland Avenue was washed out, and in 1907, so was the dam at the end of Mill Street. Also during that 1907 flood, the rushing water crossed what is now the West State Street Recreation Area, broke through the B & O Railroad embankment, and devastated the west end of Union Street.

For Ohio University, built high on the hill, the almost yearly flooding of the bottom land was merely an inconvenience, not an immediate concern. That began to change, however, during the 1940s. President John C. Baker realized that the G.I. bill would bring students to Ohio University in greater numbers than ever before and that more living quarters and academic buildings would be needed. Because space

In the spring of 1960, the Hocking overflowed and flooded the campus. The underground garage below Jefferson Dorm was emptied of all vehicles except one, a V.W. bug. A group of twenty enterprising students jumped into the water and played water polo, using the V.W. as the ball. The "match" lasted six to eight hours.

—Dave Jeffrey, '65

Students enjoyed the flooded Hocking. *Courtesy* Athena Yearbook, *1968.*

We lived in the McKinley Street apartments, which were located down the hill near McCracken and over the railroad tracks and adjacent to the golf course. At the time, the Hocking River flowed right past the golf course. In the spring of 1968, the Hocking spilled over and inundated most of the golf course, and stranded most of the students in two or three dorms, including the McKinley Street apartments.

Our children loved it, as their view from the fifth floor was fantastic! In the few days that it took the water to subside, we survived on sandwiches and quick prepared foods. The unique thing about our situation was to watch our milkman, who delivered to us, without fail, until the waters went down.

—Bill Moore, M.A. '68

Courtesy Athena Yearbook, *1968.*

In the spring of 1967 students watched the flood waters rise on West Green. *Courtesy* Athena Yearbook, *1967.*

I recall the water . . . being up to the tops of the parking meter in front of Jefferson Hall. The last straw . . . was when the Grover gym floor was warped ten feet in the air. After that, the Army Corps of Engineers was called in to re-route the river.

—Ranaldo Lawson, '65

Back when I was a freshman, the river ran through the campus. Parks Hall, which is now the office of the Osteopathic College, was where all the wrestlers stayed. (We called it the animal house.) Well, right out from it, where the water swirled, there was a little island, and these guys put a flag on it and named it Parks Hall Island. They had a canoe, and they'd just about gotten to the island when these wrestlers swam out and upset the canoe.

The flood made it very interesting. The only place you could stand above the water on the East Green was on the railroad tracks.

—Tim Lairson, '69

was limited around the College Green, the administration began to acquire land in the flood plain to the east and south of the campus.

With the beginning of dormitory construction, the river for the first time came to the students. Always before, the students had gone to the river—parties of boaters, the short-lived rowing team of the 1880s, summer school students and the town's young people at the swimming hole under the south bridge, zoology and botany students studying birds, water creatures, and plants along its shores. Up until that time, the river "was just there," to be cursed when it misbehaved but mostly to be enjoyed as it flowed peacefully in its bed, its beauty recognized in paintings and poetry.

Photographs show the old riverside O.U. stadium inundated in 1913 and Grover Center, built on the same spot, surrounded by the water of the 1964 flood. And it was during the '64 flood that the Faculty Club had a dance at the Millview Inn, where some people watched parts of White's Mill dam crumble as others listened to a jukebox playing Chubby Checkers and learned to do the Twist. There are pictures taken during later floods of students canoeing through West Green; National Guard trucks carrying students and O.U. personnel up Richland Avenue; and machinery used to build Seigfred Hall surrounded by three feet of water.

There are stories of students alongside city volunteers piling sandbags to reinforce the rail embankment and of anti–Vietnam War protesters from Columbus who couldn't reach Athens because of the flooding river. But were some stories apocryphal? Did the river really deliver a case of beer to the door of a dormitory? Did a flooded first-floor elevator in McCracken Hall respond to a call to the second floor and when opened dump a full load of water on the caller?

As Ohio University expanded in the late 1960s, the regular inundation of the lowlands finally had to be addressed. At the farewell banquet for retiring President Baker, Trustee Fred Johnson's pronouncement that the river had to be moved met with a skeptical response. It took some years for the plan to come to fruition, but on April 12, 1969, President Vernon R. Alden spoke at the groundbreaking ceremony for the Hocking River Flood Control Project, which would move the part of the Hocking's channel that flowed through town.

Portions of the Hocking channel had been moved before. In the late 1800s, a small loop, near where the O.U. physical plants are today, was bypassed. In 1912 a new channel was dug to bypass a large loop in what was then Athens Mental Health Center farmland and is now the location of the Convocation Center and part of the West Green. The 1960s design was much more extensive, however, than either of the previous changes, and it was only after Ohio University had built the large dormitory complexes on East, South, and West Greens that the Corps of Engineers deemed the project cost effective.

The flood protection plan was completed in the early 1970s, and as planned, most of Athens has since been flood free. The new channel took much of the plant life in its path as well as the lakes and part of the grounds of the Mental Health Center that had been enjoyed by generations of O.U. students. But it also opened up land for the new development that has been taking place ever since.

A few aging sycamore trees still stand along West Union Street, indicating the once-threatening route of the Hocking, but the river now flows peacefully through town in its new bed. The abandoned oxbow channel between Clippinger and the Aquatic Center has been dedicated as the Emeriti Park, with a waterfall, pond, flowering plants and shrubs, and many of the tall trees that marked the earlier path.

Hocking at Dawn. Watercolor © Paul Bradford. *Courtesy of the artist.*

9

The Search for Community

1974–1988

> Our greatest need is to recapture the sense of what we are about—a sense
> of common purpose which gives value and meaning to our work as we
> commit ourselves to our tasks and the future of the university.
> —*Charles Ping, 1975*

In 1974, as Americans confronted the growing energy crisis, the revelations of the Watergate hearings, and the resignation of President Richard Nixon, Ohio University trustees discussed ways to help their institution regain its sense of community while they searched for a replacement for President Claude Sowle. The trustees selected economics professor Harry B. Crewson to serve as interim president—a good choice, for he was well known to the faculty, trusted by the nonacademic employees' union, familiar with city politics, and acquainted with state officials in Columbus.

A genial man who believed in the basic good health of the university, President Crewson resolved to take a measured approach to problems and to improve the school's image by reducing campus divisiveness. He adopted a low profile, eliminating regular press conferences, weekly appearances on WOUB's *Open Line,* and the contentious public budget hearings. To present a "more balanced" view of the university, he required the *Post* to include a weekly supplement, the *Pillar,* prepared by the university public information office.

Economics professor Harry B. Crewson assumed the presidency in 1974 after Claude Sowle's resignation. *Courtesy University Photographer's Office.*

Post staffers said the administration was trying to "seize control" of part of the newspaper, but their objections went unheeded. Student Governing Board members, shouting "We're not babies," demonstrated against the "insulting" Freshman Residential Plan, which segregated first-year students in dorms with more restrictive visiting hours, but the administration was unmoved. Members of the United Student Workers Union (formerly SWU) got a grievance procedure and a raise, but not all they wanted. Athens Citizens for United Farm Workers, who risked arrest in marches on Cutler Hall and the president's house to demand that only union produce be served in dining halls, were disappointed when the administration provided both union and non-union lettuce and grapes and let students decide what they would eat.

There were fewer options for forestalling the faculty's move toward unionization. As more teaching positions were eliminated—of the 729 existing in 1973, only 651 were expected to remain by fall 1975—concerns for job security rose. Also galling were reports that the academic area had received $3 million less than the board of regents had recommended and that the university was maintaining nonacademic areas at the expense of academics. Not surprisingly, when the faculty senate sent out a survey in December to determine support for collective bargaining, a

A sit-in at Boyd Hall publicized student opposition to the Freshman Residential Program that restricted hours for freshmen women. Spectrum Green, *1975. Courtesy* Athena Yearbook.

Athens Citizens for United Farm Workers, including Student Governing Board chair Bruce Mitchell, *center,* marched on Cutler Hall to protest the use of non-union produce in university cafeterias. Spectrum Green, *1975. Courtesy* Athena Yearbook.

majority of the faculty responded, and 75 percent of the respondents indicated approval. In spite of this apparent mandate, the trustees refused to allow a spring election of a bargaining agent. That vote, with its potentially dramatic consequences for relationships between the faculty and administration, would have to wait for the arrival of a new president.

Dr. Crewson and the trustees took a similarly strong approach to university funding problems. They razed Ewing Hall, closed more residence halls, and increased their lobbying efforts for supplemental funds from the board of regents and the legislature. The board of regents, anticipating enrollment lower than 13,000 for 1975, told the trustees they should plan for an even smaller university of 10,000 students. Board members reacted strongly. Trustee Don Spencer said the university needed to grow, not shrink; Fred Johnson asserted that such a reduction would be "absolutely disastrous" to the institution's educational programming and devastating to the economy of southeast Ohio as well. Deciding that achieving higher enrollments "may be like shooting fish in a barrel compared to problems we have solved in the past," the board of trustees proposed an ambitious plan to stabilize enrollment at 13,500 within four years. In return for a special subsidy from the legislature, far exceeding the year-to-year supplements previously recommended by the regents, the university would close more buildings, reduce expenses, and recruit zealously.

With the end of the academic year, the trustees were able to announce another success. In spite of opposition from the chancellor of the Ohio Board of Regents and from the Ohio State Medical Association, the legislature had voted overwhelmingly to establish an osteopathic medical school at Ohio University, creating a more comprehensive university and expanding its traditional programs in the helping professions.

As Harry Crewson stepped down from the presidency and accepted the title of Trustee Professor for his service, he could take pride in the year's accomplishments. Though total enrollments were down, the number of graduate and international

THE POST
Trustees reject May bargaining

Trustees rejected the faculty's plan to choose a collective bargaining agent in the spring of 1975. Post, *April 22, 1975.*

Ewing Hall, built in 1898, was razed as part of the effort to close unneeded or inefficient buildings. Spectrum Green, *1975. Courtesy* Athena Yearbook.

Director Bob Winters geared the School of Theater's production of *Jesus Christ, Superstar* to Athens and its surroundings. Spectrum Green, *1975. Courtesy* Athena Yearbook.

Angela Davis, radical black activist, author, and academic, and Katharine Graham, publisher of the *Washington Post,* spoke on campus in May 1975. Spectrum Green, *1975. Courtesy* Athena Yearbook.

students was up. The forensics team continued to sweep national contests; the music school had presented almost a hundred programs and concerts and collaborated with the School of Theater to produce *Jesus Christ, Superstar;* celebrities such as Angela Davis and Katharine Graham had come to campus to discuss national events. In addition, the federal government's passage of Title IX promised funding for women's athletics and a new name for the marching band. Voices on the campus seemed quieter in anticipation of the arrival of the new president, Charles J. Ping.

In some ways, the eighteenth president seemed to have as much in common with the university's early presidents as he did with his immediate predecessors. Charles Ping was a Presbyterian minister and an academic with a Ph.D. in philosophy. He had served one year as acting president of Tusculum College in Tennessee and six years as provost at Central Michigan University, where he had worked with a unionized faculty, written and implemented long-range budget plans, and taken time to attend Harvard's summer management program for university presidents and administrators.

At his first convocation in September 1975, President Ping expressed faith in the institution and affirmed its distinctive character. The new president noted the beauty of the university's residential campus and its connection with southeast Ohio. He recognized its traditions of complementing liberal studies with professional programs, combining teaching and research, and reaching out to a broad audience. He expressed

THE SEARCH FOR COMMUNITY

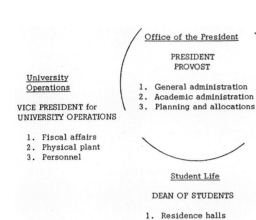

President Ping reestablished education as the defining mission of the university by reorganizing its administrative structure. *Courtesy Mahn Center.*

Charles J. Ping, O.U. president 1975–94. *Courtesy University Photographer's Office.*

his intention to use informed participation and careful planning to make hard choices, presented an organizational plan that reestablished education as the defining principle of Ohio University's existence, and shared his hope that this historic institution could recapture a sense of community.

Though President Ping intended to spend his first year in assessment and the second in planning for the future, he faced the immediate need to stabilize the university community as well as to expand it. The faculty had approved collective bargaining and were ready to move ahead with the previously delayed election of a collective bargaining agent. However, in Ping's experience, collective bargaining tended to "create tensions in university life that erode any sense of community and enhance adversarial patterns." He insisted on a carefully supervised vote and delayed it until winter. Throughout the fall quarter he met with both individuals and groups. When the votes were finally recast and counted, the union was defeated, and the issue put to rest, at least for a while.

The second task in stabilizing the university community involved gaining some control over enrollments and the budget. Realizing the seriousness of the current situation, which recalled the crisis of the 1840s, President Ping worked closely with state legislators as the admissions office stepped up recruitment. The administration managed to refinance the draining debt on the Convocation Center at a lower interest rate and began execution of a complex plan to sell ten of the empty residence halls to the state for

President Ping's administrative staff included *(left to right)* Provost Neil Bucklew, Vice President C. Eugene Peebles, Vice President Wayne Kurlinski, and Dean of Students Carol Harter. Spectrum Green, *1979. Courtesy Athena Yearbook.*

As a professor of labor relations, I had both a personal and a professional interest in the 1974-75 Ohio Education Association (OEA) campaign to organize the faculty as a bargaining unit. Though most of my colleagues in the business college viewed my activities with suspicion, if not hostility, I joined the organizing committee. Thinking we might have to strike to force an election, I suggested to Dave Stewart, the head of the organizing committee (and later provost), that we should talk to the local chapter of the American Federation of State, County, and Municipal Employees (AFSCME), which had represented the nonacademic employees in negotiations since the '60s.

The president of the local chapter, Tommy Adkins, assured us that AFSCME would support our efforts. He said his members were ready to honor our picket lines if we went on strike. Then he asked if the faculty would do the same for AFSCME. We looked at each other sheepishly, then admitted we didn't know if we could promise that. I am sure we all suspected privately that most of the faculty were not ready to go that far.

When Charles Ping became president of Ohio University, he agreed to a faculty vote on collective bargaining but asked for a chance to correct the university's problems. We knew the election would be close, with many faculty members sitting on the fence. I watched the count that night as our efforts fell forty votes short. True to his word, President Ping initiated reforms, and the support for collective bargaining evaporated.

—Lane Tracy, Professor Emeritus of Management Systems

"alternative uses," paying off high-interest bonds with the proceeds. Grosvenor Hall and Irvine were transformed from residential space to classrooms and labs for the new Ohio University College of Osteopathic Medicine. The birth of the new college in less than ten months—complete with curriculum and faculty—was overseen by Acting Dean Gerald Faverman.

Unfortunately, June brought a setback to what had been a year of progress, when a street confrontation between students and police ended in the firing of wooden bullets (knee-knockers) at the brick-throwing students. President Ping joined Athens Mayor Donald Barrett in forming a task force to look for some solution to this perennial problem, and in July the trustees approved a new student code of conduct to clarify acceptable standards of campus behavior.

The university began the fall with the extraordinary news that Dean Faverman had succeeded in preparing the medical school, welcoming its first twenty-four students, and laying the groundwork for additional Ohio University

In June 1976, a student's arrest outside Swanky's led to a violent confrontation between students and police. Spectrum Green, 1976. *Courtesy* Athena Yearbook.

THE SEARCH FOR COMMUNITY

College of Osteopathic Medicine

In 1823, the Ohio University Board of Trustees voted to establish a medical school at the university. After a delay of only 152 years, on August 18, 1975, Gov. James A. Rhodes signed Amended House Bill 229 to create the Ohio University College of Osteopathic Medicine. Following the passage of this bill, President Harry Crewson, the college Osteopathy Planning Committee, and Acting Dean Gerald Faverman set about organizing the new medical school. In the fall of 1976 the college enrolled its first class. The rapidity with which the college sprang into being astonished skeptics and detractors. A medical school had never been launched in such a short period of time.

The legislation establishing OU-COM mandated that the college emphasize the preparation of family physicians for underserved areas of the state and that it utilize existing health-care resources for its clinical training programs. Of all OU-COM graduates in practice, 64 percent are in the state of Ohio, 56 percent are in primary care, and 40 percent have "hung out shingles" in communities of less than 50,000. The college has developed linkages to support its educational programs, drawing on resources from across the state. The Centers for Osteopathic Research & Education (CORE), a medical education consortium, boasts affiliations with twelve Ohio hospitals as well as with three other colleges of osteopathic medicine across the country.

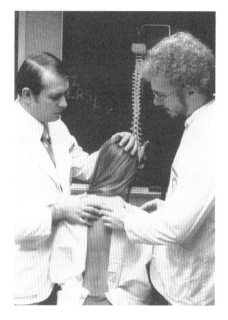

Dr. Daniel Marazon instructing OUCOM students in biomechanic procedures. Ohio University Alumni Journal, *January-February 1978.*

The Ohio University College of Osteopathic Medicine has undergone dramatic change throughout its brief history. Through the leadership of its four deans, Faverman, Frank W. Myers, Barbara Ross-Lee, and Jack Brose, as well as the efforts of countless faculty and staff members, the college has become a leader in medical education and service throughout the state, the nation, and the world. The college's two new curricular tracks replace the traditional passive, lecture-based approach with active, case-based medical education. OU-COM has also been active on the world stage with programs like the S.H.A.R.E. (Student Health Assistance Rural Experience) Kenya Project and the Charles J. Cannon Edinburgh Geriatric Tutorial, which gives students a chance to observe first-hand the way health care is provided to older citizens in Scotland.

In a mere three decades, OU-COM has become a recognized leader in producing outstanding primary care physicians. The college consistently ranks among the top five in the American Medical Student Association's Primary Care Scorecard. This annual survey ranks medical schools in terms of the percent of graduates pursuing primary care and family practice residencies. The college has found innovative ways to provide primary care in underserved areas of the state with two state-of-the-art mobile health units. These rolling "clinics" reach many of the vulnerable populations in southeastern Ohio. The college has also established two landmark programs— the Center of Excellence in Multicultural Medicine and the Center for Appalachian and Rural Health Research. The former is the only federally funded Center of Excellence in Ohio and the only one in the U.S. at an osteopathic college.

programs in healthcare. Other good news followed. Though the budget for 1976–77 was "very tight," it included a desperately needed faculty raise of 10 percent. A mission statement and a ten-year education plan were in the works, and according to Admissions Director James Walters, enrollment was up for the first time in six years.

Of course, most students were unaware of the deep significance of much of this news. They noticed changes that affected them: the ease of admission, the elimination of ABC grading (which many faculty had always called "an embarrassment"), the increase in hours needed to graduate, and the reinstatement of a first-year writing requirement. The majority of the career-minded undergraduates chose the pre-professional programs in business, communication, and the sciences rather than majors in humanities or the recently popular social sciences.

On the lighter side, streaking was popular in some circles, and according to alumnus Matt Lauer the mood was one of "Let's have a good time." He recalls sitting at the Deck on West Union, drinking beer and watching people go by, or listening to "Desperado" in every bar. For many students, the bars were the new "social melting pots," and there was one to suit every taste. The Union and the Frontier Room (where the West Coast Ramblers might be heard singing "The Milk Cow Blues") were for the socially conscious. The Cat's Den had a color TV with football games. The Tavern's chess set drew graduate students; Swanky's was a '60s holdover; and, oddly, McGoo's attracted a more refined crowd.

Students could also choose among two hundred campus organizations. Fraternities and sororities still had not regained the popularity they lost during the '60s, and activist groups had fallen on hard times with the end of the Vietnam era and confrontation politics. Intramural and club sports, however, were big. More than 15,000 names filled the rosters of seventy sports—obviously with some repeaters. Jim Herpy had his name on two. As he recalls, "I actually had to work my way through college, and the only thing I really did was play intramurals. We had a football team, and we were all-campus runner-up in water polo." Broomball was the fastest-growing intramural sport, while a newcomer, ultimate frisbee, pushed for a place in the sun. Among the club teams, karate, archery,

Streaking—a '70s fad. *Courtesy* Athena Yearbook, *1974.*

and an alpine group appeared. Rugby ruled, and everyone wanted to see the wild hockey games at Bird Arena and cheer Roger Secoy as he cleared the ice on the Zamboni. Many students joined the ranks of volunteers who ran both WOUB and ACRN, the twenty-four-hour-a-day progressive rock radio station that *Billboard* magazine called "one of the finest on any campus." Christian groups such as Campus Crusade for Christ were growing again. Choral groups, the university orchestra, and down-home bands were popular. Center Program Board members tried to book well-known groups for concerts, but given the isolation of Athens and opposition from the the new dean of students, Carol Harter, it was hard to rival the years between 1970 and 1974 when rowdy crowds had frequently filled the Convo to hear eight bands in a single weekend.

One thing Dean Harter did not oppose was an organized Halloween Party. In 1974 costumed students had spilled into the street. Police, used to being called "pigs," surprised students by being "so cool" and rerouted traffic for four hours. In 1976, Harter and the mayor agreed to close East Union Street for a block party in front of Baker Center. Rain sent revelers into Baker during the early evening but ended in time for mischief on Court Street. Nevertheless, the administration—which would come to

Matt Lauer, '97, pictured here at Homecoming 2001, has been co-host of NBC News' *Today Show* since January 1997. Before earning a place in the spotlight, he spent three years as the show's news anchor and often filled in as its host. Although Lauer left Ohio University four credits shy of a degree in 1979, he earned the missing credits and his degree in 1997. *Courtesy* Athena Yearbook, *2001.*

I attended the legendary Bruce Springsteen concert in April '76 at Mem Aud. As I remember, it was organized on the spur of the moment. Bruce was playing in Columbus, and someone realized he had the following night free and booked him in Mem Aud with only about a week's notice. Cheap 8 by 10 handbills were printed and distributed all over campus on April 1st. Many students thought it was an April Fool's Day joke. Because of the last-minute preparations, the seating was festival style, and some damage was done to the auditorium. But the concert itself was a rare opportunity to hear a great performer in a small hall. No one who was there will ever forget it.

—Dave Westrick, '77

Mimi Hart of Hotcakes was a popular performer at Swanky's and the Front Room. Spectrum Green, *1977. Courtesy* Athena Yearbook.

Hamsa

"It's the Buddha's goose, I think," he says.

"What is?"

"Hamsa, it was named after Hamsa, the Buddha's goose. It was one of the first hippie communes around here. Intentional communities, they called them. *Life Magazine* called them hippie communes, so that's what most people think they were."

"What was Hamsa like?"

"It was mostly university types. A couple of professors who hadn't really dropped out, but you might say that they were eccentric. Some graduate students. An undergrad. Others they'd call slackers today."

"But what was it like, I mean, what happened?"

"Well, it felt a lot farther away from the university than the ten miles it actually was. Twenty-five years ago, the roads were in much worse shape, and lots of people were driving beaters or Volkswagen Bugs, which were always breaking down."

"But was it all sex, drugs, and rock 'n roll?"

"The '60s didn't get to some parts of Athens County 'til the '70s. So there had to be some of that. But mostly it was people from different backgrounds and different degrees of rebelling against where they came from, learning to live in groups larger than a family. Lots of them worked at the university, studying, teaching. They were trying something new."

"Hamsa wasn't the only one either, was it?"

"Oh, yeah, there were lots of them. Lots of university types were back-to-the-landers, but the land seemed expensive enough for them to want to buy together, communally. Usually a hundred dollars an acre or so. McDougalville was a place on McDougal Road. The 86 was another. And Sunflower, New Covenant, Currents, The Edges, Susan B. But the university was always there on the edge."

"Oh, and the goose."

"The goose?"

"Hamsa was the name of Krishna's swan."

—Will Dewees, intentional community organizer

Student broadcasters kept the All Campus Radio Network, ACRN, operating 24/7 and made it one of the finest on any campus. Spectrum Green, *1977. Courtesy* Athena Yearbook.

rue this day —decided the idea was a good one and planned to sponsor a better party with Mike Schmidt, Bob Hope, the Marching 110, and a cake for thousands in the fall of 1977.

The growing community of African American students, now numbering approximately 1,200, took little part in the uptown scene or Halloween. They stuck together, seeing themselves as "a country within a country" or "a system within a system." They attended Mt. Zion Baptist Church, played bid whist and danced in Lindley Center, visited on the windowsills of Logan's bookstore, or rapped on the wall in front of Baker Center. According to Anthony Webb, the

After an unofficial Halloween party in 1974, the Athens celebration grew quickly. Spectrum Green, 1976, 1979, 1980. *Courtesy* Athena Yearbook.

soldier's monument on the Green was their gathering place. "Information was passed along, schedules were set, and last night's happenings were re-told. The statue was one place black students felt was theirs. Other students were discouraged from sitting there. The statue belonged to us."

The Black Students Communication Caucus provided academic and career counseling and sponsored Black Communications Week each spring. *Black Directions,* a WOUB radio show, featured "Black Talk," "Black His-tory," "Perspectives," and "zany" deejay Carol Ford, who epitomized the ability to communicate "soul to soul." Gospel Voices of Faith, under the

African American students used the Civil War Monument as a gathering place. *Courtesy Anthony Webb.*

International student Maleb Abou Mansour became a frisbee fan, along with many other Ohio University students. *Courtesy Mahn Center.*

African American and international students lent diversity to the campus. *Courtesy Mahn Center.*

direction of Professor Francine Childs, sang on campus and on tours. Fraternities and sororities offered social activities. A newspaper, a theater group, and Black Awareness Week were organized.

The effort to make white students aware of what it meant to be black—and black in Athens—was an ongoing task. Frances Holly Blount remembers that her three roommates, all white, did not know anything about black people. "One day I locked the door and made them stay in. I had an issue of *Ebony,* and I went through that and just taught them about black people." For some, the culture shock of coming to rural Athens remained as strong as it had been for Diana Donaldson.

I was not prepared for the fact that we were in southern Ohio. It was difficult to listen to the accents. To me it sounded like we were in the deep South. And it was more rural. I remember coming for precollege and walking uptown and standing on the corner, getting ready to criss-cross—you know, being able to go criss-cross across the street, which I thought was really cool—and watching a truck go down Court Street with cows in it. COWS! I couldn't relate to that.

Culture shock also affected some of the six hundred students who had come to Athens from fifty-five other countries, including Venezuela, Liberia, Saudi Arabia, Malaysia, Vietnam, and South Africa, drawn by the Ohio Program of Intensive English (OPIE), by the education, math, and science departments, and by recommendations from people who were acquainted with O.U. programs abroad. The newly formed Athens Friends of International Students, which included many local residents, provided personal contacts, conversation, and friendships. The Farley family created "a mini-UN" at the Oasis, where students chattered in many languages over hummus, curry rice with peas, and fried noodles. Other new restaurants—the Farmacy, Hopsing, ¿Casa Que Pasa?, and Souflaki's—spiced up Athens cuisine with miso sandwiches, egg-drop soup, tostados, and gyros.

Still, the adjustment was far from easy, especially for married students who came without their spouses

The Oasis, at the corner of University Terrace and Park Place, and other Athens restaurants changed their menus as more international students arrived in Athens.
Courtesy Dan Dry Associates.

Hopsing and ¿Casa Que Pasa?
Courtesy Mahn Center.

and children. A student from Liberia said, "The thoughts of a better job and better living conditions when [I] return home made me brave the separation, but now I'd never want to be separated from my family again." Nik, from Malaysia, who came for a Ph.D. in linguistics, agreed. "The way I forget my yearnings [for family] is to bury myself in work, but the presence of sixty other Malaysians helps me overcome my homesickness."

In 1976, students, faculty, and townspeople became better acquainted with the many cultures that were represented on the campus when the International Student Association sponsored a festival with cooking demonstrations, a Latin American Night, a Venezuelan dinner and dance, and a Casbah Bazaar with crafts and food. The event is now known as the International Street Fair, a favorite tradition of each year's International Week.

The Athens International Film Festival, another innovation of the '70s, has also come to characterize spring in Athens. Conceived in 1973 by three film students, the festival was intended to "create a meeting place for independent film and video producers as well as provide an opportunity for independents to meet Hollywood producers, directors and writers." In 1976,

For anyone interested in working with international students, O.U. is the best place. For example, this year I wrote a paper about the effect of new rice production technology on women in Southeast Asia. Right there alongside me in class were women from Malaysia and Indonesia who could comment.

—Natalie Zimmerman, '82, for OHIO UNIVERSITY TODAY

The International Street Fair began in the late '70s and became a favorite feature of each spring's International Week. *Courtesy University Photographer's Office and Kanta Devi.*

legendary filmmaker Howard Hawkes graced receptions and gave workshops. The following year, European and Japanese directors were featured. The festivals lasted sixteen days, offered sixteen feature films, judged 300 competition films and videos, and gave prizes to the winners.

In the fall of 1977, President Ping presented The Educational Plan 1977–1987, the first of several long-range planning documents that would come to define his administration. From it he distilled six commitments to guide the university over the coming years. Stated simply, they were commitments to ensure quality; to enhance intellectual community by reforming the curriculum and redefining faculty roles; to encourage educational justice, international community, and lifelong learning; and to value the residential campus with its traditions of lib-

Flags on the Green during International Week. *Courtesy David Tilahun and International Students and Faculty Services.*

eral arts and professional programs, teaching, and research. Each of these commitments reflected the university's historic traditions or developing programs. What perhaps was new was the conviction that achieving these now formally defined goals depended on hard choices, sound plans, and the determination to put those plans into action.

The choice to try to stabilize enrollment at 13,500 by 1978 had already been made. As the state legislature honored its agreement to provide a special subsidy, the administration took action on its plans to improve recruiting and public image and reduce both space and expenses—especially those connected with dormitories. Admissions Director Walters initiated prospective student weekends and used the university's natural beauty as a selling point. He knew that after touring the College Green, many students would feel like Mary Ann Samad Lohmueller, who said she stayed in Athens for another degree "just so I could watch the leaves fall and blow across the campus one more time." The administration addressed the problem of being 25 percent "over-spaced" (space had increased 46 percent between 1967 and 1970) by razing more buildings and selling more residence halls to the state for new uses. A long-range Space Utilization Management Plan was developed, maintenance on residence halls was deferred, and, after the cold winter and energy crisis of 1977, the university calendar was changed to include a winter break that extended from Thanksgiving until early January.

The decision to adopt the ten-year educational plan required a mechanism for keeping the individual plans of nineteen planning units in line with the university's larger goals. UPAC—the University Planning Advisory Committee—became that mechanism. Composed of representatives of the planning units, the group collaborated to review and evaluate unit proposals and then recommend the allocation of a small portion of the budget to correct salary inequities, to adjust for inflation, and to support initiatives for enhancing or creating programs.

Of course, no amount of planning could guarantee quality. Adequate resources were imperative, and the state's support of Ohio University and

Giulio Scalinger and two other film students began the Athens International Film Festival in 1974. Still successful, the event is now known as the Athens International Film and Video Festival. *Courtesy Ruth Bradley and Center for Film and Video.*

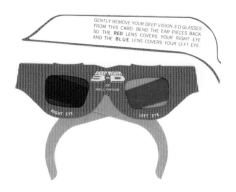

3-D glasses for the Athens International Film Festival. *Courtesy Ruth Bradley and Center for Film and Video.*

A literary festival, sponsored by the English department, brings writers to the campus each May. *Courtesy Department of English.*

The first Athens International Film Festival was held in April 1974. *Courtesy Ruth Bradley and Center for Film and Video.*

Ohio University's Spring Festivals

Between the end of April and the middle of May, critically acclaimed writers, film-makers, media notables, and visitors from around the world share their ideas, work, and cultures with the university and Athens communities in a series of festival events. The oldest, Communication Week, comes first.

In 1968 journalism faculty in the newly established College of Communication organized the first Journalism Week. They also created the Carr Van Anda Award, in honor of the legendary managing editor of the *New York Times,* and named CBS anchor Walter Cronkite as one of its first recipients. Two years later, the event became Communication Week, incorporating all the schools of the college. Students play an important role in organizing events. Traditionally each school offers a day-long set of talks and workshops at which leaders in the communications world meet and speak with students and faculty. Distinguished guests have included Katharine Graham, publisher of the *Washington Post;* Gordon Parks, photographer; Marshall McLuhan, communication theorist; Shana Alexander, *Newsweek* columnist; Charlayne Hunter-Gault, *MacNeil/Lehrer NewsHour* reporter; David Brinkley, NBC news anchor; the Reverend Jesse Jackson, founder of the Rainbow Coalition; and Vint Cerf, an Internet pioneer.

Starting in October 1973, Giulio Scalinger, an undergraduate in film from South Africa, led a group of student film aficionados in creating a showcase for independent and student-produced films from around the world. The result was the first Athens International Film Festival, held in April 1974, with author and critic Susan Sontag as the guest speaker. Some ninety-three films, mostly by students, were shown, and five student filmmakers were judged competition winners. By the second festival, feature films included recent significant works by internationally known directors such as François Truffaut, Robert Altman, and Louis Malle. The broad range of offerings—animation, documentary, abstract—expanded to include a video competition in 1982. The steadily growing success of the Athens International Film and Video Festival was apparent at its twenty-fifth anniversary in 1998, when a record 495 works were entered in its competition. By that date the festival had screened almost 6,400 works and brought 334 artists, producers, critics, and scholars to the university.

International Week, celebrated since 1982, has become a time when all of Athens focuses on the world beyond southeast Ohio. The culmination of the week's conference, discussions, films, and music is the festive street fair, coordinated by the Office of International Student and Faculty Services and International Student Union in collaboration with the Athens Area Chamber of Commerce. The street fair is a day of education and celebration on which Ohio University's international students turn Court Street into a global marketplace, sharing the dances, food, music, art, and crafts of their homelands.

The Spring Literary Festival, the newest of the spring celebrations, was first offered in May 1986 to bring some of the world's most distinguished authors to the university. Carolyn Chute, Andre Dubus, Michael S. Harper, Robert Hass, Stanley Plumly, and Tobias Wolff offered a three-day series of readings and lectures. Response was so enthusiastic that the College of Arts and Sciences and the English department have made the festival a permanent spring event. Graduate students in creative writing work with faculty to select each year's writers, produce a tabloid flyer to promote the event, and commit to a host of other errands while the writers are in town. For some of these aspiring writers, spending time with charismatic writers such as William Stafford can be a life-changing experience.

C. Paul Stocker, '26, understood the importance of faculty and equipment to engineering programs and contributed generously to support the Russ College of Engineering and Technology, housed in the C. Paul and Beth K. Stocker Engineering and Technology Center. Stocker invented the Sub Cycle static frequency converter, an innovation that became a buzzword among telephone equipment operators throughout the nation, and received more than fifty foreign and domestic patents. The converter was the first product Great Britain asked for under an exchange of patents agreement during World War II. Stocker's firm, Lorain Products, manufactured more than three hundred products at six plants in the United States and Canada; he retired as its president after a merger with Reliance Electric.

Courtesy Mahn Center.

of higher education was increasingly unpredictable. Year after year, the university had to cut its budget in reaction to state cuts, sometimes in midsummer, sometimes in midyear. The results were constant adjustment and repeated tuition increases. Consequently, in 1978 the president announced the launch of the 1804 Fund, designed to coincide with the celebration of the university's 175th anniversary in February 1979. The goal was set at $14 million, $7.5 million of which had already been received from the estate of 1926 alumnus C. Paul Stocker, an electrical engineer who well understood that "much depends on the scholarly climate in which men live and work." His bequest tripled the university's endowment and provided a chair in electrical engineering, $250,000 annually for engineering equipment, and other undesignated funds. The campaign increased the university's endowment from $3 million to over $20 million, adding, among other things, $35,000 a year for the library; merit, Honors Tutorial, and athletic scholarships; and grants for both research and creative activities. Cherry trees sent by Chubu Institute, O.U.'s sister institute in Japan, as a gesture of friendship decorated the bike path, and the Grosvenor house on University Terrace, the gift of fund chairman Wilfred Konneker, became the Konneker Alumni Center.

The year 1978–79 was also notable for strengthening liberal studies. Many American colleges and universities (including Harvard) were reinstating

Class outdoors on the Green.
Courtesy Dan Dry Associates.

core requirements, and the Ohio Board of Regents agreed that Ohio's schools should do the same. President Ping and the committee he appointed to prepare a "Discussion Document for General Education" were well aware of Ohio University students' current tendency to choose degrees in business, engineering, and communication over arts and sciences, and agreed that "the time has come for a reassertion of the intrinsic values of General Education."

The plan, agreed upon by the many departments it affected, included three sets of General Education requirements, or tiers: Tier I quantitative and writing courses, Tier II "breadth of knowledge" courses (often but not exclusively from arts and science departments), and a Tier III "capstone"

Brother Jed's admonitions challenged students each spring. *Spectrum Green, 1981. Courtesy Athena Yearbook.*

course, for the "special integrative study . . . of important themes or problems cutting across the main areas of the student's college experience and involving a confrontation of value issues." The tiers would be instituted in stages, with Tier III slated for 1982. Intended to make Ohio University a "distinctive and vigorous institution," the program depended for its success on faculty mentors who, along with departmental rather than University College advisers, would meet frequently with students to guide their selection of classes and stimulate their involvement in the intellectual life of the university.

The residence halls were also seen as venues for student involvement. Life in university housing was much improved since the overcrowded days of the 1960s. Both programming and supervision of residence halls was better. The two new greens had lost much of their bare, raw look, and students now seemed to identify with their particular greens in ways that former President Alden had hoped for. Residents of East Green said their stomping

Students played and studied under the trees on the College Green. *Courtesy Mahn Center.*

ground, with its old trees and a winding roadway, was "homey, the most civilized, and had the best academic atmosphere." Residents of "Wild West" loved Mae West and Locolymics weekends and sunbathing at Boyd Beach. South Green, with catwalks and mods, was tranquil-looking but known for parties. In 1979 Tim Caskey's indoor beach party brought tons of sand into the Nelson Rec Room, attracted 2,000 students, and started a new campus fad. At the Big Snooze Pajama-Rama that same year, students shared late-night reruns, rock, and a simulated sunrise. As for the residents of the College Green,

Vending in Athens

People who remember the Muffin Man, the Bagel Man, the Crepe Lady, and Skip the Weeny Man knew Athens in the '70s at the height of its vending days. Alternative food delivery schemes were not new to the area. Katherine Cocanower remembers the early 1920s. "We had to be in the dorm at 7:30. But the boys would sometimes yell up to the window to ask if we were hungry after that. If we were, they'd go uptown and get us some hamburgers, and we'd lower a rope down and pull the food up." Twenty years later, student vendors like Frank Blakely, Bob Wren, and Leo and Isabelle Wilcox were more organized, making boxes of sandwiches and peddling them door to door in women's dorms to earn their spending money.

The Burrito Buggy (detail). Alkyd © Gary Pettigrew. *Courtesy of the artist.*

In the late '60s two enterprising students putting themselves through school brought a narrow, one-person buggy to the bottom of Jeff Hill. In their mini convenience store they sold pop, chips, and sandwiches. But it was Louie Stevens, the Bagel Man, who got the Athens street scene rolling in the fall of '72 with bagels that were reasonably priced and delicious. The operation seemed to pose a threat to the Athens police and City Council. City regulations did not include street vendors, and besides, what was he really selling in there after dark?

Louie resisted all efforts to get rid of him, collecting 2,000 signatures on a petition to put the vending issue on the ballot. As citizens turned out to vote in the Nixon/McGovern election, many also cast their votes for Louie. He won his vending rights and afterward worked with Athens City Council to establish vending laws. As Dave Brennan of Munchie Muffin fame tells it, the streets of Athens became like the Wild West as vendors came and went. Some were students who paid for their educations and left. Some were students who stayed on. And others were "hippies" who were drawn to the cheap land and thriving counterculture of the Athens area. All of them gave Athens a new and special ambiance.

Sandwich vendors in the 1940s. *Courtesy Athena Yearbook, 1946.*

Some vendors found the long hours, frequent foul weather, and need for real business acumen more than they wanted to deal with. By 1984, when the city changed its vending laws, many of the smaller carts were disappearing, and gradually larger, more expensive buggies took their places. Mark Bernards and Paul Wildeck hit on a Mexican theme and brought a Burrito Buggy to town. Late Night Pizza followed and eventually invented an artichoke parmesan pie. Nisar Shaikh's Flying Saucer, re-named Ali Baba's, continued to offer exotic Middle Eastern treats. In the '90s, the Red Wagon offered sandwiches on Big Chimney Bread, and buggy lunches became as popular as late-night snacks.

Louie Stevens, the original bagel man. Spectrum Green, *1978. Courtesy* Athena Yearbook.

By the end of the '90s, many vending spaces on Union Street stood empty; then only the Burrito Buggy and Ali Baba's wagon remained to carry on a long tradition. But eating on the street is fun, the clientele is loyal, and as Paul Wildeck says, Athens is a town that appreciates something different. In spring 2002, something different appeared—alligator meat, gumbo, and hot dogs at the Express. The menu was new, but the buggy was the old Red Wagon with a new coat of purple paint. With luck and the passing on of a few more unused licenses, buggies will continue to add their special flavor to the uptown scene.

Dave Brennan selling fruit. Spectrum Green, *1978. Courtesy* Athena Yearbook.

Jody Blinder, Beth Gillespie, and Jaycee Human prepare for the Styx concert, circa 1979. *Courtesy Jody Blinder, '83.*

one said sitting on the memorial and chatting with friends "seems to make the load and pressure of my schoolwork a lot lighter." Another liked listening to Brother Jed and the spring evangelists, to the sound of church bells, or to people playing guitars.

Students' musical tastes in the mid-1970s showed an appreciation of both popular and classical groups. They listened to bands brought in by UPC (the Beach Boys, the Doobie Brothers, Styx, and the Southern Revival), as well as to guests of the Artist Series, such as jazz great Dizzy Gillespie, pianist Ruth Laredo, and the Osaka Philharmonic. Many also attended concerts and recitals presented by music majors and faculty and contributed to the success of elaborate productions—*Carmen, La Bohème,* and *Madame Butterfly*—that resulted from collaboration between the music and theater schools.

The Doobie Brothers put on a colorful show in 1979. Spectrum Green, *1979. Courtesy* Athena Yearbook.

Ohio University was equally supportive of theater and dance. Since the 1887 performance of *Fashion,* its students had taken to the stage both formally and informally. They had often shared the spotlight with professors in productions that ranged from *Othello* to the *Pirates of Penzance.* They had built props and lighted scenes, invented stunt carnivals, written one-acts, and joined townspeople in a theater department spin-off, Ohio Valley Summer Theater, under the leadership of Professor Robert Winters. When the School of Dance celebrated its tenth anniversary in 1979, successful graduates of the program returned to campus and performed works they had choreographed in honor of founder Shirley Wimmer, saying it was "her vision that makes Ohio University a unique place for dancing and dancers, teachers and students."

Students also benefited from the university's commitment to educational justice. A federally funded work-study program offered jobs for more than 1,200 students. The Student Development Center provided tutoring and a popular study skills course for eager beavers who just wanted to get a step ahead as well as for some of the 30 percent of students who lacked adequate preparation in math, writing, and reading.

The School of Dance, established by Shirley Wimmer, celebrated its tenth anniversary in 1979. *Courtesy Mahn Center.*

In 1979 the center added the College Adjustment Program with a grant from the federal government. Black studies courses now enrolled more than three hundred students (sixteen as majors). By the early 1980s, LINKS peer mentors and the summer programs in the colleges of engineering and medicine eased minority students' transition into the university.

Though a mid-1970s O.U. yearbook said there was a backlash against women's liberation, some coeds appreciated the designation of 1975 as International Year of the Woman, Ohio University's 1977 Woman's Place Conference, and a new Women's Center. Supported by the provisions of Title IX, O.U. coeds cut their hair to rejoin the previously all-male band and competed for new scholarships and berths on the four women's intercollegiate teams coordinated by Peggy Pruitt. They won accolades for softball prowess, hustled on the hockey field, and formed the Rugby Club with male ruggers.

Women also had an increasing number of role models on campus. Though only 52 of the 510 tenured faculty members were female, students could look up to the dean of students and the directors of home economics, dance, the Honors Tutorial College, and nursing. In 1979, when the College of Health and Human Services opened, African American Hilda Richards became the university's first female academic dean. With the creation of

During the '70s and early '80s, women filled several senior administrative positions. *Left to right:* Dean Hilda Richards, Health and Human Services; Vice President Martha Turnage; Vice President and Dean of Students Carol Harter; Dean Dora Wilson, Fine Arts; and Dean of Ohio University–Chillicothe Ann Jones. Ohio University Today, *Fall 1984.*

courses devoted to women's issues by Professors Joy Huntley, Patricia Richard, Barbara Daniel, and Nancy Bain, students could earn certificates in women's studies by the early 1980s. In 1981, the Affirmative Action Plan was revised.

The university's commitment to international community enriched campus life in other ways. In the spring of 1978, Nigerian Ambassador Olujimi Jolaoso attended Nigeria Week. That fall, an eleven-member delegation from the People's Republic of China included Ohio University in its tour of American universities. The visitors liked the science programs, the physics department's accelerator, the small-town atmosphere, and the presence of 900 international students. Within two years, sixteen Chinese scholars would be studying for graduate degrees. In December, Malaysia's ambassadors to the U.S. and the U.N. and its deputy prime minister came to campus for the ninth annual Malaysian Students Association Convention. The following spring, the national media spotlighted Ohio University's

The College of Health and Human Services is housed in Brandon T. Grover Center, which was rededicated in November 2001 after a $24.5 million renovation. Dean Gary Neiman and Brandon T. Grover Jr. and Jane Grover Scheel, children of the building's namesake, take part in a ribbon-tying ceremony symbolizing the uniting of all academic units of the college in one complex. *Courtesy College of Health and Human Services.*

World Communication Conference. A part of the journalism school's Communication Week, it pitted NBC's *Nightly News* anchor David Brinkley and Assistant Secretary of State Hodding Carter III against representatives of third-world wire services in discussions of communication issues. During the next academic year, the Chubu Institute of Technology, which already had an exchange program with Ohio University, established a fund to pay for visiting

College of Health and Human Services

The Educational Plan 1977–1987, adopted in October 1977, set twelve goals in the area of health and human services, stating: "There can be no question that many health and human service disciplines have matured to a level of complexity that placement in an institution of higher learning is not only appropriate, but mandatory." The College of Health and Human Services, the university's ninth degree-granting college, was approved on January 28, 1979, and was operational by July 1 of that year.

The new college already had a rich heritage of service and achievement because its three academic units and two centers had existed in other parts of the university. The School of Health, Physical Education, and Recreation; the School of Home Economics; the Center for Human Development; and the Nursery Child Care Center all moved from the College of Education. The School of Hearing and Speech Sciences joined them from the College of Communication. One year later, in 1980, the School of Nursing completed the college under the direction of Dean Hilda Richards. The School of Physical Therapy was created in 1984, and a separate college division was established in 1994 to administer campus recreation and wellness programs.

Over the years, changes and additions to the college units have reflected the changing needs and focus in health and human services career fields, and most of the original academic units have undergone name changes. In 1993 the School of Home Economics became the School of Human and Consumer Sciences as a result of expanded program offerings. The Nursery Child Care Center in that school is now the Child Development Center. The School of Health, Physical Education, and Recreation, which underwent name changes in the interim, divided into two schools in 1994: the School of Health Sciences and the School of Recreation and Sport Sciences. In 2001 the School of Hearing and Speech Sciences changed to the School of Hearing, Speech, and Language Sciences, in alignment with professional standards. Despite these changes, the college continues to follow founding principles, maintaining emphasis on an interdisciplinary approach to education within the field of health and human services and providing the community with services through experiential learning centers, including Ohio University Therapy Associates hearing, speech, language, and physical therapy clinics; the Child Development Center; the Atrium Cafe; WellWorks wellness and fitness program; and the Heartworks cardiac rehabilitation program.

Though the college is the youngest at the institution, it has rapidly grown into one of the largest. With nearly ninety full-time faculty, the college offers about twenty-five majors to nearly 2,600 undergraduates and graduate students, including nationally recognized programs in sports administration and in hearing, speech, and language.

For twenty-one years, the college's programs were scattered across the campus, but in the fall of 2001, the college was united in the newly renovated Brandon T. Grover Center, fulfilling one of the original goals set in 1977. The comprehensive complex is one of several facilities administered by the college. Additionally, the college operates the Child Development Center on the Ridges and several recreation facilities, including the Charles J. Ping Student Recreation Center, Bird Arena, the Aquatic Center, the Golf and Tennis Center, Challenges Courses, and intramural fields.

professors at its Kasugai campus; the Malaysian government endowed the Tun Abdul Razak Chair for Southeast Asia Studies; and the education college signed a contract to provide teacher training in Botswana.

Closer to home, African American Trustee Don Spencer challenged the university's trustees to listen to students who thought it was immoral to continue investing in South Africa under apartheid. Though most trustees agreed, they hesitated. Spencer, however, insisted: "Don't say you abhor it and then allow it to continue." Eventually, they followed his advice.

Though international enrollments were rising, statistics indicated that by the mid-eighties Ohio University's total enrollment was likely to drop because of a decrease in the pool of college-age students. One solution was to broaden the base of students by including more adults. As a result, the Office of Lifelong Learning was established in 1979, and continuing education was expanded. By 1981, 4,500 students (some of whom were incarcerated) were taking Independent Study courses from 250 faculty members. The Belmont campus offered a weekend program that invited working adults to come to campus on weekends over several years to earn Associate in Arts degrees, and Lancaster's Executive MBA program allowed people with careers to earn advanced degrees without being on campus for extended periods of time. In addition, Betty Menson supervised a program in experiential learning, which granted credit for documented learning experiences outside the classroom, and English Professor Edward Quattrocki used a grant from the National Endowment for the Humanities to offer an M.A. in Liberal Studies to adults.

In 1981, Dean McWilliams and I were the first participants in an exchange program between O.U. and our university in Toulouse, France. I had been a student and a lecturer at U.B.C. in Vancouver, S.M.U. in Dallas, and U.C.L.A. in Los Angeles. But Athens gave me the opportunity to discover what small-town life in America was like. I found out quickly that Athens, Ohio, is not a sleepy town, and I fell in love with it. Every night there is something going on at the theater, in the concert hall, and through the streets—the memory of the "Take Back the Night" march will remain in my mind forever. Walking through Athens is pleasant, partly thanks to Alvi McWilliams's persevering and successful efforts to beautify it. If you want to get out in the hilly countryside just rent or borrow a bike: the scenery is gorgeous, particularly in the fall.

—Professor Marcienne Rocard, Toulouse, France

In spite of the generally mellow tone of campus life during the mid-to-late 1970s, each year seemed to end in conflict and bad publicity, and 1979 was no exception. For the tenth time in eleven years, on a warm evening, students left bars late, lingered uptown, and eventually battled police for control of Court Street. This yearly "hooliganism," the growing popularity of Halloween (now the "Mardi Gras of the Midwest"), and the presence of twenty-seven uptown bars combined to reinstate Ohio University as one of the country's top party schools.

Fortunately, during the next two years good publicity became more frequent and widespread than the reports on uptown disturbances and parties. In the spring of 1981, the *Wall Street Journal* reported that President Ping had created "something of a model in adapting the planning process to the collection of fiefdoms and other vested

"This is Chief Jones of the Athens police department. I believe this crowd constitutes a riot situation. You have 10 minutes to disperse."

From SPECTRUM GREEN, 1977

interests that constitute the campuses of higher education." Certainly his planning and budgeting were leading the university closer to the six goals defined by Educational Plan 1977–1987. Enrollment—now over 20,000 on the combined campuses—had exceeded projections as well as the growth at most other Ohio schools. Despite a recession and declining state support for higher education, the university no longer needed a special subsidy, and the residence halls were self-sustaining. The new programs in medicine, health and human services, visual communication, and communication systems management, along with enhancement of programs in engineering, attested to a commitment to professional education and research, while the three-tiered general education program promised a revitalization of teaching and liberal arts. The university was more diverse and far reaching than it had ever been. The Institute for Local Government Administration and Rural Development (ILGARD) was ready to provide assistance to government organizations in twenty-eight southeast Ohio counties. The library had replaced its card catalog with a computerized retrieval system (soon to be named ALICE). Thanks to the efforts of the president's wife, Claire Ping, the beautifully kept Campus Green was named a historic district on the National Register of Historic Places.

The fall of 1981 brought extraordinary publicity, first from the *Washington Post* and then from media around the world. Ohio University professors Thomas Wagner and Joseph D. Jollick had made a major scientific breakthrough by transferring hemoglobin genes from rabbits to mice, which then

Ohio University Libraries replaced the wooden card catalog with ALICE, an online catalog system. *Courtesy Mahn Center.*

Edison Biotechnology Institute

Founded in 1984, Ohio University's Edison Biotechnology Institute (EBI) is an interdisciplinary biomedical genetics research institute housed in a 40,000-square-foot facility on the Ridges. The institute and its faculty have achieved international recognition for the development of new research technologies and treatments for disease. Building on that success, EBI has served as a focal point for creating a community of campus scholars who are interested in developing a multidisciplinary biomedical research environment that promotes collaboration and synergy. Efforts to develop new therapeutics and diagnostic tools for human diseases, such as diabetes, cancer, autoimmune diseases, and cardiovascular complications, have been bolstered by the State of Ohio's Technology Action Fund, which awarded EBI grants in 2000 and 2001. The latter provided support for a university collaboration with Battelle, an international research and development organization based in Columbus, Ohio.

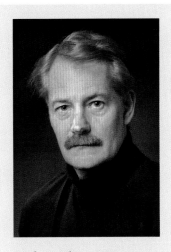

Professor Thomas Wagner, who worked with Professor Joseph Jollick to transfer hemoglobin genes from rabbits to mice. *Courtesy University Photographer's Office.*

Originally known as Ohio University's Edison Animal Biotechnology Center (EABC), EBI was among the first of six advanced technology centers established by Governor Richard Celeste under the Edison Program, designed to spur economic development in high-technology industries within Ohio by creating industry-university alliances.

Dr. Thomas Wagner, one of the institute's founders and its first director, was joined in 1986 by Dr. John Kopchick, molecular biologist and Goll Ohio Eminent Scholar. Both have made international headlines for their biotechnology breakthroughs, which include creation of the first successful transgenic animals in the early 1980s and discovery of a growth hormone antagonist (GHA), the first in a new class of peptide antagonist therapeutics.

Through new partnerships with academic departments at the university, the institute has grown to include five faculty scientists. It has generated more than two dozen patents and continues its focus on basic scientific discovery and the transfer of those discoveries to the public via the marketplace. Institute creativity and innovation have contributed substantially to a record of accomplishment in technology productivity that puts Ohio University in the top 10 percent of academic institutions nationally and that is unmatched within the state of Ohio.

were able to produce rabbit hemoglobin. This work led to new funding and new collaborators. The 1804 Fund helped provide a state-of-the-art laboratory with the equipment for transplanting genes—one of only six such labs in the world. Funds from the state's Thomas Alva Edison Foundation led to the establishment of the Edison Animal Biotechnology Center (later the Edison Biotechnology Institute). A company called Embryogen was incorporated as a conduit to the business world from the Edison Center. Directed by alumnus Wilfred Konneker, who volunteered his time, the company was housed in Old Morton Hall with the expectation that it and other start-up companies would eventually move to the old asylum grounds, which had recently been transferred to the university. By 1983 the university was able to offer an interdisciplinary doctoral degree in molecular and cellular biology. When the program won one of the first Eminent Scholar endowments from the Ohio Board of Regents in 1984, the *Columbus Dispatch* called Ohio University the "new mecca of science."

The Eminent Scholar award was a part of the state's Excellence Awards, a new initiative to base some funding on excellence rather than on sheer growth in numbers. Three other awards came to Ohio in the first round of competition among universities. The School of Telecommunications received funds that allowed it to become a national center for broadcast computer applications; the unique Institute of Visual Communication got a computer editing lab and a remodeled home in Seigfred Hall; and honors tutorial students got computers for their honors dorm. The awards were welcomed by students as well as by faculty and administrators. A student in VisCom said, "I came here because I had heard this is the best visual communication program in the country and Chuck Scott is the most highly thought of visual communication professor. I've found out it's true." Honors tutorial student Bruce Brege said of his experience, "It was new, different, revolutionary. No one in the U.S. had done this. It was brand new. I liked the idea of one-on-one with professors and the chance to really immerse myself in learning." Jason Stone said his HTC experience helped him become a critical thinker. "Being thrown to the dogs . . . gave me confidence to know that I could work my way through something that I didn't understand at first."

Other programs and professors were winning praise from students as well. Award-winning writers William Heyen, Stanley Plumly, and Dave Smith, all graduates of the English department's program in creative writing, returned for the 1983 honors convocation to pay homage to their former teachers Jack Matthews and Hollis Summers. "There is never a moment," they said, "when these two men are not present with us and we are not the only ones who are part of this tradition."

Graduates of the film department—Jack Wright, Daniel Saez, Eran Preis, Yin Tingru—described it as a place where there is "an intense and very open relationship between students and faculty." In only a few years, it had gained a reputation as one of the top ten programs in film production and was well on its way "to becoming the best small film department in the

Professors Hollis Summers and Jack Matthews were
recognized at the Honors Convocation in 1983.
Ohio University Today, Winter 1984.

The Winter Walks in Athens, Ohio

Some bricks in the walks of Athens, Ohio,
Are marked with ATHENS, OHIO,
Encouraging students and other pedestrians
To pretend to belong where they go.

Some feet echo comfort in Athens, Ohio,
Moving from ATHENS to ATHENS
While firmly ensconced in Athens, Ohio,
No matter how studiously pedestrian.

Perhaps I should mention that harsh winds blow
In passing through Athens, Ohio,
And some bricks are nameless, I know,
And some are crippled in Athens.

Hollis Summers,
THE WALKS NEAR ATHENS, 1954

*Courtesy University Photographer's
Office.*

United States," thanks in large part to the boost it got in the early 1970s from the film festival. Not only had the festival spawned the well-known magazine *Wide Angle,* it now attracted large numbers of film-makers and film buffs each year.

The avionics department, directed by Richard McFarland, a world authority on instrument landing systems, received over $1 million in 1984–85, bringing total outside funding since the program's inception to $7 million. The journalism school, which received $1.5 million from the Scripps Howard Foundation in 1982, was now rated as one of the top journalism programs in the country. Psychology Professors Harry Kotses and Tom Creer received a grant of $1 million to further their studies of adult asthma. The Baker Peace Conference, funded by a 1983 gift from former president John Baker and his wife, Elizabeth, attracted a multidisciplinary audience to the campus each year.

In 1986 both engineering and education celebrated significant birthdays. The engineering college was fifty, and it got a new home. Crook Hall had been completely renovated. Now named the C. Paul and Beth K. Stocker Engineering and Technology Center, for its benefactors, it provided what Dean Richard Robe called "perhaps the finest, most up-to-date facilities of any comparable engineering program in the nation." The College of Education

Master teacher Jean Harlan reading to children in the College of Education's Putnam Child Care Center.
Courtesy Mahn Center.

celebrated its centennial. It could point with pride to its 30,000 living graduates and the addition of new teacher training programs for Africa.

By the mid-eighties, both the recession and the state's funding crisis were over. The university was stable. It had received an excellent evaluation from the North Central Association of Colleges and Schools. Reviewers of the comprehensive ten-year self-study, prepared by English professor John Hollow, called it "one of the best they had ever seen," showing clearly that the university had prepared "perhaps better than most universities for the future and whatever it may hold." In 1985, *Best Buys in College Education* also gave the school a thumbs up. The *Fiske Guide* said "Socrates would have loved it." It singled out the university's programs in general education, honors tutorial, creative writing, photography, psychology, physics, journalism, business, and electrical engineering and noted that this university gave its students a "sense of community that few public institutions manage to achieve."

Several classes have been exceptional, and some professors. We take professors, not classes, and a network exists to get the word around. The best recommendation is, "the prof is tough, but good," and I've had some of them, like Frank Henderson in political science, Hal Arkes in psychology, and Dwight Pugh in quantitative methods.

—Mark Deaton, '83

Russ College of Engineering and Technology

The first record of Ohio University students' engaging in the science of engineering appeared in the trustees' *Minutes* of 1824 with the mention of a test in "Mensuration, Guaging [*sic*], Surveying and Navigation." By 1857 the catalog listed civil engineering courses, taught in what is now Wilson Hall. In 1891 the curriculum expanded to include several courses in electrical engineering. Students performed their experiments in the lighting plant that until 1913 was housed in Ewing Hall.

The College of Applied Science opened in the fall of 1936 with Albert A. Atkinson as its first dean and offered courses in civil and electrical engineering, agriculture, and industrial arts, as well as others through the School of Home Economics. Construction of an engineering building—currently the Research and Technology Building—began in 1948, but by the time it was completed in 1950, it was already overflowing, and even after a second section was added in 1958, many classes remained scattered around campus. During these years, the programs of mechanical, civil, electrical, architectural, and chemical engineering earned full accreditation from the Engineering Council for Professional Development.

In 1963, with the beginning of the computer age and advanced technology, the college was renamed the College of Engineering and Technology, and the Avionics Engineering Center became a part of the School of Electrical Engineering. When university enrollments declined during the early 1970s, the administration, faced with serious budget problems, considered phasing out engineering. Dr. Richard Mayer, dean of the college since 1971, persuaded President Claude Sowle to keep the program intact.

The growth of excellent programs, along with generous endowments from C. Paul and Beth Stocker, Fritz and Dolores Russ, and other trustees and engineering alumni, brought the college national recognition. The Stockers' gift of $8 million in 1978 has supported research and equipment, faculty enrichment, graduate fellowships, and two visiting professor chairs. In 1985 state funds paid for the renovation of Crook Hall, which became the C. Paul and Beth K. Stocker Engineering and Technology Center. The state-of-the-art facility houses the School of Electrical Engineering and Computer Science and the college's six departments—Aviation, Chemical Engineering, Civil Engineering, Industrial and Manufacturing Systems Engineering, Industrial Technology, and Mechanical Engineering.

In 1992 the college was named the Russ College of Engineering and Technology —the only named college at the university—to honor Fritz J. and Dolores H. Russ. In 2001 these outstanding alumni created the biannual $500,000 Fritz J. and Dolores H. Russ Prize, administered by Ohio University and the National Engineering Academy, in appreciation of the contributions of engineers to humankind.

The Russ College now includes several well-known centers and institutes of research. The centers include the Avionics Engineering Center, the Center for Geotechnical and Groundwater Research, the Ohio Coal Research Center, the Center for Automatic Identification Education and Research, and the Center for Advanced Materials Processing. The institutes include the Ohio Research Institute for Transportation and the Environment, the Institute for Corrosion & Multiphase Technology, and the Robe Leadership Institute. Through the generous support of alumni, friends, corporations, and foundations, the college has achieved recognition and excellence.

Spectrum Green, *1977. Courtesy Athena Yearbook.*

Fredrick Hagerman

In 1986 Fredrick C. "Fritz" Hagerman, professor of physiology, was runner-up for a national teaching award. His students were not surprised. They had repeatedly selected him for the University Professor Award, which recognizes each year's most memorable teachers. When they chose him for the fifth time in 1992, the dean of University College (which administered the program) took him out of the competition by naming him University Professor for Life.

In research, "Doc" Hagerman set the pace for the study of exercise physiology the world round. Faced with the difficulty of finding research equipment to study the complex phenomena, he used his own body as a laboratory device and subjected himself to regimens of work and exercise one has to view his lab films to appreciate. His commitment to these studies inspired many others to follow him.

In addition to chairing his department and serving on university committees and task forces, Fritz has been intimately involved with both professional and Olympic athletes in the role of consultant and trainer. The Cincinnati Reds baseball team used his knowledge and insights to develop stronger, fitter, and healthier players. His alterations to the U.S. Olympic rowing teams' training procedures helped them vault from relative unknowns to serious Olympic contenders.

Student government, abandoned in the '70s, reappeared in the '80s. *Courtesy Mahn Center.*

Ohio University's student community was becoming more conservative. Designer jeans replaced ragged Levi's, and students were "surprisingly spiffed up" much of the time. Oktoberfest was old hat, and a traditional Homecoming with a fancy parade seemed worth reviving. So did Student Senate, which reappeared in 1981 to replace the Student Governing Board, which had abolished itself in 1975. Many students saw no reason to object to ROTC. The library was a popular hangout. Dean of Students Carol Harter saw these students as eager to develop management and leadership skills and described them as the "post-Watergate generation," brought up on MTV and media. They described themselves as "realistic."

In spite of their relative conservatism, many students admired Professor Edgar Whan, the "maverick" professor who had championed most of the '60s and '70s liberal grading policies and programs, and voted him University Professor in Perpetuity. They enrolled in classes in humor writing, the history of baseball, the philosophy of sex and love, the sociology of sport, history of espionage, and popular literature, taught by Professors Mel Helitzer, Charles Alexander, Robert Trevas, Eric Wagner, Alan Booth, and John Hollow. They waited in long lines on weekends to get into uptown

bars and admitted that the weekend began on Wednesday and ended on Tuesday with time off for good behavior on Sundays and Mondays. Dancing was popular, especially at the Greenery, the Nickelodeon, Gee Willikers, and the Hangar. Everyone recognized "Rock Me Amadeus," Tears for Fears, and Duran Duran. Dating was out; groups were in, and so were fads. Some students spent hours in the fantasyland of Dungeons and Dragons, while others played Pac-Man or euchre. For many, *General Hospital* in front of Baker Center's big TV was de rigueur. Students were eager to continue the revival of that favored entertainment of the early '70s, the rowdy spring music festival.

The May 1980 festival brought 9,000 students onto the Mill Street fields to be entertained by Balinese dancers, the O. J. Anderson Mime Troupe, the Karate Club, Cameo, Jay Ferguson, McGuffey Lane, backgammon, frisbee, and beer. The next year merrymakers heard the Dregs, Willie Phoenix, and a repeat of McGuffey Lane. Beer trucks, hotdogs, and dancing were the order of the day. By 1984 Springfest had a new twist with an airband competition and dancing in the totally mudsoaked field. The Goodyear blimp

Springfest became a highlight of the spring social scene. *Left,* Spectrum Green, *1980. Courtesy Athena Yearbook. Right, courtesy Mahn Center.*

This place opens you up to so many things. For example, the other day I was walking on the College Green and stopped to watch some theater students putting on a play alongside Memorial Auditorium, while on the other side three Hari Krishnas went about their business. I don't want to go back to Dayton, where it's "normal"; people shouldn't lead such sheltered lives. I don't agree with everything I see and experience here, but the awareness is good. I'm not afraid of the unknown or the challenge. It's a philosophy this place has helped shape.

—Barry Grubs, from Ohio University Today, Summer 1982

The Beach Party in Bird Arena, with volleyball and sand castles, raised funds for Springfest. *Courtesy* Athena Yearbook, *1986.*

was invited to the '86 party, but declined. Never mind. The event was about to get a new source of funding—a Beach Party in Bird Arena where over two feet of sand encouraged volleyball, sandcastles, and beer drinking.

At the Convo, Bobcat basketball coach Danny Nee arrived in 1980 and built an exciting team from the ground up. By the time he left in 1986, his team had compiled a 107–67 record, won two regular-season MAC championships and two MAC tourney titles, and made two appearances in the NCAA (winning a first-round game in 1983) as well as two trips to the NIT. Lady Bobcats were equally impressive. Their star was Caroline Mast, MAC player of the year and a member of the All-MAC team for two consecutive years, who helped the team to a MAC championship in 1986.

By 1987, a renewed sense of pride pervaded the air as students, faculty, staff, and friends prepared to celebrate the 200th anniversary of the Northwest Ordinance that had laid the groundwork for the Ohio University. They were joined over the

Caroline Mast, Ohio University's all-time leading basketball scorer, led her team to a MAC championship in 1986. *Courtesy O.U. Athletic Department.*

Coach Danny Nee led the Bobcats to two MAC championships and two appearances in the NCAA. *Courtesy O.U. Athletic Department.*

Kermit Blosser

Kermit Blosser's life has been intimately linked with that of Ohio University for more than seventy years. Kermit arrived on campus, fresh from a Hocking County farm, in the fall of 1928. He worked his way through the university by washing dishes and shoveling coal, but still found time to participate in football and wrestling. As a sophomore, he played end on the football team that inaugurated Peden Stadium. He lettered each of the next three years as his team won all but one game and captured three Buckeye Conference titles. In 1932 he was NCAA champion wrestler at 191 pounds and an alternate on the Olympic wrestling squad, though he had only taken up wrestling to become stronger for football.

After graduation, Kermit became a high school coach, leading his team to a state basketball championship. But Navy service in the Pacific theater during World War II interrupted that career.

After the war, Athletic Director Don Peden decided to bring in new coaches who were O.U. alumni. He invited Jim Snyder, Jim Johnson, Bob Wren, and Kermit Blosser. Kermit began coaching football and assisting Thor Olson with wrestling. Soon Peden decided that O.U. needed a golf team, and Blosser discovered, to his surprise, that he was supposed to start it, even though he knew nothing about the sport and didn't even own a set of clubs. Fortunately, Kermit was a quick learner, for he led his golf team to eighteen MAC championships, the greatest domination by any MAC team in any sport. But he was always modest about his success. To him the thing that made being a teacher and coach worthwhile was having his students come back and say, "If it weren't for you, I wouldn't have graduated."

Kermit "retired" in 1988. Despite this fact, and the fact that he is legally blind, Kermit is a daily presence in the Convocation Center where he maintains contact with the athletic staff and alumni. An All-American and a member of ten different sports Halls of Fame, Kermit Blosser epitomizes the values of distinguished achievement and unstinting service to his alma mater.

Courtesy O.U. Athletic Department.

year by guests such as Daniel J. Boorstein, Martin Marty, Walter E. Williams, Maya Angelou, Benjamin Hooks, and Attallah Shabazz. Members of the university could congratulate themselves for having come together again, as a community, just as President Ping had hoped and expected they would. By adhering to the goals of the ten-year Educational Plan and what the president called a "stubborn striving for excellence," the university had renewed its commitment to liberal education, developed two new professional colleges, achieved fiscal stability, and supported remarkable research results. Now it was time to create a new education plan, launch a second fund-raising effort, and begin to look toward the third century of education at Ohio University.

There are several professors who stand out in my memory. I had Don Norris for freshman algebra. I hated math, but Professor Norris stated in class that if we had any problems we should come and see him. He is the only math professor I had who could come up with seven different ways to do a problem. He would keep coming up with solutions until you got it.

Dan Keyes was an inspiring creative writing teacher. His expectations were so high that you worked your tail off just so you wouldn't let him down. My final story of his class was published in an anthology of short stories and poetry put out by the University of Cincinnati.

Don Lambert taught a writing and editing class where he timed you in class to see how quickly you could put a story together. During speed week, you wrote five to six stories in fifty minutes and were graded on the accuracy of your typing (on an electric typewriter), grammar, syntax, and how well your lead was constructed.

—Tracy Green Corrigan, '89

The campus in autumn.
Courtesy Mahn Center.

THE SEARCH FOR COMMUNITY

Ohio University and the World:
Two Hundred Years of Global Connections

Ohio University was born with international features. The new university town was named Athens for Athens, Greece, the ancient seat of wisdom and learning. However, it was not until later in the nineteenth century that faculty members studied and traveled abroad and the first students came to Athens from other countries. Daniel Lindley, an O.U. graduate and son of President Jacob Lindley, served for thirty-seven years as a missionary to Africa. President Charles Super studied in Tuebingen, Germany. President Elmer B. Bryan served as general superintendent of education in the Philippines.

Senator John Glenn and President Ping welcome H. E. Zain Azraai, Malaysia's ambassador to the United States, to the convention of the Malaysian Students Association of North America, December 1977. *Courtesy Mahn Center.*

Wartime President Herman James studied at the University of Berlin and served as lecturer at the University of Leipzig

The first international student came to Ohio University in 1895 from Japan. His presence was such an exotic curiosity that he was able to augment his income by selling copies of a photo of himself clad in his traditional Japanese costume. At the turn of the twentieth century, students from East Asia formed an active Chinese student club.

World War I focused the attention of the campus on Europe, and many O.U. students, staff, and faculty served overseas. But it was World War II that brought more comprehensive global awareness to the campus. More than 5,000 O.U. alumni served in the war and 221 were killed. Nearly 20 percent of the faculty was granted leave to serve in the military.

At war's end, veterans flooded onto the campus under the G.I. Bill. These older, war-seasoned, worldly-wise students changed the character of student life. In this postwar period, a succession of internationally minded presidents began a transformation of the university from a small parochial institution into an astonishingly cosmopolitan one.

John Baker came to Athens in 1945 with strong international experience. While O.U. president he served as U.S. representative to the United Nations Economic and Social Council and nurtured many international friendships and connections. In 1950 he approved scholarships to support international students. The diversity of the student population expanded within two years to include thirty-seven nationalities, including students from Eastern European bloc countries.

Federal support for university international activities grew during the Cold War. In 1958, the College of Education secured the first of several Agency for International Development (AID) contracts to assist in curriculum development and teacher training in Nigeria. An AID project to improve secondary education in South Vietnam was also undertaken.

President Baker enticed international leaders such as Dag Hammarskjöld to Athens. Making global activities a priority agenda item, he created a distinctive international profile for Ohio University; in 1982, he and his wife endowed the Elizabeth and John Baker Peace Studies Program.

President Vernon Alden, with prior experience in Asia, Europe, and Latin America, was enticed from Harvard to Athens partly because of the university's nascent international programs. By the early 1960s, the university was administering five sponsored overseas projects, as well as beginning its long involvement with the Peace Corps.

A campuswide interdisciplinary Center for International Studies was established in 1964. Its first director was historian J. Norman Parmer, formerly a Peace Corps director in Malaysia. Master's degree programs in African Studies, Southeast Asian Studies, and Latin American Studies were launched between 1964 and 1970. Both the African Studies and Southeast Asian Studies programs earned the coveted designation as National Resource Centers by the U.S. Office of Education. An interdisciplinary undergraduate major in International Studies was established in the late 1970s, during the tenure of Center Director Ed Baum.

In 1968, the Ohio Program of Intensive English began training international students in English as a Foreign Language. Study abroad programs enhanced opportunities for language study in Austria, France, and Mexico, and the study of art history in England and Italy.

During the presidency of Charles Ping, the university's reputation for international achievement grew as some university personnel assumed leadership roles in prominent international organizations. Scholarly studies of international education selected Ohio University as a model case study, and feature articles on its exemplary international activities appeared in national publications such as the *Chronicle of Higher Education.*

Building upon a program begun in the late 1960s that brought staff from Malaysia's Mara Institute of Technology (ITM) to Athens for advanced degrees, the College of Business launched its cooperative OU/ITM Bachelor of Business Administration in 1975, and Ohio University faculty traveled to Malaysia to offer courses. Later an MBA program was added at ITM and at other Malaysian sites.

International students numbered more than a thousand in the 1980s. Many assumed leadership positions in the public or private sectors upon returning to their home countries. Where numbers permitted—in Nigeria, Malaysia, Japan, Hong Kong, Indonesia, Singapore, and Thailand—they formed local Ohio University alumni associations, and typically they maintained great loyalty to their alma mater. For example, with the help of alumni like Haji Mohd Arif Bador, the Razak Chair, named in honor of the second prime minister of Malaysia, was established at Ohio University in 1980 in cooperation with the Malaysian government and the American private sector. It was the first endowed chair of its kind in Malaysia and in the United States.

During his twenty-one-year tenure (1978–99) as dean of libraries, Hwa Wei Lee helped form many of the university's international connections. Alden Library became an official government depository for the governments of Swaziland, Botswana, Guatemala, and Malaysia, and the Shao You-Bao Overseas Chinese Documentation and Research Center was established.

During President Ping's administration, the university's formal linkages with overseas institutions for research, staff development, faculty/student exchanges, and other educational services grew to more than 120, involving the university in virtually every part of the world. In recognition of this expansion of global programs, Felix Gagliano was named Vice Provost for International Programs in 1981. Efforts were made to expose all faculty, students, and campus units to the educational benefits of overseas programs. Special funding initiatives encouraged faculty to increase international content in their courses. Every university planning document after 1977 articulated the university's special commitment to international education. The first General Education Plan stressed the importance of exposing all undergraduates to international topics. The University Planning and Advisory Council (UPAC) gave funding preference to international activities such as an international travel fund, a scholarship fund for study abroad in the College of Arts and Sciences, and the hiring of additional language faculty.

The university also shared international resources with its regional campuses and communities. The Ohio Valley International Council, formed in 1983 and directed by Mary Anne Flournoy, placed special emphasis on the public schools. OVIC developed a model for teaching Americans about the wider world through mobilization of its international students as cultural consultants. As a fifth grader wrote to her visitor, "I used to think Nigeria was a mean place but I don't anymore. Thank you for coming to Trimble. Most people wouldn't bother."

During the 1980s, the College of Education was extensively involved in Africa with USAID contracts in Botswana, Swaziland, and Lesotho; in the 1990s it helped establish relationships with Namibia and South Africa. The College of Communication conducted training projects in the Baltic States, the former East Germany, and West Africa and began a joint degree program in Thailand. Study abroad programs and exchanges proliferated beyond the traditional Western European settings to locales such as Japan, Swaziland, and Hungary. The Colleges of Arts and Sciences, Education, Business, and Communication were particularly active in seeking opportunities for their students abroad.

President Robert Glidden has built upon the foundation of his predecessors, adding his own innovative focus upon the powerful new technologies that promise to shrink the globe and diminish age-old educational barriers of time and space. All colleges now have international programs. The College of Business's MBA Without Boundaries includes cohorts of students in Hubei Province in China and provides training in American business practices for a thousand Brazilian professionals a year. The College of Osteopathic Medicine offers a field experience in Kenya and, with the College of Health and Human Services, a Traditional Medicine in China training program. The College of Arts and Sciences offers numerous study abroad programs, including one at a residential center in Germany, the Ohio-Leipzig European Center.

The College of Communication has involved faculty in training programs for communication professionals from Eastern Europe and the former Soviet Union; its School of Journalism hosts the Sing Tao Center for International Journalism. The Russ College of Engineering and Technology maintains exchange and research ties with universities in Pakistan, the PRC, Russia, Germany, the Netherlands, Poland, and Switzerland. The College of Fine Arts involves faculty and students in performance training and filmmaking in

Croatia. The College of Education allows students to satisfy part of their student teaching requirement abroad.

The Global Learning Community (GLC), the university's first residential international program, began in 1998 and now involves students from all colleges in a unique two-year certificate program. Project-based learning and international experiences such as consulting, internships, and study abroad are its hallmarks.

The Center for International Studies has been headed since 1996 by Associate Provost Josep Rota. The programs in African Studies and Southeast Asian Studies rank among the top ten in the nation. The Institute for the African Child of the Center for African Studies has provided a thematic focus and unique research emphasis. By early 2002, there were 220 faculty affiliated with these and other Center for International Studies programs.

The terrorist attacks of September 11, 2001, added new urgency and meaning to international studies and to campus discussion of world issues. This tragedy underscored the urgency of the university's mission to nurture the competencies required to understand the larger global context. On the eve of its 200th birthday Ohio University is well prepared for this challenge. The university's myriad global activities mark the campus as the most international of the state's higher learning institutions and rank it among the most globally oriented institutions in the United States.

After Peking University president Chou Pei-Yuan was introduced to Ohio University by President Ping, Chinese students began to enroll. Spectrum Green, *1979. Courtesy* Athena Yearbook.

10

Toward the Third Century

> Those who would shape the third century of Ohio University hold a trust from the past for the future. . . . Born of a revolutionary understanding of government and the role of education in society, the university owes its life to the conviction that knowledge is ". . . necessary to good government and the happiness of mankind."
>
> —*Colloquium on the Third Century, 1987*

At the end of the 1980s, Ohio University was riding the crest of a wave of success. Total enrollment was nearing 25,000; residence halls in Athens were virtually full, and entering students were better prepared. The annual budget of over $172 million typically included as much as $8 million in gifts from loyal alumni and more than $21 million in government contracts and grants. Frequent news reports highlighted the beauty of the campus, the scholarship of professors, and awards to innovative programs.

Not surprisingly, when the trustees adopted a new long-range planning document in 1988, its tone was self-congratulatory. Though the plan did recognize the challenges presented by a rapidly changing society—the end of the Cold War, the shift from a manufacturing to a service economy, an increasing reliance on technology, the growing gap between rich and poor, the crisis in health care—it emphasized continuity. It said Ohio University should prepare for its third century by perfecting its own distinctive identity as an institution of opportunity that fostered both teaching and research and complemented

In the fall of 1989, Ohio University trustees heard encouraging reports on enrollment, housing, minority faculty hires, and the most recent class of graduates. Athens Messenger, *September 17, 1989.*

Everything's coming up roses at Ohio U.

liberal studies with professional programs. To build on its reputation for quality, the university would have to continue to make hard choices about the interrelated issues of programming, funding, and size.

The immediate choices included a continued commitment to the university's burgeoning research efforts and to its distinctive centers of excellence in both undergraduate and graduate programs. To balance the growth of research and professional programs, the General Education program was to be reformed to better integrate required courses and students' majors. To increase funding without having to dramatically increase enrollment (the state's funding formula primarily rewarded constant growth in numbers), the report proposed a major fundraising campaign.

Students focused their fundraising efforts on the wildly popular Beach Party, now the chief money-maker for Springfest. The 1988 event planners, hoping to be included in the *Guinness Book of World Records,* dumped tons of sand in Bird Arena, set up the volleyball net and a hot tub, and welcomed students in Hawaiian shirts and leis. But a new law that raised the legal drinking age from eighteen to twenty-one cut beer consumption, and only $5,000 —half the previous year's total—was raised for Springfest. Nevertheless,

Springfest went off that year without a hitch. Twenty-five thousand students blanketed the fields near Lakeview Apartments for what was later called the Woodstock of Ohio. Folks who wanted to listen to the Outlaws and other bands without paying for the privilege perched across the river on Bong Hill; others plied their homemade watercraft up and down the shallow Hocking. Asked to recall the event years later, Tracy Green Corrigan smiled and said simply, "God, it was fun."

The next year, the university complied with the new drinking law by banning beer sales at all campus events and turning the Frontier Room into a coffee shop. Springfest went dormant until its 1994 revival at a Court Street parking lot. However, in the

Musicians at Springfest '88 drew 25,000 people to the recreation fields east of campus. A few music lovers enjoyed the show from river rafts, while others listened from Bong Hill. *Courtesy* Athena Yearbook, *1988.*

fall of 1990, residents of Palmer Street had a party for friends. The following spring, they expanded with T-shirts and four bands. Two thousand people showed up, and a new tradition of neighborhood street fests was born.

Of course the new drinking age was not the only social change affecting students. Information-Age careers led students to select the hot majors in computer science, engineering, management information systems, communication, or health and human services. They took leadership seriously, volunteering at Careline, Big Brothers/Big Sisters, and a host of other Athens service agencies. As a national pro-life movement threatened *Roe v. Wade,* some showed their support for women's reproductive rights. Others protested CIA recruiting on campus, organized blood drives, contributed funds for the homeless in Athens, and planted trees for Earth Day '90.

Students' responses to social and environmental issues included planting trees on Earth Day and holding blood drives as well as demonstrating against the CIA and volunteering at community service agencies such as Big Brothers/Big Sisters. *Courtesy* Athena Yearbook, 1990.

Governor Richard Celeste *(left)* presented the Ohio Board of Regents' Program Excellence Awards to representatives of the General Education program, the School of Visual Communication, the School of Journalism, and the Honors Tutorial College and an Eminent Scholar Award to the School of Film on June 15, 1990. *Courtesy Samuel Crowl.*

By 1990 the university's externally sponsored research had grown by 15 percent for three successive years, and its "centers of excellence" were increasing in strength and number. People and programs outside the sciences were also winning awards, including Pat Dewees, Jack Matthews, the regional campuses, Alden Library, a humanities institute, and the university's program in General Education. The Ohio Board of Regents awarded funds for the fledging literary festival. The university's second and third eminent scholar awards went to a unique new Contemporary History Institute, proposed by Professor John Gaddis, and to the thriving film school.

Other exciting news came from the Third Century Campaign for the university's endowment: generous donors had already contributed $68

Professor John Gaddis helped develop the Contemporary History Institute, founded in 1987. *Courtesy Mahn Center.*

Contemporary History Institute

The Contemporary History Institute (CHI) performs a unique function in American higher education: it provides interdisciplinary graduate-level training in the application of historical analysis to recent events and contemporary policy issues. Founded in 1987 with major support from the John D. and Catherine T. MacArthur Foundation, CHI is centered in the Department of History, and many members of the history faculty concentrate their research on the period from World War II to the present. But the institute also draws on faculty from the departments of Economics and Political Science and the E. W. Scripps School of Journalism, who lend their distinct disciplinary and methodological perspectives to the enterprise. The resulting synergy of interdisciplinary insights provides a powerful analytical foundation for understanding the recent past and the issues confronting us today.

Since its inception, CHI has played an active role in bringing prominent speakers to campus, including Peter Arnett, McGeorge Bundy, Jimmy Carter, Pat Choate, Natalie Zemon Davis, John Kenneth Galbraith, Doris Kearns Goodwin, Tom Hayden, George Kennan, Paul Kennedy, Mary Matalin, David McCullough, William H. McNeill, Don Oberdorfer, Richard Pipes, and Sander Vanocur.

I frequently remember a certain Thursday night class with Wayne Dodd. It's amazing how such seemingly innocent choices shape us. I well recall how disappointed I was to learn that the course was in writing poetry, not fiction. I was determined to drop the class until Dodd urged me to just stick around for the night. It became one of the most important experiences in my life. It proved to me that I really could write and opened my mind to so many wonderful ideas. What a great gift that course was— it, to a large extent, made me who I am. Would that I might serve my own students so ably.

—Mark C. Parchmann, '83

The *Ohio Review,* edited by Professor Wayne Dodd, marked the end of its successful thirty-year run with special retrospective issues in 2001.

million of the $100 million goal. President Ping pointed out that these gifts would provide "a margin of difference" for the university through enhancement of the library, scholarships, endowed professorships, PACE positions (offering students the chance to acquire career-related skills), equipment, and campus beautification. Campaign co-chair Wilfred Konneker was among the supporters who earmarked their gifts for the new Manasseh Cutler Scholars program. Jeanette Grasselli Brown and Glenn R. Brown designated their gift for an endowed professorship for a woman in the sciences and for the Frontiers in Science lecture series. Edwin and Ruth Kennedy's magnificent collection of Southwest Native American art sparked the creation of a museum at the Ridges.

Less satisfying was the faculty's response to a proposal for a new, more cohesive general education program. Though some professors found the proposal innovative, others deemed it impractical, and faculty senate members rejected it. The senate responded equally strongly to an *Athens Messenger* report on the cost of intercollegiate athletics at various MAC schools that pegged Ohio University's expenses at $3.5 million: a senate committee recommended that the president encourage MAC schools to drop from Division I-A to I-AA status. The president, however, took the position that intercollegiate athletics was part of the fabric of university life. Though the football team had been wallowing in a slough of despond for almost ten years and had won only three games in the past two years, the president could point to the women's swim team 1991 MAC championship, the baseball team's prowess, coach Larry Hunter's success with the basketball team, and a strong record of graduation rates for athletes.

FRONTIERS in SCIENCE

Jeanette Grasselli Brown, '50, is a research chemist who served as director of research and development at BP America for thirty-eight years. An expert on infrared spectroscopy, she was the first woman inducted into the Ohio Science and Technology Hall of Fame. She has served Ohio University as a member of the board of trustees, as a distinguished visiting professor and director of research enhancement, as a co-founder of the Frontiers in Science lectures (with Glenn R. Brown), and as the sponsor of a Cutler scholar.

Courtesy University Photographer's Office.

Focus on these local issues was diverted in January 1991 by Operation Desert Storm. Tension had grown in the country and on the campus throughout fall quarter as President George Bush ordered troops to the Middle East to protect Kuwait from an Iraqi invasion. On January 16, as American military action against Iraq seemed imminent, the Athens Peace Coalition held an antiwar protest on the Green. However, its members were soon outnumbered by Bush supporters who wrapped themselves in the flag in support of American troops. Kristan Collins Runyan recalls her own reaction.

I remember turning on my tiny television in Voigt Hall and hearing Tom Brokaw break into the scheduled programming to announce that Operation

Coach Scott Hammond congratulates members of the women's swim team after their third consecutive MAC championship in 1991. Ohio University Today, *Spring 1991.*

During the Gulf War of 1991, some students showed their support of President Bush's plan to protect Kuwait against Iraq. Others who opposed Operation Desert Storm tussled with police following a peace rally on January 17, 1991. *Courtesy* Athena Yearbook, *1991.*

Desert Storm had begun. My roommate's brother was over there, and we spent the rest of the evening watching TV. At about midnight, we could hear hundreds of students rallying for the troops. . . .

We ran down Jeff Hill and through the East Green, gathering numbers as we went. From the East Green though South, then West, and still more students joined in. By the time we left West Green, there were more than 1,000 students. Up the Richland hill we went, still running and cheering. We turned up Court Street and marched right up to the Armory. The crowd stood and cheered before finally disbanding. It was quite a show. News reports noted the irony of a campus known for its hippies and throw-backs rallying in support of the U.S. troops forced into action.

The next day, the "hippies and throw-backs" returned for a sit-in at Court and Union, and the pro-Bush faction reappeared to jeer and berate them. Police were forced to carry most of the antiwar group—including one member who had lost his clothes in the tussle—to the buses waiting to take them to jail.

Less combative activities occupied the rest of the winter. Black History month offered dancers, songs (by the Gospel Voices of Faith), and lectures

Courtesy University Photographer's Office.

Leon Harris, '83, anchor of *CNN Live Today* and *CNN Presents,* oversaw the satellite services used in CNN's coverage of the 1991 Gulf War. He is also well-known for coverage of such diverse events as the 1995 Oklahoma City bombing, the 1999 search for John F. Kennedy Jr.'s plane along the shores of Martha's Vineyard, and the terrorist attacks of 9/11/01. Harris, who began his CNN career in 1983, was honored as Best Newscaster at the 17th and 19th annual CableACE Awards. In 1999 he addressed the graduating seniors at commencement.

throughout February. The Bobcat hoopsters raced toward a MAC championship. As spring arrived, there was Jell-o wrestling for Moms Weekend, chariot racing and the old favorite Tug of War for Greek Week, and a two-day mini-carnival on each green. Carnival booths offered tie-dye, frisbee throw, and watermelon seed spitting; rappers warned of the dangers of alcohol and drugs; and Students for Reproductive Choice organized Condom Olympics.

At commencement that year, Governor George Voinovich, '58, spoke to the graduating seniors, almost a third of whom wore red ribbons to protest severe cuts in the state's funding for higher education. For Ohio University the cuts meant, among other things, a virtual hold on hiring, an increase in the size of classes, and the possibility of faculty layoffs, even as the number of students increased. Enrollment at the

In May of 2000, the Student Senate voted our home on Mill St. the worst off-campus residence in Athens. My friend, Darin Painter, wrote a Turnstile column in the POST about our life there:

"Every house has its array of quaint features, and the humble abode on Mill St. had plenty. For instance, slope. Like a tricky downhill putt, my upstairs bedroom broke slowly from left to right, then quickly back to the left just before the hole in the wall. Paint our beloved estate red and white, toss on a funny hat, shake it twice, and it becomes a Dr. Seuss sketch. One fish, two fish, red fish and other nutritious items we never, ever kept in the fridge would have stayed cold, provided the duct tape was replaced regularly. Otherwise, it was green eggs and ham and, time permitting, Taco Bell. . . .

"Our Mill St. house looked like a hundred damn dollars when we left O.U., and I'm sorry members of Student Senate don't see it that way now. . . . Here's the truth: My friends and I took something awful and turned it into something awful with sand and seashells and laughter dumped all over the place. We loved that house. Loved walking into it every evening and seeing friends gathered by the "captain's chair." Loved maneuvering the mower around those shrubs. Loved grilling on the patio, inviting anyone inside. . . . They [Student Senate] could have felt, like the rest of us living in the best worst house on Mill Street, as if it were home."

—Jim Jolley, '99

Jim Jolley, '99, and friends at home on Mill Street. *Courtesy Jim Jolley, '99.*

Athens campus had moved well past the 15,000 that the administration had called an ideal size in 1985. Though the goal for each freshman class was held near 3,000, better retention rates meant more students—18,283 in 1992. The residence halls were full; classes were full; and so was Athens. The perennial parking problem was now acute. Housing costs were prohibitive for many local people. Old residential neighborhoods had become "student ghettos" that were sometimes noisy and often shabby. Many permanent residents simply moved farther from town, while others formed neighborhood associations and fought for a balance of owner-occupied and rental property in their areas.

The uptown area was also being transformed. Fires had destroyed several locally owned businesses in the Carpenter Block; the Gevas family had closed the Town House; the Varsity Theater became a Taco Bell; the Woolworth building stood empty. Once a vibrant small-town shopping district serving the diverse county population, uptown Athens had become an extension of the campus, catering to students. More fast-food restaurants appeared, and the number of students living in the uptown area increased. Growing tension between students and their landlords led student senate's Fish Party to "wage a war on housing violations." To empower student tenants, the student senate sponsored a "gripe night," published a study that ranked landlords by the number of their code violations, and established close

Matt Myerholtz, *(left)* and Edward Freeman, '95, were the first students out after the surprise storm of '94 dumped eighteen inches of snow and shut the campus down for a week. *Photo by Suzanne Oswald Freeman.*

contact with local government offices. The frustration of local residents came out in rants against the university's continued growth.

In April 1993 President Ping announced that in July of the following year he would leave the presidency and return to teaching and involvement in the Charles J. Ping Institute for the Teaching of the Humanities. As his final year as president came to a close, the trustees approved plans for a new $24 million student-funded recreation facility, which would also be named in honor of Dr. Ping. Other gratifying news came from the Third Century Campaign, which had exceeded its $100 million goal by $32.7 million, and from the Carnegie Foundation for the Advancement of Teaching, which announced that Ohio University now ranked, along with only 125 other American institutions, as a Research University II.

In his nineteen years as president, Charles Ping had awarded more than half of all Ohio University degrees. One of the last ones he awarded went to

The 1994 MAC champs, led by Gary Trent (no. 20), went on to compete in the NCAA tournament. *Courtesy O.U. Athletic Department.*

his wife Claire in appreciation for the work she had done to protect the land at the Ridges and to preserve the character of Court Street. As he and the university paid their respects to her, Charlie Ping could be sure that he too had the affection and respect of the community he had fostered. In his praise, Professor Alan Booth said he "brought us an institutional sense of self." Professor Nick Dinos agreed: "I will remember Charlie

A Court Street facade by Sue Wall, '73. *Courtesy Patricia Grean.*

President Ping awarded an honorary degree to Claire Oates Ping for her contributions to the university and to the Athens community at commencement in 1994. *Courtesy Mahn Center.*

because he brought a sense of value and decency [that] made everybody believe it was worthwhile to be here, that what we were doing counted for something and that it was terribly important to do something with these young minds."

Charles Ping had made Ohio University a stronger, more confident, better unified university, offering more opportunities and challenges for its students, both in the U.S. and abroad. His greatest gift, however, may have been that he recognized and valued the institution for what it was—not Harvard, but Ohio on the Hocking, a university whose own history, setting, and distinctive characteristics were the constants in the face of change.

In the fall of 1994, the possibility of change seemed more palpable than usual. The massive Ping Center (the first major campus building in more than twenty years) was going up on South Green Drive; the renovation of Copeland Hall was almost complete; Gordy Hall was being transformed with modern classrooms and equipment and with site-specific art by alumna Jenny Holzer. Every hour a green-and-white bus arrived from a new private apartment complex on Shafer Street. Among the nearly 19,000 students making their way to classes were 3,314 freshmen—the largest class since 1970, in spite of more selective admissions standards. In classrooms and offices there were more new professors and administrators than usual—the first wave of replacements for the many faculty and staff members who had come in the '60s and would soon be retiring.

Both these new recruits and veterans of the university community were looking forward to meeting their new president, Robert Glidden, who had

Jenny Holzer, '72, is a graduate whose work is permanently on display as a part of the design of the renovated Gordy Hall. Her work stands out in the visual arts because words, not images, are her primary means of expression. Some of her texts offer provoking comments on life in general ("PRIVATE PROPERTY CREATED CRIME") while others focus on the specific (*Lustmord*, a multimedia installation, takes on the subject of rape with phrases such as "I am awake in the place where women die"). Holzer's texts have been made into books and video films.

Courtesy Athena Yearbook, *2001*.

served as professor and dean of music at several institutions as well as vice president and provost at Florida State University and had a reputation as a friendly, open, consensus builder. Now they were eager to know his plans for leading their university into its third century.

In his inaugural address, President Glidden emphasized continuity. He promised to honor Ohio University's traditions and rich legacy as a residential campus and reaffirmed its commitments to teaching, research, and service to the area. However, he told his audience that the university would pursue the newest methodologies in teaching and research. He also spoke of the need to develop both a learning environment that could prepare students for the demands of the twenty-first century and a "model community" whose members shared the values of collegiality, respect for every individual, and the free exchange of ideas.

Soon after, President Glidden demonstrated his commitment to an open administration by revealing his e-mail address, visiting with students in residence halls, and hearing from academic departments about the need for more faculty and facilities, especially in biological science, now the largest department on campus. To demonstrate his commitment to collegial governance, he appointed eight all-university committees to review policies, from academic program assessment and teaching excellence to community development and international programs. As other groups joined the Pew Higher Education Roundtable discussions of mission and goals, the agenda for the future was defined. Ohio University would develop its learning environment by enhancing the benefits of its residential campus in Athens; by using technology and innovative formats to engage students in learning; by revising the General Education program to offer students skills for lifelong learning; by developing distinctive graduate programs and supporting

On her arrival in Athens, First Lady René Glidden took on the task of supervising the renovation and redecoration of 29 Park Place, the home of the university's presidents. She later led the effort to reclaim a building at the Ridges for a child-care center and supported the continued development of the Kennedy Museum of Art. *Courtesy University Photographer's Office.*

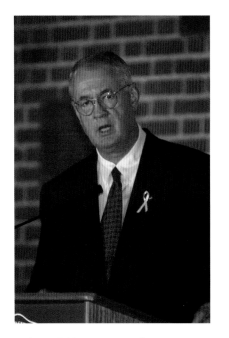

Robert Glidden, O.U. president 1994–. *Courtesy University Photographer's Office.*

research. As a "model community," the university would serve the region, promote diversity, broaden its international perspective, and value accountability, civility, and ethical behavior.

The first visible changes involved technology. In January 1995 students returned from winter break to find their residence hall rooms wired for cable TV. While many students were delighted at the easy connection to news of the world, they also realized they would have to resist watching too many sports programs, *90210, Melrose Place,* and *The Simpsons* (featuring former student Nancy Cartwright as the voice of Bart), as well as the less-known *Raving Reviews* and *My New Roommates,* produced by the members of Athens Video Works for ACTV-7.

The next fall, students applauded the introduction of a computerized I.D. card, with Bobcat Cash that could be used in washers, dryers, and vend-

As a member of the Student Alumni Board, I once had the opportunity to fly to Cincinnati with President and Mrs. Glidden on the university plane, and it was wonderful to get to know President Glidden as more than just the head of Ohio University. I distinctly remember how he and Mrs. Glidden interacted with each other. It was obvious they have great senses of humor, and they kept me laughing as they defended their decorating choices for the renovation of the president's residence. When we arrived in Cincinnati, our new president moved into his official role effortlessly. Overall, it was an experience I won't forget.

—Darrell Lausche, '97

The number of computer labs increased on campus.
Courtesy Mahn Center.

ing machines as well as for meals in dining halls, admission to ballgames, and checking out books at Alden Library. The university's new interactive home page on the World Wide Web, designed over the summer by Tom Reid and Rich Barrette, made it easier to find out about university resources and programs and to use the library, since its catalog, ALICE, was now available online.

As students prepared for tests, checked out body piercing at Crow's, listened to Psycho Suitcase at ACRN's Battle of the Bands, and waited for the opening of the magnificent Ping Center with its weight rooms, track, and climbing wall, they heard of other changes affecting campus life. A new MAC ruling demanded an average attendance of 17,000 for its Division I-A teams. The football team, with a record of 8–42–2 over five years, attracted an average of only 11,000 fans to its games. To maintain the team's status in the MAC, President Glidden and the trustees agreed to take a "more assertive and aggressive approach to athletic administration" and to bring in both a new coach and a new athletic director. As Tom Boeh arrived to take over as A.D., he spoke of the pep rallies, ticket packages, and additional seats in Peden that would boost attendance. He had the support of fans as he outlined his goals of winning more MAC championships, attracting national attention, and making Ohio University "the Michigan of the MAC."

In the spring of 1996, A.D. Boeh unveiled a new logo—a snarling Attack Cat under the word "OHIO." The Cat was intended to be more distinctive

A 36-foot-high, double-sided climbing wall, five basketball courts, eight racquetball courts, a four-lane running track, and two gymnasiums are among the features of the 168,000-square-foot recreation center, which was named for president Charles J. Ping. *Courtesy University Photographer's Office.*

than the Paw, which had been used since 1978, and more aggressive. However, to Boeh's surprise, loyal Paw fans (who were used to being asked their opinion on such matters as the school song, colors, and team name) mounted a Save the Paw campaign. In May, during student senate elections, the Cat was pitted against the Paw and lost, 1,775 to 158.

By August of that year, when the new lights came on at Peden Stadium for the football team's first night game, the focus on the logo had shifted—from the Attack Cat to the word "OHIO." As the athletic department pushed "Ohio" as a more distinctive identifier than either "O.U." or "Ohio U.", Ohio State officials made an effort to control use of the name. When O.S.U. filed an objection with the federal office of patents and trademarks opposing Ohio University's copyright, the national media tuned in to a disagreement that extended over the next two years. By then, President Glidden had pledged to meet the gender requirements of Title IX by 2000, football fans had packed Peden Stadium, ending the attendance crisis, and "Ohio" athletic teams were on the move.

In fact, the whole campus seemed to be on the move in the fall of 1996. Nick Dinos, of the chemical engineering department, was named Ohio Professor of the Year. The Kennedy Museum of Art opened in a beautifully restored building on the Ridges. With a gift from John Deaver Drinko, two Distinguished Teaching Professors—Lois Vines and Alan Booth—began their work with the Ping Institute for the Teaching of the Humanities. Thanks to the generosity of private donors, the first prestigious Manasseh Cutler Scholarships had been funded, and twelve Cutler Scholars with academic

Fans of the Paw were slow to warm up to the Attack Cat, unveiled in 1996. *Courtesy University Photographer's Office.*

and leadership potential were being recruited for the next year's class of freshmen.

In October, First Lady Hillary Clinton's second visit to Athens brought huge crowds of cheering students onto the Green. Later in the year, at a Kennedy Lecture debate between "Ragin' Cajun" James Carville and Bush in-fighter John Sununu, many so-called Gen-Xers belied their reputations for political apathy. They and other Ohio University students were proving themselves worthy members of the model community President Glidden promoted. Josh Woolley and Erik Burmeister, who were active in student senate, succeeded in getting approval for a Student Advocacy Center to provide legal advice and representation for students. Rollerbladers raced in support of Habitat for Humanity. The Campus Greens made a stand against logging and mining in the Wayne National Forest and strip mining at Dysart Woods, the university's old-growth forest in Belmont County. Others with environmental concerns helped clean up the Hocking River. With the assistance of the university's Center for Community Service, students signed on as volunteers for local nonprofit agencies such as Careline, Good Works, United Campus Ministry, My Sister's Place, and the Hickory Creek Nursing Home. Honors tutorial students worked with talented and gifted seventh graders from Alexander Middle

Hillary Clinton received a warm welcome on her second visit to Athens in 1996. *Courtesy* Athena Yearbook, *1997.*

Rollerbladers raced to benefit Habitat for Humanity. *Courtesy* Athena Yearbook, *1995.*

The Dysart Defenders walked 120 miles from Dysart Woods, a 455-acre land laboratory with 50 acres of old-growth virgin forest, to the statehouse in Columbus to raise awareness of the threat of longwall mining. *Courtesy* Athena Yearbook, *1999.*

Remembering Martin Luther King Jr. *Courtesy Mahn Center.*

School. Students whose classes included a service learning component planned public relations campaigns for area "clients." A few years later, 5,000 would battle city council for the right to keep overstuffed couches on their off-campus porches.

African American students on campus were among those who promoted respect for all individuals. Though there were fewer of them than there had been in the '70s, they continued to work against racism in Athens. After an ugly event uptown, they sponsored a panel discussion and met with Athens police officers to protest the harsh treatment of blacks. They continued the annual week-long celebration of Kwanzaa, with its focus on black culture and identity, by inviting the campus community to discussions, a poetry jam, gospel music, and a soul food dinner. They also pushed for more tenured faculty for the African American Studies department and for a new cultural arts center to replace the center in Lindley Hall.

The annual Take Back the Night march began on campus in 1979. *Courtesy* Athena Yearbook, *1998.*

Women also spoke out, as they had since 1979, to raise awareness of violence against women and to call for safer streets. At the end of a week of programs, they held a healing ceremony for victims of rape and then moved through the dark campus and streets of Athens, carrying candles and chanting slogans to show their determination to Take Back the Night. In conjunction with National Coming Out Day, members of the uni-

TOWARD THE THIRD CENTURY

My first week in Bush Hall where my group came together. And homesickness.

Attending every home football game, rain or shine, to watch the Marching 110. And witnessing the O.U. Alumni Band fighting with the Miami team.

Talking to Dean Rudy while walking across the Green.

Dean Nelson's INCO 101. His true/false pop quizzes had patterns: T/F/T/F/T/F.

Doc Hagerman's anatomy class—it taught me how to study.

Karaoking at Baker and bowling in the basement. Playing euchre until the wee hours of the morning. Joining the rest of the campus during the "screw exams" riot that started on the South Green, worked through every green, went through town, and ended at President Ping's house for Christmas carols.

Palmerfest every year; getting tattoos by Crow on Union Street; and Halloween.

Brother Jed and Sister Cindy.

Learning to budget money as I funded my own education.

Declaring a dual major and studying hard.

The 1994 blizzard. We felt like kids again. School closed and we slid down Jeff hill for the whole week using Shively cafeteria trays as sleds.

Being introduced to the diversity on campus. Becoming involved in the Gay/Lesbian community and coming out to my friends while experiencing a serious growth period, not only in my personal life, but in my academic life. And feeling at peace after being at O.U. for those 5 years.

Playing women's rugby on the South Green and traveling with the team to colleges around Ohio and Kentucky. Running on the bike path. Stroud's Run.

Leaving Athens with tears but visiting often.

—Amy Kessler, '96

Coming Out Day. *Courtesy* Athena Yearbook, *2001.*

versity's Lesbian, Gay, and Bisexual Commission sponsored a rally on the Green and invited students to speak of their own experiences in coming out. The newly organized Swarm of Dykes left messages on the Graffiti Wall, though some did not survive censorship. A group of men made plans to establish the university's first gay fraternity, Delta Lambda Phi; several years later, the O.U. Interfraternity Council became the nation's first to officially recognize a gay greek group.

Though Ohio University students could be hard working, generous, and community minded, they were also loyal to their old

Graffiti Wall messages announcing OUT Week did not always survive intact. *Courtesy* Athena Yearbook, *2001.*

A new feature of Halloween 1996 was the presence of policemen patrolling on horseback. *Courtesy* Athena Yearbook, *2001*.

pastimes—Halloween and the street fests, which expanded to Oak Street and High Street. The Athens Halloween celebration was two decades old. From a gathering of five hundred costumed students in the street, it had grown to an annual crush of thousands that gave university administrators year-long headaches though they spoke against it, no longer sanctioned it, and tried to control its effects on the campus and residence halls. The Clean and Safe Halloween Committee, a group of local businesspeople, was the new sponsor and looked forward every year to the stream of cars that poured into Athens, filling the fairgrounds and every parking place within a mile or two of town. In 1996, as usual, the ghosts, goblins, and witches crept out of their lairs by eleven o'clock on Saturday night and streamed uphill to join vendors, the bands, and a sea of other friendly celebrants. The new twist was the presence of policemen on horseback who helped keep order as, inevitably, the crowd took over the street, women bared their breasts, riot was narrowly avoided, and some people had a really good time.

Halloween, never fun for the university staff, was at least expected. That was not the case with the event of April 5, 1997. When the clocks were set

On April 5, 1997, when clocks were set forward for Daylight Savings Time, students created a disturbance, recalling the riots of the '70s. Ohio University Today, *Summer 1998*.

forward for Daylight Savings Time, students left bars (early by their reckoning) and gathered in clumps on sidewalks where some kind of fracas occurred. By the time the police arrived, people were dancing on cars and throwing things. Though ordered to disperse, most refused. After an hour and a half of continued wrangling, the police decided to clear the

TOWARD THE THIRD CENTURY

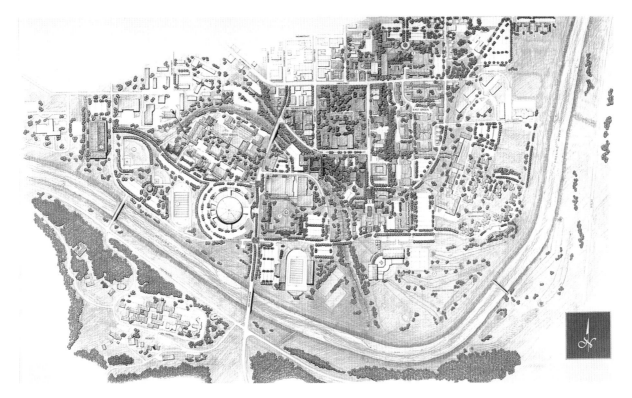

street by firing wooden and foam bullets. The disturbance recalled the un-explainable annual riots of the '70s and once again made the national news. President Glidden, surprised and dismayed, wondered how the same students who contributed so genially to the campus community could under-cut a year of good work with a few hours of irresponsible behavior. He began to consider ways to avoid such incidents in the future.

Fortunately, June's commencement, with Hillary Clinton as one of the speakers, provided its usual joyful atmosphere. Then, the trustees unveiled a master plan for the campus—perhaps the most ambitious in the university's history. A sports mall, following the curve of the river, would flow from an indoor tennis complex east of the Ping Center to a new practice field near an enlarged Peden Stadium, and continue west toward a new soft-ball field, an improved soccer field, and a new track. In addition to constructing a storage facility and a lab for Professor William Paul Jepson's work on transmission pipes for petroleum products (already announced), they proposed to redesign Grover Center to house the College of Health and Human Services, expand Bentley Hall, extend the golf course across the river, and remodel Memorial Auditorium. Other projects on the wish list included a new performing arts center, a much-needed modern student center, a biological science building, and perhaps a parking garage.

A campus master plan, approved by the trustees in 1997, proposed ambitious projects for developing and improving the campus.
Courtesy Mahn Center.

The CI was one of Court Street's popular hangouts.
Courtesy Dan Dry Associates.

Activities at Baker Center offered alternatives to the uptown scene.

The following fall, President Glidden began a discussion of the importance of ethics and responsible behavior for both students and staff. Soon after, he appointed a special ethics assistant to promote a dialog on ethical behavior. A program called PATH was developed to encourage personal accountability, trust, and honor; in 1999 the Templeton Foundation recognized the program by adding Ohio University to its Honor Roll of twenty character-building institutions.

The president also addressed the dangerous epidemic of binge drinking, prevalent across the country and obvious in Athens, where the relatively new rite of passage—the Court Street Shuffle—called for a stroll down Court Street and a drink in every bar from the Greenery to Night Court. To encourage more responsible drinking behavior, the university's Health and Wellness programs offered education. A Binge Drinking Prevention Coalition was organized; the *Post* began carrying messages urging responsibility; and Campus Activities began sponsoring alternatives to the uptown scene with Baker Nights, movies, and Frozen Fridays at Bird Arena.

There were plenty of other reasons for cheer. *Money* magazine rated the university as the twenty-fifth best buy in the country and the best buy in Ohio. Students discovered swing dancing. The *Athens News* praised the university's great music scene. President Glidden's goal of enhancing the learning environment through the use of technology and interactive learning was succeeding. The number of computers on campus had increased dramatically since his arrival; students now had e-mail accounts and could con-

tact professors, classmates, and friends at will. Within a year the president
would be able to announce that the number of personal pages on the university's site had grown from zero in 1994 to 21,519, that 500 were dedicated
to student organizations, and that 16,000 were created by students.

A number of departments, such as chemistry and physics and astron-
omy, were using computer programs to provide interactive, individualized
problem-based instruction. Both Business 20/20 and the MBA Without
Boundaries (one of the first of its kind) relied extensively on technology. The
College of Education was using distance learning to connect schools with
Ohio University through its "Learning Community Link."

Changes in class formats proliferated rapidly over the next
few years. With a technology grant from the Ohio Board of
Regents the university established the Center for Innovation
in Technology and Learning, which assisted faculty in revising their methods of engaging students in learning. By 1999,
O.U. Summer Online offered eleven courses to 220 students;
the university was part of the Ohio Learning Network, which
provided a clearinghouse for courses offered through distance
learning; and Alden Library's technological advances allowed
faculty and staff to access databases from anywhere in the
world.

However, the most dramatic moment in the move toward engagement through technology came in the fall of

Someone asked me recently, "Who
was your favorite teacher at O.U.?"
I didn't have to think—it was David
Descutner. I'm not alone; everybody
loved him. He was great because he
let us learn from one another as he
guided us. Some of the best ideas
and insights came from students in
the class, and Dr. Descutner wasn't
intimidated by that. He made us
think we were smart, that we had
good ideas.

—Mindy Rex, '87

The last person I expected to meet on an overnight train ride from Bergen, Norway, to Oslo was an Ohio University graduate. He took one look at the pawprint on my backpack and asked, "Are you from O.U.?" His name was Rocco, and he was on a business trip. Heather and I were in a study abroad program, we explained, on fall break from Odense University in Denmark, and we were trying to enjoy as much of Scandinavia as we could afford. The three of us shared a few stories about Athens, and then Heather and I got down to dinner: a bread roll and an apple. I think we shared a pat of butter. In retrospect, we were a pathetic sight.

The next morning, as we were debarking, Rocco approached us to say goodbye, and to wish us good luck. As we shook hands in turn, he pressed a few bills into our palms. "Oh, no," we both protested, "we can't take your money!" But Rocco just smiled and said, "From one Bobcat to another."

—Amy Shough Isler, '00

In 1999, the university announced plans to extend its study abroad program with a residential center, the Ohio-Leipzig European Center in Leipzig, Germany. *Courtesy* Athena Yearbook, *2001*.

1999, when the trustees, following the suggestion of Vice President for Administration Gary North, agreed to put a computer in the rooms of all first-year students —2,121 computers in 1,945 rooms in 72 days. This obvious commitment to its students by a publicly assisted university drew the attention of popular media as well as the *Chronicle of Higher Education*. The following year, rooms of second-year students were also equipped with new Gateway computers.

The university also expanded its international focus. Many faculty members, especially in the business college, were adding a global perspective to their courses. The journalism school had opened its Sing Tao Center for international journalism in 1997, and the following year the business and communication colleges established a residential Global Learning Community in Bromley Hall for students who lived together, served as interns in foreign countries, and worked with corporations to develop new products. In 1999, the university added to its more than forty study-abroad opportunities in some twenty countries by planning to open a new center in Leipzig, Germany. More students were studying abroad than ever before.

Other programs maximized students' opportunities to engage with their work and each other: University College and Residence Life sponsored a First Year Enrichment Program in which several hundred students participated in discussions of environmental issues through residential learning

I had always known I would go to school in Cincinnati, Ohio. I saw a musical when I was fourteen that kept repeating the name of that city. In 1989 Xavier University and O.U. both accepted me, but I thought O.U. looked picturesque in the brochures. So I checked the map of Ohio and figured the two towns couldn't be that far apart. I arrived at O.U. from Singapore on a rainy late summer night to find old buildings, and I was even more depressed when I found out Cincinnati was four hours away. I stayed anyway, because I couldn't admit to my parents I had made a mistake.

It was pride that made me stay at O.U., but it was O.U. that won my heart. Wherever I go, I will see images in my head of squirrels chasing each other up a tree as I cross the Green or trudge up Morton Hill with my buddies from Shively Hall. Uptown Halloween. Now, how can I forget that? The magical walks I took by the Hocking River, the quiet as I walk to the Catholic church early on Sunday mornings, the beautiful trees with their multicolored leaves in the fall. My adviser, the best adviser ever, Dr. Joe Bernt, who gave me confidence and made me so much a part of the J-school, where international students were rare.

With the money from my first paying job—as international peer adviser—I bought myself an 18K gold class ring, and I wear it proudly.

—Angelina Loh, '91

communities; Supplemental Instruction provided out-of-class sessions for discussing class lectures and concepts; the Writing across the Curriculum Program allowed students to use the concepts they learned in large classes as the basis for writing in their small "linked" composition classes. The most far-reaching program affecting what and how students learned was General Education, the foundation of the undergraduate curriculum. President Glidden appointed University College Dean Patti Richard and Charles J. Ping Professor of Humanities Tom Carpenter to head a steering committee to redesign the twenty-year-old program for twenty-first-century students.

Though undergraduate education remained a strong priority at Ohio University, the president was equally committed to enhancing graduate programs and support for research. Because the Ohio Board of Regents had put a limit on new doctoral programs, Ohio University focused on increasing the number of graduate students in existing strong Ph.D programs and creating trend-setting master's programs that would serve the needs of students and the state. Since 1994, faculty members had developed degree programs in physical therapy (the first in Ohio), in social work, and in communication technology and policy.

Though external funding for research was up 30 percent between 1996

Mudwrestling remained as popular as ever. Courtesy *Athena Yearbook*, 1991.

and 1999, the effort to identify new sources increased. Faculty members were submitting more grant proposals and having more of them funded, and the president hoped to attract other successful researchers by increasing the number of endowed chairs and professorships. As a result, the university ranked in the top 15 percent of the country's 187 research institutions and could boast of being seventh in the number of inventions disclosed per dollar expended. One confirmation of its efforts came in a $1.4 million grant from the National Institutes of Health to support construction of a $5.6 million life science building.

As students, faculty, and staff returned to campus in the fall of 2000 to open the last academic year of the second millennium, they could take comfort that the country had survived the impeachment of the president; the seventeen-year cicadas would not return to Athens for another sixteen years; and the university was thriving in spite of the state's meager support of higher education. There was also comfort for students in the fact that, even in a new century, many of their revered traditions endured. Ohio University was still a place of opportunity and friendliness. Court Street—once described as the only main street in the country that went from nowhere to nowhere—remained kind to jaywalkers. The College Green welcomed readers, jugglers, nappers, and dogs. Mothers filled every available hotel room

Students entertained their sisters and brothers for Sibs Weekend each year. *Courtesy* Athena Yearbook, *2000*.

When I first arrived in Athens in 1996, I was not quite sure what my major would be, but one thing was certain. I needed to be in a choir, preferably the best. What I discovered in the sweltering heat at Baker Center freshman march was a group that shaped who I am today. This group is the Singing Men of Ohio. SMO is both an ensemble of the School of Music and a student organization. To join SMO, an audition with the director and an interview with the executive committee have to be completed. I approached Dr. Ira Zook's office door in the Music Building apprehensively. Gave it a hearty knock and his tenor voice echoed with a sharp "COME IN!" And just as easy as that, I was a member for life.

—Corey Todd, '00

on Moms Weekend, and the kids from home filled Baker, Bird, and the Aquatic Center on Sibs Weekend. Halloween was in no danger of fading away, despite stricter policies for guests, and the Greek Games, the Marching 110, mudwrestling, club sports, and intramurals were as popular as ever.

On the other hand, the number of students on campus continued to rise as the size of the freshman class increased each year. These larger freshman classes—intended to bring in the revenue to support Provost Sharon Brehm's initiative to add thirty new faculty positions over three years—also created the need for new facilities. No one doubted that the campus needed a life science building, a "smart classroom" building, and a new student center. However, some members of the university community, including students, questioned whether the newly completed Athletic Mall enhanced the university's reputation or warranted the expense. And there were objections, sometimes loud and long, from various segments of the Athens community as the university made plans for several off-campus projects.

Such town/gown tensions were hardly new. During the 1800s, tenants of university lands had opposed the trustees' right to raise their rents. In the 1960s, homeowners along the Hocking River corridor had questioned the urban renewal project that moved the river and constructed the South Green. The development projects that drew comment in the late 1990s included a student apartment complex on Richland Avenue, the expansion of the university airport, and a new shopping center on university land on East State Street. On the other hand, there was only praise for the university's purchase and restoration of the Athena Theater, which had gone out of business, leaving downtown Athens without a theater for the first time in almost a century.

The university purchased the Athena Theater in early 2001 and gave it a welcome facelift. *University Photographer's Office.*

From the beginning, it was fun. The place was small; it was almost at the back of beyond; and I worried a bit about the remark a friend and colleague made when I left the east coast: "You're going all the way out there where no one knows what's going on?"

As many of us said at the time, we were certainly not going to stay here for more than, maybe, three years. So why did we stay? In part because we had the freedom to get away on occasion, and we had considerable freedom to do what we wanted to do professionally. Teaching was fun; trying to develop a research program was fun; and having the opportunity to meet people professionally and socially from a great variety of disciplines was a joy.

Being able to contribute to and watch the growth and maturation of the university and the town could not have been more fulfilling. In spite of the usual problems, there was always something interesting happening, especially in the '60s and '70s. And the stream of musical and theatrical events, as well as the stunning parade of visiting lecturers, remained astonishing. By the way, it really is a beautiful place. Terrific for raising kids, who leave home and then wonder why Mom and Dad do not.

—Norman S. Cohn, Distinguished Professor Emeritus,
Environmental and Plant Biology

As President Glidden met with the university community to review the agenda for 2000–2001, he made two important announcements. First, Ohio University would compete more aggressively for national recognition. Ohio University Libraries ranked as one of the top hundred research libraries in the U.S. and Canada. The Ohio University Press published fifty books each year, written by scholars from around the world. With over $41 million dollars in external support for research, the institution would compete for a federally sponsored research center in science or engineering. Faculty members Judith Yaross Lee and Joseph Slade had already won a planning grant in the National Endowment for the Humanities competition to host a regional humanities center. The Office of Nationally Competitive Awards in the Honors Tutorial College was helping students compete for and win Goldwater, Truman, and Mellon Fellowships. "Ohio University Without Boundaries"—online courses modeled after the MBA Without Boundaries —promised to be a productive university niche for new programs. Moreover, the revised General Education Plan was ready for discussion by the faculty. The innovative program proposed to weave competencies in written and oral communication, quantitative reasoning, ethical judgment, aesthetic reasoning, cultural perspectives, and research into the fabric of "knowledge"

The university's first online degree program, the College of Business's MBA Without Boundaries, was launched in 1997.

courses in humanities and fine arts; mathematics, science, and technology; and social sciences. Students would gain competency over the course of their degree programs through stand-alone competency courses and through "enriched" elective and major courses. The ideal would be increased rigor, increased engagement, increased learning for career and life.

The president's second announcement was that these efforts, and the success of the university's third century, would be supported by a Bicentennial Campaign to raise $200 million for named professorships and endowed chairs, for scholarships and fellowships, for innovative programs, technological advances, and new facilities.

This optimism was dramatically interrupted in the fall of 2001 by the horror of 9/11—the terrorist attacks on the Pentagon and the World Trade Center. For Christina Franks, the day was one in which she experienced Ohio University as a community.

As I got ready that Tuesday morning, my roommate called me into our living room to look at television. A plane had hit one of the towers at the World Trade Center. As we kept watching, the second plane slammed into the second tower. In horror, we recognized that this was no accident.

I wanted to be with my friends on Student Senate, so I headed up to the offices in Baker. As I entered, I witnessed something eerie. Baker was not its usual hub of activity. People in the Front Room were not studying or talking, but standing around the large television in silence. Other televisions with the same scenes were being wheeled into the hallways and lobbies. No one said a word. When I got to the Senate office, my friends and I watched, like the rest of the nation, in disbelief, as other planes came down at the Pentagon and in Pennsylvania, and the Trade Towers collapsed into mountains of rubble.

Grief stricken, several of us went to the president's office in Cutler to help decide what to do for the students. With administrators, we discussed everything from a possible ethnic backlash on campus to a ribbon campaign to honor those who died. We decided that Ohio University needed to come together as a community, so we planned a vigil for that night, where people could pick up white ribbons and then join discussion groups.

A candlelight vigil on the College Green brought students together after the events of September 11, 2001. *Courtesy University Photographer's Office.*

It felt like such a feeble gesture when people were sifting through concrete looking for survivors. Who were we going to help with a bunch of white ribbons? I couldn't have been more wrong. Several hundred people showed up at the West Portico of Mem Aud to say prayers and hear President Glidden's words of comfort. I was surprised by the numbers, but I shouldn't have been. Ohio University has a strong sense of community, and when this event changed all of our lives, we needed to come together with friends and remember how precious each moment is.

Many other students at Ohio University responded to the crisis by giving blood and collecting goods to send to New York City. One group of fifteen went to Ground Zero and offered their hands and help to the Red Cross and other emergency agencies.

Gradually, as the country and the campus dealt with the shock of this event, people went back to their routines. The university bought Bromley Hall. The College of Health and Human Services moved into Grover Center; construction continued on the Life Sciences Building, the Voinovich Center for Leadership and Public Affairs at the Ridges, and Bentley Hall. Professors Carolyn Tice and Delysa Burnier received the first Presidential Teaching Awards; Professor Arthur Smith received an Early Career Award for Scientists and Engineers; classics professor Lynne Lancaster and English professor Mark Halliday, both recipients of the prestigious Rome Prize, set off for extended stays and work in Italy. University administrators made new plans to recruit more women to the faculty and minorities to both the faculty and student body.

One minority student, Sara Flores, a King-Chavez-Parks scholar from Lorain, Ohio, said in 2001 that recruiting minorities continued to be difficult because "O.U. is far from their homes, and the shock of being with a majority of whites makes them clam up, stay in their own little circles, and finally want to leave." But she also called the university "honorable" for

Professors Carolyn Tice and Delysa Burnier received the first Presidential Teaching Awards in 2001. *Courtesy University Photographer's Office.*

recruiting at even the poorest schools in her hometown, and for working hard to help students once they are on campus. "I'm in the LINKS program, and they go out of their way to help us all the time. They really want us to succeed. For me, it's the ideal setting." Jesse Raney, who came to O.U. as a Templeton scholar, also liked the feel of the campus—"homey, like a community where you don't feel overwhelmed"—but sometimes felt "on the edge of things" and was disappointed that socially it was difficult to "cross."

New Provost Stephen Kopp, who arrived in July 2002, hoped to increase campus diversity and dialogue as well as further the development of the learning-centered community the president had promoted since the beginning of his tenure. The provost began to frame a discussion about how learning occurs and is measured. He announced his intention to encourage faculty to become designers of educational experiences and students to approach learning opportunities as inquirers. He also announced that he would begin an examination of the budget and a possible reallocation of some university funds from administrative to academic functions.

President Glidden spent time educating Ohio University students, parents, and legislators on the critical need for the state of Ohio to increase its support of higher education. He also took time to visit with alumni and friends of the university. As he did so, he reminded these loyal constituents of the university's traditions. He spoke of the goals of the institution and sought support for its programs through gifts to the Bicentennial Campaign. Teaching, long the university's first priority, would be enhanced by a redesigned General Education Program and by the creative use of technology. Graduate education and research were supported by funds that totaled almost $54 million in 2001. An increasing number of faculty members received

The Emeriti Park on South Green Drive was built to honor former faculty and staff of the university. *Courtesy University Photographer's Office.*

> I am attached to the place, and it's been a place that's rewarded our attachments—a receptive institution where we've been able to lead the kinds of professional lives we wanted. We could teach classes we wanted to teach, get involved in the programs we were interested in. This university is responsive, open. We didn't have to take one little field and mine it but could stake out the kinds of teaching and research we wanted to do.
>
> —Samuel Crowl, Trustee Professor of English

funding and recognition each year for their notable research and creative work. For example: composer Mark Phillips, sociologist Martin Schwartz, and botanist Gar Rothwell had received the university's first Presidential Research Scholar awards; Professor Lawrence Witmer drew national attention for his reconstruction of the soft tissues of dinosaurs; Assistant Professor Daniel Phillips was named an Outstanding Junior Investigator in Physics. The university's success in developing and supporting high-tech start-up companies received the attention and the strong approval of Governor Bob Taft as he pledged to use such expertise to help "make Ohio a leader in the knowledge economy."

The residential campus in Athens, though larger and still relatively inaccessible, was more beautiful than ever and graced by new trees and flowering gardens. Traffic flowed more smoothly from a new front door off of Richland Avenue, past new buildings and the fountains of the Emeriti Park.

The university's commitment to opportunity, diversity, and innovation remained strong. Scholarships, PACE positions, and work-study jobs provided financial aid. LINKS, the First Year Enrichment Program, residential learning communities, the College Adjustment Program, and Supplemental Instruction provided academic support. The Honors Tutorial College, departmental

After I arrived at Ohio University, my adviser immediately enrolled me in the College Adjustment Program (CAP). The profound effect this program had on me was to improve my study skills and time management habits. The program encouraged deeper accountability outside the classroom and allowed me to excel in my classes as a result of understanding my values and objectives. Today I still utilize many of the strategies provided by the program, especially the time management skills. I owe a great deal to Ohio University and the CAP program.

—Jeffery D. Chaddock, '88

honors programs, and the Bachelor of Specialized Studies allowed both accelerated and innovative approaches to degrees. International study programs were widely available.

These opportunities were repaid many times over. For example, Fritz Russ, '42, and his wife, Dolores, provided a multimillion-dollar endowment for the Fritz J. and Dolores H. Russ Prize, which was awarded in 2001 by Ohio University and the National Academy of Engineering to Earl Bakken and Wilson Greatbatch, inventors of the human heart pacemaker. Betty Thomas, '69, Emmy Award–winning actress and movie director, returned to campus to share her expertise with film students. David Wilhelm, '77, who served as chairman of the Democratic National Committee during President Clinton's administration, formed a venture capital group to invest in businesses in southeast Ohio. Frank and Margaret Krasovec made a record-breaking gift to the College of Business, while Robert and Peggy McGreevey Walter of the class of 1967 des-

Lee Kliesch of the Academic Advancement Center shares her knowledge of learning strategies. *Courtesy* Athena Yearbook, *1995.*

ignated their gift to help cover the costs of the "smart classroom" building. Lisa Miree, Miss Black USA of 2001, encouraged responsible sexual behavior among young people. Adonis Bolden, '01, a young man of great discipline, committed himself to the classroom in order to bring his compassion and influence to young black men. Patrick Davison used his photographic skills to document the tragedy at Columbine and added his name to the

Lisa Miree, '97, '00, was chosen Miss Black USA in 2001. *Courtesy Miss Black USA Organization.*

Fritz and Dolores Russ. *Courtesy University Photographer's Office.*

Fritz Russ, '42, and his wife, Dolores, elevated the image of engineers and brought recognition to Ohio University and the Russ College of Engineering and Technology by establishing one of the top two engineering prizes in the world. In 2001, the first recipients of the Fritz J. and Dolores H. Russ Prize were the inventors of the human heart pacemaker. Russ founded Russ Venture Group, a Dayton consulting firm. The Russes also founded Systems Research Laboratories, a leader in the electronics and automation industries before its acquisition by Arvin Industries in 1987.

list of university graduates who have won Pulitzer Prizes. Dance student Chia Chi Chiang's choreography was recognized by the National American College Dance Festival.

On the eve of the Ohio University bicentennial celebration, President Glidden could assure alumni and friends that even as the institution continued to change, the spirit of its founders was still alive. Although no one could know precisely what the third century would bring, it was certain that each year students would enter to grow in knowledge, wisdom, and love and that each year others would follow the instructions on Alumni Gate to "serve thy fellowman, thy country, and thy God." It was also true that many of those who left would come to feel about Ohio University as Lt. G. R. Jolley had in the 1940s when he wrote:

David Wilhelm, '77, venture capitalist and former chairman of the Democratic National Committee during the Clinton administration, returned to his alma mater in 2002 to give the commencement address. *Courtesy University Photographer's Office.*

As I close, I must confess a feeling of inadequacy. It is impossible for me in mere words to do what I should like to do: to express the idea of the true Ohio University—the spirit, the tradition, the memories of the past, the hopes for the future that mean so much more than even buildings and campus. For Ohio University is much more than the sum of its parts; it must be seen and felt and experienced to be appreciated. And when the truth is told, to those who know her best, the history of O.U., the thing that makes her unique and beautiful and haunting to those who know her, must be expressed in the memories of what she has been to each person associated with her—must be expressed in his or her memory of the soft smell of spring over the campus, the misty

Commencement. *Courtesy University Photographer's Office.*

beauty of the Hocking in the early dawn, the twinkling lights of Athens from atop North Hill, the gay laughter of students ringing in the late of night, the clear, firm clang of old Cutler's bell on a winter morning—in short, what I have done is only to speak about the factual history of Ohio University. Her real story must remain forever locked in the hearts of those who know her, a secret to be shared by her favored few.

The Ohio University Campus Gate. *Courtesy Mahn Center.*

Presidents

Jacob Lindley, A.M., D.D.,
1774–1857
First President, 1808–22

Dr. Lindley was pastor of the Presbyterian church in nearby Waterford, Ohio, before becoming the first president of Ohio University. In addition to organizing the academy and the college and implementing the curriculum, President Lindley taught all the classes without assistance until 1814. During his administration the first two baccalaureate degrees were conferred and the College Edifice (Cutler Hall) was completed.

President Lindley was a native of Pennsylvania and was educated at Jefferson College and the College of New Jersey (Princeton). After retiring from the university, he continued to work in the ministry.

James Irvine, A.M., 1793–1835
Second President, 1822–24

(No known portrait exists.)
Professor Irvine became a professor of mathematics at Ohio University in 1821;

the following year, he became president. Suffering ill health, President Irvine served only two years, concluding his tenure with a travel leave.

Born in New York, President Irvine attended Union College. He resumed his career in the ministry after leaving Ohio University.

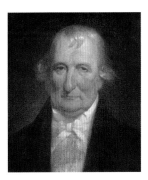

Robert G. Wilson, D.D., 1768–1851
Third President, 1824–39

Dr. Wilson was pastor of Chillicothe Presbyterian Church when he was chosen to be president of Ohio University. During his tenure, a department of English studies was added to provide teachers for the common schools and to qualify men for business careers. East Wing and West Wing (Wilson and McGuffey Halls) were constructed, and the university raised revenue by selling some of its land.

A graduate of Dickinson College, President Wilson was a native of North Carolina. He resumed his ministerial career after retiring from the university.

William Holmes McGuffey, D.D., LL.D., 1801–1873

Fourth President, 1839–43

After graduating from Washington College (now Washington and Jefferson) in 1826, William McGuffey, an ordained Presbyterian minister, took a position as professor of Latin, Greek, and Hebrew at Miami University. When his theological conservatism put him at odds with the Miami administration, he left to become president of Cincinnati College.

In 1839 McGuffey accepted the presidency at Ohio University, where he integrated the functions of the academy into the college, instituted a more practical academic calendar, and extended the range of course offerings. However, his strict disciplinary measures caused many students to leave, and when the state legislature ruled in 1843 that the university could not revalue its lands, financial problems and discord increased. Soon after, President McGuffey resigned and returned to Cincinnati, where he took a position at Woodward College.

Alfred Ryors, D.D., 1812–1858

Fifth President, 1848–52

When Alfred Ryors, a former professor of mathematics at Ohio University, became president, the institution had been closed to all but preparatory students for almost three years. President Ryors significantly reduced the university's debt, restored authority to the faculty, and regained the public's confidence. He left Ohio University to become president of Indiana University in 1852, ending nearly a half-century of control by ministers and members of the Presbyterian church.

Solomon Howard, D.D., LL.D., 1811–1873

Sixth President, 1852–72

President Howard was the first member of the Methodist faith to lead Ohio University. Prior to being selected for the position, he was president of the Springfield Female Academy of the Ohio Methodist Conference. An ordained minister, he was active in the founding of Ohio Wesleyan University.

During the early years of his administration, Howard established a scientific course for students interested in practical pursuits. He also worked to restore fiscal stability to the university and in 1859 was able to declare the institution debt free for the first time in more than forty years.

The Civil War and the state of Ohio's failure to provide Morrill Act proceeds caused financial problems, but Howard kept the university stable. A highlight of his twenty-year tenure was the decision in 1870 to admit women to Ohio University.

William Henry Scott, A.M., LL.D., 1840–1937

Seventh President, 1872–83

William H. Scott was an Athens County native and the only Ohio University graduate to become president. An ordained Methodist minister and professor of philosophy, he was thirty-two years old when he took office as acting president in 1872. The trustees elected him to the permanent position a year later.

Perhaps the university's first fundraiser, Dr. Scott sought "subscriptions" from townspeople, alumni, faculty, and friends and worked diligently to secure direct support from the state. He used the funds to repair the buildings, construct a chapel, obtain equipment, and purchase library books. He also encouraged more rigorous academic standards, introduced a teacher training course, and hired the university's first female faculty member.

In 1880, Dr. Scott took an interest in a plan put forth by the president of Ohio State, proposing that Ohio University, Ohio State, and Miami merge. In 1883 he left Ohio University to assume the presidency at Ohio State and reportedly still cherished the idea of the merger some fifty years later.

Charles William Super, Ph.D., LL.D., 1842–1939

Eighth President, 1883–96 and 1899–1901

Charles W. Super was named president *pro tempore* in 1883 and was soon given the job on a permanent basis. Fluent in German, Greek, and Latin, Dr. Super also knew French, Spanish, Italian, Arabic, Hebrew, and Sanskrit and held three honorary degrees.

President Super succeeded in securing the university's first direct appropriation of money from the state legislature in 1885. Funding for additional requests indicated the legislature's commitment to annual appropriations.

Dr. Super oversaw the establishment of a normal department in 1886. "Commercial courses" to prepare students for business careers, a department of music, and the implementation of stipends to support graduate students followed.

In 1896, President Super—who was also teaching Greek and philosophy, interviewing prospective students, and supervising all university record-keeping as well as all buildings and grounds—asked to be relieved of his presidential duties so he could return to the classroom.

When Isaac Crook, Charles Super's successor, resigned the presidency after only two years, Professor Super was named dean of the faculty. When a new president had not been found after a year's search, he agreed to return to the office, where he served until 1901.

Isaac Crook, D.D., LL.D., 1833–1916

Ninth President, 1896–98

After President Super's resignation in 1896, Rev. Isaac Crook was named to the office. Another Methodist minister, he had previously served as president of the University of the Pacific and chancellor of Nebraska Wesleyan University. Though President Crook was active in recruiting students, enhancing faculty rights, and acquiring books for the library, trustees who had not been in favor of his election refused to support him. President Crook tendered his resignation in 1898 and returned to the ministry.

Alston Ellis, Ph.D., LL. D., 1847–1920

Tenth President, 1901–20

Alston Ellis was a nationally recognized leader in public school education and administration when he came to the presidency of Ohio University, and it was during his term that the normal department became a full-fledged Normal School. Programs in music, commerce, and engineering also flourished as the

university's budget and enrollments expanded. Seven new building were constructed, summer school became a standard part of university course offerings, and the first alumni director and dean of women were hired. In 1913 the university was accredited by the North Central Association as one of its charter members.

Dr. Ellis helped protect the university's name and programs during several legislative attacks, and he led it through the dark times of World War I. He died unexpectedly in 1920.

Edwin Watts Chubb, 1865–1959

Acting President, 1920–21 and 1934–35

Dr. Chubb, who had been on the faculty at Ohio University since 1900, was selected to serve as acting president after Dr. Ellis's death. At the time, he was dean of the College of Liberal Arts. During his brief tenure, the board of trustees was reorganized: lifetime appointments were discontinued, and new appointments were made on a staggered basis so that the board's composition changed each year.

After his term as acting president, Dr. Chubb returned to his position as dean of the College of Liberal Arts. In 1931, Edwin Watts Chubb Library was named in his honor.

In 1934, following the death of President Elmer Bryan, the trustees asked Dean Chubb to serve as acting president for the second time. He did so until the arrival of President Herman James in 1935.

Elmer Burritt Bryan, A.B., LL.D., L.H.D., 1865–1934

Eleventh President, 1921–34

Dr. Bryan had served eleven years as the president of Colgate University when he accepted a similar position at Ohio University. Previously he had taught in public schools as well as at Butler College and Indiana University.

President Bryan undertook to increase the enrollment of men to balance the number of women attending the normal college. He constructed a new gymnasium for men only, purchased a building where all the men of the university could share a common meeting place, and approved both a 14,000-seat football stadium and a new building to house classes and laboratories for engineering courses.

Other significant accomplishments during his administration were the construction of Alumni Memorial Auditorium and Chubb Library, acceptance of the university into the Association of American Colleges and Universities, recognition of the university's women by AAUW, and installation of a chapter of Phi Beta Kappa.

In 1925 a series of health problems caused President Bryan to submit his resignation. The trustees, however, persuaded him to accept two additional five-year contracts. In June 1934, Dr. Bryan's health declined further, and in October he died.

Herman Gerlach James, J.D., Ph.D., LL.D., 1887–1959

Twelfth President, 1935–43

Dr. James was serving as president of the University of South Dakota when he was offered the presidency of Ohio University. Author of nine books, he earned degrees from the University of Illinois, the University of Chicago, and Columbia, studied at the University of Berlin, and lectured at the University of Leipzig, with which Ohio University has a strong relationship today.

One of President James's first acts was to create University College, in which all entering freshmen would spend their first year. To develop a true university and reduce the duplication of offerings in the two existing colleges, Liberal Arts and Education, President James reorganized the university into five degree-granting colleges: Arts and Sciences, Education, Commerce, Applied Science, and Fine Arts. He also formed a Graduate College and the faculty advisory council, which eventually evolved into today's faculty senate. President James approved a controversial voluntary Reserve Officers Training Corps on campus and created innovative branch campuses at Portsmouth and Zanesville, the start of the university's regional campus system.

When America became involved in World War II, President James sought a leave of absence from the presidency in order to utilize his expertise in South America to aid the United States government. He became seriously ill shortly after leaving on his mission and in April 1943 resigned the presidency.

Walter Sylvester Gamertsfelder, Ph.D., LL.D., 1885–1967

Thirteenth President, 1943–45

Dr. Gamertsfelder, who came to the university as a faculty member in philosophy in 1921, was serving in the dual roles of dean of the College of Arts and Sciences and dean of the Graduate College when he was asked to become acting president. Though he was familiar with the campus and had the knowledge and experience to serve, he faced the impact of World War II on the campus. Women outnumbered men five to one, enrollment had dropped by nearly 2,000 students, and about 17 percent of the faculty had taken leaves of absence to join the armed forces or government service.

Because of the importance of relationships with the U.S. War Department, the trustees determined that Dr. Gamertsfelder needed the powers of a full-fledged president, and accorded him that status on July 1, 1943. When John Baker agreed to accept the presidency, Dr. Gamertsfelder resumed his responsibilities in the Graduate College, in Arts and Sciences, and in the classroom. For his devoted service and effective administration, the trustees named him the university's first Trustee Professor on his retirement in 1951.

John Calhoun Baker, M.B.A.,
D.C.S., LL.D., L.H.D., 1895–1999
Fourteenth President, 1945–61

Dr. John C. Baker is generally regarded as the father of the modern Ohio University. When he left his position as associate dean of the Harvard Business School to accept the presidency, World War II was just ending, and the university was on the verge of a period of expansion in both enrollments and facilities. President Baker oversaw this expansion, reinstituted the regional campus system, created the Ohio University Fund, Inc. (now The Ohio University Foundation), implemented the Distinguished Professor awards, and initiated various international relationships. Dr. Baker championed research as a component of effective teaching and instituted programs to strengthen faculty rights. He also directed a successful major scholarship drive during the university's sesquicentennial celebration in 1954.

After he retired in 1961, President Baker remained active in a variety of educational, business, and international affairs. He continued his involvement with Ohio University, serving as a valued advisor and mentor to each president who succeeded him. Dr. Baker and his wife, Elizabeth, shared an avid interest in promoting the academic study of conflict resolution, and the Baker Peace Studies Program at Ohio University is the result of that interest.

Vernon Roger Alden, M.B.A.,
LL.D., L.H.D., 1923–
Fifteenth President, 1962–69

Vernon Alden was associate dean of the Harvard Business School when he was selected as president of Ohio University. President Alden's administration saw a doubling of enrollment and faculty, a great expansion of the campus area through urban renewal, and the continuation of a construction program that included completion of the West Green, the development of the South Green, and a new regional airport. Dr. Alden also spearheaded the development of southeastern Ohio, including rerouting the flood-prone Hocking River and constructing highways to provide easier access to Athens.

Dr. Alden was an advocate of faculty research and of innovative academic programs such as the Ohio Fellows Program, the Cutler Program, the Honors College, and a Black Studies Institute. During his administration both tuition remissions for university employees and their families and sabbatical leaves were implemented, and the faculty senate and the Ohio University Press were established.

When Dr. Alden left the presidency of Ohio University, he embarked on a career in private business with the Boston Company and continued his involvement with international affairs.

Claude R. Sowle, J.D., 1928–1997
Sixteenth President, 1969–74

Claude Sowle, former dean of the law school at the University of Cincinnati, served as president of Ohio University during a turbulent time. Soon after he took office, college campuses across the country were torn by protests against the United States' involvement in Cambodia and Vietnam. Ohio was no exception, and within a few days of the shootings at Kent State University in 1970, Ohio University—in the midst of antiwar agitation—was forced to close before the end of the spring quarter.

Despite the turmoil on campus, President Sowle's tenure was characterized by a determination to encourage student, faculty, and staff input into administrative processes. Perhaps the clearest evidence of that determination was his decision to hold open budget hearings that were broadcast live over the campus radio station. He also appeared on a weekly call-in program on WOUB.

President Sowle initiated a systematic appraisal of university programs and services, approved the innovative Bachelor of General Studies degree, established the position of ombudsman, and called for more opportunities for women at Ohio University. Dr. Sowle left the presidency for a position in the law school at Ohio State University.

Harry B. Crewson, Ph.D., 1913–2003
Seventeenth President, 1974–75

During the year he served as president, Harry Crewson endeavored to restore calm to the campus. His approach to problems was reasoned, deliberate, and forthright: he addressed students' demands fairly, and though enrollment continued to decline, he worked to stabilize the university's budget. At the end of his tenure, the state approved the establishment of a medical school for Ohio University. When a new president was named, President Crewson returned to the classroom as Trustee Professor of Economics, only the second person in the university's history to be honored with this title.

Charles J. Ping, Ph.D., 1930–
Eighteenth President, 1975–94

A philosopher and Presbyterian minister, Charles Ping became president of Ohio University in 1975, after one of the campus's most difficult periods. President Ping was determined to

reclaim the stability and devotion to academic excellence that had long characterized the institution.

His tenure was highlighted by the creation of the University Planning Advisory Council (UPAC), a budget advisory group composed of faculty, administrators, and students from across campus. Dr. Ping was committed to long-range planning, and directed creation of a ten-year planning document for the institution. He envisioned Ohio University as a community and encouraged professors, staff, and students to share in that vision. He also took a leadership role among university presidents and was a vigorous spokesman on behalf of public higher education with the Ohio legislature.

The Ping years saw the creation of two new colleges—Osteopathic Medicine and Health and Human Services—as well as the establishment of the Innovation Center, the Institute for Local Government Administration and Rural Development (ILGARD), and the Edison Biotechnology Institute. Two highly successful capital fundraising efforts—the 1804 Campaign and The Ohio University Third Century Campaign—significantly increased the university's endowment.

Dr. Ping earned a bachelor of arts degree from Rhodes College, a bachelor of divinity from Louisville Presbyterian Theological Seminary, and a doctoral degree from Duke University. Prior to coming to Ohio University, he taught and held top-level administrative positions at Alma College in Michigan, Tusculum College in Tennessee, and Central Michigan University. When he retired from the presidency in 1994, Dr. Ping was named President Emeritus by the board of trustees. He accepted the position of director of the Cutler Scholars Program and Trustee Professor of Philosophy and Education.

Robert Glidden, Ph.D., 1936–
Nineteenth President, 1994–

An Iowa native, Robert Glidden began his academic career in music and taught at both the high school and college levels before moving into academic administration. He was dean of music at Bowling Green and dean of the School of Music and then provost and vice president for academic affairs at Florida State University.

When Dr. Glidden assumed the presidency of Ohio University in 1994, he was both mindful of its rich traditions and cognizant of the need for changes as the institution approached its 200th birthday and the world approached the new century. One of the key accomplishments during President Glidden's tenure was the move to embrace and incorporate technology across the institution. Perhaps the most visible manifestation of this effort was the installation, in fall 2000, of a computer in the residence hall room of every first-year student. Ohio University was the first public school in the state to provide computers for its students, and by 2001 every residence hall room on campus was equipped. Dr. Glidden also urged the use of technology in classrooms as a tool to encourage active learning.

President Glidden sought to draw national attention to the institution's solid general education program, focused graduate programs, and carefully targeted research emphases. In addition, President Glidden spearheaded the university's third major fund-raising effort, The Bicentennial Campaign, and directed the group that planned the university's bicentennial celebration in 2004.

Distinguished Professors

The Distinguished Professor Award recognizes outstanding scholarly and creative accomplishments. It is the highest permanent recognition attainable at Ohio University. Recipients have tenure and a minimum of five years' service at the university. Among their privileges is the honor of naming an undergraduate student annually to receive a year's full-tuition scholarship. The award, first made in 1959, is supported by an endowment from Edwin and Ruth Kennedy to the Baker Fund. The sketches reflect the recipients' achievements at the time of their recognition.

1959

John F. Cady, History, Ph.D.,
University of Pennsylvania

Before coming to Ohio University in 1949, Professor Cady taught at a number of colleges and universities and then spent six years with the Office of Strategic Services and the State Department, becoming an authority on Southeast Asia. He used that expertise to develop courses in the history of Southeast Asia and the Far East. His scholarly publications include *The Roots of French Imperialism in Eastern Asia,* which won the Carnegie Award of the American Historical Association in 1954; *A History of Modern Burma,* winner of the Ohio Academy of History Achievement Award in 1959; *Thailand, Burma, Laos and Cambodia; Southeast Asia: Its Historical Development;* and *Postwar Southeast Asia.* He won Guggenheim, Fulbright, and Rockefeller fellowships as well as the

Distinguished Service Award from the Ohio Academy of History. In 1971, the year of his retirement, John F. Cady Hall was dedicated in his honor. The following year he was named an honorary alumnus of Ohio University.

Harvey C. Lehman, Ph.D., Psychology,
University of Chicago

Professor Lehman came to Ohio University in 1927 as an associate professor after holding positions as a high school principal, a physical education teacher, and a psychology teacher. He wrote more than 150 articles, focusing primarily on the correlation between men's ages and their greatest achievements. His book, *Age and Achievement,* was praised as among the most important contributions to the literature of genius.

*Paul Murray Kendall, Ph.D., English,
University of Virginia*

Professor Kendall joined Ohio University's English department in 1937. He won international praise for his historical biographies: *Richard III,* a 1956 best seller and runner-up for the National Book Award; *Warwick the Kingmaker,* a 1957 winner of the Ohioana Book Award Medal; *The Yorkist Age;* and *Louis XI: The Universal Spider.* He served as general editor of *The Complete Works of Shakespeare* and co-editor of the six volumes of *Dispatches with Related Documents of Milanese Ambassadors in France and Burgundy, 1450–1483.* Dr. Kendall received fellowships from the Guggenheim and Ford Foundations and grants from the American Philosophical Society, the Rockefeller Foundation, and the Baker Fund. In 1969, after being named a Regents Professor for three consecutive years, he was honored by the Ohio Board of Regents with the title of Regents Professor of English for the duration of his tenure at Ohio University.

1960

*Robert L. Morton, Ph.D., Education,
Ohio State University*

Professor Morton, a 1913 alumnus of Ohio University, returned to Athens in 1918 to join the education faculty.

Devoted to the teaching of mathematics, he published nine books and co-authored junior high and elementary school mathematics textbooks whose sales exceeded $50 million. The series *Making Sure of Mathematics* was used in schools for more than fifteen years and was followed by an equally popular series, *Modern Mathematics through Discovery.* Dr. Morton retired in 1960 after forty-two years of teaching but continued to be a loyal alumnus, endowing two academic chairs to create the Robert L. Morton Professorship in Mathematics, the university's second named professorship. In 1972 Ohio University presented him with a Founders Citation, its highest award for service, in recognition of his scholarship, loyalty, and generosity. The new mathematics building, completed in 1973, was named Robert Lee Morton Hall in his honor.

*Dwight O. Mutchler,
Lecturer in Drawing*

Professor Mutchler studied at the Chicago Art Institute, the Academy of Art in Chicago, and the University of Chicago and worked as a professional artist for twenty-five years before coming to Ohio University in 1950. Over the next decade, he won frequent awards, including first prizes from the Columbus Graphic Arts Exhibit, the Columbus Art League, and both the Akron and Canton Art Institutes. To celebrate the university's sesquicentennial in 1954, he created a seal depicting Manasseh Cutler, Rufus Putnam, and the cupola of Cutler Hall. His best-known work is his 1957 mural, *The Wright Brothers and Their Accomplishments,* commissioned by the Ohio Historical Society for the Statehouse Rotunda in Columbus. He retired in 1968 and was honored in 1987 when the Mutchler Room in Baker Center was dedicated to him.

1962

*John E. Edwards, Ph.D., Physics,
Ohio State University*

Professor Edwards, an Athens native and Ohio University alumnus, joined the physics faculty in 1932. He was the first member of his department to use radioactive isotopes on campus and, in the 1950s, established the isotope committee that eventually evolved into the present Radiation Safety Committee. His work in the field of x-ray spectroscopy and nuclear physics, his numerous research publications, and his three laboratory manuals made him nationally known in his field. In 1971, when a building was completed to house its newly acquired 11 million-volt Tandem Van de Graaff accelerator, the physics department began operation of the John E. Edwards Accelerator Laboratory, named to honor Dr. Edwards and his research.

1963

*George E. Hill, Ph.D., Education,
Northwestern University*

Professor Hill came to Ohio University after extensive experience at Macalester College, the University of Pennsylvania, Morningside College, and Kansas State

Teachers College. He served as the Director of Guidance in the College of Education and as a member of the Advisory Committee on Guidance and Counseling of the U.S. Office of Education. Both the North Central Association of Colleges and Secondary Schools and the Ohio School Counselors Association awarded him honorary life memberships. Along with some eighty articles on guidance and counseling, he published *Management and Improvement of Guidance, Improving Teacher Education,* and, after his 1972 retirement, *Prof,* a nostalgic look at the teaching profession.

1964

Hollis Summers, Ph.D., English, Iowa State University

Poet and fiction writer Hollis Summers joined the English department faculty in 1959. His previous positions were at Georgetown College in Kentucky and then at the University of Kentucky, where he was named a distinguished professor. Between 1935 and 1988, he published five novels, including *The Weather of February, The Day After Sunday,* and *The Garden;* two collections of short stories; and nine books of poetry, including *Sit Opposite Each Other* and *The Walks near Athens.* Dr. Summers was frequently invited to give lectures and readings both in the United States and abroad and often taught at writers' conferences such as the Breadloaf Writers Conference in Vermont. In 1978 he was a Fulbright Lecturer at the University of Canterbury in New Zealand. The Ohio Arts Council honored him with its Individual Artists Award for his contributions as an outstanding instructor of literature and poetry.

1965

Troy W. Organ, Ph.D., Philosophy, University of Iowa

Professor Organ taught at Parsons College, the University of Akron, and Chatham College before coming to Ohio University in 1954. He was the author of fourteen books and numerous articles on philosophy and religion as well as a textbook on logic as a problem-solving tool. Much of his work was based on his interest in Indian philosophies and his conviction that "Buddhism is the most charming and winsome way of life man ever created." He received two Fulbright senior research grants to India as well as fellowships from the Ford Foundation and the American Council on Education. In 1987 he was awarded Ohio University's Distinguished Scholar award. Residents of Athens remember his dedication to long-distance running, which, he said, "freshened his attitude."

1966

Edward Stone, Ph.D., English, Duke University

Professor Stone joined the English department in 1956, having taught at the University of Virginia, Georgia Institute

of Technology, Duke University, and Newcomb College. He was one of the instigators of the controlled-materials method of teaching the writing of research papers and was a productive author himself. As a specialist in American literature he published more than seventy scholarly articles on authors such as Herman Melville and Henry James as well as seven books, including *Henry James: Seven Stories and Studies, What Was Naturalism?* and *The Battle of the Books.* Fulbright teaching grants took him to the National University of Mexico in 1966 and to the University of Buenos Aires in 1968. On his retirement in 1984, his colleagues in the English department established the Edward Stone Award to honor each year's outstanding English major.

1968

William D. Huntsman, Ph.D., Chemistry, Northwestern University

Professor Huntsman received a B.S. from Ohio University in 1947 and returned to Athens in 1951 to join the chemistry faculty. Dr. Huntsman was the recipient of numerous research grants for exploring the boundaries of organic chemistry. A 1957 U.S. Department of the Air Force grant allowed him to complete research on the mechanisms of various reactions of unsaturated hydrocarbons; a 1962 National Science Foundation grant helped him complete research on thermal cyclization reactions. He was a Fellow in the Ohio Academy of Science. A 1957 Ohio University Outstanding Teacher Award recognized his encouragement of student scholarship.

Norman S. Cohn, Ph.D., Botany, Yale University

Professor Cohn joined the botany faculty in 1959. He published numerous articles in the field of radiation genetics and the chemistry of genetic materials as well as two books, one of which, *Elements of Cytology,* was made available in a Spanish edition. Dr. Cohn lectured in the United States, Scotland, England, Italy, and Czechoslovakia and received fourteen research grants, including two Fulbright research scholarships to the University of Leiden in the Netherlands. His professional memberships included the Genetics Society of America, American Association for the Advancement of Science, American Society for Cell Biology, and the New York Academy of Sciences. In 1970, Dr. Cohn was appointed dean of the Graduate College and director of research for Ohio University.

1969

Roma A. King, Jr., Ph.D., English, University of Michigan

Professor King taught at Baylor University and the University of Missouri at Kansas City before joining the English department faculty in 1963. Focusing his research on nineteenth-century British literature, and especially on the poetry of Robert Browning, he served as gen-

eral editor of a definitive seventeen-volume edition of Browning's poetry. His sixth book, *The Focusing Artifice: The Poetry of Robert Browning,* published in 1968, was chosen by the MLA Book Club for distribution as part of the club's Scholar's Library. Dr. King was also a co-founder and associate editor of *Mundus Artium: A Journal of International Literature* and a member of the advisory board of *Victorian Poetry* and of the editorial board of the Ohio University Press.

1970

William U. Snyder, Ph.D., Psychology, Ohio State University

Before coming to Ohio University in 1962, Professor Snyder held positions with the U.S. Employment Service, the Des Moines Child Guidance Clinic, Ohio State University, and Pennsylvania State University. As the chair of the psychology department and director of clinical training, he secured a federal training grant in clinical psychology as well as numerous research grants to support his work. He wrote *Dependency in Psychotherapy,* co-authored *The Psychotherapy Relationship,* and was editor of *Casebook of Nondirective Counseling.* He also served as consulting editor for the *Journal of Counseling Psychology, Psychological Review,* and *Psychotherapy, Theory and Research.* Dr. Snyder was certified as a Diplomate in Clinical Psychology and was an active member of such professional organizations as the American and Ohio Psychological Associations, the Pennsylvania Psychological Association, Psychologists Interested in the Advancement of Psychotherapy, and the American Academy of Psychotherapists.

William W. Paudler, Ph.D., Chemistry, Indiana University

Professor Paudler was a postdoctoral research associate at Princeton and a research chemist for Procter and Gamble before coming to Ohio University in 1962. He was awarded fourteen research grants and contracts to further his work on the isolation and structure determination of new alkaloids and was invited to lecture in fifteen foreign institutes. His work *Advances in Heterocyclic Chemistry* was published as Volume 12 of *Naphthyridine Chemistry.* He served on the editorial board of the *Journal of Heterocyclic Chemistry* and as a referee for publications of that journal as well as for the *Journal of the American Chemical Society* and the *Journal of Organic Chemistry.* Dr. Paudler was elected as a Fellow of the American Institute of Chemists and as a member of the New York Academy of Science and of the executive committee of the International Society of Heterocyclic Chemistry.

1971

Carl G. Gustavson, Ph.D., History, Cornell University

Professor Gustavson joined the history faculty at Ohio University in 1945 as a specialist on twentieth-century Europe. His five books include *A Preface to His-*

tory (1955), *The Institutional Drive* (1966), *Europe in the World Community since 1939* (1970), and *The Mansion of History* (1976). Three Fulbright research grants allowed him to work in Germany, Sweden, and Israel. He also received grants from the American Philosophic Society, a fellowship from the Ford Foundation, and an award from the Baker Fund. Dr. Gustavson received the Ohio Academy of History Award in 1956, served as president of the Academy (1964–65), and received its Distinguished Achievement Award in 1978. Ohio University students of the class of 1957 voted him Best Teacher; the university later recognized his service by naming him an honorary alumnus.

1972

Raymond O. Lane, Ph.D., Physics,
Iowa State University

In 1966 Professor Lane left a position at Argonne National Laboratory in Illinois to come to Ohio University. Dr. Lane, an experimental nuclear physicist, gained recognition for his work in the penetration of electrons in matter, beta ray spectroscopy, neutron scattering, and nuclear structure as well as for his contributions to the development of instrumentation and techniques for obtaining and analyzing new data. He was the author of twenty-two professional publications and read papers at colleges, universities, and research institutes. In addition, Dr. Lane was instrumental in helping the university secure the 11-MeV accelerator from the Atomic Energy Commission in 1968. In 1969 he was elected a Fellow of the American Physical Society, an award given only to members who have made significant original contributions to the advancement of physics.

1973

Karl F. Ahrendt, Ph.D., Music,
Eastman School of Music,
University of Rochester

Professor Ahrendt came to Ohio University in 1950 as director of the School of Music after teaching violin and theory at Florida State University and directing the music department at Augustana College. He was an effective administrator and an active composer whose works brought him national recognition. His compositions include more than thirty works for piano, voice and chorus, orchestra, and chamber ensemble. They have been performed by groups such as the Modern Art Quartet of Woodstock, New York; the New York Baroque Ensemble; the Provincetown Orchestra in Massachusetts; and the Cleveland Orchestra. His honors included first prize in the Eurydice National Choral Competition, sponsored by the Philadelphia Arts Alliance; honorable mention in the National Delius Composition Competition; and a first prize for "Three Poems for a Calendar" in the 1972 Ohio Music Teachers' Association Composition Contest.

1974

Lowell E. Gallaway, Ph.D.,
Economics, Ohio State University

Professor Gallaway held positions with the University of Pennsylvania, the Social Security Administration, the University of Minnesota, San Fernando Valley State College, and Colorado State University before joining the economics faculty in 1967. Dr. Gallaway's publications include *Manpower Economics* (1971), *Poverty in America* (1973), and three other books as well as numerous monographs and journal articles dealing primarily with labor mobility, union organization, economic history, and the economics of poverty. He was awarded summer fellowships to the University of Chicago and to Stanford University and served as editor of the *Review of Social Economy* and of *Regional Science Perspectives*.

1976

Lee C. Soltow, Ph.D., Economics,
University of Wisconsin

Professor Soltow joined the faculty in 1950 as an economics instructor in what was then called the Department of Statistics. He had taught previously at the University of Wisconsin. In 1961 he received a Ford Foundation fellowship to

Norway and in 1965 published *Toward Income Equality in Norway*. Two Rockefeller Foundation grants supported his work as visiting professor at Ibadan University in Nigeria, 1965–67. Dr. Soltow continued his study of wealth and income distribution with grants from the National Endowment for the Humanities, the National Institutes of Health, and the National Science Foundation. He received recognition for his many journal articles and especially for his 1975 book, *Men and Wealth in the United States, 1850–1870*, which traced the distribution of wealth in mid-nineteenth-century America.

1977

John M. (Jack) Matthews, M.A., English, Ohio State University

Professor Matthews came to Ohio University in 1964 and took over as director of the Creative Writing Program. Two of his books have won Ohioana Awards, and his novel *Hanger Stout, Awake!* was praised by Eudora Welty and listed by NBA-Award-winning poet William Stafford as "one of the neglected books of the 20th century." Matthews was the first at Ohio University to be named both Distinguished Professor and University Professor. He has had a Guggenheim fellowship and Ohio Arts Council Major Artist's Award, and has published hundreds of poems, short stories and essays, six novels, collections of short stories, and works of nonfiction that reflect his passion for book collecting including *Collecting Rare Books for Pleasure and Profit* (1977). Anthony Burgess wrote that his novel *The Charisma Campaigns* (1972) "already has the feel of an Ameri-

can classic"; *Charisma* was also nominated by Walker Percy for the NBA Fiction Award.

1978

Wai-Kai Chen, Ph.D., Electrical Engineering, University of Illinois

Professor Chen came to Ohio University, his undergraduate alma mater, in 1964. He was the author or co-author of more than 100 papers as well as several books, including *Network Topology and Its Engineering Applications,* which discussed the topological techniques used in the analysis of linear networks and systems for computer application, and *Theory and Design of Broadband Matching Networks,* an advanced text in network theory. Three National Science Foundation research grants, two NASA grants, two Ohio University Research Committee grants, and a Baker Fund grant supported his work. He was elected as a fellow of both the Institute of Electrical and Electronics Engineers and the American Association of Science.

1979

George R. Klare, Ph.D., Psychology, University of Minnesota

In 1954 Professor Klare came to Ohio University where he became an expert on the readability of texts. He was author or co-author of five books, including *Know Your Reader* and *The Measurement of Readability,* as well as eighty articles and book chapters. The Institute for Scientific Information honored him through research counts making his 1974 article "Assessing Readability" a Citation Classic. The International Reading Association later inducted him into its Reading Hall of Fame. Dr. Klare held research grants from national agencies and was frequently invited as a consultant and lecturer on readability and programmed learning. In addition, he helped charter the Ohio University Faculty Senate, served as dean of the College of Arts and Sciences, and was acting associate provost for graduate and research programs.

1980

Peter R. Griffiths, Ph.D., Chemistry, Oxford University

Professor Griffiths joined the chemistry faculty in 1972. He was awarded grants from agencies such as the National Science Foundation, the Environmental Protection Agency, and the National Institutes of Health and from Alcoa Foundation, Upjohn Company, Standard Oil Company, and the Coal Research Laboratories Association to support his work in transform spectroscopy. He published *Chemical Infrared Fourier Transform Spectroscopy* in 1975, received the Coblentz Award for research in that field in 1977, and edited *Transform Techniques in Chemistry* in 1978. In the summer of 1979 he was at the University of Lausanne, Switzerland, as a visiting professor and in 1981 served as the general chairman for the conference on Fourier Transform Spectroscopy.

1981

Jacobo Rapaport, Ph.D., Physics, Massachusetts Institute of Technology

Professor Rapaport taught at both Universidad de Chile and MIT and joined

the physics faculty in 1969. An authority on nuclear physics, he was recognized for the 89 journal articles and 106 papers presented at national and international conferences and for the book *The (p,n) Reaction and the Nucleon-Nucleon Force,* which he edited for 1980 publication. Dr. Rapaport secured major research grants of more than $1.1 million. He received both Guggenheim and Fulbright fellowships, was named a Fellow of the American Physical Society in 1979, and in 1981 was elected to the executive committee of the Division of Nuclear Physics of that organization. His work with students won him an Ohio University Outstanding Graduate Physics Professor Award.

1982

Guido Stempel III, Ph.D., Journalism, University of Wisconsin

Professor Stempel became a recognized authority on the technique of content analysis while he was still a student at the University of Wisconsin. He came to Ohio University in 1965 and continued his research, authoring numerous articles and papers and editing *Journalism Quarterly,* the most prestigious journal of research in the field of mass communication. His *Research Methods in Mass Communication* became known as the standard on research methods in journalism. Dr. Stempel also served as director of Ohio University's Bush Endowment for Journalism Research, as chairman of the Research Committee of the National Council of College Publications Advisers, and as a member of both the executive and research committees for the Association for Education in Journalism.

1983

John L. Gaddis, Ph.D., History, University of Texas

Professor Gaddis joined Ohio University's history department in 1969. He gained national recognition for his work in American diplomatic history when his first book, *The United States and the Origins of the Cold War,* won the 1972 Bancroft Prize. In 1978 he published *Russia, the Soviet Union and the United States* and in 1982 *Strategies of Containment,* a widely praised interpretation of the Cold War from Kennan to Kissinger. For two years (1977–79) he worked at the U.S. Naval War College as a visiting professor and in 1980 was Bicentennial Professor of American Studies at the University of Helsinki. He held Fulbright and National Endowment for the Humanities fellowships and grants from the American Council of Learned Societies, the Harry S. Truman Research Fund, and the American Philosophical Society. Dr. Gaddis also served as coordinator of the John and Elizabeth Baker Peace Studies Fund.

1985

Richard K. Vedder, Ph.D., Economics, University of Illinois

Professor Vedder, who specializes in U.S. and European economic history, public finance, labor economics, and public policy analysis, came to Ohio University in 1965. The recipient of grants from the Ford, Rockefeller, Earhart, and other foundations, he has been visiting professor at Washington University in St. Louis, Claremont McKenna College, and the University of Colorado. He served as an economist with the Joint Economic Committee of Congress and Visiting Scholar at the American Enterprise Institute. Often collaborating with his colleagues, Dr. Vedder has authored or edited *Essays in Nineteenth-Century Economic History; The American Economy in Historical Perspective; Variations in Business and Economic History;* and *Poverty, Income Distribution, the Family and Public Policy,* as well as numerous articles. He writes frequently for newspapers such as the *Wall Street Journal, Investor's Business Daily, USA Today,* and the *Washington Post* and is consulted by political leaders throughout the world. He was named a University Professor, Honors Tutorial College Tutor of the Year and an honorary Ohio University Alumnus.

1986

Gladys Bailin, B.A., Dance, Hunter College

Professor Bailin joined the dance faculty in 1972. Her previous experience included performance, teaching, and choreography. As a member of the Alwin Nikolais Dance company, she performed at Lincoln Center, the Spoleto Festival in Italy, and the Connecticut Festival; working with the Don Redlich Company, she performed at the Paris International Festival of Dance. As a teacher, she worked with Nikolais Dance Theater Lab, the Henry Street Playhouse, and at the New York University School of the Arts. Her choreography, performed at numerous universities, was supported by four fellowships from the National Endowment for the Arts and by an Ohio University Research grant. In 1983 she became the director of the School of Dance and was also recognized by her students as a University Professor.

1989

Charles C. Alexander, Ph.D., History, University of Texas

Professor Alexander taught at the Universities of Houston and Georgia before coming to the Ohio University history department in 1970 to teach intellectual history. He published several books and articles on such subjects as the Ku Klux Klan, the American space program, and the diplomatic history of the Eisenhower administration before beginning in the 1980s to focus on the history of sports. A biography, *Ty Cobb,* was not only praised by critics but serialized in several newspapers. A second biography, *John McGraw,* was also well received. In 1980 Dr. Alexander began teaching Sports in American History, a new course for Ohio University and one of the first such courses at any university. In 1985 he developed and taught another unique and popular course, The History of American Baseball.

1991

Roger Finlay, Ph.D., Physics, Johns Hopkins University

Professor Finlay joined the physics department just as it was developing its doctoral program. As its first experimental nuclear physicist, he is credited with beginning the university's nuclear experimental program. His research was funded by federal agencies, the National Science Foundation, and the National Institutes of Health. He lectured frequently at research laboratories around the world and was a consultant to the Lawrence Livermore and Los Alamos laboratories, the Max Planck Institute in Heidelberg, and the Institute of Nuclear Physics in Germany. In 1984 he was the organizer and editor for an international conference on neutron-nucleus collisions; in 1986 he was selected a Fellow of the American Physics Society. The College of Arts and Sciences recognized his innovation in developing new courses and awarded him its 1989 Dean's Teaching Award.

1993

Thomas E. Wagner, Ph.D.,
Molecular and Cellular Biology,
Northwestern University

Professor Wagner held positions at Wellesley College/Harvard and Sloan-Kettering Institute for Cancer Research at Cornell University before coming to Athens in 1970. With research interests in control mechanisms in the regulation of gene expression, genetic recombination in eukaryotes, mammalian recombinant gene transfer, and biotechnology, Dr. Wagner led a group of researchers who, in 1980, discovered the process of DNA microinjection, the method by which genes are transferred from one animal to another. In 1981 his research team's successful transfer of a rabbit gene into a mouse focused national attention on the university. In 1983 Dr.

Wagner became the director of Ohio University's Mammalian Recombinant Genetics Institute, and a year later he founded and became the director of the Edison Biotechnology Institute, which conducted pioneering work in genetic engineering throughout the 1980s. In 1989 he was awarded a patent for his microinjection process, which became widely used in medical and agricultural research. Dr. Wagner's work was supported by grants of more than $9 million from such groups as the American Cancer Society, the National Cancer Institute, the Ohio Department of Development biotechnology fund, the National Science Foundation, and the National Institute of Child Health and Human Development. His more than 170 publications appeared in such journals as *Biochemistry, Biopolymers, Development in Mammals,* and the *Journal of Animal Science.* He was often invited to deliver the key lecture at national and international conferences and was a consultant to both governmental and commercial groups. Three biotechnology companies were founded based on the discoveries from his lab.

Wayne Dodd, Ph.D., English,
University of Oklahoma

Professor Dodd taught at the University of Colorado before coming to Ohio University in 1968. In 1971 he became the founding editor of the *Ohio Review,* which came to be recognized as one of the nation's leading journals of contemporary writing. A special Ohioana Award for Editorial Excellence from the Martha Kinney Cooper Foundation and the Fels Award for Outstanding Editing from the Coordinating Council of Literary Magazines honored him for this work. His major publications include

the novel *A Time of Hunting,* critical essays on poetry, and several volumes of poetry, including *The Names You Gave It, Sometimes Music Rises,* and *Echoes of the Unspoken.* In addition he wrote essays, book reviews, and interviews for scores of literary and scholarly magazines and journals, anthologies, and collections. His work was supported by fellowships from the National Endowment for the Arts, the Rockefeller Foundation, and the Ohio Arts Council.

1996

Alonzo L. Hamby, Ph.D., History,
University of Missouri

Professor Hamby came to Ohio University in 1965 as a specialist in twentieth-century American political history. His first book, *Beyond the New Deal: Harry S. Truman and American Liberalism,* won the David Lloyd Prize from the Harry S. Truman Library Institute, the Ohio Academy of History Book Award, and the First Book Award from Phi Alpha Theta. Other equally well-received books followed: *The Imperial Years: The United States since 1939* in 1976, *Liberalism and Its Challenges: F.D.R. to Reagan* in 1985, and *Man of the People: A Life of Harry S. Truman* in 1995. Dr. Hamby received eighteen study and research grants from ten foundations and institutes, lectured widely, and served as a member and officer of the Ohio Academy of History, the Organization of American Historians, and the American Historical Association.

Robert Hikida, Ph.D., Biological Sciences, University of Illinois

After postdoctoral work at Columbia University, Professor Hikida came to Ohio University in 1969. His research on the development, maintenance, and rejuvenation of muscles, particularly in birds and humans, was supported by numerous grants from the National Institutes of Health, the National Science Foundation, the U.S. Olympic Committee, and Ohio University and published in journals such as *American Journal of Anatomy, Cell and Tissue Research,* and *Science in Sports and Exercise.* Dr. Hikida contributed to the university not only through his well-known research, but through his contributions to students. He has been named the Outstanding First Year Basic Science Faculty of the Ohio University College of Osteopathic Medicine for twelve years, was voted Outstanding Graduate Professor in 1976, received the Jeanette G. Grasselli Faculty Teaching Award in 1992, and was named
the Outstanding Faculty Member at OU-COM in 1993.

Robert J. DeMott, Ph.D., English, Kent State University

In 1969 Professor DeMott came to Ohio University and established himself as an effective teacher of undergraduates and a dedicated mentor of the many graduate students who worked with him. His teaching awards include Outstanding Graduate Professor, University Professor, the Jeanette G. Grasselli Faculty Teaching Award, and the Honors Tutorial College's Outstanding Tutor Award. He won international respect for his work on the novelist John Steinbeck, publishing *Steinbeck's Reading* in 1984; *Working Days: The Journals of the* Grapes of Wrath, a 1989 *New York Times* Best Book; and *Steinbeck's Typewriter: Essays on His Art,* co-winner of the 1998 Nancy Dasher Award from the College English Association of Ohio. Dr. DeMott also served as editor of the three-volume Library of America series on Steinbeck (published in 1994, 1996, 2001).

Edward W. Stevens, Ph.D., Education, University of Rochester

Professor Stevens joined the education faculty in 1971. The focus of his work and research was the history of education and of literacy in particular. He edited several books on the subject with

other Ohio University faculty members; other publications include *The Grammar of the Machine: Technical Literacy and Early Industrial Expansion in the United States* and *Literacy, Law, and Social Order* as well as numerous articles. The need for literacy programs in southeast Ohio was of special interest to him and he secured several grants to support such projects, serving as director of the Adult Basic and Literacy Education Regional Resource Literacy Project and of the Ohio Appalachian Literacy Project. He also worked to initiate the Center for Study and Development of Literacy and Language. His distinguished professorship was awarded posthumously.

Surender K. Jain, Ph.D., Mathematics, University of Delhi, India

Professor Jain came to Ohio University in 1970 from a position as Reader in Mathematics at the University of Delhi. Focusing his research on ring theory, a branch of abstract algebra, he co-authored *Basic Abstract Algebra, Linear Algebra, Noncommutative Ring Theory, Applied Abstract Algebra,* and *Advances in Ring Theory.* Some eighty-five professional articles appeared in journals such as *Transactions of the American Mathematical Society, The Pacific Journal of Mathematics,* and *The Journal of Pure and Applied Algebra.* Dr. Jain also received two Fulbright senior scientist awards, held grants from the German Academic Exchange Service, the National Science Foundation, and the United Nations, and was frequently invited as visiting professor to other universities.

Ursula Belden, M.F.A., Theater,
Yale University

Professor Belden joined the theater department in 1986 to head its professional
Design Production and Technology program. Her distinguished professional
design career spans the past twenty-five
years and features work On Broadway,
Off-Broadway, in Europe, and in
Canada. Broadway credits include *Quil-*
ters, Waiting in the Wings, and *Amadeus.*
Off-Broadway she has designed more
than two dozen American and/or New
York premieres and many classics, including the award-winning revival of
Strindberg's A Dream Play. Recent international credits include productions in
Berlin, Prague, and Canada. Her extensive regional theater credits stretch from
coast to coast. A recipient of numerous
New York and national awards, her
work has regularly been selected for inclusion in the United States exhibition at
the Prague Quadrennial. Belden has received grants to conduct research in
Berlin (1998), Ireland (1990), London
(1995, 1997), and Prague (1997, 1999).

Steve Grimes, Ph.D., Physics,
University of Wisconsin

Professor Grimes came to Ohio University from the Lawrence Livermore
National Laboratory in 1981. A nuclear
physicist, his research interests include
MeV neutron cross sections with time-
of-flight techniques, neutron-induced
charged-particle producing reactions,
inelastic and exchange reactions, nuclear
astrophysics, and medical applications
of nuclear physics. His more than 100
articles appeared in technical journals
such as *Physical Review, Nuclear Science*
and Engineering, and *Medical Physics.* In
addition he delivered papers at more
than ninety professional conferences,
both in the United States and abroad;
more than forty of these were published
as a part of the conferences' proceed-
ings. Dr. Grimes became the director of
the John Edwards Accelerator Laboratory in 1985; in 1991 he was a visiting
professor at the University of Kentucky.

Kenneth Holroyd, Ph.D., Psychology,
University of Miami (Florida)

Professor Holroyd, a clinical psychologist and health psychologist, joined the
psychology department in 1975. His
research focused on understanding and
alleviating the suffering associated with
chronic pain disorders. This work includes laboratory studies that shed light
on the psychobiology of chronic pain
and clinical studies that combine state-
of-the-art drug and non-drug therapies
to more effectively treat chronic headache problems. He published more than
a hundred scientific articles and book
chapters, edited two books, was an
invited speaker at national and international scientific meetings, and served as
a consultant to pharmaceutical companies, the World Health Organization,
and health maintenance organizations.

Distinguished Teaching Professors

The Distinguished Teaching Professor award honors outstanding teachers of the humanities and appoints them as professors in the Charles J. Ping Institute for the Teaching of the Humanities. Created by the Ohio University Board of Trustees in 1992 and named for the university's eighteenth president, a philosopher, the institute supports the teaching of the humanities in schools and universities by funding projects such as library acquisitions, curriculum revisions, teaching colloquia, public forums, and summer workshops for teachers.

1994

Alan R. Booth, Ph.D.,
Boston University

Professor Booth, J. Richard Hamilton/Baker and Hostetler Professor Emeritus of Humanities and Professor Emeritus of History, joined the faculty in 1964 to teach African history. His teaching awards include the Outstanding Graduate Faculty Award, the College of Arts and Sciences' Outstanding Teacher Award, and the Jeanette G. Grasselli Faculty Teaching Award, as well as the Class of 1950 Teaching Award and University Professor award. He was active in service to the university as chair of a number of major committees, his department, and the faculty senate and beyond the university as a consultant and lecturer on African affairs. His publications include books on southern Africa, including *The United States' Experience in South Africa, 1783–1870; Swaziland: Tradition and Change and a Southern African Kingdom;* and *The Historical Dictionary of Swaziland.*

Lois Davis Vines, Ph.D.,
Georgetown University

Professor Vines, James S. Reid/Standard Products Company Professor of Humanities and Professor of French, who came to Ohio University in 1969, is an internationally recognized Edgar Allan Poe scholar. For her teaching, she received the College of Arts and Sciences' Outstanding Teacher Award, the Jeanette G. Grasselli Faculty Teaching Award, the University Professor Award, and the Alumni Teaching Award. In 1990 the Ohio Foreign Language Association named her Outstanding College Teacher in Ohio and the National Committee on Teaching as a Profession honored her as co-recipient of the Pioneer in Collaboration Award. For her teaching and research she was named *Chevalier dans l'Ordre des Palmes Académiques* by the French government. Dr. Vines published more than thirty articles, monographs, and book chapters, as well as *Valéry and Poe: A Literary Legacy* and *Poe Abroad: Influence, Reputation, Affinities.* In 1991 she received the Ohio Foreign Language Association Outstanding Publications Award.

1996

Thomas H. Carpenter, Ph.D.,
Oxford University

Professor Carpenter, Charles J. Ping Professor of Humanities and Professor of Classics, taught in secondary schools in Massachusetts and Rome for ten years after completing his Master of Theological Studies at Harvard. Convinced that good teaching is supported by involvement in research, he pursued his doctorate at Oxford University. During this time he explored his interest in the relationship between imagery and religion in the ancient Greek world, focusing particularly on the god Dionysus. After completing his degree, he stayed on at Oxford as the chief researcher for the Beazley Archive, where he was responsible for establishing a database of ancient Greek figure-decorated pottery while also working on various publications including the much used text, *Art and Myth in Ancient Greece.* In 1986 he returned to the United States to take a joint position in the Department of Art History and Center for the Humanities at Virginia Tech. In 1996 he joined Ohio University's classics department and became director of the Ping Institute for the Teaching of the Humanities.

1998

Dean McWilliams, Ph.D.,
University of Oregon

Professor McWilliams, J. Richard Hamilton/Baker and Hostetler Professor of Humanities and Professor of English, came to Ohio University in 1969 to teach comparative literature. He also was frequently invited to universities in Mexico, the Philippines, Germany, and, most frequently, France to teach as an exchange, Fulbright, or visiting professor. Dr. McWilliams was named an Outstanding Graduate Teacher finalist in both 1972 and 1982; he has been recognized as a University Professor and received the Jeanette G. Grasselli Faculty Teaching Award. His publications include books on Michel Butor and John Gardner and critical editions of two novels of Charles W. Chesnutt as well as a number of articles.

University Professor Honorees

The University Professor Award, introduced by University College in 1971, recognizes outstanding undergraduate teaching. The honorees, who are tenure-track faculty members, are selected for their teaching excellence by students on the Athens campus. The award provides release from part of normal teaching duties and $2,000 for professional development, allowing each professor to develop and teach two unique courses.

1970–71

James Bruning, Psychology
Richard Doolen, History
Edgar Whan, English

1971–72

Robert Borchard, Art
James Bruning, Psychology
Brian McHugh, Education
Algis Mickunas, Philosophy
Dwight Pugh, Business Administration
Shirley Wimmer, Dance

1972–73

Jerry Adams, Physics
Abraham Clearfield, Chemistry
Elliot Entin, Psychology
Richard Harvey, History
Larry Hlad, Sociology
Meno Lovenstein, Economics
Algis Mickunas, Philosophy
Evan Rudolph, Interpersonal
    Communication
Robert Trevas, Philosophy
Ray Wagner, Interpersonal
    Communication

1973–74

Robert Baker, Journalism
Maung Gyi, Interpersonal
    Communication
Fredrick Hagerman, Zoology
Robert Hobbs, Theater
Ronald Isele, Hearing and Speech
    Sciences
Dwight Pugh, Business Administration
Manuel Serna-Maytorena, Modern
    Languages
Hari Shankar, Mathematics
James Tilling, Political Science

1974–75

Donald Borchert, Philosophy
Samuel Crowl, English
Nicholas Dinos, Chemical Engineering
Sung Ho Kim, Political Science
Richard Mason, Sociology
Roger Quisenberry, Electrical
    Engineering
Jerome Rovner, Zoology
Geoffrey Smith, Geology
Edgar Whan, English
Kenneth Williams, Interpersonal
    Communication

1975–76

Irvin Badger, Civil Engineering
Joseph Berman, Radio-TV
J. Frank Henderson, Political Science
Lewis Hicks, Mechanical Engineering
Peter Kousaleos, English
Ronald Kroutel, Art

1976–77

Harry Kaneshige, Civil Engineering
Arthur Marinelli, Law
Algis Mickunas, Philosophy
Walter Tevis, English
John Timmis, Interpersonal
  Communication
Richard Wetzel, Music

1977–78

Samuel Jasper, Mathematics
Gary Sarver, Psychology
Shirley Slater, Home Economics
Hubert Wilhelm, Geography
David Williams, Political Science
Weldon Witters, Zoology

1978–79

Roger Bennett, Journalism
Francine Childs, Afro-American Studies
Robert DeMott, English
Elliot Entin, Psychology
Fredrick Hagerman, Zoology
Laurence Larson, Botany

1979–80

Gifford Doxsee, History
Terrill Eiler, Art
James Graffius, Botany
David Hostetler, Art
Robert Trevas, Philosophy
David Watts, Sociology

1980–81

Burton DeVeau, Economics
David Heaton, English
Peter Kousaleos, English
Donald Norris, Mathematics
Jerome Rovner, Zoology
David Stewart, Philosophy

1981–82

Dana Hewins, Economics
Ronald Isele, Hearing and Speech
  Sciences
Samuel Jasper, Mathematics
Dean McWilliams, English
Ed Payne, Music
Eric Wagner, Sociology

1982–83

James Barnes, Political Science
Melvin Helitzer, Journalism
J. Frank Henderson, Political Science
William Kaldis, History
Jack Matthews, English
Byron Scott, Journalism
Edgar Whan, English (in perpetuity)

1983–84

Gladys Bailin, Dance
Frank (Ted) Bernard, Geography
John Collier, Chemical Engineering
Donald Fucci, Hearing and Speech
  Sciences
Fredrick Hagerman, Zoology
Hubert Wilhelm, Geography

1984–85

Clifford Houk, Chemistry
William (Gene) Kaufman, Mathematics
Thomas Peters, Journalism
Dwight Rogers, Curriculum and
  Instruction
Madeleine Scott, Dance
George Wood, Curriculum and
  Instruction

1985–86

Hugh Bloemer, Geography
Girard Krebs, Sociology
William Reeves, Industrial Technology
Donald Richter, History
Richard Vedder, Economics
David Williams, Political Science

1986–87

David Descutner, Interpersonal
  Communication
Gifford Doxsee, History
J. Frank Henderson, Political Science
Ronald Isele, Hearing and Speech
  Sciences
Gary Pettigrew, Art
Michael Smilowitz, Interpersonal
  Communication

1987–88

Raymond Gusteson, Political Science
Fredrick Hagerman, Zoology
Brian Manhire, Electrical Engineering
Lynn Phelps, Interpersonal
  Communication
Dwight Pugh, Finance
Eric Wagner, Sociology

1988–89

Frank (Ted) Bernard, Geography
Alan Booth, History
Michael Bugeja, Journalism
Bruce Carlson, Psychology
Steven Miner, History
Donald Norris, Mathematics

1989–90

Linda Bellush, Psychology
Donald Borchert, Philosophy
Francine Childs, Afro-American Studies
Jeffrey Falkel, Physical Therapy
Marsha Gathron, Health and Sport
  Sciences
Reid DeBerry Huntley, English

1990–91

Thomas Calhoun, Sociology
J. Frank Henderson, Political Science
Justice Hill, Journalism
William Kaldis, History
Joan McMath, Curriculum and Instruction
Donald Richter, History

1991–92

Nicholas Dinos, Chemical Engineering
Michael Mumper, Political Science
Barry Roth, English
Gary Sarver, Psychology
John Schermerhorn, Management Systems
Arthur Zucker, Philosophy

1992–93

Carl Remus Bridges, Management Systems
Schuyler Cone, Home Economics
Fredrick Hagerman, Zoology
Calvin B. L. James, Zoology
Albert Mosley, Philosophy
Dwight Pugh, Finance

1993–94

James Barnes, Political Science
Loreen Giese, English
Reid DeBerry Huntley, English
Girard Krebs, Sociology
Valerie Perotti, Management Systems
Carolyn Tice, Social Work

1994–95

Bruce Carlson, Psychology
Marsha Gathron, Health and Sport Sciences
John Gilliom, Political Science
Richard Greenlee, Social Work
J. Frank Henderson, Political Science
Linda Ross, Biological Sciences

1995–96

Samuel Crowl, English
Dennis Dalen, Theater
Katherine Jellison, History
Joan McMath, Curriculum and Instruction
Joan Safran, Curriculum and Instruction
Lois Vines, Modern Languages

1996–97

Alice Blake-Stalker, Curriculum and Instruction
David Chappell, Management Systems
Nicholas Dinos, Chemical Engineering
Ernesto Randolfi, Health Sciences
Jerry Sloan, Journalism
Matthew White, Biological Sciences

1997–98

Eddith Dashiell, Journalism
Daniel Dolata, Chemistry
Richard Harvey, History
Daniel Modaff, Interpersonal Communication
Patricia Weitsman, Political Science
Julie White, Political Science

1998–99

No University Professors were selected for 1998–99

1999–00

David Descutner, Interpersonal Communication
Ronald Hunt, Political Science
Calvin B. L. James, Biomedical Sciences
William (Gene) Kaufman, Mathematics
Marcia Nighswander, Visual Communication

2000–01

Michael Bugeja, Journalism
Richard Harvey, History
Paul Nelson, Interpersonal Communication
Gary Sarver, Psychology
Carolyn Tice, Social Work
Patricia Weitsman, Political Science

2001–02

Tom Carpenter, Classics
Jenny Chabot, Human and Consumer Sciences
Caryn Medved, Interpersonal Communication
Joan McMath, Teacher Education
Jan Palmer, Economics

2002–03

Raymond Frost, Management Information Systems
Paula Popovich, Psychology
Nagesh Rao, Interpersonal Communication
Arthur Trese, Plant Biology

2003–04

Delysa Burnier, Political Science
Terry Eiler, Visual Communication
Donald Fucci, Hearing, Speech, and Language Science
David Kirch, Accountancy
James Petrik, Philosophy

Trustees

An Ohio University Legacy Family

A story recounted by Professor Willis Boughton in "The Genesis of a University" describes one pioneer family's persistence in sending its children to Ohio University. The Reads lived on a farm near Urbana, Ohio, 150 miles from Athens.

> They had a large family of boys and one daughter. It was determined to give the boys the best educational advantages that the west afforded, so the Ohio University was selected. There were in succession seven boys to educate. In the spring their help was needed at home to plow and to plant, and in the fall, to gather in. It was necessary for them to journey back and forth at these seasons. As there were no public conveyances, the father had to make the journey with a large two-horse carriage. It took three days to make the trip each way, and Mr. Reed [sic] made it one hundred and twenty times. Did it pay? Daniel, the oldest boy [an 1825 graduate], became a college president; three became lawyers, and one of these a judge of the Supreme Court of Ohio; two became doctors; and the seventh was shot while commanding a vessel in the attempt to run the blockade between New Orleans and Baton Rouge in the civil war.

Since those early days, other family names have appeared repeatedly on university rosters. When the Reverend

James McAboy became a trustee in 1831, he began such a tradition in his family. Now, generations later, his descendants continue to enroll at Ohio University, contribute to their communities, and often serve in the professions the institution was founded to support.

1826–33   Rev. James McAboy, an early teacher in the first schoolhouse in Athens, served the university as a trustee.

1869   **John L. McMaster** served in the Union Army before enrolling at Ohio University. He had a successful career as a lawyer in Indianapolis and also served as the city's mayor.

1915–16   Natalie S. Rutherford Myers, great-niece of John L. McMaster and related to James McAboy through her mother, Carrie Stevens Rutherford, received a teaching certificate and taught in a one-room school.

1920–23   James K. Rutherford, Natalie Rutherford Myers's younger brother, missed graduation by one semester but was successful in the field of mechanical engineering.

1926   Dwight H. Rutherford, first cousin of Natalie and James K. Rutherford, became a civic leader in Athens and a charter member of the Trustees Academy. He was awarded an honorary degree in 1977.

1941   **Janet Rutherford Lee**, niece of Natalie and James K. Rutherford, married Dr. Arnold Lee, class of '41.

328

1944 **Mary V. Myers Clark**, daughter of Natalie S. Rutherford Myers (1915–16), became a high school teacher and also served as a field staff assistant with the American Red Cross.

1947–48 Harriet Jane Rutherford Brownlow, daughter of James K. Rutherford (1920–23) and his wife Ruth, married Ben W. Brownlow, class of '49.

1948–49 Janet Theobald Morris, great-niece of John L. McMaster, became a deputy chief clerk of the Meigs County Court. Her sons James, Mark, and John graduated from Ohio University in 1977, 1978, and 1985.

1951–53 Nancy Rutherford Whitacre, another daughter of James K. and Ruth Rutherford, married David Whitacre, class of '53.

1954 Nancy Rutherford Penn, the daughter of Dwight H. Rutherford (1926) and his wife Rose, was a founding member of the Ohio Village Volunteers of the Ohio Historical Society in Columbus.

1969 **Barbara Lee Rutherford Birkhimer**, the daughter of 1941 graduates Arnold and Janet Rutherford Lee, became an elementary school teacher.

1977 **James Morris**, a son of Janet Theobald Morris (1948–49), became a U.S. Air Force officer as well as a high school teacher and coach.

1978 **Mark Morris**, also a son of Janet Theobald Morris, became a U.S. Air Force officer.

1985 **John Morris**, the third son of Janet Theobald Morris, followed his brothers James and Mark into the USAF.

1997 **Kristen N. Reynolds**, a granddaughter of 1941 graduates Janet R. and Arnold Lee, earned a nursing degree on the Zanesville campus.

1998 **Ellen Birkhimer**, the daughter of 1969 graduate Barbara L. Birkhimer, followed her mother into elementary school teaching. Her husband is Tuyen D. Cao, '00.

Source Notes

This bicentennial book was conceived as an effort to present the total character of Ohio University by describing the development of its administrative policies, campus facilities, academic programs, and cultural life, including the activities of its students. Many reference materials on these topics are available in Ohio University's Alden Library, Athens, Ohio. The library's Robert E. and Jean R. Mahn Center for Archives and Special Collections is an especially rich repository.

The ongoing record of the decisions that shape Ohio University's administrative policies, physical facilities, and academic programs is *Minutes and Resolutions of the President and Trustees of the Ohio University*. The legal documents found in William E. Peters's *Legal History of the Ohio University, Athens, Ohio* (Cincinnati: Press of the Western Methodist Book Concern, 1910) are good supplements to the early trustee minutes, and the presidents' annual reports to the trustees give interesting year-by-year accounts of the institution's progress from 1839 to the present. President Charles Ping's annual reports have been collected in two volumes: *Ohio University in Perspective: The Annual Convocation Addresses of President Charles J. Ping, 1975–1984* (Athens: Ohio University Press, 1985) and *Ohio University in Perspective II: The Annual Convocation Addresses of President Charles J. Ping, 1985–1993* (Athens: Ohio University Press, 1994). President Robert Glidden's annual convocation addresses, 1994–2002, have been printed as pamphlets by Ohio University Graphic Communications and are available from the Office of the President, Cutler Hall, Athens, Ohio 45701.

The papers of Presidents Wilson, McGuffey, Howard, Scott, Super, Ellis, Bryan, Gamertsfelder, James, Baker, Alden, Sowle, and Ping offer a wealth of information on the day-to-day work of each man. (The Gamertsfelder papers include manuscripts describing Presidents Bryan and James.) In addition, a few letters by Jacob Lindley provide some insight into his thinking; a number of letters in the Ezra Walker Collection by President McGuffey clarify his position on the financial problems of the 1840s; and the Coe Collection contains both letters and documents.

Other material by and about the presidents can also be found in the Mahn Center. A few pages of "The History of the McGuffeys" by Alice McGuffey Ruggles (1950) describe President McGuffey's problems with Athens residents. Charles Super's book, *A Pioneer College and Its Background (The Ohio University)* (Salem, Mass.: Newcomb & Gauss, Printers, 1924), gives his view of the university; his locally printed pamphlet, *A Retrospect and a Protest* (1908), presents a candid assessment of his successor, Alston Ellis. A taped interview with Robert Mahn, former secretary to the board of trustees, provides descriptions of the university during the administrations of Presidents James, Baker, and Alden. Two books about President Baker's administration are *Ohio University: The Baker Years* by Paul Fontaine (Athens: Ohio University Press, 1961)—a year-by-year review of campus events from 1945 through 1961—and *John C. Baker: An Oral History* (Athens: Ohio University Libraries, 1995), in which he discusses his years at the university. Three books provide insights into President Alden's tenure at Ohio University. President Alden reviews his years in Athens in *Speaking for Myself: The Personal Reflections of Vernon R. Alden* (Athens: Ohio University Libraries, 1997) and discusses his presidency in *Vernon R. Alden: An Oral History* (Athens: Ohio University Libraries, 1999), edited by archivist Doug McCabe. *The Decade of the University: Ohio University and the Alden Years* by Professor Meno Lovenstein (Athens, Ohio: Lawhead Press, 1971) is a philosophical account of the university in the '60s. I also found the papers of Vice President James Whalen particularly helpful in understanding the foment of that period. A taped interview with President Claude Sowle is useful in understanding his approach to the problems of the early '70s. A similar interview with Donald A. Spencer, a trustee from 1975 to 1983, provides insights into the work of the board of trustees.

A record of the faculty's concerns with students and curricular matters during the nineteenth century is available in *Records of the Faculty of Ohio University, 1837–97*. A manuscript prepared by former provost Thomas C. Smith follows the development of faculty governance at Ohio University from the 1920s, when a chapter of the American Association of University Professors was formed at the university, through the days of the Faculty Advisory Council, to the creation of Faculty Senate in the early '60s. Faculty Advisory Council annual reports (1940—64) and the minutes of Faculty Senate (1972–98) give further evidence of the faculty's contributions to university decision making. A quite different source, a diary kept by Professor Raymer McQuiston during the 1950s and 1960s, offers a personal reflection on the daily round of classes, grading, and meetings.

Various official university publications suggest how the decisions made by trustees, presidents, and faculty members were implemented. The annual catalogues/bulletins, from 1804 to 2002, describe the school's changing facilities, faculty, students, and programs and sometimes have photographs. The Fact Book kept up-to-date by university archivists and the publications of the Office of Institutional Research give facts and figures about facilities, administration, academics, and a variety of awards. Successive alumni journals, including the *Ohio Alumnus* (Alumni Association, 1923–69);, the *Ohio University Alumnus Magazine* (Office of University Publications, 1972–78), *Ohio University Today* (1979–99), and *Ohio Today* (Division of University Communications and Marketing, 1999–present), contain stories about buildings, programs, faculty and staff, and a wide variety of campus and alumni activities. The *Campus Communicator* (September 1970–July 1972) provides news of the campus from the administration's point of view, as does *Outlook* (University News Services, 1975–). Alumni directories published in 1923, 1989, 1993, and 2002 by the university's Alumni Association are useful, as are the news releases from the Office of Public Information.

Reports about the university are plentiful in area newspapers, most of which are available on microfilm in Alden Library. The university's opening in 1808 was announced in the *Ohio Gazette and Virginia Herald* (Marietta, Ohio, 1803–11). The *Scioto Gazette* (Chillicothe, Ohio, 1801–15) sometimes printed letters from professors or students. Other early reports on the university exist in the *Athens Mirror and Literary Register* (1825–30), the *Athens Messenger and Hocking Valley Gazette* (1850–64 and 1872–1903), and the *Athens Messenger and Herald* (1894–1902). The *Athens Messenger* and especially the *Athens News* (1977–) continue to be good sources of information on university personnel and events.

For background on American education in the eighteenth and nineteenth centuries I referred to *American Collegiate Populations: A Test of the Traditional View* by Colin B. Burke (New York: New York University Press, 1982) and *". . . Schools and the Means of Education Shall Forever Be Encouraged": A History of Education in the Old Northwest, 1787–1880* (Athens: Ohio University Libraries, 1987), a collection of essays edited by Paul H. Mattingly and Edward W. Stevens. For a history of the university that uses many of the primary sources noted, I recommend Thomas N. Hoover's *The History of Ohio Univerisity* (Athens: Ohio University Press, 1954), a readable and thorough account of the university's first 150 years. Other brief accounts of Ohio University history include Willis Boughton's "The Genesis of a University, the Ohio University, Athens," reprinted from an article in the *Magazine of American History* (New York, 1893); Clement L. Martzolff's *Ohio University, the Historic College of the Old Northwest* (Athens, Ohio: The University, 1910); and "The Crisis at Ohio University," in the *Moorsfield Antiquarian; A Magazine of American History* 2, no. 3 (1928), edited by Hugh McClellan and Charles W. McClellan (Champlain, N.Y.: Moorsfield Press). A manuscript by Connie Perdreau, a copy of which is in the Mahn Center's topical files, provides a history of African Americans at Ohio University. Beverly J. Price's "Report on the Status of Women at Ohio University" (1972) reveals women's positions in the early '70s.

For details of student life, the Mahn Center was again a rich repository of information. There I found two unpublished chapters on student life written by Thomas N. Hoover, minutes of two long-lived literary societies (the Athenians and the Philomatheans), a number of letters from early students at the university, the short diary entries of Samuel Bright (1866) and Frank H. Super (1896), and the diary kept by Margaret Boyd (1872–73). *The First Ninety Years: A History of Beta Chapter of Delta Tau Delta of Ohio University* by F. Darrell Moore (n.p., 1953) is a good descriptor of college life from the 1860s to the 1950s. The papers of the first dean of women, Irma Voigt, give a picture of activities from 1915 until the 1940s. A few existing issues of early student publications were helpful, including the *Echo and University Record* (1843), the *College Mirror* (1874–76), the *Current* (1886–92), the *Daily Yell* (1890), the *Daily News* (1891), *Ohio University Panorama* (1892–93), the *Mirror* (1902), the *Green and White* (1911–39), and the *Green Goat* (1922 to the mid-1950s). The *University Post*, now called the *Post* (1939–present), remains an excellent resource for information on student activity, interests, and opinion. The *Athena Yearbook*, first published in 1892, was invaluable for both commentary and pictures of the changing campus scene. I also found interesting photographs and memorabilia in the Mahn Center's scrapbooks. "Ohio University Scenes" was undated and unidentified, but the others belonged to Percy R. Stout, '13; Clarence Carr Liggett, '16; Loah Frost (Dow); Harry E. Secrest, '17; Lois Hays (Parker), '18; Margaret Katherine Lawless, '18; Doris Woodworth, 1900s; Katherine E. Dague (Cocanower), '23; G. Caswell, 1928–29; Mrs. Eleanor Crites, '28; Leona Hughes, '32; Mrs. Viola F. Keairns, '33; Alpha Phi Alpha; Alliance Française, 1914–57, and Maurel Hunkins, dean of men (1946–59) and then director of public occasions (1959–72). A slide show, "I'm Here for Work" (1986), is a wonderful history of women at Ohio University. I also benefited from the loan of the scrapbooks of William Fenzel, '15; Ruth Thomas (Downing), '18; Anne Downing LaFollette, '56; Jan Rienerth, '66; and Treudley Hall.

The character and spirit of Ohio University are linked to its founding by pioneers, in an "embryonic town," on what was America's western frontier. The most recent and most comprehensive history of this town, the university's home, is *Athens, Ohio: The Village Years* by Robert L. Daniel (Athens: Ohio University Press, 1997). *Getting to Know Athens County* by Elizabeth Grover Beatty and Marjorie S. Stone (Athens: The Stone House, 1984) discusses the county—its agriculture, industries, communication, transportation, and health services—and includes the development of Ohio University in the section on education. The earliest general history of the county is *History of Athens County, Ohio* (Cincinnati: Robert Clarke, 1869) by Charles M. Walker. Walker includes information on Manasseh Cutler, Rufus Putnam, and the settlement of the area and provides documents concerning the transfer of lands from the United States to the Ohio Company of Associates and the founding of Athens and the Ohio University. He also offers biographical sketches of settlers, including the Ewings, the Perkins, the Browns, and Jacob Lindley, all of whom were intimately involved with the university in its earliest days. A. B. Walker's *Reminiscences* (Athens, Ohio: October 1876) discusses his family, including its relationship with the Ewings, the arrival of the railroad, and the university's founding. Harriet Connor Brown's biography of Maria Brown Foster, *Grandmother Brown's Hundred Years 1827–1927* (Boston: Little Brown & Co., 1920), gives a highly readable account of everyday life in Athens. Mildred A. Bleigh's collection of newspaper clippings, *It Happened in Athens County: (in the early 1900s)* (Athens, Ohio: M. A. Bleigh, 1989), is a good guide to exciting local events.

Several early atlases reveal the development of the county, town, and university by providing pictures of people and places. I appreciated *The Atlas of Athens County, Ohio,* edited by D. J. Lake (Philadelphia: Titus, Simmons & Titus, 1875); *Athens County, Picturesque, Industrial, Commercial,*

1797–1897, by J. C. Tipton (Athens: Messenger and Herald, 1897); *The Centennial Atlas of Athens County, Ohio* (Athens: Centennial Atlas Association, 1905); and especially *The Athens Home Coming Reunion, June 14 and June 15, 1904,* compiled by Captain A. H. Mattox, which provides photographs of men who were among the university's first students as well as photographs of Athens and the university. *Athens County, Ohio* by William E. Peters (Athens: n.p., 1947) includes scenic views of the area, and *The Harris History: A Collection of Tales of Long Ago of Southeastern Ohio* by Charles H. Harris (Athens: Athens Messenger, 1957) profiles families and shows photographs of their homes and workplaces. Marjorie S. Stone varies this approach in *As Time Goes By: A Pictorial Journal of Athens, Ohio* (Athens: The Stone House, 2001) by showing buildings as they were years ago and as they are today.

Dan Dry's *Then and Now, Ohio University* (Louisville: Harmony House Publishers, 1992) provides contemporary color photographs of the university. *Ohio University Campus Master Plan, The Campus Green* (Columbus, Ohio: NBBJ, 1997) provides a look at future campus facilities. The Mahn Center also contains many archival photographs, including the Thomas Oldfield and O'Bleness collections. The Snow Collection and the James Anastas Collection at the Athens County Historical Society and Museum are excellent supplements.

Many other reference materials are available in the Mahn Center, including biographical and topical files on people and programs and the papers of numerous administrators, professors, and alumni. For short, contemporary descriptions of university programs and student activities, the university's website at www.ohio.edu is good place to begin.

I was also fortunate that a number of people were willing to share their own photographs and scrapbooks or to participate in lengthy interviews. Their names are included with those of other generous contributors in the acknowledgments pages.

Index

Page references in italics denote illustrations.

Center for Innovation in Technology and Learning, 289
Center for International Studies, 266, 267
Center of Economic Development, 189
Chaddock, Jeffery D., 299
chapel, *78, 86, 87. See also* Galbreath Chapel
Chase's Collegians, 127
cheerleaders, *121, 193*
chemistry, 18, 86, 87, 97, 148, 158, 170, *173*, 193, 289
Chen, Wai-Kai, *314*
Chiang, Chia Chi, 300
Child Development Center, 65, 251
Childs, Francine, 240
Chillicothe campus, 148, 150, 151
China, People's Republic of, 250, 267
Chinese Club, *105*, 265
Choral Union, O.U., 107, *108*
Chubb, Edwin Watts, 90, 106, 118–19, 130, 131, *305*
Chubb Hall, 214. *See also under* library
Chubu Institute of Technology, 245, 250, 252
CIA recruiting, 270
circus, 38, 61, 69, *70*, 85
civil rights movement, 181, 185, 200
Civil War, 55, 57; veterans at O.U., 59–61, *60, 63*
Civil War Monument, 83, *85, 239*
Claire Cottage, 95
Clark, Henry, 77
Clark, Kenneth S., 113, 122
Clark, Lewis, *72*
Clark, Mary V. Myers, *329*
Clayton, Jefferson B., *107*
Clearfield, Abraham, 193
Clinton, Hillary, *283*, 287
Clinton, William, 299
Clippinger, Donald R., *173*
Cocanower, Katherine Dague, 247
Cohn, Margaret, 210
Cohn, Norman, 294, *312*
College Adjustment Program (CAP), 133, 249, 298, 299
College Edifice (Cutler Hall), *16*, 27, 28, *29*, 34, 37, 42. *See also* Center Building; Cutler Hall
College Green (Campus Green). *See under* greens
Comedians, *129*
commencement, 16, 22, 28, *30*, 40, 54, 56, 59, 62, 71, 81, 83, *278*; speakers, *274, 275, 287, 300*
Commerce, College of, 132, 134, 173, 186. *See also* Business, College of
commercial branch, *97*, 134
Commons, 9, 27–28, 38, 67, 78, 83, 85
communes, 238
Communication, College of, 136, 200, 203, 244, 250, 251, 254, 266–67, 270, 290, 291
Communication Week, 203, 244, 250, *252*
comparative arts. *See* Fine Arts, College of

computer science, 259, 270
computers on campus, 288–90
concerts and music festivals, *202, 220, 221,* 223, 237, 248, *261;* Southern Ohio Folk Festival, 218. *See also* Springfest
Connett, Raymond, 122
Contemporary History Institute, 271
Continental Congress, 2, 3, 4, 5, 6, 7
Convocation Center, 76, 77, 193–94, 195, *196,* 220, 233, 262, 263
Cook, Tiff, 172
Coonskin Library, 17, 88
Copeland, Charles M., 97, 134
Copeland Hall, 134, 278
Corbin, James Carter, 31
Corp, Benjamin, 16
correspondence courses, 150. *See also* extension program
Corrigan, Tracy Green, 264, 269
Corts, Robert, 211
Court Street, 28, *48, 98, 114, 237, 240, 242,* 244, *253,* 269, 277, *278,* 288, 292
Cox, Samuel Sullivan "Sunset," *44*
Craig, Florence, *72*
Cranz, Kate, 80, *81*
creative writing program, 200, 244, 256, 258, 264, 272
Creer, Thomas, 257
Creps, Richard H., 144
Crewson, Harry B., 175, 224, 229, *230, 231,* 235, *308*
Cronkite, Walter, 203, 244
Crook, Isaac, *88, 305*
Crook Hall, 257, 259
Crowl, Samuel, 298
Culbert, Taylor, 187, *188,* 218, 220–21
Cunningham, John K., 153–54
Curry, Thomas H., *173*
Cutler, Manasseh, 2–3, *3,* 5, 7, 18, 20, 34
Cutler, William Parker, literary medal, *18*
Cutler Hall, *29,* 105, 133, 147, 148, *158,* 201, 211, 230, 295, 301. *See also* Center Building; College Edifice

Dad's Day, 127
Dailey, Edward, 199
Dana, Joseph, 16, 42
Dance, School of, 136, 248–49, *249,* 300
dances, 108, 125, 126, *127, 139, 140, 143, 144,* 154, *160, 164, 166, 167, 176, 178,* 288
Daniel, Robert L., 10
Darnton, Donald C., *188*
David, Margaret, 168
Davis, Angela, *232*
Davis, John Merrill, *63, 66*
Davison, Beaumont, 151–52
Davison, Patrick, 299
Day, Jesse H., *173*
Deaton, Mark, 258
demonstrations. *See* protests and demonstrations
DeMott, Robert J., *318*
Demoyne, William, 161

Denham, Joseph, 170
Dent, Elmer A., 80
Deppen, Margaret, *115,* 206
Depression, Great, 130, 132, 139
Descutner, David, 289
Devine, Wendy Weeden, *76,* 116
Dewees, Pat, 271
Dewees, Will, 238
Dilley, Frank, 133, 137
DiNicola, Dan, 199
Dinos, Nick, 277–78, 282
Distinguished Professor awards, 178, 180, 309–19
Distinguished Teaching Professor awards, 282, 320–21
Dixon, Charles Herbert, *63, 66*
Dixon, J. Floyd, 150
doctoral degrees, O.U., 90, 94, 136, 147, 170, 173, 183, 186, 190, 203, 226, 256, 291
Dodd, Wayne, 272, *317*
Dohnányi, Ernst von, 169, *170*
Donaldson, Diana, 240
Donnelly, Mary, 80
Doobie Brothers, *248*
Doolen, Richard, 218
dormitories. *See* students: housing
Drake, Professor, 37
Dunkle, Eli, 81, 93
Dupre, Mary-Blair, 214
Dybvig, H. Eugene, 155
Dysart Woods, 283

Eachus, Madge Acord, 106–7, 128
Eagleson Act, 99
Eastern campus, 151
East Green. *See under* greens
East Wing (Wilson Hall), 39, 81, 98, 102, 115, 146
Ebert, Madalene, 80
Eblin, Lawrence P., *173*
Economics, Department of, 134, 151, 187, 271
Edge Hill Cafeteria, *197*
Edifice. *See* College Edifice
Edison Biotechnology Institute (EBI), 64, 65, 255
Education, College of, 32, 94, 119, 131–32, 170, 176, 224, 251, 252, 257–58, 265, 266–67, 289. *See also* model school; Normal College; normal department; teacher training
Educational Plan: 1977–1987, 242–43, 251, 254, 263; II, 268–69
Edwards, John E., *310. See also under* accelerator
Edwards, Tom, 122
1804 Fund, 245, 255
Eisenhower, Dwight, 168, 171, 175
Elliott, Rush, 187–88, *190*
Ellis, Alston, 90, *92,* 93, 97, 98, 99–100, 104, 106, 108, 112, 113, 115, 118, 147, 150, *305*
Ellis Hall, 66, *93,* 94, 111, 142
Ellsberg, Daniel, *221*

Political Science, Department of, 32, 258, 271

Portsmouth campus, 140, 148, *149*, 150, 151, 152, 178

Post, 72–73, 140, 141, *142*, 143, 165, 184, 185, 190, 194, 196, 199, *201*, 211, 222, 229–30, 288

Poston, L., 22

Powder Bowl, 161, *162*

Precollege orientation, 133

Preis, Eran, 256

Prep Follies, 143, 145

Presbyterian church, 11, 21, 24, 27, 232

Presidential Research Scholar awards, 298

Presidential Teaching awards, 296, *297*

presidents, O.U., 303–8. *See also individual presidents*

Previtali, Giovanni, 208

Price, Aaron, 100

Price, Beverly E., 116, 219–20, *220*

Price, E. Curmie, 32, 185

Price, Tom, 199, 200

Prisley, Joanne Dove, 165

protests and demonstrations, *195, 202, 204,* 204–6, *207, 211, 212,* 213–17, *214, 215, 216,* 220, 221, 222, *230, 270,* 273–74, *274, 283*

Proudman, Peter, *176*

Pruitt, Peggy, 76, 249

psychology, 195, 257, 258

publications, student, 43, 70, 72–73, 81, 88. *See also Athena Yearbook; Green and White; Green Goat; Post*

Pugh, Dwight, 258

Pulitzer Prize, 201, 203, 300

Putnam, Gen. Rufus, 2, 4, *5,* 6, 7–10, 19, 28

Putnam Child Care Center, *258*

Putnam Hall, 94

Quattrocki, Edward, 252

Quisenberry, Roger, 186

radio station, 143, 156, 157, *157,* 180. *See also* WOUB-AM-FM-TV

railroads, 54, *55,* 69, 225

Ramey, Jesse, 297

Rapaport, Jacobo, *219, 315*

Ratelle, Eleanor Hazlett, 132

Razak Chair. *See* Tun Abdul Razak Chair in Southeast Asia Studies

Read, Amasa, 36

Read, Daniel, 38, 45, 328

Read, Ezra, 36

Rebok, Barbara Amos, 177

Red Cross, 112, *113,* 143

Reese, Jerry, 221

regional campuses, 173, 208. *See also* Belmont campus; Chillicothe campus; Eastern campus; Ironton campus; Lancaster campus; Martins Ferry campus; Portsmouth campus; Regional Higher Education; Zanesville, Ohio: campus

Regional Higher Education, 150–52, 271.

See also extension program; regional campuses

Registration Hop, *160, 164*

Reid, Tom, 281

Remsburg, Frank S., 87

Research and Technology Building, 259

residence halls. *See* students: housing; *individual buildings*

Residence Life, 133, 290

Residential/Experimental College, 209

Revelers, 129

Revolutionary War, 2, 3, 4, *5,* 6

Rex, Mindy, 289

Reynolds, Kristen N., 329

Rhodes, Gov. James, 208, 213, 215, 235

Ricci, James, 184

Rice, Mildred, *100*

Richard, Patricia, 250, 291

Richards, Hilda, 33, 249, 251

Ridges, the, 64–65, 255, 272, 277, 296. *See also* Athens Lunatic Asylum

riots and disturbances, 34, 176–77, 181–82, 202, 204, 221, 223, 234, *253,* 286, 286–87. *See also* protests and demonstrations

Riter, Carl F., watercolor, *46*

Robe, Richard, 257; Robe Leadership Institute, 259

Roberts, June Carver, watercolor, *21*

Rocard, Marcienne, 252

rollerblading, 283

Roosevelt, Theodore, 107

Ross-Lee, Barbara, 33, 235

Rota, Josep, 267

ROTC, 132–33, 143, 144, 260; protests against, 212, *212,* 213, 214, 220

Rothwell, Gar, 298

Rowland, Hal H., 179

Roye, Edward J., 31

Rucker, Bob, 104

Rudolph, Emaline Goddard, 89

Rufus Putnam Hall, 94

Rufus Putnam Training School, 94, 124

rugby, 221, *222,* 249

Runyan, Kristan Collins, 273

Russ, Dolores H., 259, 299, *300*

Russ, Fritz J., 259, 299, *300*

Russ College of Engineering and Technology. *See* Engineering and Technology, Russ College of

Russ Prize, Fritz J. and Dolores H., 259, 299, *300*

Rutherford, Dwight H., 328–29

Rutherford, James K., 328–29

Ryors, Rev. Alfred, 38–39, 45, 47–48, *48,* 66, *304*

Ryors Hall, 207

Saez, Daniel, 256

St. Patrick's Day Weekend, 177–78, 182, 183

Sargent Hall, 207

satellite: NASA, 203; tracking station, 186, *188*

Saxbe, William (Ohio attorney general), 198–99

Scalinger, Giulio, *243,* 244

Schaefer, Laurel Lee, 73

Schantz, Tom, 179

Scheel, Jane Grover, *250*

Schloss Building, 148

Schmidt, James Norman, 200

Schmidt, Mike, 77, 221, *222,* 238

Schorr, Daniel, *252*

Schuler, Geneva Elliott, 120

Schwartz, Martin, 298

Science Hall, 97

Scott, Charles (Chuck), 256; photos by, *216, 224*

Scott, William Henry, 53, 54, 62, 63, 68, 69, 70, 74, 78–79, *107, 139, 304*

Scott Quadrangle, 139, 144, 218

Scripps, E. W., 93, 203

Scripps Hall, E. W., 93, 95, 203

Scripps Howard: Foundation, 203, 257; Multi-Media Laboratory, 203; Survey Research Center, 203

Scully, Gerald, 208

Secoy, Roger, 237

Seese Bill, 91, 92

Seigfred, Earl C., 136

Seigfred Hall, 174, 186, 228, 256

senate. *See* administrative senate; faculty: senate; students: government

Shaikh, Nisar, 247

Shao You-Bao Overseas Chinese Documentation and Research Center, 266

Shawnee State University, 152

Shermer, Carl L., 176, *188*

Shively Hall, 291

Shmishkiss, Pearl Bernfled, 138

Shriver, Sargent, *186*

Sibs Weekend, *292, 293*

Sievert, Bill, 205

Simon and Garfunkel, *202*

Singapore, 266, 291

Singing Men of Ohio, 293

Sing Tao Center for International Journalism, 267, 290

Sinz, Cheryl Kimes, 194

skating, 172, *173*

Skit Show (Women's League), 108–9, *109,* 128

Slade, Joseph, 294

slavery, 22, 28, 31

Sleeper, David L., 86

Sleeper Bill, 86

Sloan, A. O., 81

Small, Irv, *131*

Smart, Charles Allen, 169

"smart classroom" building, 293, 299

Smith, Arthur, 296

Smith, Bill (drummer), 141

Smith, Bill (professor), *173*

Smith, Dave, 256

Smith, Rev. Edward, 39